BARTRAM'S TRAVELS ILLUSTRATED

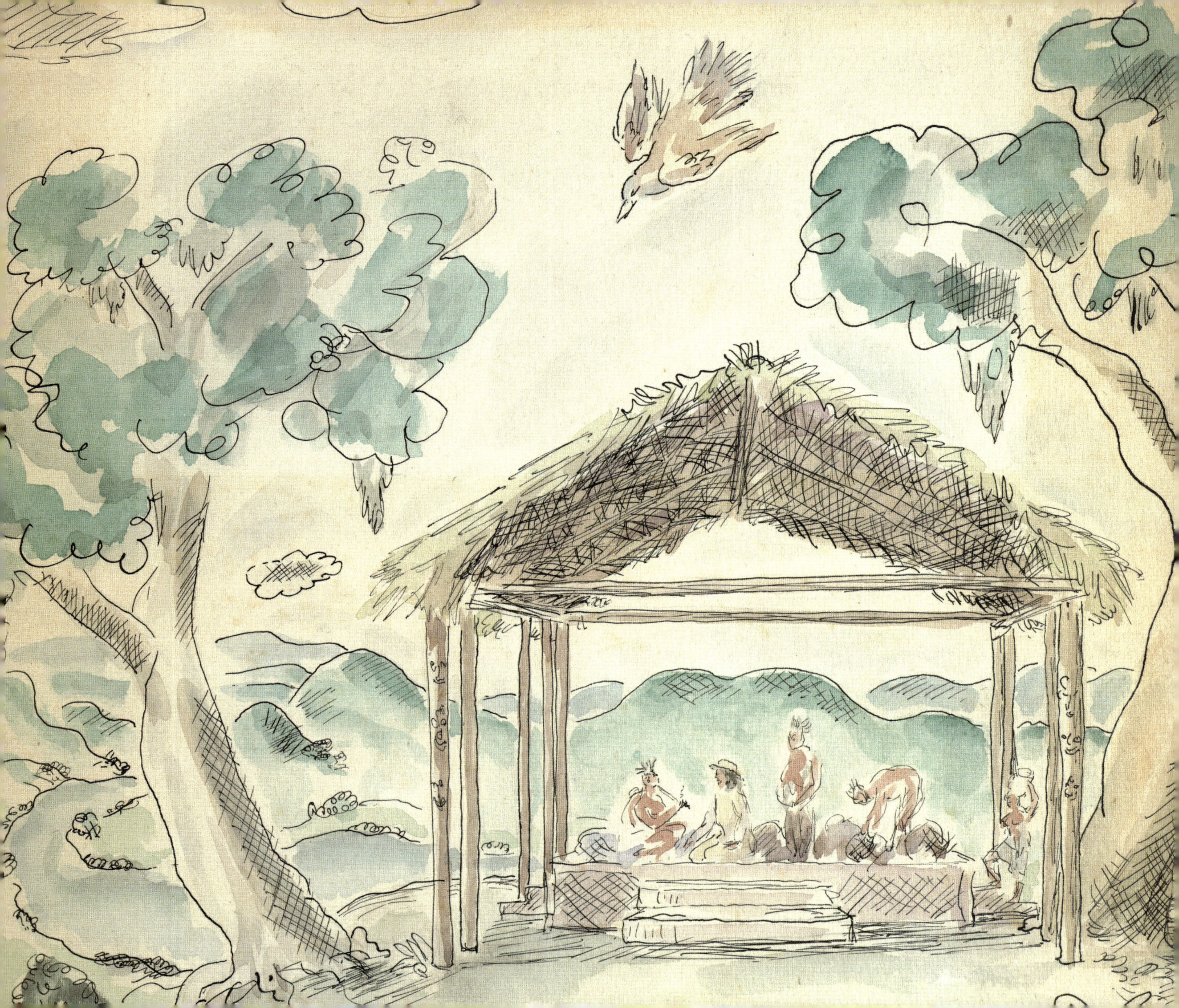

BARTRAM'S TRAVELS ILLUSTRATED

Embellished by William G. Haynes Jr.

EDITED BY DORINDA G. DALLMEYER AND HARRIET H. LANGFORD

The University of Georgia Press | Athens

A Wormsloe
FOUNDATION
nature book

Except when otherwise noted, all images by Bill Haynes are courtesy of the Hargrett Rare Book and Manuscript Library, University of Georgia Libraries.

Athens, Georgia 30602
www.ugapress.org

Designed by Erin Kirk
Set in Adobe Caslon Pro
Printed and bound by Friesens
The paper in this book meets the guidelines for permanence and durability of the Committee on Production Guidelines for Book Longevity of the Council on Library Resources.

Printed in Canada
30 29 28 27 26 C 5 4 3 2 1

EU Authorized Representative
Easy Access System Europe—Mustamäe tee 50, 10621
Tallinn, Estonia, gpsr.requests@easproject.com

Library of Congress Cataloging-in-Publication Data

Names: Dallmeyer, Dorinda G. editor | Langford, Harriet H., 1946– editor
Title: Bartram's Travels illustrated / / embellished by William G. Haynes Jr. ; edited by Dorinda G. Dallmeyer and Harriet H. Langford.
Description: Athens : The University of Georgia Press, [2026] | Includes bibliographical references.
Identifiers: LCCN 2026003753 | ISBN 9780820374734 hardback
Subjects: LCSH: Haynes, Bill—Criticism and interpretation | Bartram, William, 1739–1823. Travels through North & South Carolina, Georgia, east & west Florida, the Cherokee country, the extensive territories of the Muscogulges, or Creek Confederacy, and the country of the Chactaws—Illustrations | LCGFT: Pictures
Classification: LCC ND1839.H39 B37 2026
LC record available at https://lccn.loc.gov/2026003753

CONTENTS

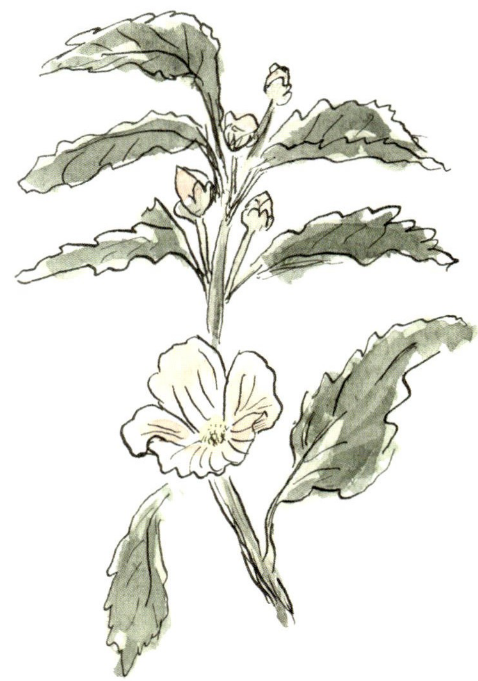

PREFACE

A Tale of Two Williams *Dorinda G. Dallmeyer and Harriet H. Langford*

William Bartram (1739–1823)

In 1739, just five miles from Philadelphia, the intellectual center of the American colonies, William Bartram was born at his family's plant nursery. As a child, William began to help his father, John, on collecting trips, learning botany and developing his artistic skills. European plant fanciers competed for the new American species that the Bartrams found and, with time, for William's drawings as well.

William matured into an extraordinary naturalist. In 1765 he joined his father on a collecting trip in South Carolina, Georgia, and Florida. What William saw inspired him to return later. However, he failed in an attempt to start a rice and indigo plantation on Florida's St. Johns River and then nearly drowned off the Florida coast while working as a surveyor's assistant. Going home was his only choice. Not a man cut out for the ordinary jobs of colonial America, he cultivated his family's long-standing contacts with members of the Royal Society who were particularly interested in the flora of the South. Finally, patience was rewarded.

One month before his thirty-fourth birthday, funded by his British patron, Dr. John Fothergill, William set off on the sojourn that would consume him for nearly four years—from the barrier islands of Georgia to the Mississippi River; from the headwaters of the St. Johns River to the heights of North Carolina's Blue Ridge Mountains.

In early 1777, William Bartram returned home and strayed probably no more than five miles away for the rest of his life. However, he was hardly a recluse. He was a storehouse of knowledge about the Southern frontier for those leading the transition from British control to American independence. He also served as a generous mentor to the rising generation of American scientists who would go on to be pioneers in fields such as entomology, ornithology, and botany. And despite the delays inherent in attempting to write and publish a book in the midst of revolution and nation building, in 1791 his tome appeared: *Travels through North & South Carolina, Georgia, East & West Florida, the Cherokee Country, the Extensive Territories of the Muscogulges, or Creek Confederacy, and the Country of the Chactaws; Containing an Account of the Soil and Natural Productions of Those Regions, Together with Observations on the Manners of the Indians*. Known familiarly as *Travels*, to this day it continues to fire the imaginations of all who love Southern landscapes.

Chief among Bartram's talents were his power of observation and his ability to capture what he saw on paper, in both words and images. Bartram wanted the reader to see the animal in motion, to appreciate the liveliness of plants, to personally experience the natural world through his words. His drawings go beyond scientific accuracy to give us living portraits of wildflowers welcoming a moth, vines threatening to twine off the page. His alligators bellow and thrash; a frog struggles in the jaws of a snake; birds stalk, strut, and hover. Indeed, Bartram was a particularly keen observer of birds: their beauty, their behavior, their appearance and disappearance with the seasons. He made systematic observations about birds that no one had recorded before.

While Bartram's drawings give us a hint of what these landscapes looked like centuries ago, it's his written descriptions that fill in the details. For example, long before the rise of mass tourism, Florida was a different kind of "Magic Kingdom," luring Bartram to explore the richness of its flora and fauna. Florida's transparent, bubbling springs gave him a window into a peaceful, natural world where he could observe the lives of aquatic animals and the depths of the earth itself.

Bartram's words and deft illustrations reflect a world of harmony and grace. As a Quaker, he was taught the book of Nature reveals all you need to know. Throughout the *Travels*, his Quaker upbringing reveals his deep spiritual connection to nature, as being a part of nature and not apart from it. What he saw in the Southeast awed him as a manifestation of Divine Creation. Or as he put it, "Nature is the work of God omnipotent."

Similarly, Bartram treated the tribes he encountered far differently than the predominant American project to either Christianize the "savages" or annihilate them. The tribes had their own sacred sites and beliefs, and ways of being on the land. The tribes with whom Bartram crossed paths found his heart different from other white men. He didn't want their animals, he didn't want their women, he didn't want their land; all he wanted to do was observe. As a result, in *Travels*, Bartram detailed such myriad aspects of Indian life that historian Kathryn Braund refers to him as "America's first anthropologist."

In sum, William Bartram was an artist, a botanist, an anthropologist, and a wonderful storyteller. He was America's first great writer, whose book appealed to a popular audience, at home and abroad. In *Travels*, readers could go with him in words where they couldn't go themselves. He combined the mind of a scientist with the heart of a poet. All you have to do is read his words, and you see it.

The great gift of Bartram's words should heighten our commitment to saving what remains of the long-gone world he described. In *Travels*, we find the starting point for reconstructing and reclaiming the natural heritage of the South. And across the centuries, William Bartram inspires us to go forward in joy, gratitude, and wonder.

Bill Haynes (William G. Haynes Jr., 1908–2001)

Unless you are a student of award-winning Southern letterpress printers, you probably will not recognize the name Bill Haynes, proprietor of the Ashantilly Press in Darien, Georgia. Bill painted the watercolors found in this book in 1934 as a student in New York City. William Bartram's influence can be traced throughout Bill's career. He initially studied to be an illustrator, but later in life he found that his artistic skills could be used in letterpress printing. He established the Ashantilly Press in 1955, with his wife, Natalie, as proofreader. For the most part, he worked alone until traditional hand-set books met new technologies in the 1970s, which made printing faster and less expensive. His book designs showcased detailed wood engravings, linoleum cuts, and beautiful typefaces on some of the era's finest papers. Bill's attention to design aesthetics put him in a small niche of well-regarded Southern letterpress printers from the mid-1950s into the 1970s.

Growing up at Ashantilly, the family home located near the mouth of the great Altamaha River delta, gave Bill the opportunity to explore and appreciate the natural world around him—a devotion that never left him. Always sensitive to coastal Georgia's Altamaha River ecosystem, Bill fought an Army Corps of Engineers proposal to channelize the Altamaha for barge traffic to connect the Georgia coast to the Gulf of Mexico. He became one of Georgia's first environmentalists with his tireless and ultimately successful environmental advocacy, so important to the coastal seafood economy of Darien and McIntosh County and its history as well.

Looking to the future of the Ashantilly property, in 1993 along with his surviving sister, Anne Lee, Bill turned their historic family home in Darien into a 501(c)(3) nonprofit, the Ashantilly Center, Inc., committed to seeing it become a center for education and interpretation of book arts, the environment, and preservation. The center has donated a large collection of both

Ashantilly Press and family papers to the Hargrett Rare Book and Manuscript Library housed in the Richard B. Russell Building Special Collections Library at the University of Georgia in Athens. It is here that this collection of Bartram-inspired paintings now resides.

The watercolor paintings collected as "Bartram's 'Travels' Embellished by Bill Haynes" were among the large collection of art, correspondence, maps, letterpress ephemera, and beautifully designed books at the Ashantilly Center. Bill painted them in 1934 at the age of twenty-six when he was studying for a career in illustration in New York City. In a charming coincidence, it was also at age twenty-six that William Bartram made his first collecting trip to the South with his father.

As the Ashantilly Center continued its work to expand the Ashantilly Press Papers collection at the Hargrett Rare Book and Manuscript Library, the discovery of a single newspaper article from 1947 produced more information about this vintage Bartram series. The *Columbia (South Carolina) Record* article entitled "Haynes Paints Bartram," by Margaret Babcock Meriwether, announced a current art exhibit by Bill Haynes and Anne Lee Haynes at the University of South Carolina. Meriwether begins the article with her assessment of Bartram's significant influence on American artists and writers, including Bill Haynes.

> Few books about America have been held longer in esteem or had a wider influence than "The Travels of William Bartram" first published in Philadelphia in 1791 and in London in 1794. . . . It has been reprinted frequently and in translation (and) was exceedingly popular on the continent as well as in Britain. . . . Bartram was able to pass on to a host of readers the joy he felt in beholding the unspoiled wilderness of the southern coast country and mountains with all the unwasted wealth of our woods and fields and waters. . . . In this case it was not a boy from far away who was drawn to see the country but a native son whose eyes were made keener and whose spirit was quickened to appropriate his home environment by Bartram's ageless enthusiasm.

The 1947 South Carolina exhibition is the only known public appearance of Bill's *Travels* illustrations until the publication of this book. Bartram would remain an enduring influence on Bill's art and advocacy throughout his life.

NOTE: All page numbers cited to *Travels* come from the edition posted on the University of North Carolina's website Documenting the American South, https://docsouth.unc.edu/nc/bartram/bartram.html. This online text is a transcription of the first edition of William Bartram's *Travels*, printed by James & Johnson (Philadelphia, 1791). Bartram's original spellings have been retained throughout; when it might not be obvious that the error was Bartram's, in the case of some proper nouns and occasional words, we've added square brackets to note the emendation.

BARTRAM'S TRAVELS ILLUSTRATED

Why Bartram Matters

DORINDA G. DALLMEYER

William Bartram's ability to marry science with poetry has ensured *Travels* a worldwide audience for more than two hundred years. What is the source of its staying power?

Bartram was born in 1739 when his father, John, a noted supplier to the international plant trade, was forty years old. Fortunately, the Bartram home and gardens lay just across the Schuylkill River from Philadelphia, known at that time as the "Athens of America."[1] Living so close to the intellectual center of the colonies, William grew up among his father's friends, who shared their knowledge of the natural sciences and helped encourage and mentor William's interests in both science and art.

As William grew, he assisted his father on collecting trips and shared John's passion not only for botany but also for the rest of the natural world. This fieldwork was not some Bartram family hobby but a business—a business connecting them closely with foreign plant collectors, especially those in Britain. This was the era when botany began to take on a more scientific bent, beyond simply the acquisition of the novel and unusual. At this time, the naming and classification of plants and animals began to be standardized across the scientific world. Unlike the rest of the Bartram children, John arranged for William to attend the Academy in Philadelphia. There William could master Latin and French in a way John never could, and he also had the opportunity to take painting and drawing lessons, although there is no evidence he did.

Instead, his budding artistic skill benefited immensely from the influence of Peter Collinson and George Edwards, both members of the Royal Society as well as botanical clients and correspondents with his father. An extraordinarily wealthy plant enthusiast, Collinson collected William's early drawings (see, for example, figure 1), even sending William fine drawing paper, delivered to him by no less a personage than Benjamin Franklin on his return to America from a trip abroad.[2]

Similarly, Edwards used his influence to have drawings that William had done in his early teens published in a popular scientific magazine. In his scientific treatises, Edwards also credited William not simply for supplying him with bird and reptile specimens but also included William's observations on the habitats and behaviors of these animals. Absolutely the prodigy, William Bartram was born to be a natural historian. According to Edwards,

> Mr. Bartram says they (blue-winged warbler) arrive in Pennsylvania from the south in April, and feed upon the insects they find on the leaves and buds of trees, and continue with them the greatest part of the summer; and he believes they breed there, though he never found any of their nests. . . . The larger bird, or *Tringa*, Mr. Bartram says, comes from the south to them in April. He opened the hen, and found in her pretty large eggs: but by accident he lost the hen, so that the bird he sent me is the cock. They continue, he says, with them the greatest part of the summer. I believe this bird is common both to Europe and America.[3]

As an alternative to waiting for the birds to come to him in Pennsylvania, William got his first immersive experience in Southern landscapes when he accompanied his father on a collecting expedition during 1765–1766 along the coasts of South Carolina and Georgia and then as far south as the headwaters of Florida's St. Johns River.[4] If

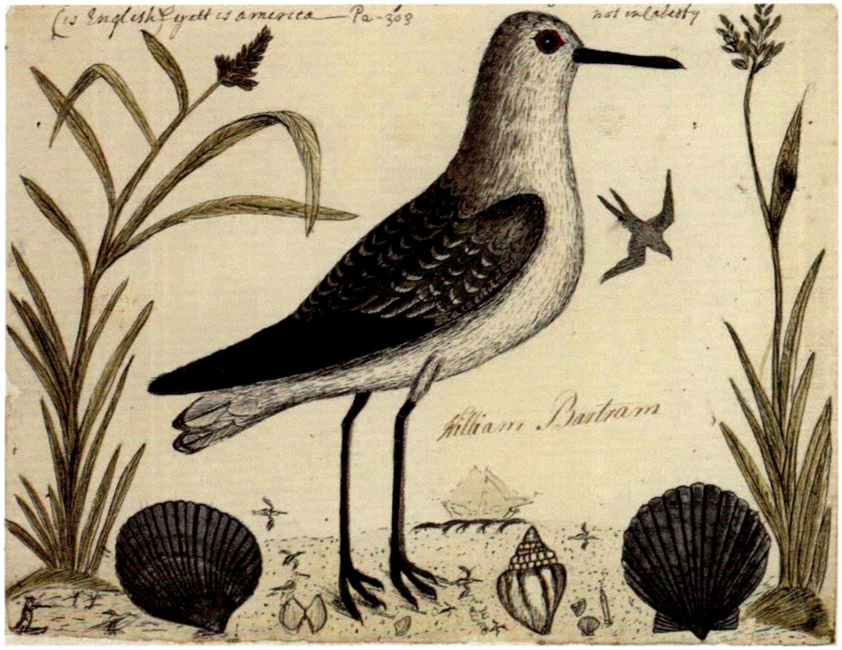

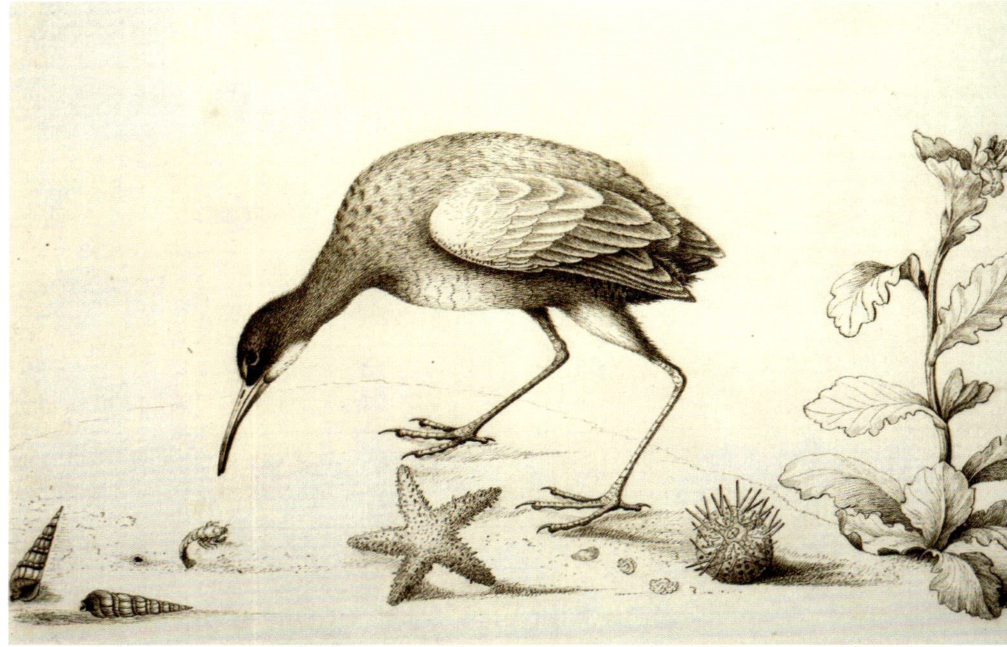

FIGURES 1–2. The painting on the left was done when William was in his early teens; the one on the right was done when he was a mature artist. Although both center on a long-legged shorebird, the early drawing is action-packed on its periphery, while the "mature" image is as spare and delicately rendered as a Japanese screen. *Left:* Arader Galleries, New York and Philadelphia. *Right:* Courtesy of the Trustees of the Natural History Museum, London.

William kept a journal of the trip, none of it has survived, but he must have been entranced by the experience of such novelty and abundance. Asking his father to advance him the value of the inheritance he would otherwise receive at John's death, William purchased rights to a land parcel along the St. Johns so he could return to Florida to start a rice and indigo plantation.

This experiment lasted all of six months. The land allotted to him by the British agents was poor, and he knew nothing about managing the enslaved people whom his father had purchased to clear the land and work the crop.[5] As a further complication, William also spent most of those months leveled by tropical diseases. Abandoning this plantation dream-turned-nightmare, William took a job assisting a survey party working along the Florida coast but nearly drowned in a shipwreck offshore. He returned to Philadelphia with nothing to show for his efforts.

Luckily, a patron was standing in the wings: Dr. John Fothergill, a British plant collector, who encouraged John to let William do what William did best. As William's patron, Fothergill promised him twenty-five pounds a year to support his undertaking a multiyear trip to botanize all the way to the Mississippi River and back. Thus, one month before his thirty-fourth birthday, William Bartram set off on the travels that would consume him for nearly four years. Resuming his place at his father's gardens on his return, Bartram continued his botanical studies and used his field journals to craft the manuscript for *Travels*, which was finally published in 1791.[6]

For those interested in natural history, the narrative of his 1773–1777 sojourn in the South

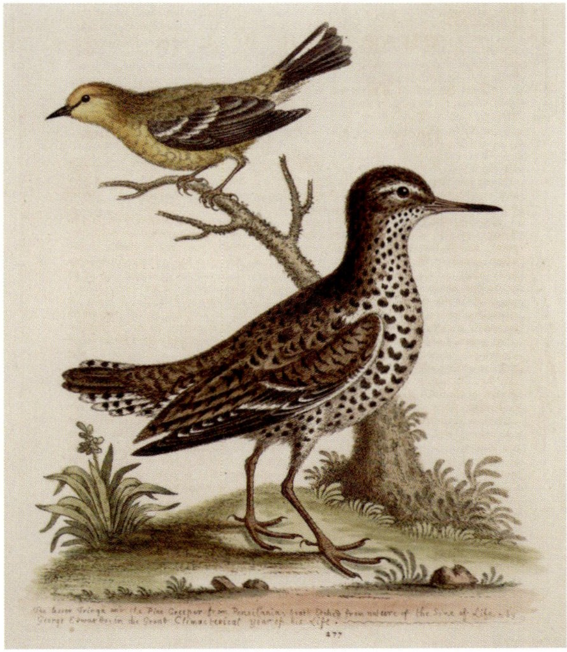

FIGURE 3. George Edwards's blue-winged warbler and spotted sandpiper. Private collection.

marks a baseline for understanding the Southern landscape at that time. Bartram's journey was foremost a biological expedition, and thus *Travels* is replete with descriptions of the plants and animals he encountered as he made his way west from the southeast coast to the Mississippi River and back. William Bartram was the first person to describe, collect, or illustrate forty-two species of native plants. He also was the first to describe twenty-three species of animals, including such Southern icons as black vultures and cottontail rabbits.[7]

Through Bartram's words, modern readers can visualize the South of the 1770s, a landscape that resounded with vast roosts of passenger pigeons and the wingbeats of Carolina parakeets, where old-growth hardwoods and millions of acres of longleaf pine forests stood, and clear rivers ran free to the sea. *Travels* is groundbreaking also because it is not merely a listing of species. Instead, Bartram provided some of the first descriptions of what we would now call "ecosystems" as well as notable details of animal and plant behavior, including unprecedented insights into bird migration.

Travels also has a way of showing how science can be interspersed with poetry. The reader may come upon a long list of Latin plant names, which can be skipped over, but when Bartram launches into descriptions of those plants, he brings them to life in your mind's eye. Similarly rich observations of the animals who crossed his path detail encounters that sometimes were far from idyllic. On several occasions, he had to contend with pests ranging from alligators intent on stealing the fish he'd caught for his own meal to the biting flies that plagued him and his horse.[8] And nature itself could threaten him, as when he found no escape from a tempestuous thunderstorm on the Altamaha River.[9]

Beyond the plant and animal world, Bartram is particularly important for his descriptions of the culture of the Indigenous peoples he met. In many instances he was utterly dependent on their goodwill and assistance not only to collect plant specimens but also to find his way in the wild South. Bartram notes both their good and bad points, even suggesting how they could be exemplars for the people he knew back in Philadelphia.

Bartram also observes the impacts of white settlement on the Southern landscape. He writes disapprovingly of the wanton killing of predators, wasteful slaughter of wildfowl, and destructive farming practices—the settlers' perception of a seemingly endless bounty clouding their appreciation of the very real limits of the land's carrying capacity. His philosophy rejects the elevation of humans over animals and plants in favor of seeing all life as a continuum, with humans an integral part of nature rather than apart from nature. And throughout the book, Bartram reveals his deep spiritual connection to nature as a manifestation of Divine Creation.

Once Bartram returned to Philadelphia in early 1777, he spent time working with his brother John, who had inherited the nursery business from their father. Given William's deep knowledge of all facets of natural history, Thomas Jefferson invited him to accompany expeditions into the vast area of the Louisiana Purchase. Despite the temptation, Bartram declined due to his advancing age.

However, he was hardly a recluse. Upon its publication, *Travels* would spawn a truly American strain of nature writing and go on to influence not only scientists in America and Europe but also Romantic poets such as William Wordsworth and Samuel Taylor Coleridge.[10] Bartram interacted extensively with the burgeoning scientific community in Philadelphia, including contributing botanical illustrations for a major compendium on the botany of the United States.[11]

Figure 4 pictures a medicinal plant, *Zanthorhiza apiifolia*, commonly known in the South as yellowroot. The plant, highly sought after by Indians and settlers alike, has anti-inflammatory and antibiotic properties. The Cherokee also used it to make yellow dye.[12]

In gratitude for the guidance he received as a young man, William happily invested much time mentoring younger botanists, ornithologists, entomologists, and artists.[13] All manner of people came to visit him because he could tell them what he had seen in the Southeast. Finally, after all his adventures in such exotic regions, he died one morning in July 1823 under a tree at home in the family garden—a most fitting place to take his rest.

In terms of American natural history, and particularly that of the Southeast, it is important to tell the story of William Bartram because he tells *our* story—from a time we cannot know personally. *Travels* is as close as we can get: this man's vision of what the Southeast looked like in the mid-1770s. It is a treasure trove of information that not only educates but inspires our generation to pursue a commitment to take care of the natural world all around us. William Bartram is the person who tells Southerners and people who love the South what it looked like, what it was like, and what it could be again.

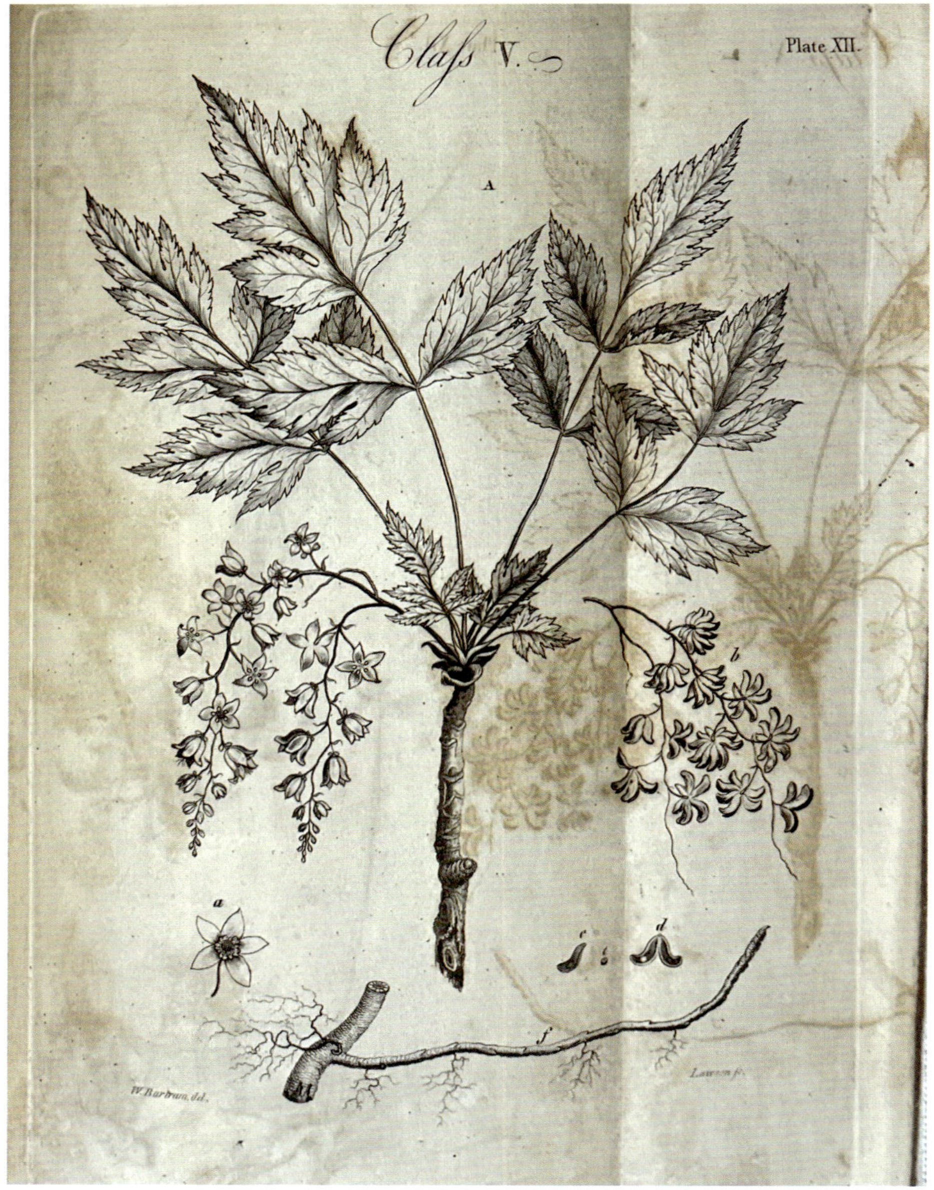

FIGURE 4. Benjamin Smith Barton noted in the preface to *Elements of Botany*, "Plate XII (engraved from one of Mr. Bartram's drawings) was kindly presented to me by my friend and colleague, Dr. James Woodhouse, Professor of Chemistry in the University of Pennsylvania." Hargrett Rare Book and Manuscript Library, UGA Libraries.

2 Bill Haynes (William G. Haynes Jr., 1908–2001)

HARRIET H. LANGFORD

The watercolor paintings assembled as *Bartram's Travels Illustrated* were discovered among the large collection of art, correspondence, maps, letterpress ephemera, and beautifully designed books at the Ashantilly Center in Darien, Georgia, in the Ashantilly House, which was Bill Haynes's historic home. After Haynes's death in 2001, the nonprofit Ashantilly board began sifting through the material Haynes had produced throughout his adult years studying art and, later, letterpress. Eventually, a large collection took shape at the Hargrett Rare Book and Manuscript Library at the University of Georgia, including the images in this book. A look at who William G. Haynes Jr. was and how William Bartram and his *Travels* became such an influence on Haynes's journey as an artist—and later an award-winning letterpress book designer and printer—can enhance our enjoyment of these vintage 1934 watercolors.

William Greaner Haynes Jr. (1908–2001), known as Bill to his family, was born in Columbia, South Carolina, where his father was working in the cottonseed oil business. A Sandersville, Georgia, native, Will Haynes Sr. married Laura Williams Grant. Laura's grandfather was the railroad tycoon L. P. Grant from Atlanta. Two older sisters, Anne Lee (1896–1997) and Frances (1897–1989), had been born there. On a business trip, Will saw that the historic marsh-side property on the outskirts of Darien, named Ashantilly, was for sale. Ashantilly was the historic mainland home of Thomas Spalding, an early plantation owner on Sapelo Island in McIntosh County. Laura Haynes purchased it, and the family returned to Georgia.

The eighty-acre tract, consisting of forty acres of high ground and forty of marsh, was originally a land grant from the British crown to William McIntosh. McIntosh's family of Scottish Highlanders was brought to this country by James Oglethorpe, the founder of the Georgia colony. McIntosh's daughter Margery inherited the property and married James Spalding, a Highland Scot living on St. Simons Island, in 1772. Their son, Thomas, was born in 1774 on St. Simons Island near Oglethorpe's home at Ft. Frederica. An interesting coincidence for the Haynes family was that William Bartram mentions in *Travels* that he was "well received and entertained" by James Spalding at his Frederica home.[1]

As the only son, Thomas Spalding inherited the Ashantilly property, a name it shared with the Spalding holdings in Perthshire, Scotland. Around 1820, Thomas had enslaved workers build an elegant tabby house to be used as his mainland home where his wife and mother could more easily visit neighbors.[2]

Sapelo Island, just off the McIntosh coast, was Thomas Spalding's primary plantation where enslaved people grew very lucrative sea island cotton. Despite having misgivings about the institution of slavery, Spalding nevertheless enslaved more than 350 people. He utilized the task system of labor,[3] and enslaved workers were supervised not by the typical white overseer but by a Black manager. Bu Allah (or Bilali), a Muslim, served as Spalding's trusted second-in-command on Sapelo.[4]

Spalding died in 1851 of pneumonia at Ashantilly after returning from arguing against secession at the state legislature. The property went to his son Charles, who was not interested in the problems associated with maintaining the old house (figure 5). Consequently, the property changed hands numerous times after the Civil War and became known as the "Old Tabby,"

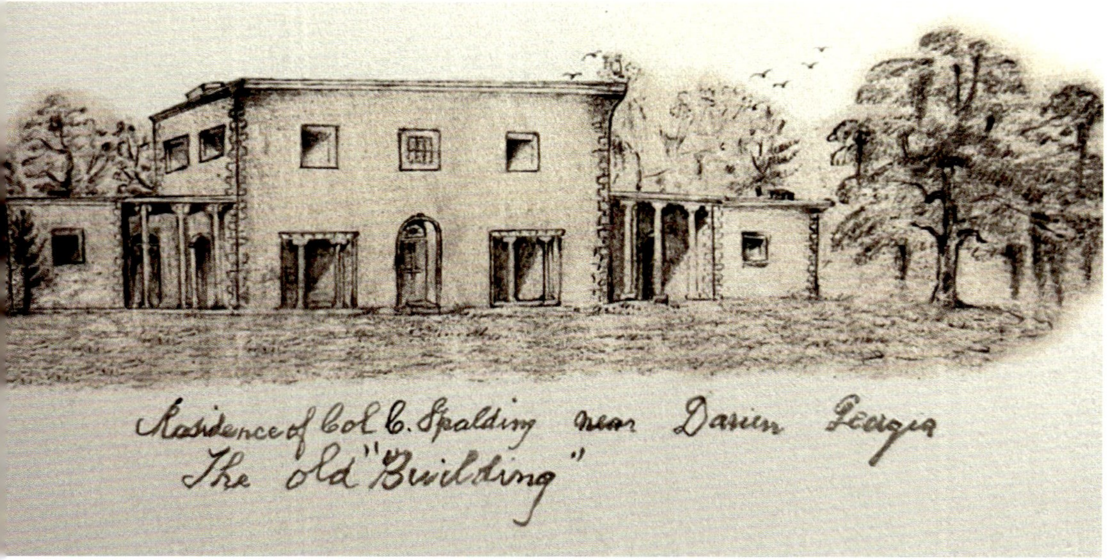

FIGURE 5. This 1860 sketch of Ashantilly shows how it looked during Thomas Spalding's life. Ashantilly Center Archives.

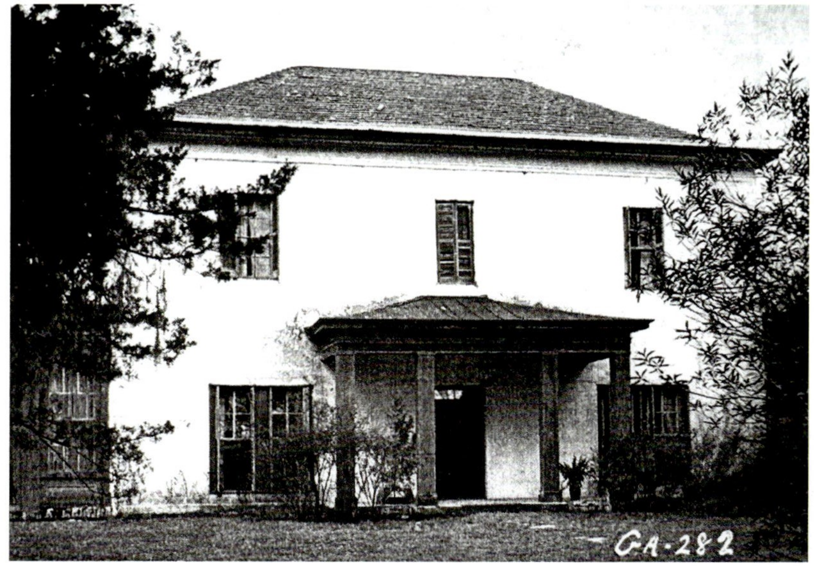

FIGURE 6. Ashantilly, February 1936. Ashantilly Center Archives; Historic American Buildings Survey, Library of Congress.

honoring Spalding's tabby building material used in the early 1800s.

The house was renovated in the 1880s by the William A. Wilcox family, who removed most of Spalding's European decorative columns, a front piazza, and open loggias between the wings. The historic two-story house gained a hipped roof, front portico, and enclosed loggias (figure 6).[5]

This home fronting Black Island Creek in the Altamaha River delta served as an inspiring location for young Bill Haynes, who had an early eye for visual detail coupled with appreciation for the natural inhabitants of the sprawling marshes and Spalding's former rice fields. His two older sisters encouraged his wide-ranging artistic talents, which reportedly included pottery and sculpture in addition to drawing. According to journalist Susan Garrett Mason, Haynes's life "centered around his family. And in turn, his family's life centered around books. Books of all sorts. Books read aloud by his mother. Books read aloud by his father. Books that were to become not only his passion but also his profession."[6] The family's large library, now housed at the Ashantilly Center, contains an original copy of the 1849 edition of William Darlington's *Memorials of John Bartram and Humphry Marshall: With Notices of Their Botanical Contemporaries*. Haynes may have heard of Bartram during those family readings or simply had been told of John and William's trips into Georgia by his schoolteachers or one of the McIntosh family's descendants still living in the county.

Haynes graduated from Darien High School and, at age nineteen, took a steamer from Savannah to New York City to begin his formal training in illustration at the Grand Central School of Art and the Art Students League. He lived with his sister Anne Lee, who was working in the commercial graphic arts field and teaching at the Grand Central School of Art. Haynes's other sister, Frances, a research librarian at Florida State University, secured a part-time job for Bill through her Columbia University library school connections.

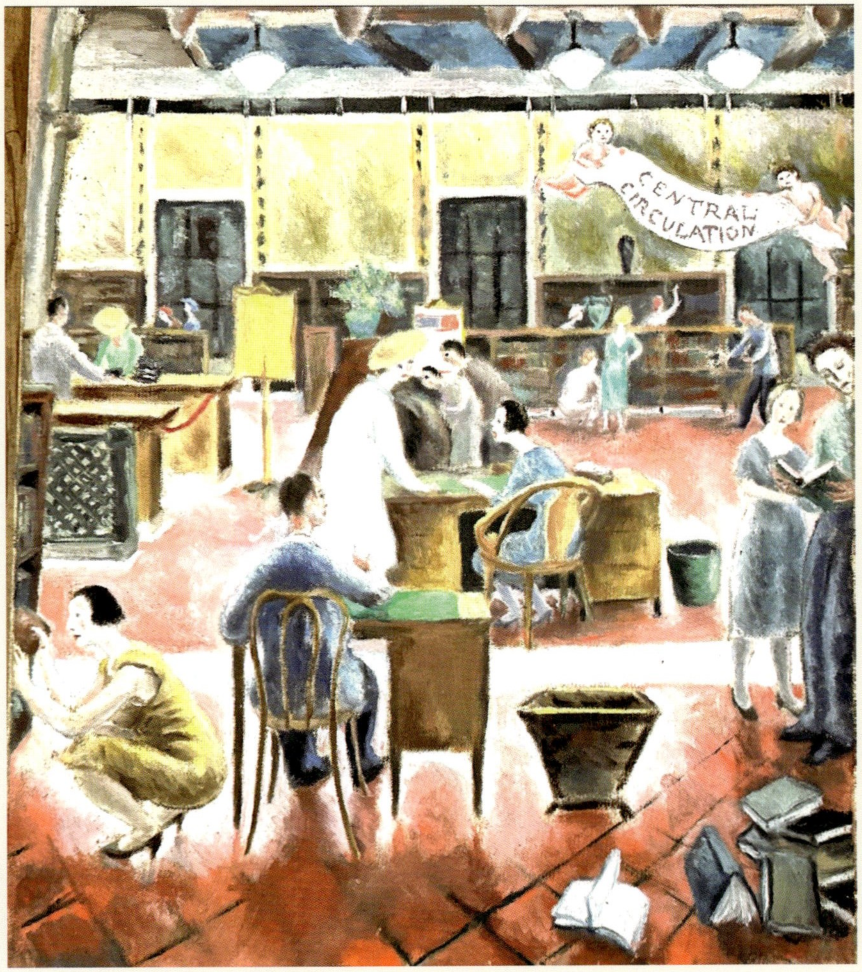

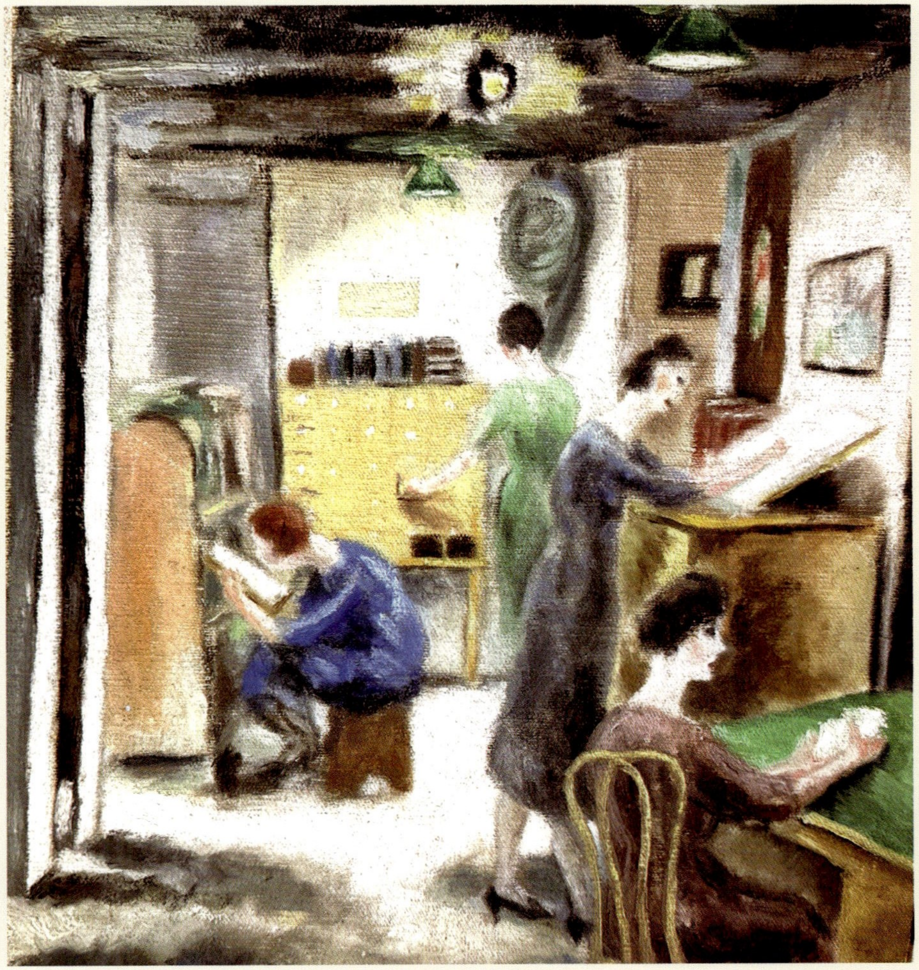

FIGURES 7–8. Bill Haynes, scenes from the New York Public Library, dates unknown. Ashantilly Center Archives.

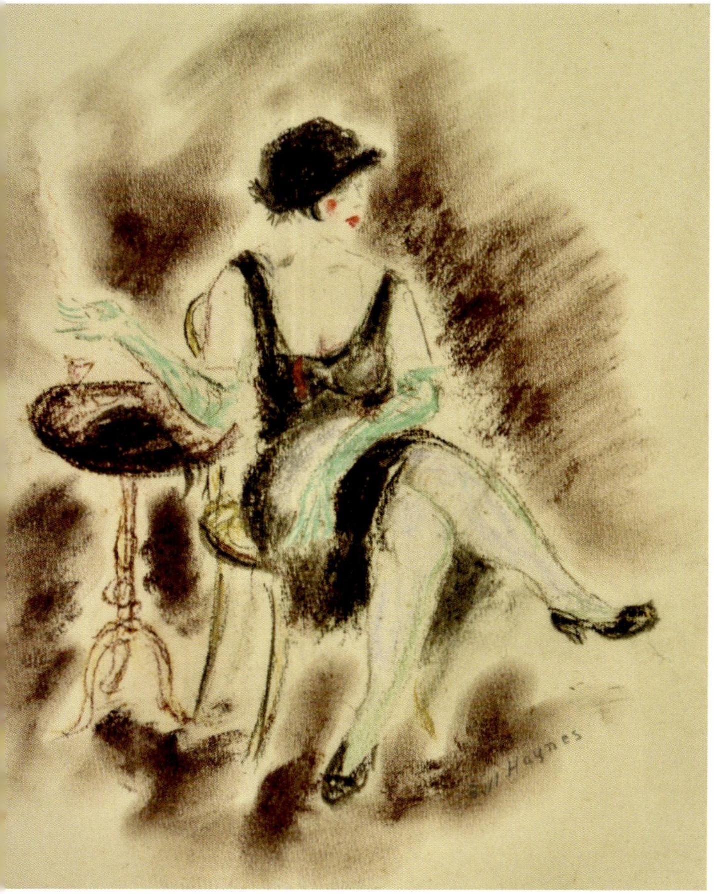

FIGURE 9. Undated portrait of an unidentified young woman enjoying New York's nightlife. Ashantilly Center Archives.

Reshelving books as a page in the New York Public Library and later becoming a clerk was likely eye-opening for a boy hungry for the knowledge and art of a broader world. In the morning, he would start work in the children's library, move to adult sections, and then go to art school in the afternoons.[7] We can confidently assume that Haynes, ever the voracious reader, was aware of the popular *Travels* edited by Mark Van Doren, which was published to great acclaim in 1928.[8]

A collection of magazines from the late 1920s into the later 1930s stored at Ashantilly Center's on-site archives details Haynes's and his sister's broad interests in the culture of the era. Among the magazines are issues of *Creative Art*, *Americana*, *Apollo*, *Art News*, *Asia*, *Revue de l'Art Ancien et Moderne*, and *Theatre Arts*. In his off-hours from the library, he haunted New York's museums, art galleries, and antiquarian bookstores. "I was learning about art and getting experience in what was good and what was not," Haynes commented. "I was training my eye in what were good proportions and what were not."[9] Poring over Haynes's archived magazine clippings yields his interests in works as diverse as the wood engravings of Albrecht Dürer and Winslow Homer's realism. He revealed to longtime friend Virginia Shields in 1982 that he was "slowly building up a private research library on art and printing."[10]

Because Haynes left few written documents that would point to favored artists, the rosters of instructors and students at both the Art Students League and at the Grand Central School of Art have been helpful in determining which teachers may have influenced Haynes's style seen in the "embellished by Bill Haynes" version of *Travels*.[11] During his work and study in New York (1927–1936), he was most likely studying with some of the early American modernists such as William and Marguerite Zorach as well as Harvey Dunn at the Grand Central School of Art.[12]

As one of the illustration instructors, Dunn was renowned for his realistic paintings of World War I battlefields.[13] However, in the postwar era he often brought a softer touch to his illustrations, which may have inspired Haynes's portrait of an unidentified young woman enjoying New York's nightlife (figure 9).

Dunn also made numerous woodcuts of images and initial letters to include in printed matter. With time, Haynes would do the same at Ashantilly (see pages 26 and 58).

Also teaching at the Art Students League was John Marin, whose early landscape technique is reflected in many of Haynes's New Guinea landscapes painted while he served in World War II (figure 10).[14]

Marin also sketched and painted the Brooklyn Bridge many times.[15] Haynes's self-portrait may have been inspired by Marin's early work (figure 11).

Another important American artist, Thomas Hart Benton, was an instructor at the Art Students League. According to Robert Torchia and Catherine Southwick, "Benton began to paint in a naturalistic style that was influenced by the Spanish master El Greco (Greek, 1541–1614) and he became known as the most innovative practitioner of mural painting in a decade of great importance for this medium in America."[16] Benton was known to have admired El Greco's work, specifically the *View of Toledo*, as did Bill Haynes (figures 12 and 13).

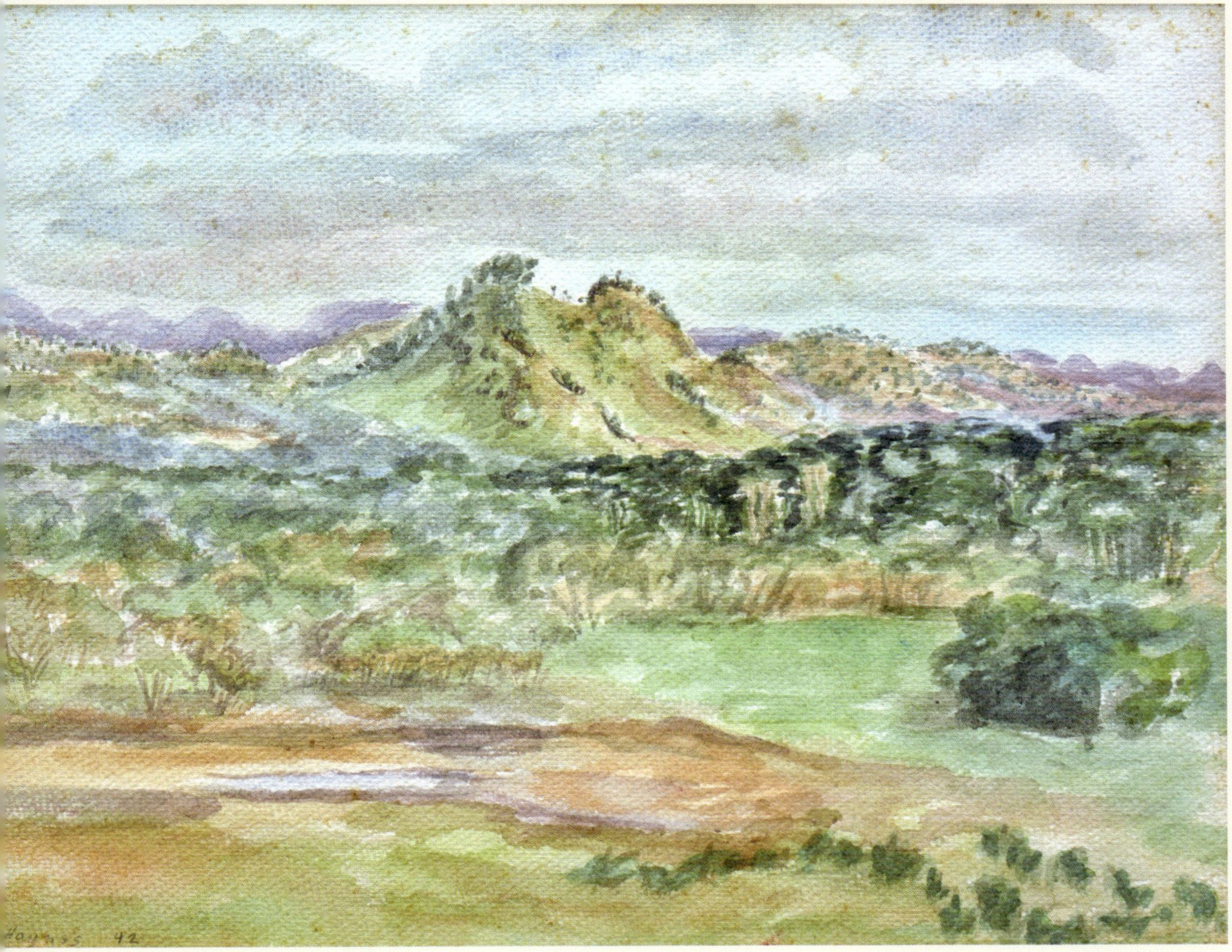

FIGURE 10. Bill Haynes, Milne Bay, New Guinea. Ashantilly Center Archives.

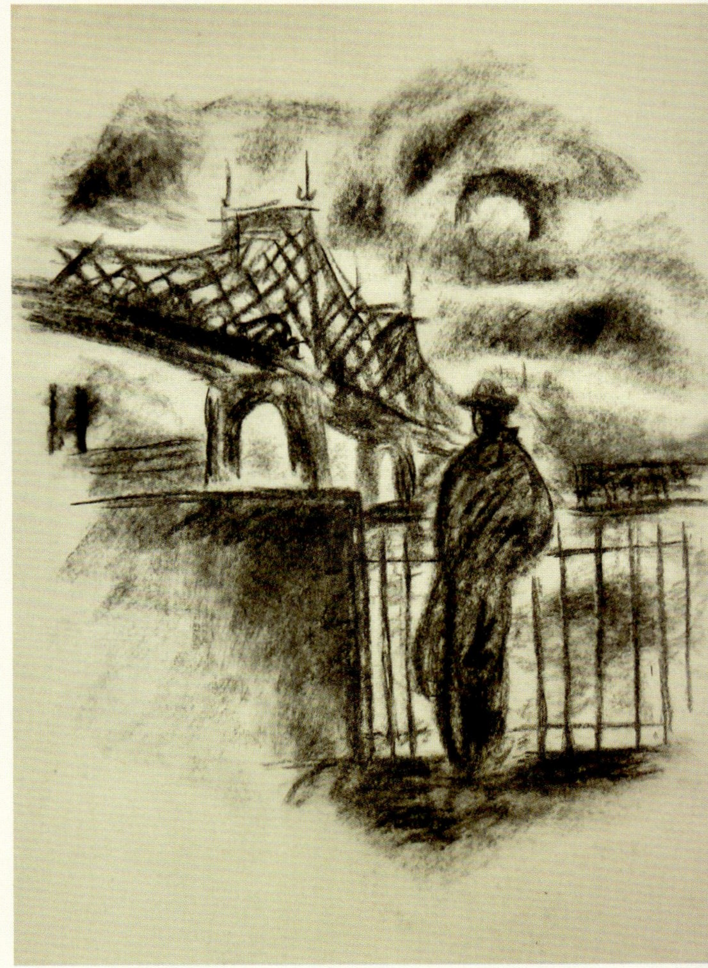

FIGURE 11. Bill Haynes (self-portrait, undated). Ashantilly Center Archives.

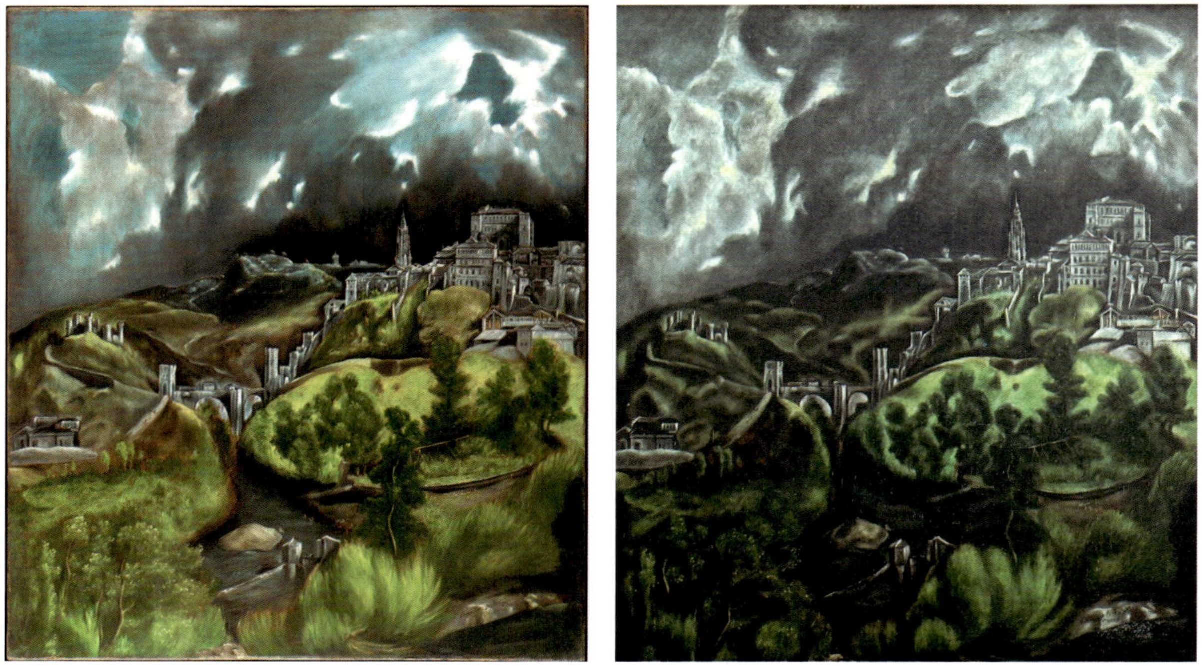

FIGURES 12–13. Original El Greco, *View of Toledo*, and Bill Haynes's student copy. *Left:* Metropolitan Museum of Art. *Right:* Ashantilly Center Archives.

Haynes's full-size copy of El Greco's *View of Toledo* is in the Ashantilly Center Archives. Information on the back of the canvas confirms that Haynes and fellow students copied famous paintings such as this one as part of their training.

Benton, who became known as a regionalist and turned his focus on American prairie life, also became an established muralist and certainly could have influenced the style and subject matter of Haynes's numerous mural studies. Indeed, Benton's monumental *Indiana* mural project undertaken for the 1933 World's Fair in Chicago may have inspired the following class assignment: to illustrate the history of the Mississippi River and the American West in a six-part set of mural panels (figure 14).[17] In Haynes's painting of river traffic, he included Black laborers toiling under the supervision of white men (figure 15).

Haynes left New York in 1936 to return home to Darien and ponder his career choices. Upon his return, many of his mural studies from the Depression years were painted in hopes of gaining a commission for executing a full-sized work. Figure 16 shows a man astride a mule offering a package to a barefoot woman in the mountains. Obviously, the terrain in this image is not the Georgia coast; however, Haynes's family owned property in the Blue Ridge Mountains near Rabun Gap, Georgia, where poverty rates were astonishing even before the Depression. Figure 17 is Haynes's proposed mural for the post office in Conyers, Georgia, illustrating farmwork, a textile mill, and a granite quarry. Note the ubiquity of mules for farm labor in these murals.[18] Also note that contour plowing had yet to be adopted to control agricultural erosion in the Southeast. Haynes painted the lively scene of *Florida Industries*, shown in figure 18, perhaps influenced during his studies in New York by the renowned Mexican muralist Diego Rivera. Although it's unclear what kinds of crops are being harvested from the field in the background, men and women carry oranges and grapefruit from the lush orchards to buyers at the boat dock. At left, a man holds stalks of sugarcane. On the right, men using crosscut saws and axes produce a neat stack of timber. Fishermen unload fish large and small on a dock. And in the foreground, divers prepare to land a boat full of sponges harvested in nearshore waters.

Most of Haynes's student artwork was never formally exhibited and is currently in either the Ashantilly Center Archives in Darien or the Ashantilly Press Papers collection at the Hargrett Rare Book and Manuscript Library. Many are undated, but the bulk of the sketches, watercolors, and charcoal work were likely class projects revealing his preference for interpreting the people, creeks, birds, and other animals of his coastal Georgia world. Viewing these images, it's easy to recognize Haynes's similar style in the landscapes and figures in his 1934 Bartram watercolors, which were filed away with the rest and would not be seen again until exhibited in 1947.

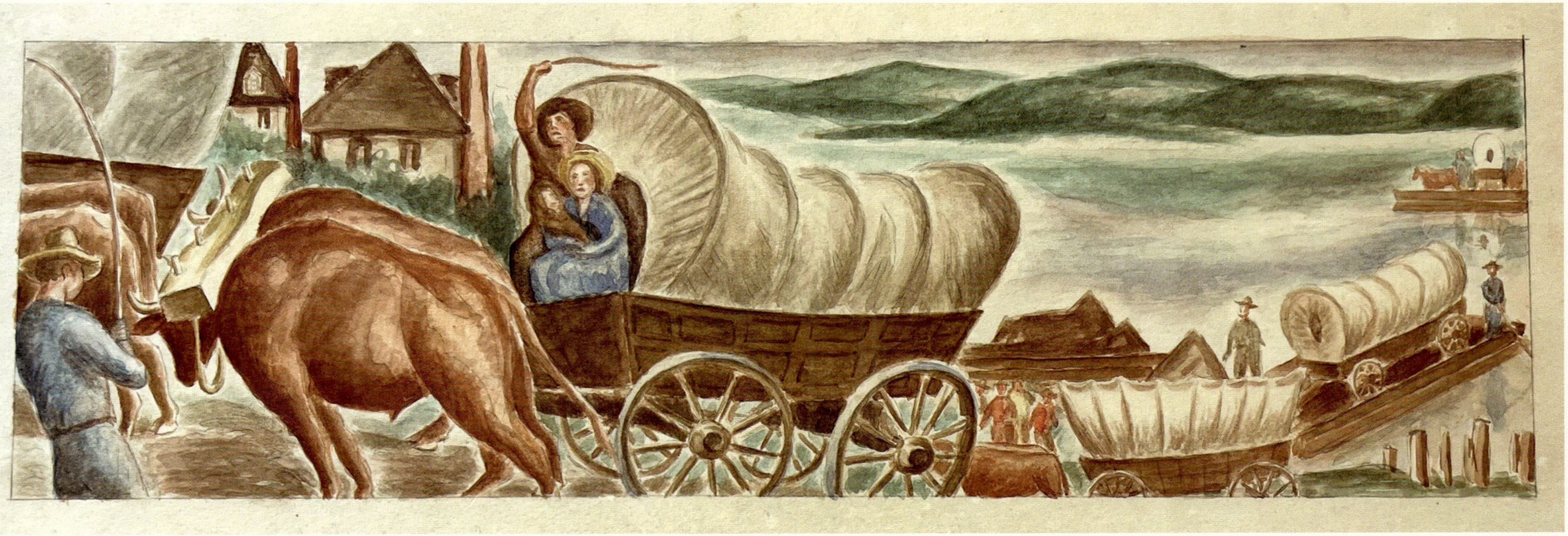

FIGURE 14. One of Haynes's mural illustrations in response to a class assignment to document the history of the Mississippi River and the American West.

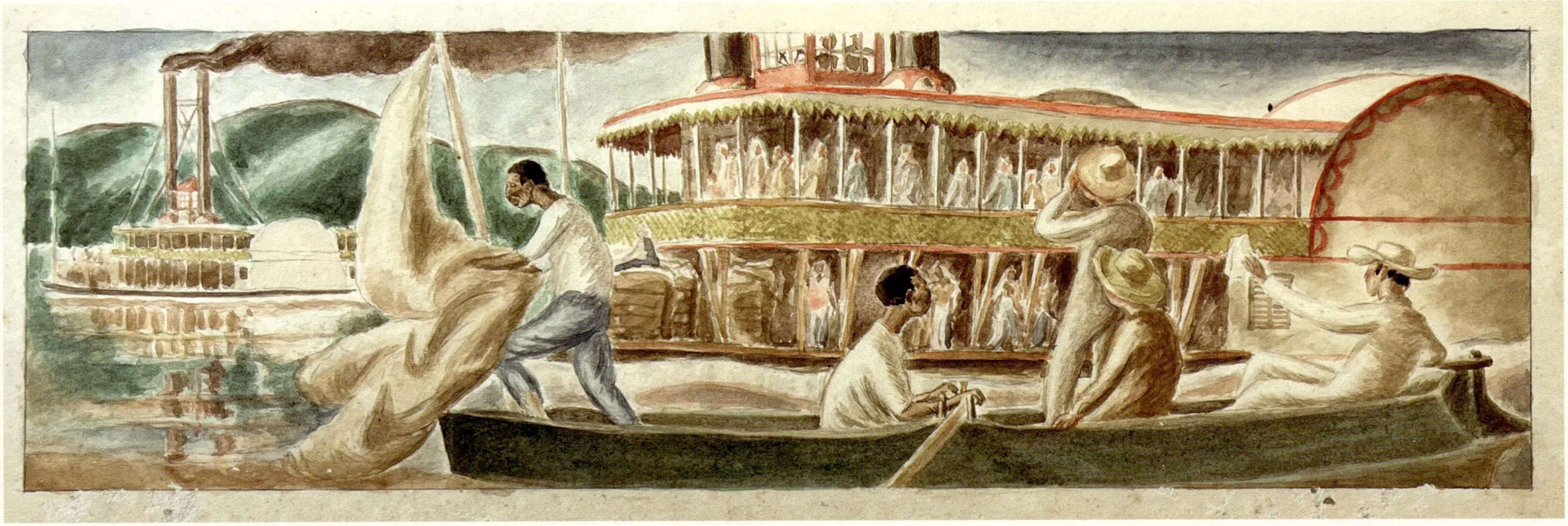

FIGURE 15. Another of Haynes's mural illustrations in response to the Mississippi River class assignment.

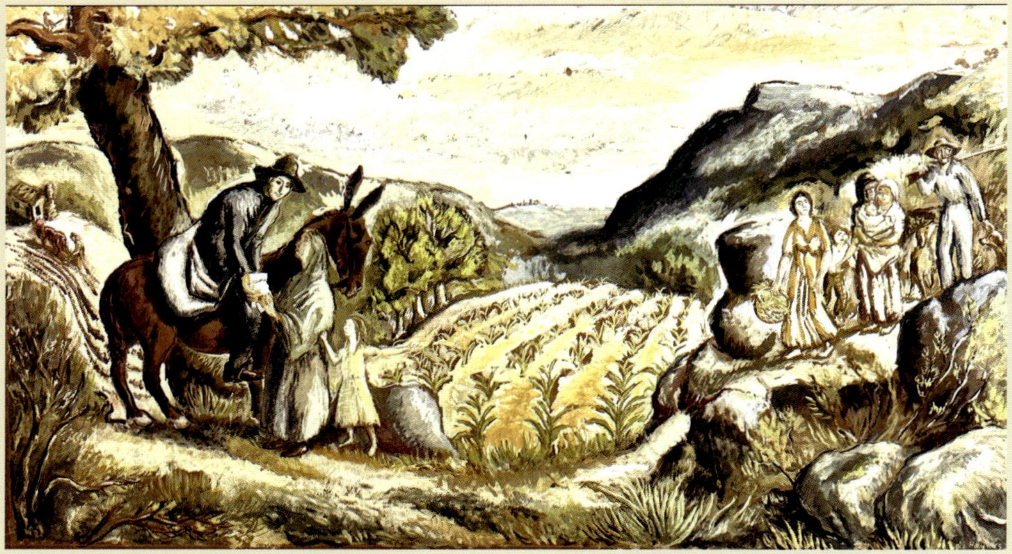

FIGURE 16. A mural study by Bill Haynes from the Depression years. Ashantilly Center Archives, date unknown.

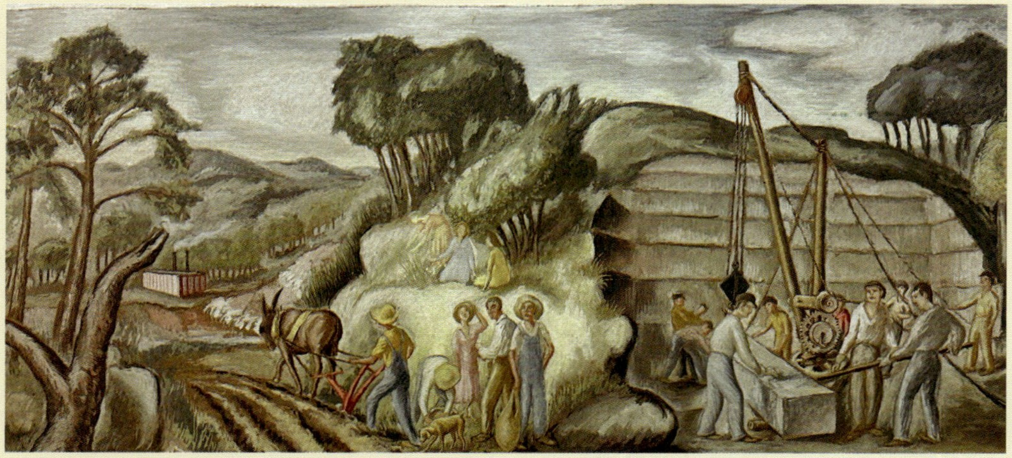

FIGURE 17. Another mural study from the Depression years. Ashantilly Center Archives, date unknown.

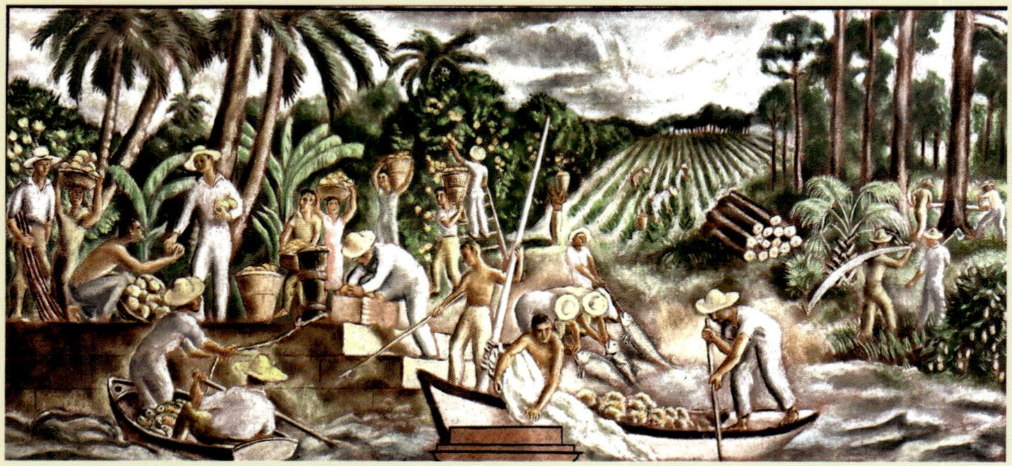

FIGURE 18. Yet another mural study from the Depression years. Ashantilly Center Archives, date unknown.

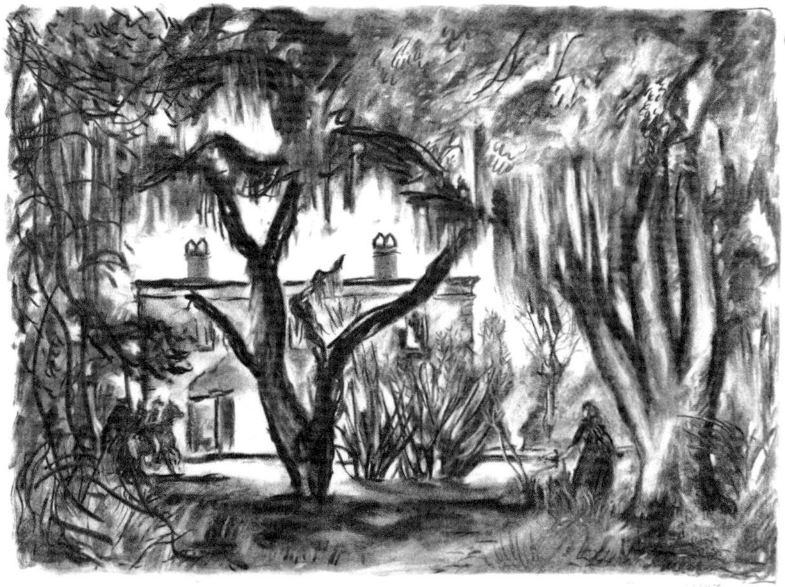

FIGURE 19. Charcoal sketch of Ashantilly prior to the 1937 fire. Ashantilly Center Archives.

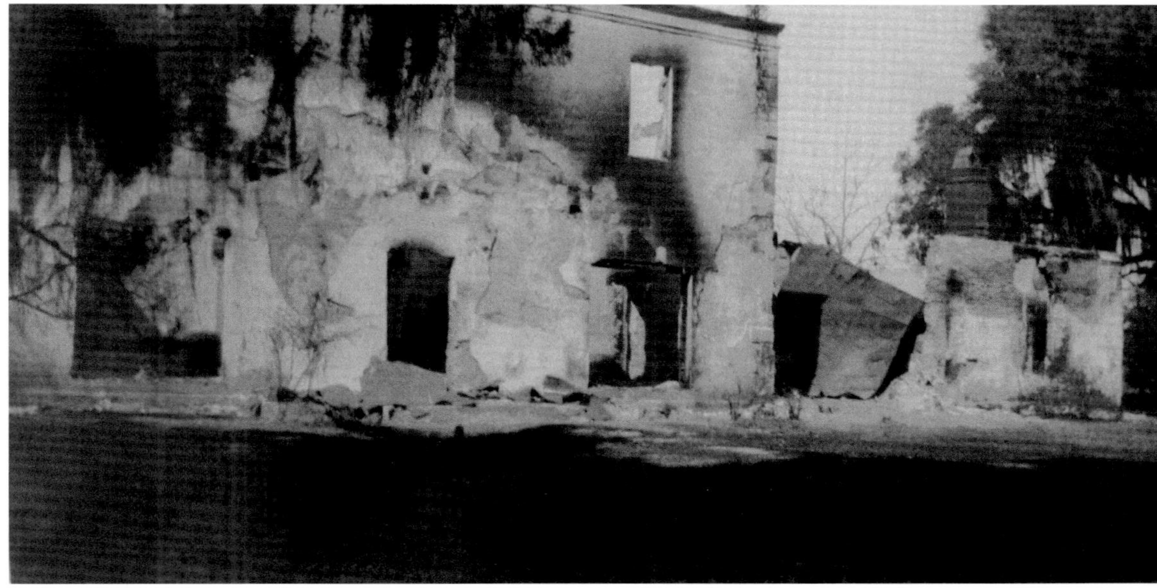

FIGURE 20. Bill Haynes's photograph of the fire's aftermath. Ashantilly Center Archives.

In February 1937 the family home suffered a devastating fire started by a chimney spark. As the fire spread through the cypress shingles added in an 1880s renovation, the family quickly removed as many of their possessions as possible. Sadly, fire service in Darien was not equipped to extinguish the two-story blaze, which left only a stark, two-story tabby core. The family moved to a nearby rental house and considered moving to Savannah where Anne Lee was teaching.

Haynes wanted to do his part to support his family, especially in the depths of the Depression, but how? His sister Anne Lee, through her friendship with Edward Rowan, assistant director with the Treasury Department's Section of Painting and Sculpture, was able to help Haynes get a position as an artist with the Civilian Conservation Corps on Blythe Island at Camp Harwell near Brunswick, Georgia. He served from May 25 to September 25, 1937, and submitted twenty-two watercolors featuring the men working at various physical tasks on the wooded property between the South Brunswick and Turtle Rivers. Haynes captured the spirit and hard work of the men who created what is now a regional park.[19] These images, as shown in figures 21–23, also reflect the influence of regionalism on his work.

After completing his term at the CCC camp, Haynes was given the opportunity to illustrate handmade limited editions of at least three individual Gullah-Geechee stories for his friend A. H. "Bertie" Stoddard, a native of Daufuskie Island, South Carolina, and Savannah, Georgia. "When I returned to Darien," Haynes recounted, "I designed a small booklet, *Br'er Partridge Out Hides Br'er Rabbit*, for Bertie Stoddard. That was my first book!"[20] These stories in Gullah dialect are folktales from 1939. The two men collaborated on three stories from Stoddard's collection.[21] Fortunately, in 1949 Mr. Stoddard recorded a number of these folktales in dialect for the folklore collection of the Library of Congress. His recordings were subsequently transcribed and published along with illustrations by other artists.

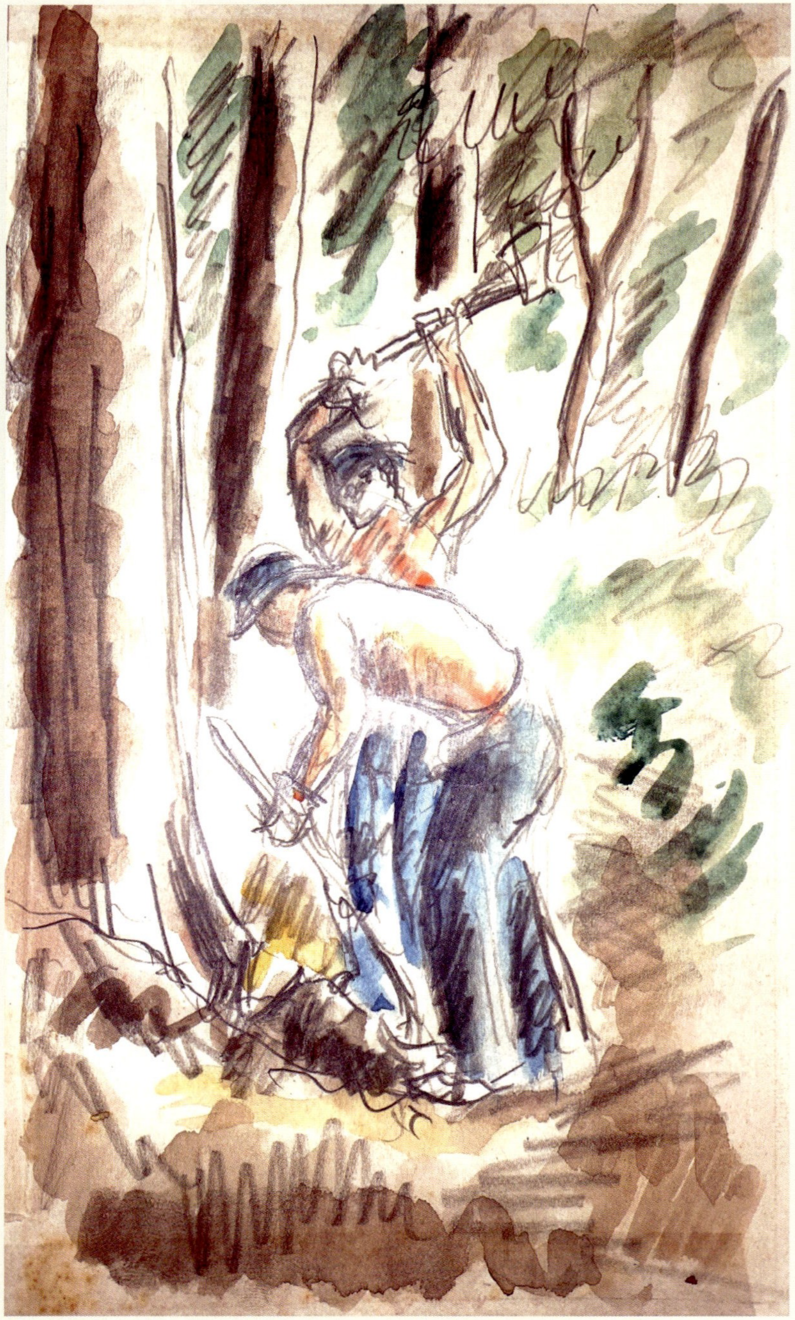

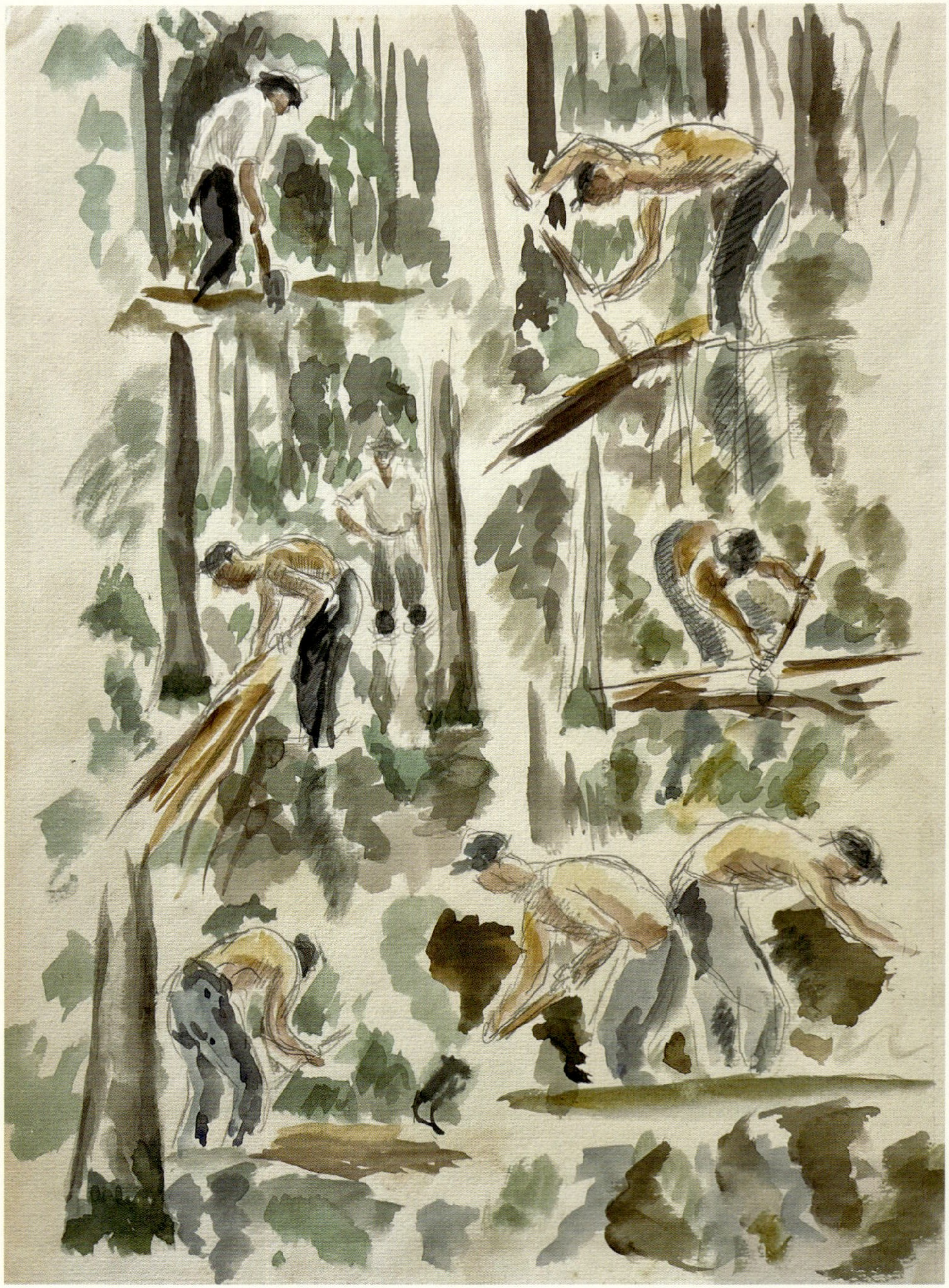

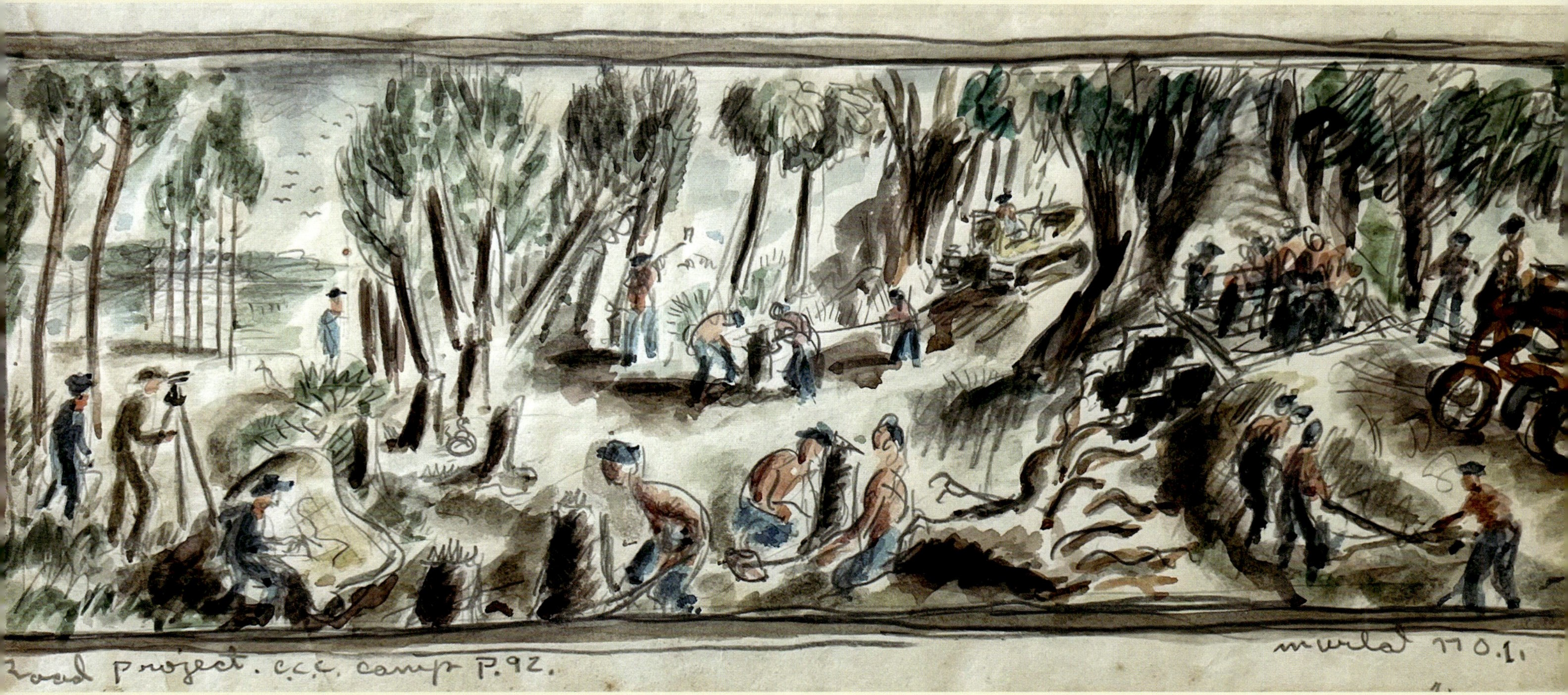

FIGURES 21, 22, and 23. Some of Bill Haynes's Civilian Conservation Corps watercolors. Ashantilly Center Archives.

The 1938 death of Haynes's great-uncle Dr. Robert Simpson of Washington, Georgia, brought an inheritance that provided more capital for the upcoming restoration of Old Tabby, which Haynes persuaded his family to begin. Savannah architect John LeBey prepared blueprints, and a local Black construction crew—likely the descendants of Thomas Spalding's enslaved workers—was directed by Haynes to begin the multiyear project. He was determined to locate vintage materials to keep to the house's early Regency style. While he added a third floor with dormers and metal gabled roof to the new structure, as well as a west-facing exterior grand staircase, he kept Spalding's original room layout for the interior. He sought materials in salvage yards in Charleston and Savannah. He also purchased architectural features such as doors, casings, windows, and assorted shutters as well as beautiful hardware. Haynes and a local crew worked until 1941, when Bill was called to wartime army duty. Although the interior was not fully completed, fortunately, the house was habitable. Haynes reported to nearby Camp Stewart in Hinesville, Georgia, and served in an army artillery battalion, eventually seeing combat duty in New Guinea.

The army was known to use the talents of draftees, so Haynes spent much of his time designing and painting camouflage patterns on tents and netting during his stint in Milne Bay, New Guinea. Having art materials handy allowed Haynes to create a collection of watercolors illustrating both the war as well as the beautiful scenery of the South Pacific.

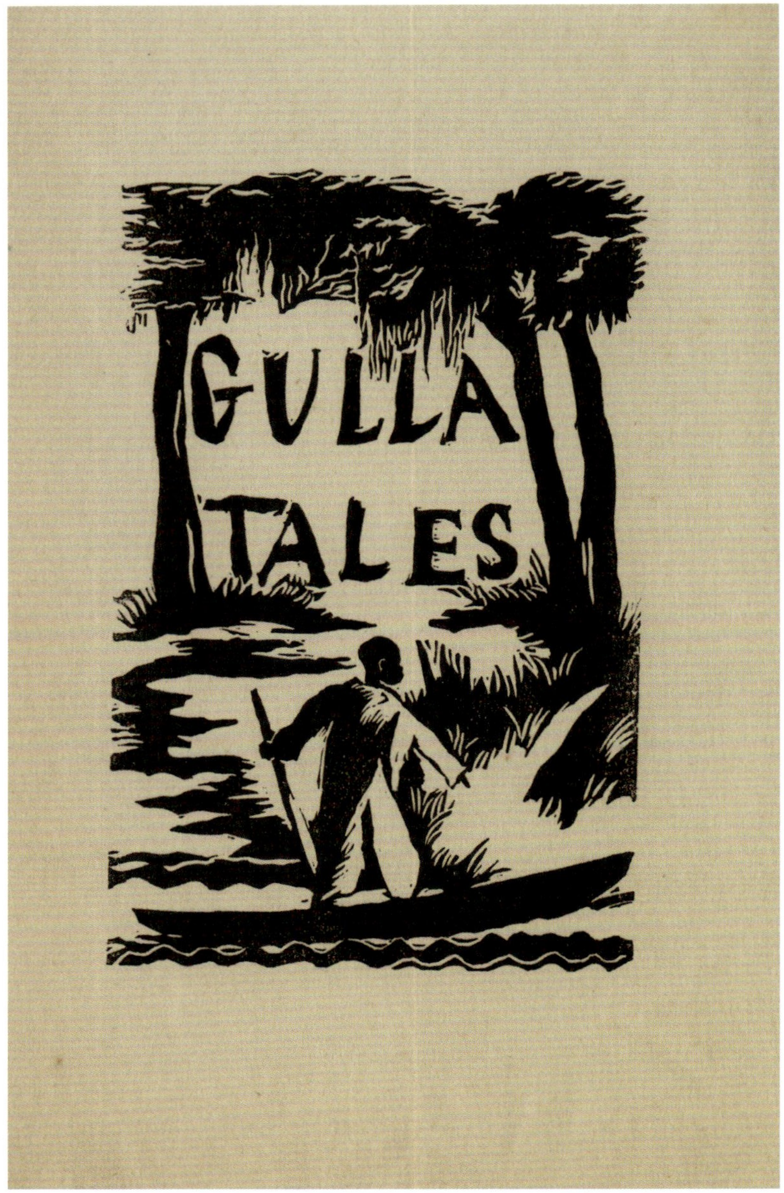

FIGURE 24. A hand-bound original of *Gulla Tales* is in the Hargrett Rare Book and Manuscript Library and contains the four illustrations shown in figures 25–28.

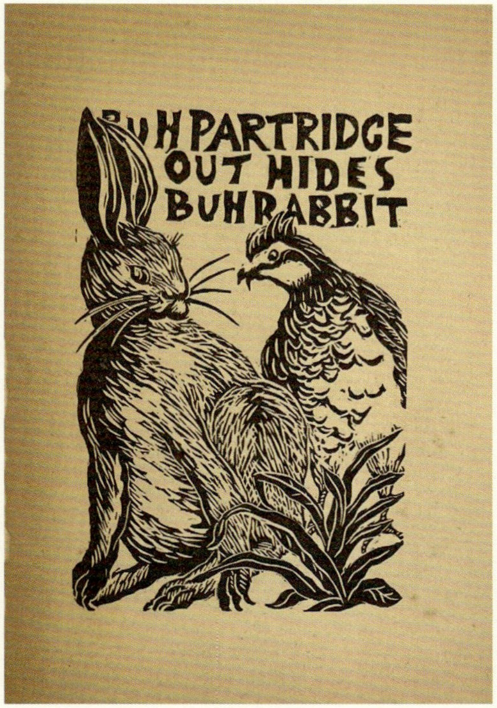

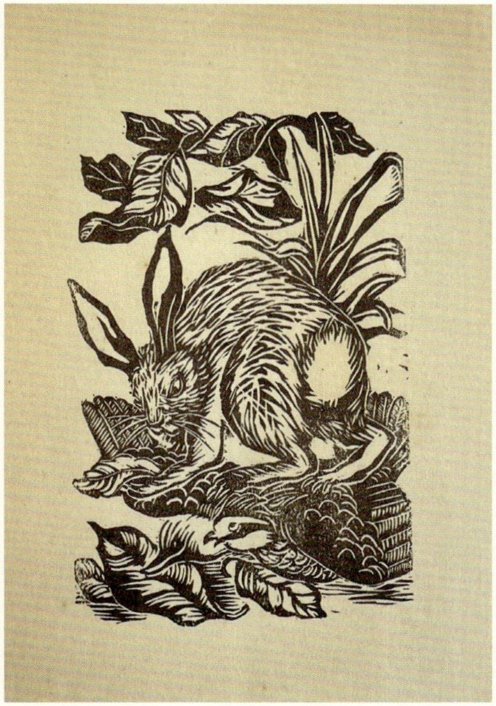

FIGURES 25–26. "Buh Partridge Out Hides Buh Rabbit" (Brother Partridge Out Hides Brother Rabbit).

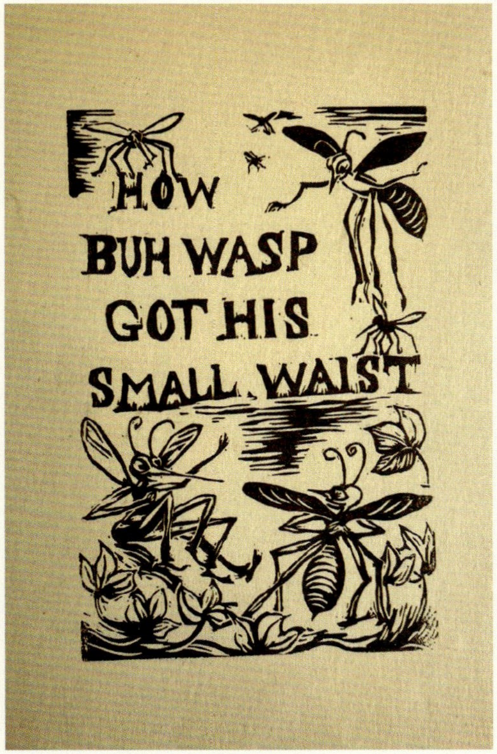

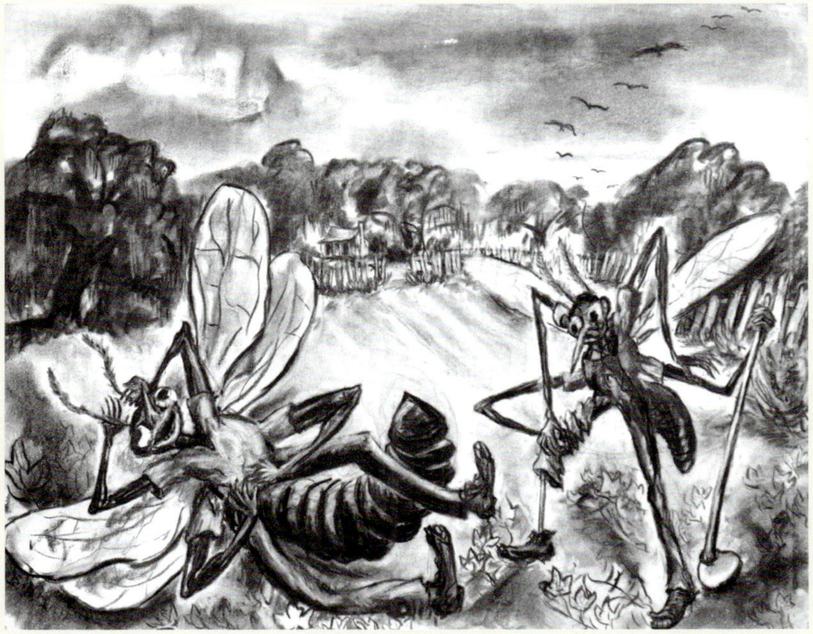

FIGURES 27–28. Title page: "How Buh Wasp Got His Small Waist." This original charcoal sketch for that story is held in the Ashantilly Center Archives.

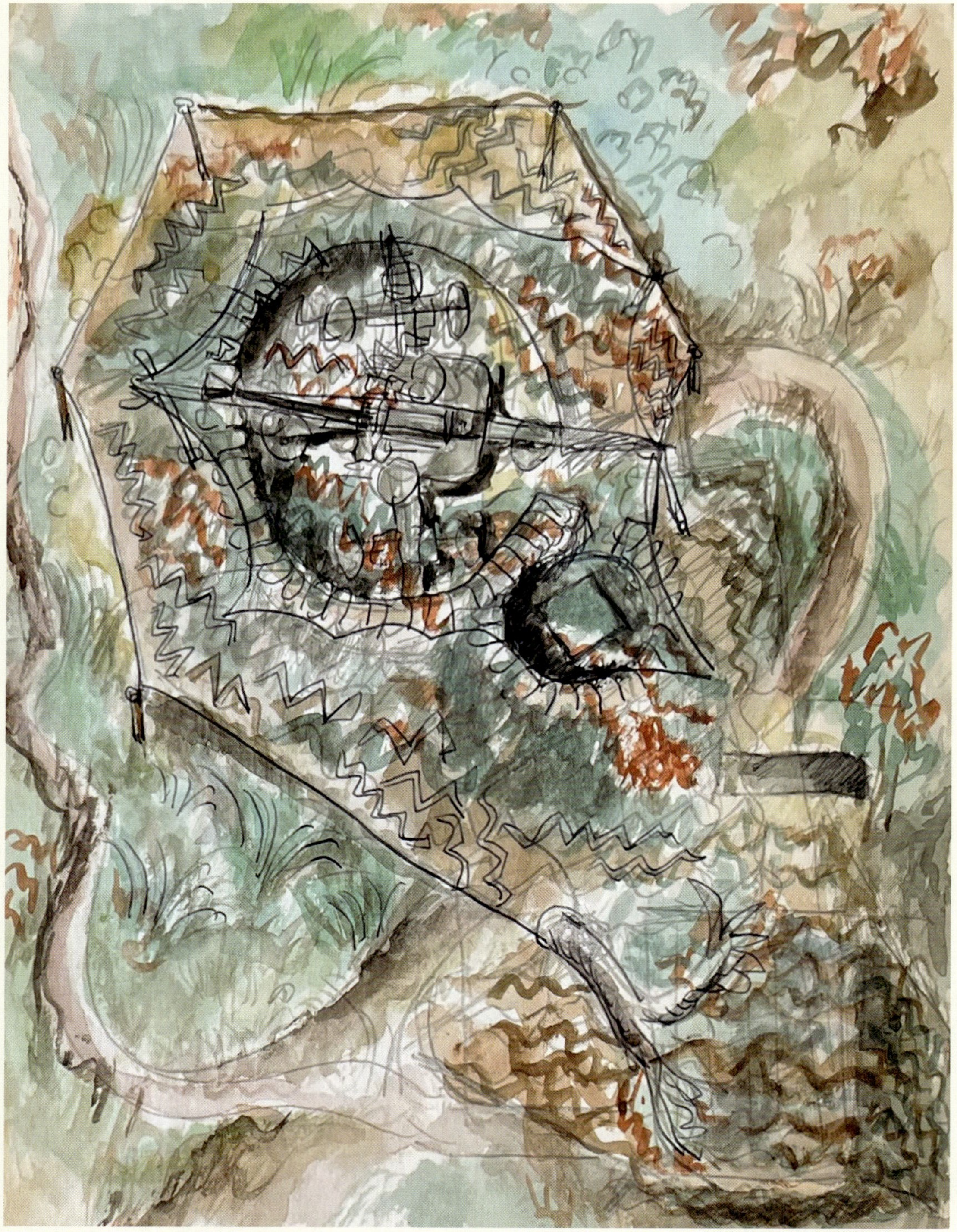

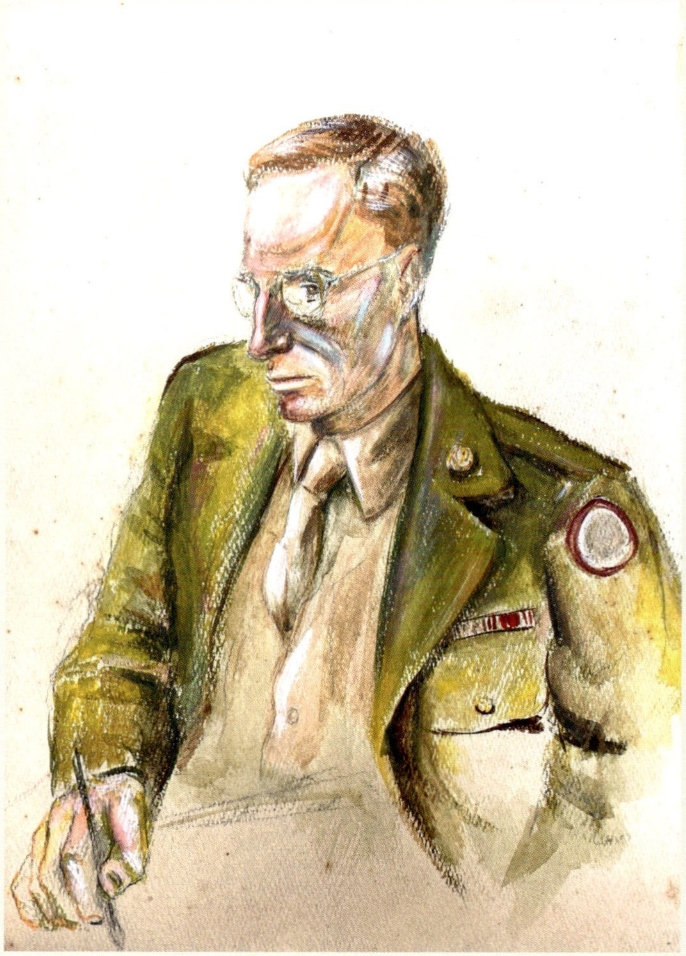

FIGURE 29. Self-portrait (date unknown). Ashantilly Center Archives.

FIGURE 30. Bill Haynes, aerial view, camouflage design for an artillery emplacement.

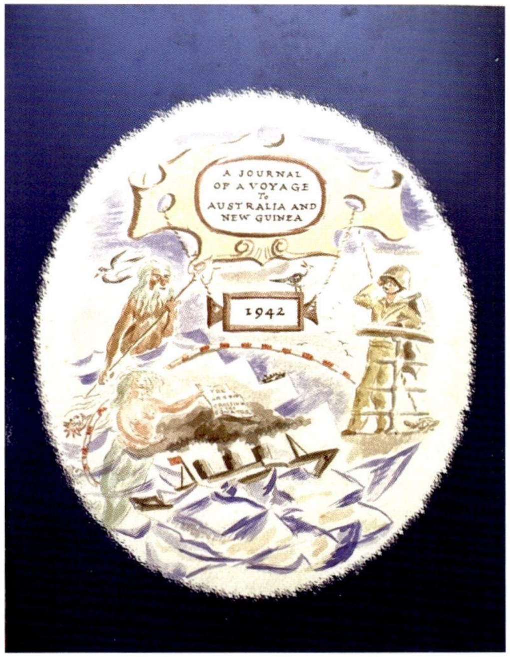

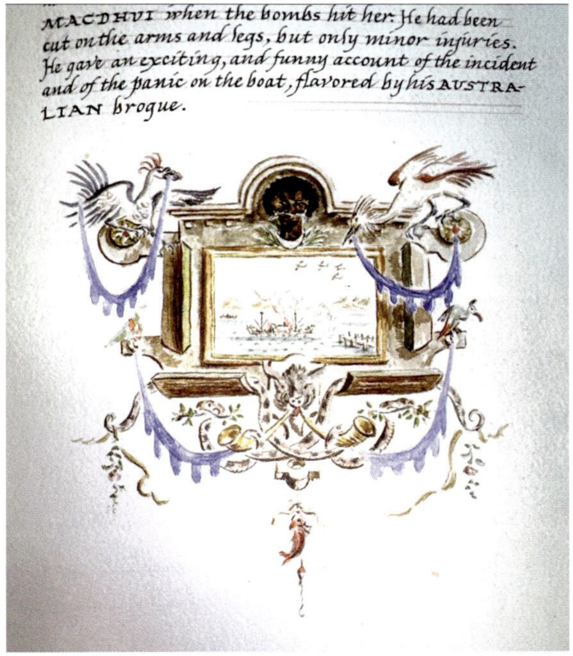

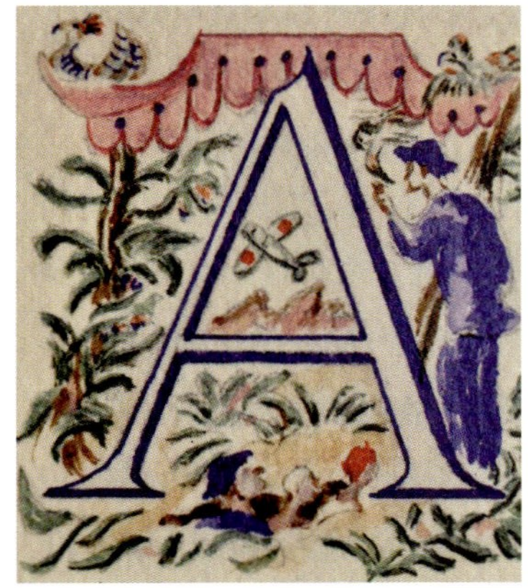

FIGURES 31, 32, and 33.
Haynes's watercolor sketchbooks and calligraphy for "A Journal of a Voyage to Australia and New Guinea." Ashantilly Center Archives.

In his two years in New Guinea, Haynes created a numbered series of watercolor sketchbooks titled "A Journal of a Voyage to Australia and New Guinea."[22] He was fascinated by the colorful, lush landscape and friendly people and created art while the war raged. Haynes's personal narrative in calligraphy was added later to accompany his watercolor sketches. Sixty-six years later, the Henchard Press in Macon, Georgia, published those images with Haynes's calligraphy narrative.[23]

Haynes also brought home a separate set of lively watercolors from New Guinea that followed the life and adventures of a fictional native boy named "Eena" (figures 34–35).

Florence Bethea, assistant librarian at Florida State University and friend of Haynes's sister Frances, wrote an outline for this story and encouraged Haynes to find a publisher. Unfortunately, he could find no takers. Haynes returned home in 1945 with many lovely watercolors but few prospects for a job.

However, partnering with his sister Anne Lee, Haynes's Bartram watercolors debuted in their first public exhibition in 1947. The recent discovery of a newspaper article in the Ashantilly Center Archives yielded vital documentation about Haynes's vintage 1934 Bartram paintings.[24] In the April 3 issue of the *Columbia (South Carolina) Record*, an article by Margaret Babcock Meriwether announced a current art exhibit at the University of South Carolina, "Haynes Paints Bartram," naming Bill Haynes and his sister Anne Lee as co-exhibitors of their artwork.[25] As quoted earlier, Meriwether begins the announcement with Bartram's significant influence on American artists and writers.[26] She mentions John Bartram, William's father, who also published his *Diary of a Journey through the Carolinas in 1765–1766.* Meriwether cites the English Lake District poets and American "wilderness lovers" such as Donald Culross Peattie, Mark Van Doren, and Francis Harper, "who recently paid devoted tributes of appreciation to the Bartrams and showed how deeply indebted to them are both modern naturalists and historians."[27] William Bartram was able to "pass on to a host of readers the joy he felt in beholding the unspoiled wilderness of the southern coast country and mountains with all

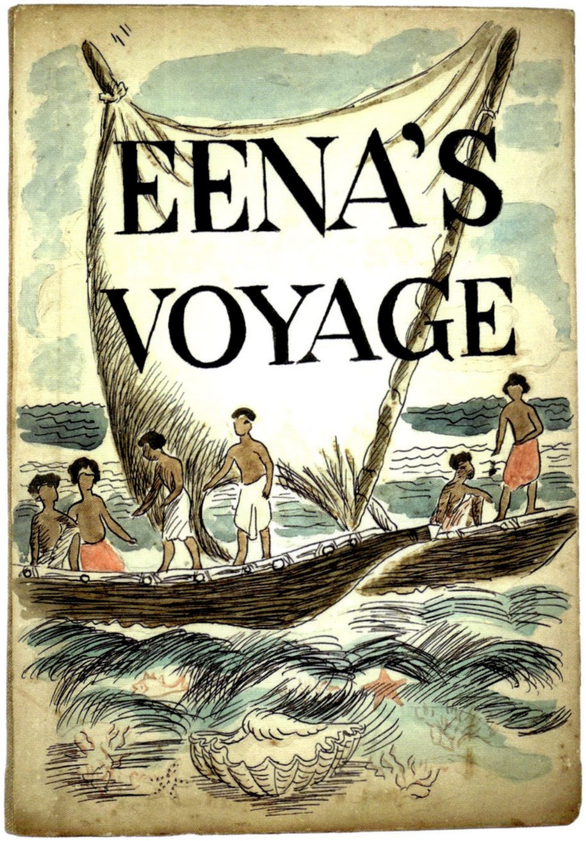

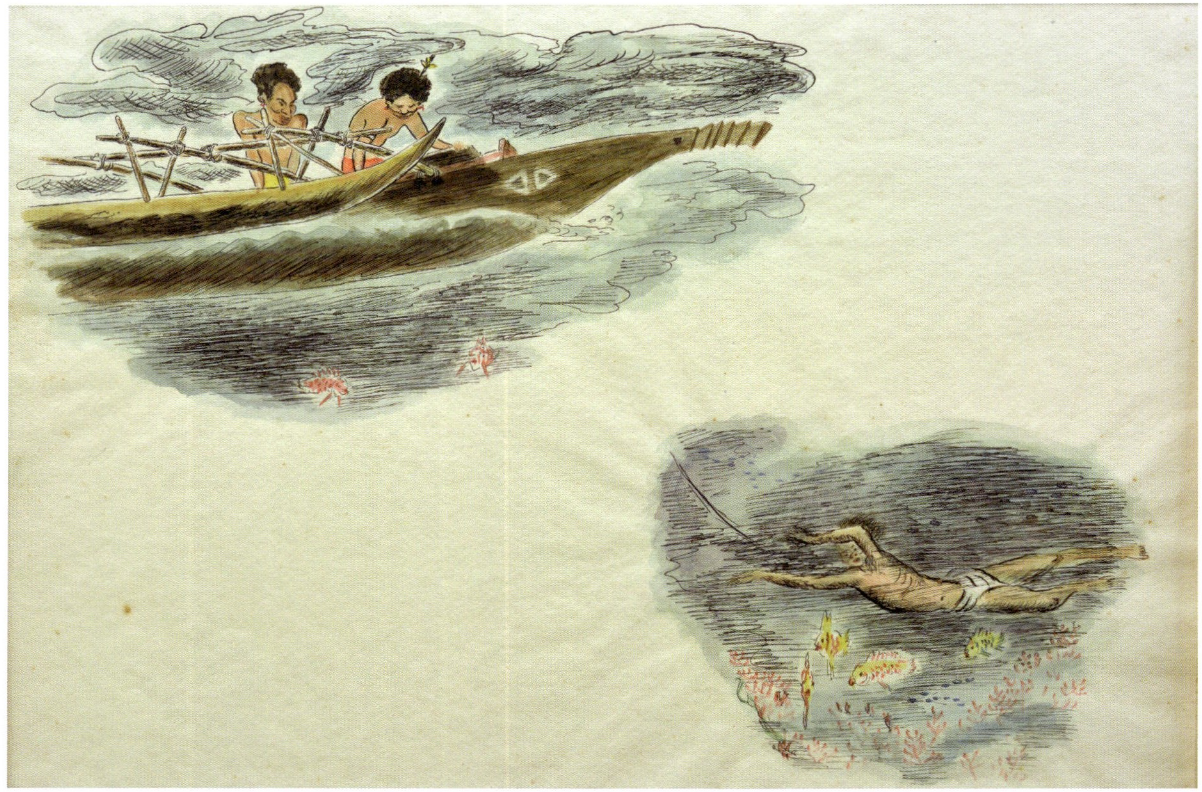

FIGURES 34–35. Bill Haynes's *Eena's Voyage*. Ashantilly Center Archives.

the unwasted wealth of our woods and fields and waters."[28] Introducing Bill Haynes as one of the admirers, she writes:

> William Bartram's happy approach to the outdoor world appeals with special force to young people. Now on exhibit at the South Caroliniana Library of the University is a book which is further proof of Bartram's charm as a guide to an interpreter of the southern scene for young disciples. In this case it was not a boy from far away who was drawn to see the country but a native son whose eyes were made keener and whose spirit was quickened to appropriate his home environment by Bartram's ageless enthusiasm.[29]

Haynes soon went back to New York City and enrolled at Cooper Union. He received a certificate in illustration and design in 1948, expecting to go into commercial work. He also took evening and weekend classes in typography at the American Institute of Graphic Arts, where his introduction to letterpress printing immediately appealed to him. Haynes also found a bride in New York City, Natalie Erdman. Staying in New York City required Haynes to quickly find more substantial employment. One of his graphic arts instructors, Jim Hendrickson, sent a recommendation for Haynes to join Bruce Rogers's Thistle Press in printing the Frick Art Collection catalog. Rogers's project managers, Bertram L. Clarke and David J. Way, were delighted to get an eager pupil who had an artist's training. According to Haynes:

> What they wanted was somebody (as assistant) who knew absolutely nothing, and I fitted the case. That's why I got the job. It was a wonderful experience for me

> because it was not in one of those dirty job shops with horrible type and slovenly habits, but a place where everything was to be done just right and to the highest standards. Not only that, but it was coming under the eye of probably the most important person in the typographic field at that time . . . and that was Bruce Rogers.[30]

FIGURE 36. Scrolled detail from the title page of the Frick catalog, 1949, Pittsburgh, printed at the University of Pennsylvania. Ashantilly Center Archives.

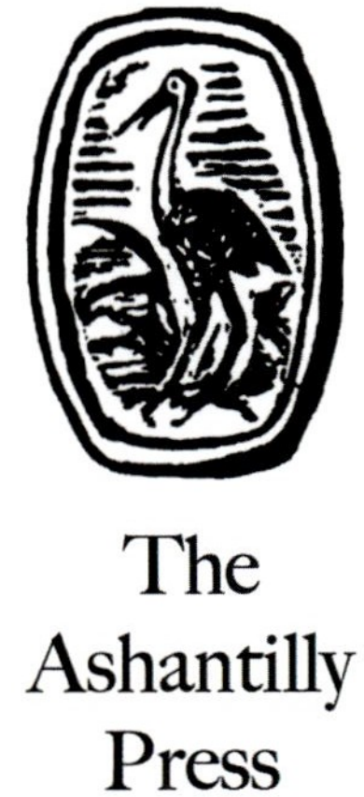

FIGURE 37. Bill carved the Ashantilly Press mark, or "device," which features a heron in the reeds. Ashantilly Center Archives.

Haynes worked there for three years, learning from these well-known letterpress legends. He made many friends for life during this period in New York City, but more importantly, he had finally found a vocation that fit his talents and interests. In a 1997 interview he said, "I was caught fast like Brer Rabbit by the Tar Baby. From that moment all my efforts were directed toward gaining useful knowledge in the art of printing."[31]

Returning to Ashantilly in 1954, the first project at the new Ashantilly Press was a commission by Bessie Lewis, McIntosh County historian and one of Haynes's former teachers. Researchers at the Georgia Archives recently had discovered a map of the original Fort King George, constructed in 1721 on the lower bluff of the Altamaha River close to Darien.[32] Miss Lewis asked Haynes to create a silkscreen reproduction of it as a four-color, hand-screened map complete with delicate compass roses and cartouche.

Maps continued to be one of Haynes's interests, dating back to his "embellished" version of Bartram's *Travels*; on page 42, you see Haynes's very creative cartouche and lovely compass roses.

The first book Haynes printed as sole proprietor of the Ashantilly Press was a reprinting of Elfrida DeRenne Barrow and Laura Palmer Bell's *Anchored Yesterdays*, graced by wood-engraved illumination at the beginning of each watch.[33]

Haynes had only a small platen press and limited amounts of Caslon type. He said of the one-year undertaking, "I didn't know the first thing about what I should charge. I had to print the first part, then redistribute and reset the type to print the other half. . . . Boy was I glad when it was finished!"[34]

This was the first of many books printed by Haynes at Ashantilly Press to win the Southern Books Competition. According to Haynes, the award was "one of the things that put me on the map."[35] *Johnny Leber* received "Top Winner" in 1962, a new designation from the Southern Books Competition jury, as the "best designed book among the ninety-seven submitted."[36] Haynes's printing of his grandfather Haynes's *The Field Diary of a Confederate Soldier* in 1963 was the only private press book to receive recognition. His exquisite wood engravings, the intricate borders, and charming linoleum-block illustrations showcased his talent and skill year after year on the larger Chandler and Price motorized press acquired in the 1960s.

As a result, Ashantilly books regularly met with positive critical response. They were selected for the Southern Books Competition exhibits almost annually from 1956 to 1976, a total unmatched among Georgia private presses. The American Institute of Graphic Arts selected titles for two of its shows: *Fifty Books of the Year in 1967 (The Things I Want)* and *One Hundred Best Children's Books of 1967–1968*. Titles were added to the private press collections of the Newberry Library and the Rare Books Division of the New York Public Library. Copies of *The Country Place*, by poet Marie E. Reddy, printed by Haynes and

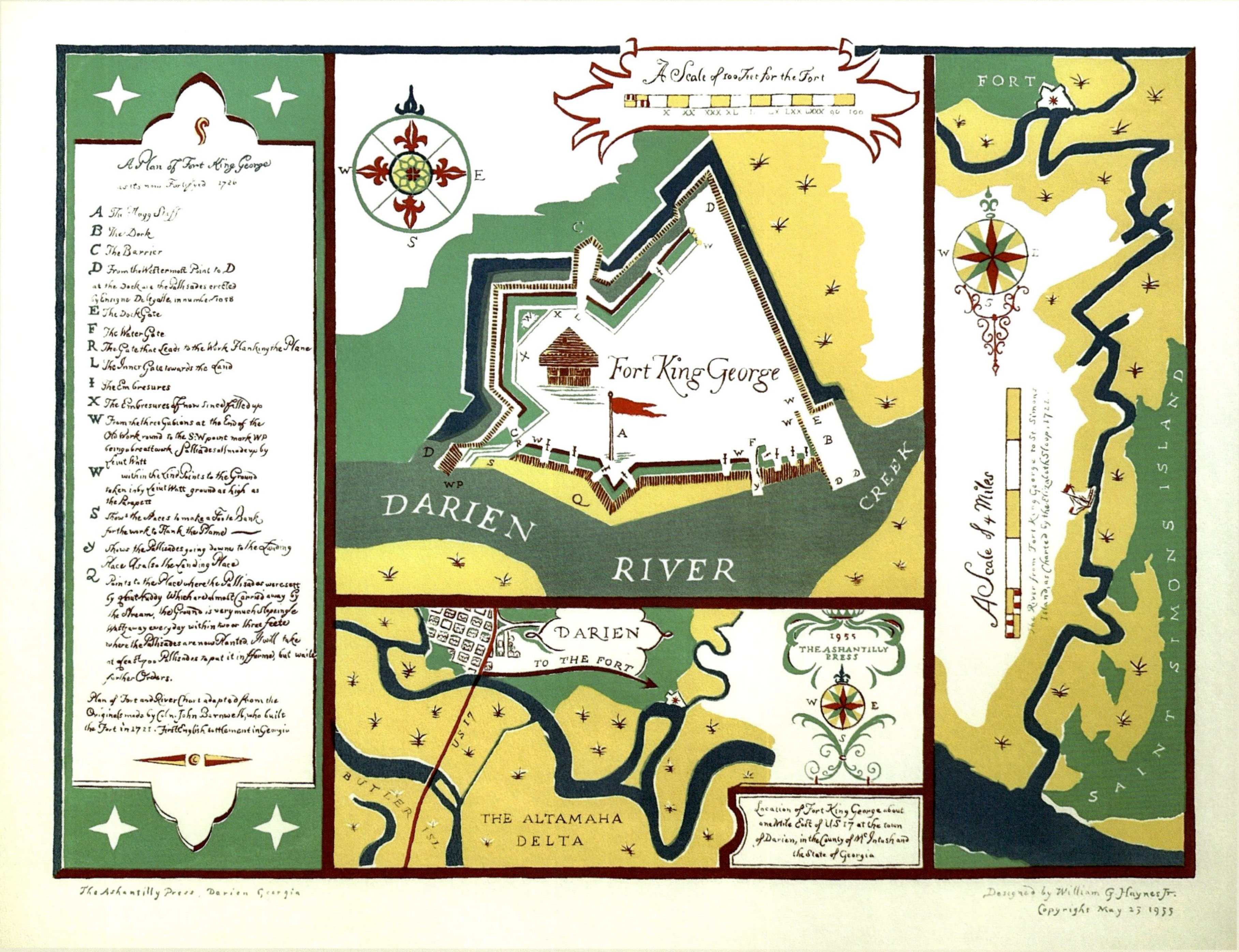

FIGURE 38. A map by Bill Haynes. Ashantilly Center Archives.

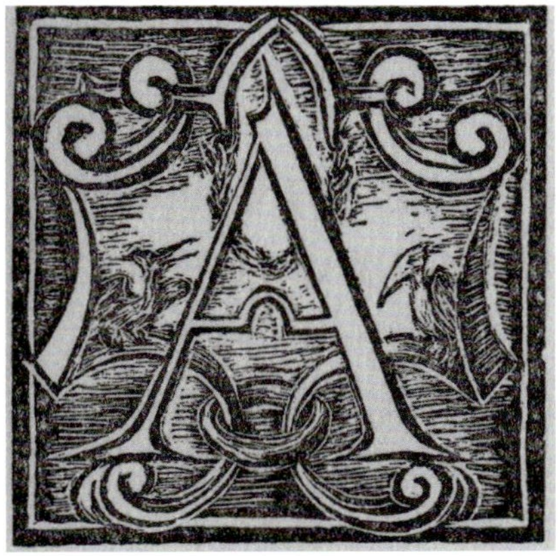

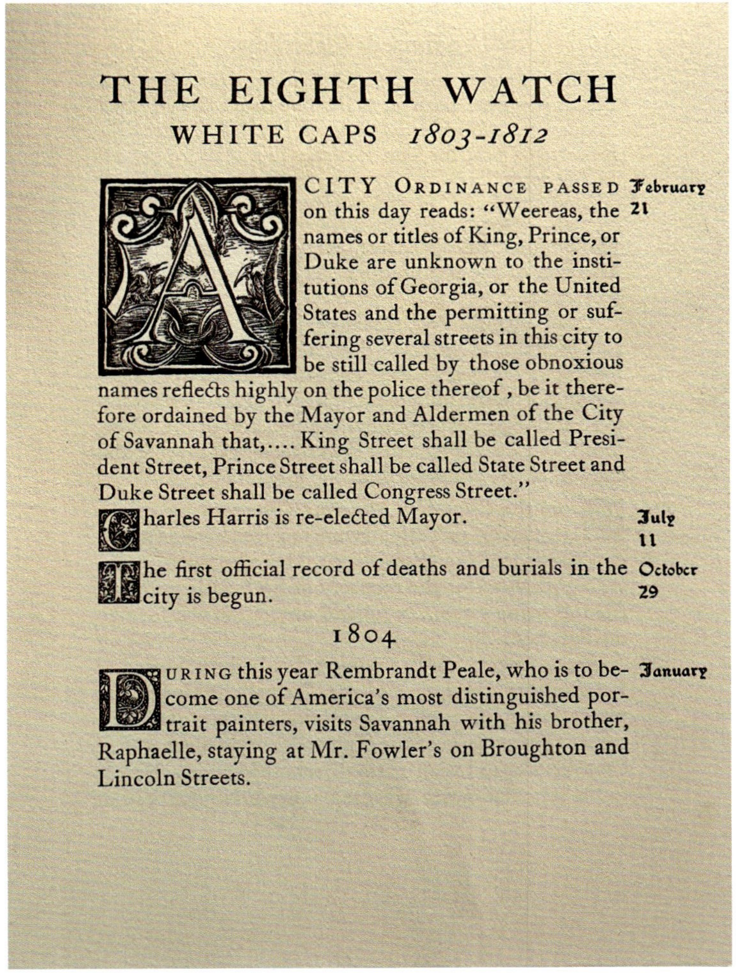

THE EIGHTH WATCH

WHITE CAPS *1803-1812*

A CITY ORDINANCE PASSED on this day reads: "Weereas, the names or titles of King, Prince, or Duke are unknown to the institutions of Georgia, or the United States and the permitting or suffering several streets in this city to be still called by those obnoxious names reflects highly on the police thereof, be it therefore ordained by the Mayor and Aldermen of the City of Savannah that,.... King Street shall be called President Street, Prince Street shall be called State Street and Duke Street shall be called Congress Street." February 21

Charles Harris is re-elected Mayor. July 11

The first official record of deaths and burials in the city is begun. October 29

1804

DURING this year Rembrandt Peale, who is to become one of America's most distinguished portrait painters, visits Savannah with his brother, Raphaelle, staying at Mr. Fowler's on Broughton and Lincoln Streets. January

FIGURES 39–40. Bill Haynes's Ashantilly Press version of *Anchored Yesterdays*. Ashantilly Center Archives.

featuring linoleum-cut illustrations by his sister Anne Lee, were added to every children's reading room in the New York Library system. As another fine printer in Georgia said, "Bill Haynes is the closest thing we have to a living national treasure!"[37]

The Barrow and Bell families became intimate friends with Haynes and his family when Bill printed *A Letter from Benjamin Franklin to Noble Wimberly Jones*. His cover design was inspired by one of Mrs. Barrow's gorgeous Chinese rugs at Wormsloe, the family home in Savannah.[38] All books are in both the Ashantilly Center Archives and in the Hargrett Rare Book and Manuscript Library collection. They are occasionally found on rare-book sellers' sites as well.

In 1965 Haynes worked on a small booklet entitled *John and William Bartram in McIntosh*, but no complete copy can be located. Bartram continued to inspire and influence Haynes's art, and the few prints now in the Hargrett collection are in a bold style similar to William Zorach's wood engravings. They exemplify another interpretive style that Haynes envisioned for Bartram's famous *Travels*.[39]

As commercial handset letterpress waned in the transition to new technologies, Haynes's focus in the late 1960s and early 1970s was on coastal Georgia's environmental challenges. The Corps of Engineers planned a potentially devastating channelization of the Altamaha River to support barge traffic from Darien to the Gulf of Mexico. Haynes organized and rallied the local crabbers, shrimpers, and fishermen, called in many prominent leaders, academics, and local businessmen, and

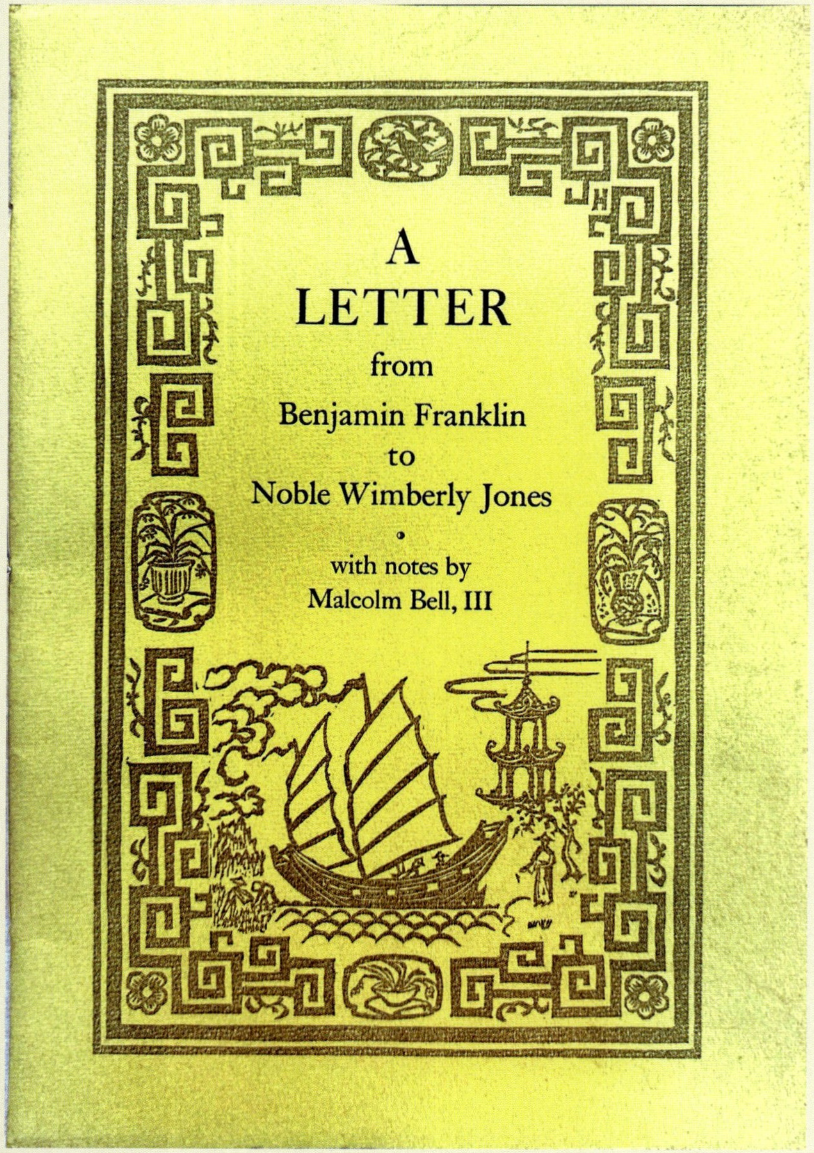

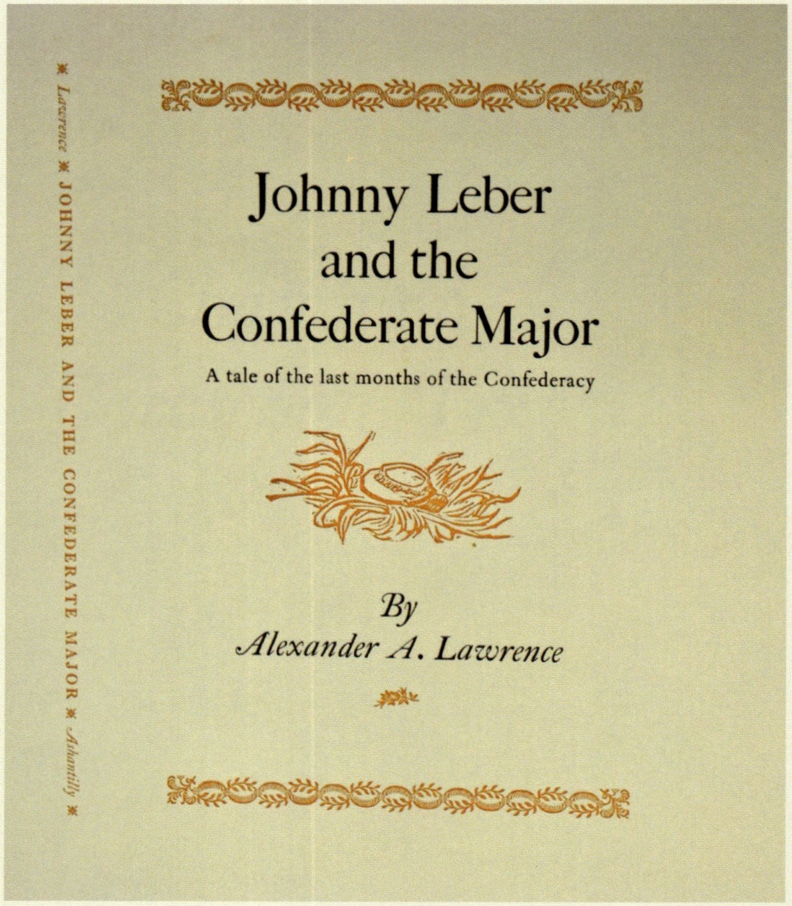

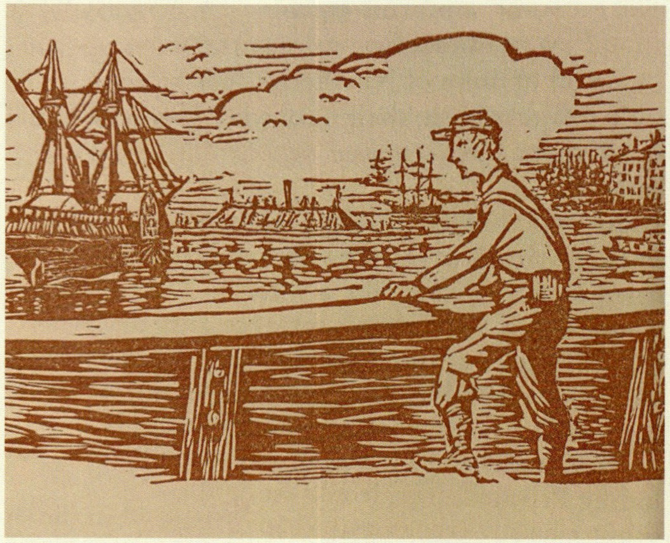

FIGURES 41, 42, and 43. Some of Bill Haynes's Ashantilly books and accompanying artwork. Note that Leber is "Rebel" spelled backward. Ashantilly Center Archives.

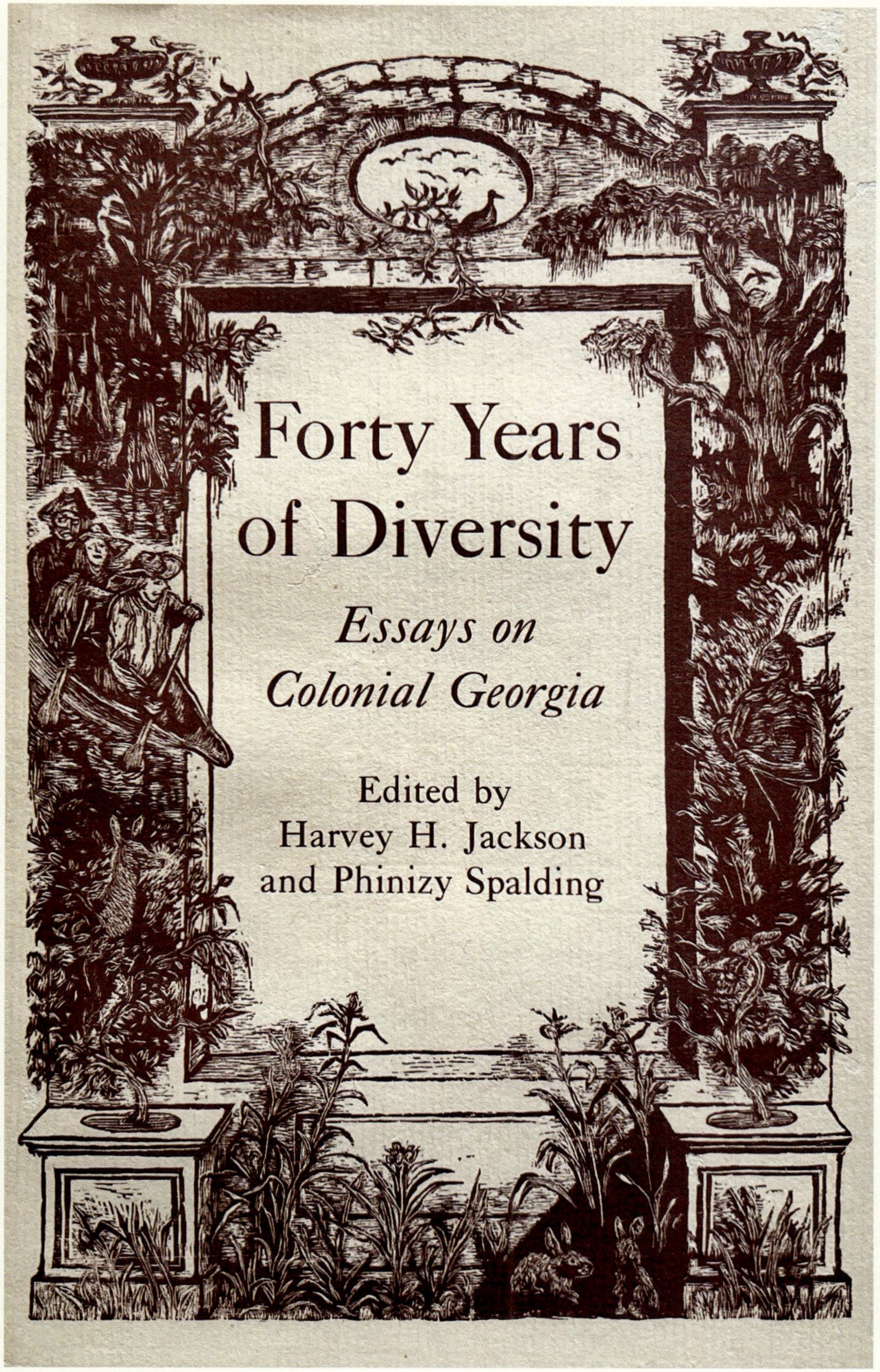

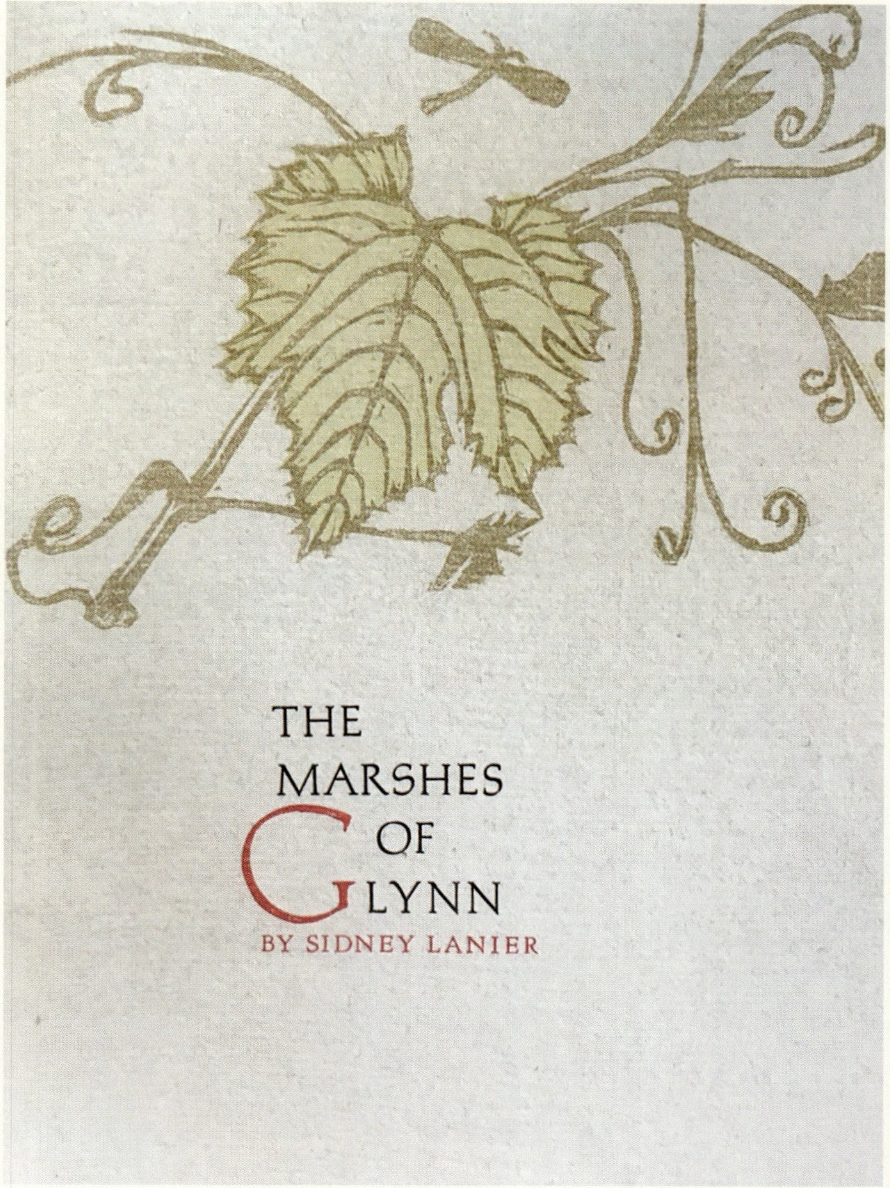

FIGURES 44–45. On the left, an example of intricate nature-based wood engraving. On the right, a perennial favorite, Sidney Lanier's *The Marshes of Glynn*, which Haynes illustrated and hand-printed, has been reprinted many times. Ashantilly Center Archives.

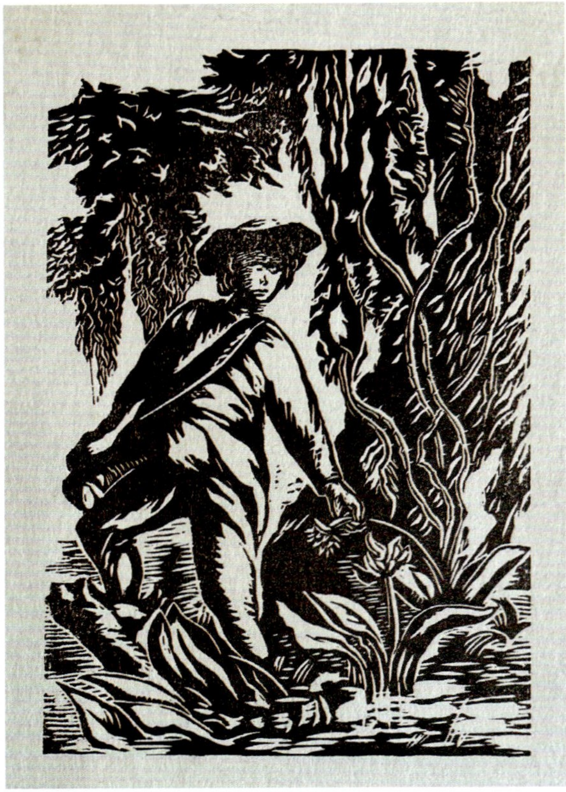

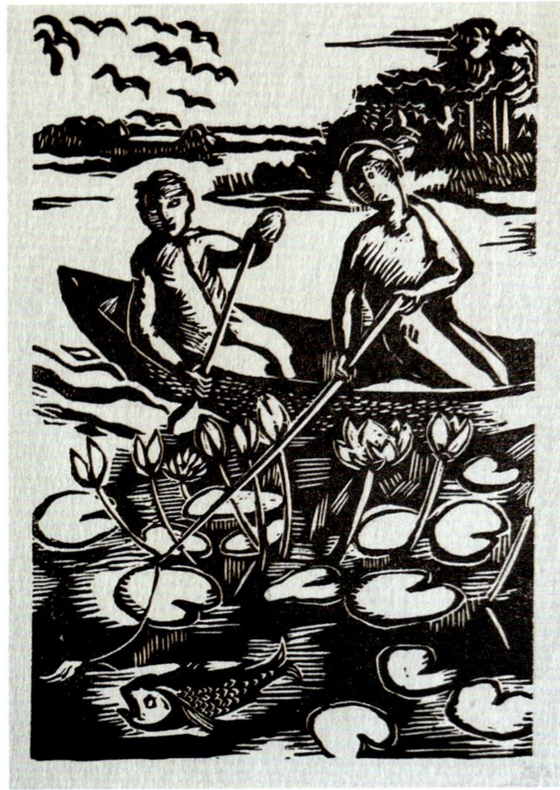

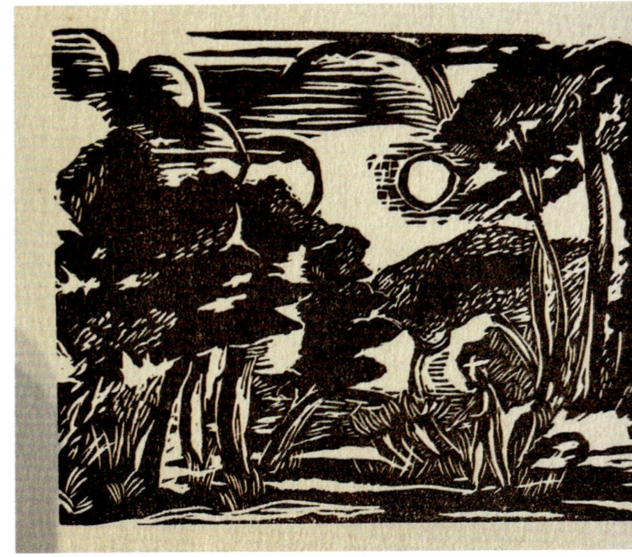

FIGURES 46, 47, and 48. Illustrations from "John and William Bartram in McIntosh." Ashantilly Center Archives.

held the Rally for the Protection of the Altamaha River Basin in 1971.

Haynes created a beautiful wood engraving of a single paddler on the Altamaha and set type for the "O Alatamaha" quote from part I, chapter V of Bartram's *Travels*, confirming Bartram's role in another phase of the art of Bill Haynes.[40]

Haynes's activism continued beyond the campaign against channelization to encompass broader issues of water quality in Georgia's coastal zone. Haynes invited scientists based at Sapelo Island's Marine Institute, where early research was being done on Georgia's coastal saltmarshes, to provide substantive evidence for better water quality regulation. He used his personal contacts to assemble the influential state leaders who were recognizing pollution threats to Georgia's pristine coastal waters. These years marked the beginnings of Georgia's environmental protection movement within the Department of Natural Resources.

During this period, we see more evidence of Haynes's enduring appreciation for William Bartram. During the 1970s, Haynes became a charter member of the Georgia Bartram Trail Society. He and landscape architect Clermont "Monty" Lee organized the Bartram Bicentennial Conference in Savannah, Georgia, in 1973.[41] In an article in the July 1973 *Savannah* magazine, Haynes wrote about Bartram's year in Georgia and of the influence of editor Mark Van Doren's 1928 edition of the *Travels* and the "subsequent articles published in scientific journals."[42] The conference featured Dr. Joseph Ewan of Tulane University, who gave a keynote speech entitled "William Bartram's Hidden Role in the Beginnings of Natural History in the United

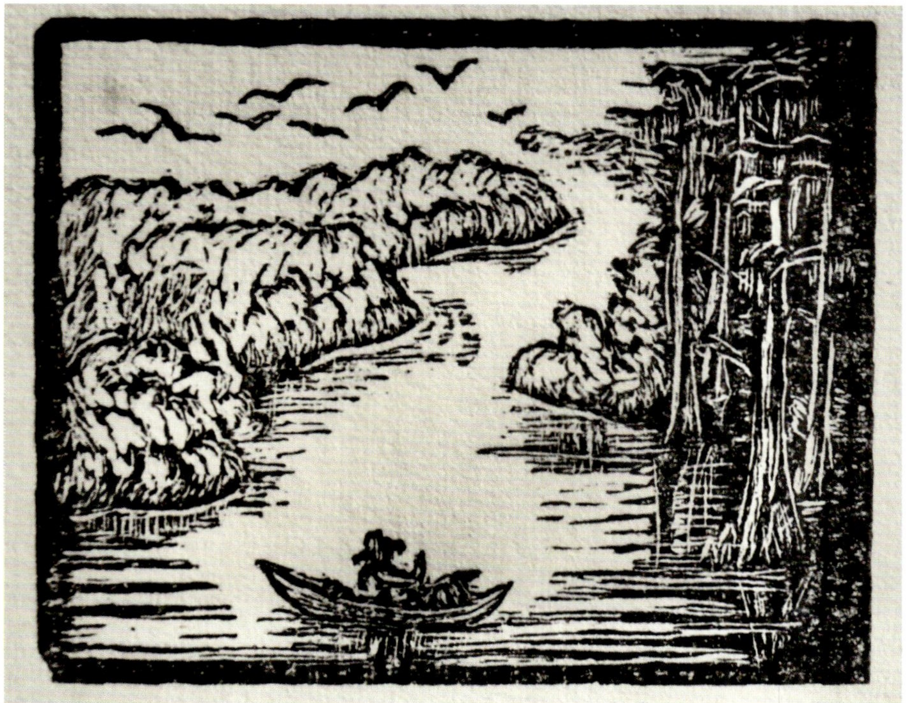

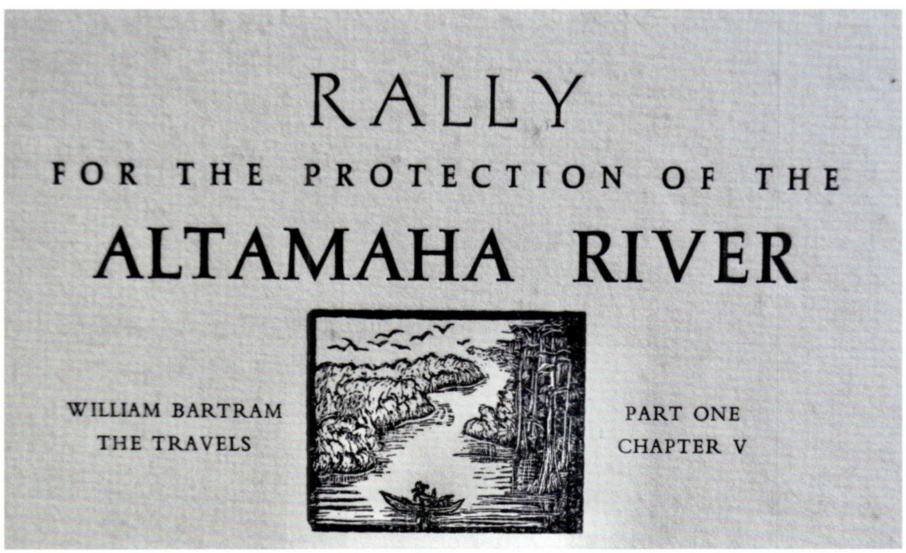

FIGURES 49–50. Illustrations as part of Haynes's Altamaha preservation work. Ashantilly Center Archives.

States."[43] At that time the Bartram Trail Society in Georgia was an advocate for locating and marking trails in Georgia to connect with Bartram's path throughout the Southeast.

In 1976 Haynes led a group of dedicated coastal citizens who organized Man in the Landscape, a conference held in Darien to bring to Georgia's coastal community the concept of promoting its natural beauty and unique cultural history as tourist attractions.[44] The title page of the conference proceedings begins with Haynes's homage to William Bartram:

> William Bartram, the eighteenth-century American naturalist, was the pivot around which the conference revolved. When William Bartram and his father visited the Georgia coast, they observed man's use and dependence on the natural world around him. As we look toward the future, man's relation to the landscape will be of increasing importance. The purpose of the conference was to enquire into ways of harmonious use of the resources of our historic and natural areas positively, profitably, and to ensure their many values will not be diminished.[45]

This 1976 bicentennial conference yielded the concept we now know as "ecotourism," so relevant to the current coastal seafood and tourism economy in today's McIntosh County. Recognizing his tenacious advocacy for Georgia's coast, Haynes was awarded the 1983 "Rock" Howard Award, granted by Georgia's Department of Natural Resources—its highest recognition given to a citizen. In his acceptance speech, Haynes likened "Rock" Howard to Bartram, and his "profound influence on the imagination of Georgians . . . did imply an insistence on preserving the natural environment as necessary to his well-being."[46] A charter member of the Bartram Trail Society in Georgia and cofounder of the Lower Altamaha Historical Society, Haynes also served on the Georgia Conservancy's Board of Trustees.

In 1993 the last remaining Haynes family members, Bill and his sister Anne Lee, created the Ashantilly Center, Inc. The culmination of Bill's lifework is seen in the founding documents:

> The mission of the Ashantilly Center, Inc., a 501(c)(3) nonprofit, is to organize and implement a program of conservation, including Ashantilly property and its legacy, to provide a vehicle for continuing education, scientific advancement and charitable endeavor which focus on the natural and built environments integral to the Georgia Coast.

At the center, a variety of programs and partnerships pursue this mission. The Ashantilly board has reopened the Ashantilly Press print shop to join a resurgence of letterpress printing as art with an artist-in-residence program and with various book arts classes and workshops. In 2015 Ashantilly Center was named to the National Register of Historic Places. Memberships, grants, and donations fund the center's ongoing commitment to Haynes's vision.[47]

More than 150 years separated the existence of these two Williams. William the naturalist from Pennsylvania was exploring and detailing nature in Georgia before the United States even existed. The second William, Bill, the twentieth-century artist and printer, was inspired by Bartram's details of early Georgia's natural state, illuminating and strengthening the Bartram legacy through his lifetime of art and advocacy, which lives on into the twenty-first century.

3 Bartram's *Travels* Illustrated

PAINTINGS BY WILLIAM G. HAYNES JR.,

ACCOMPANIED BY QUOTATIONS FROM WILLIAM BARTRAM;

ANNOTATIONS BY DORINDA G. DALLMEYER

NOTE: All page numbers cited to Bartram come from the edition of *Travels* posted on the University of North Carolina's website Documenting the American South, https://docsouth.unc.edu/nc/bartram/bartram.html. This online text is a transcription of the first edition of William Bartram's *Travels*, printed by James & Johnson (Philadelphia, 1791).

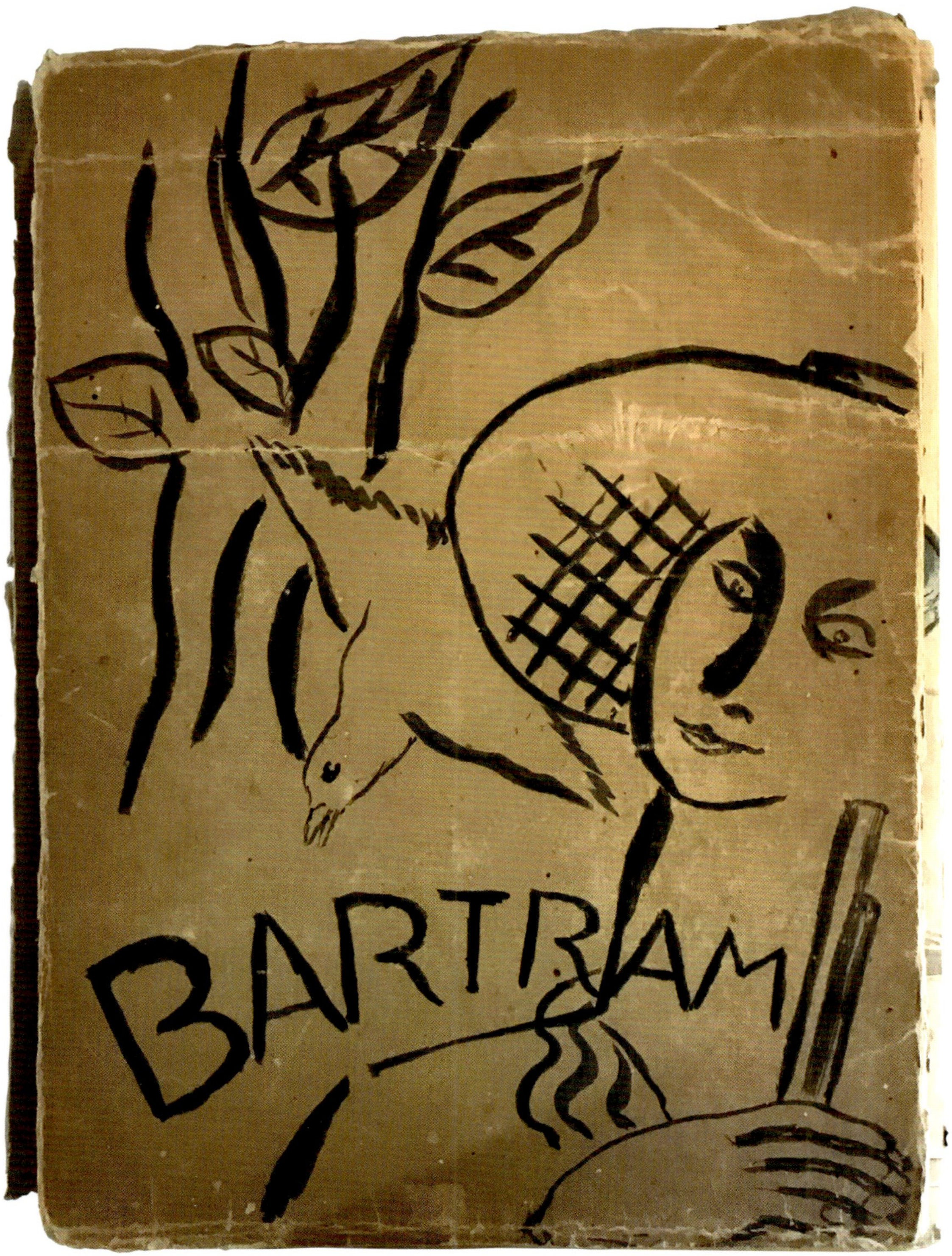

The cover for the scrapbook in which the watercolors were arranged shows William Bartram with a tree and a bird in flight over his shoulder. A colorful bird in flight appears as a motif many times throughout the suite of watercolors.

➤ The frontispiece shows *Magnolia grandiflora* in fruit, with what will become the familia figure of William Bartram, this time propelling a boat upstream. Haynes uses the short title "William Bartram's *Travels*," by which the book usually is known, rather than Bartram's more detailed *Travels through North & South Carolina, Georgia, East & West Florida, the Cherokee Country, the Extensive Territories of the Muscogulges, or Creek Confederacy, and the Coun of the Chactaws; Containing an Account of the So and Natural Productions of Those Regions, Togeth with Observations on the Manners of the Indians. Embellished with Copper-Plates.*

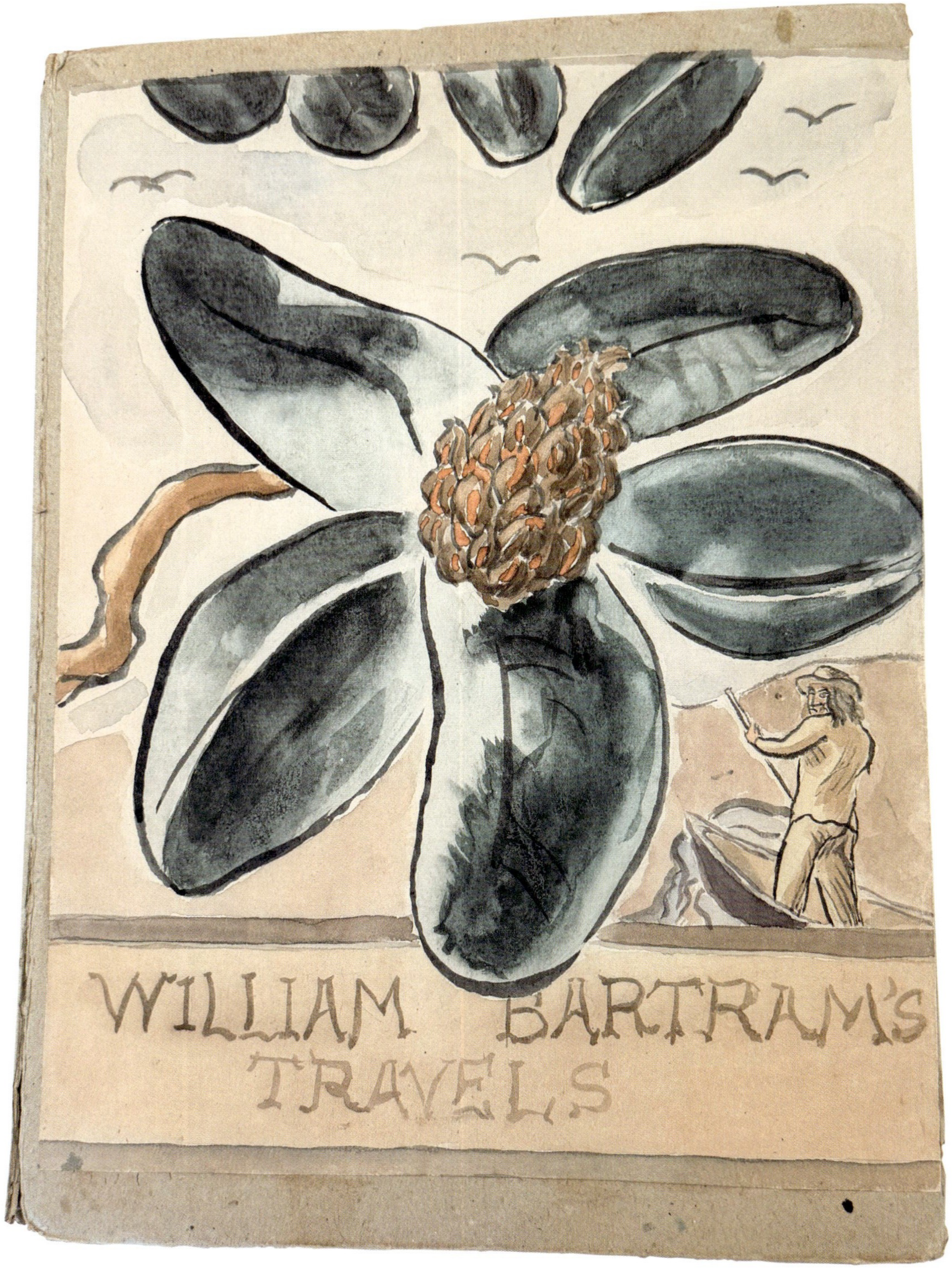

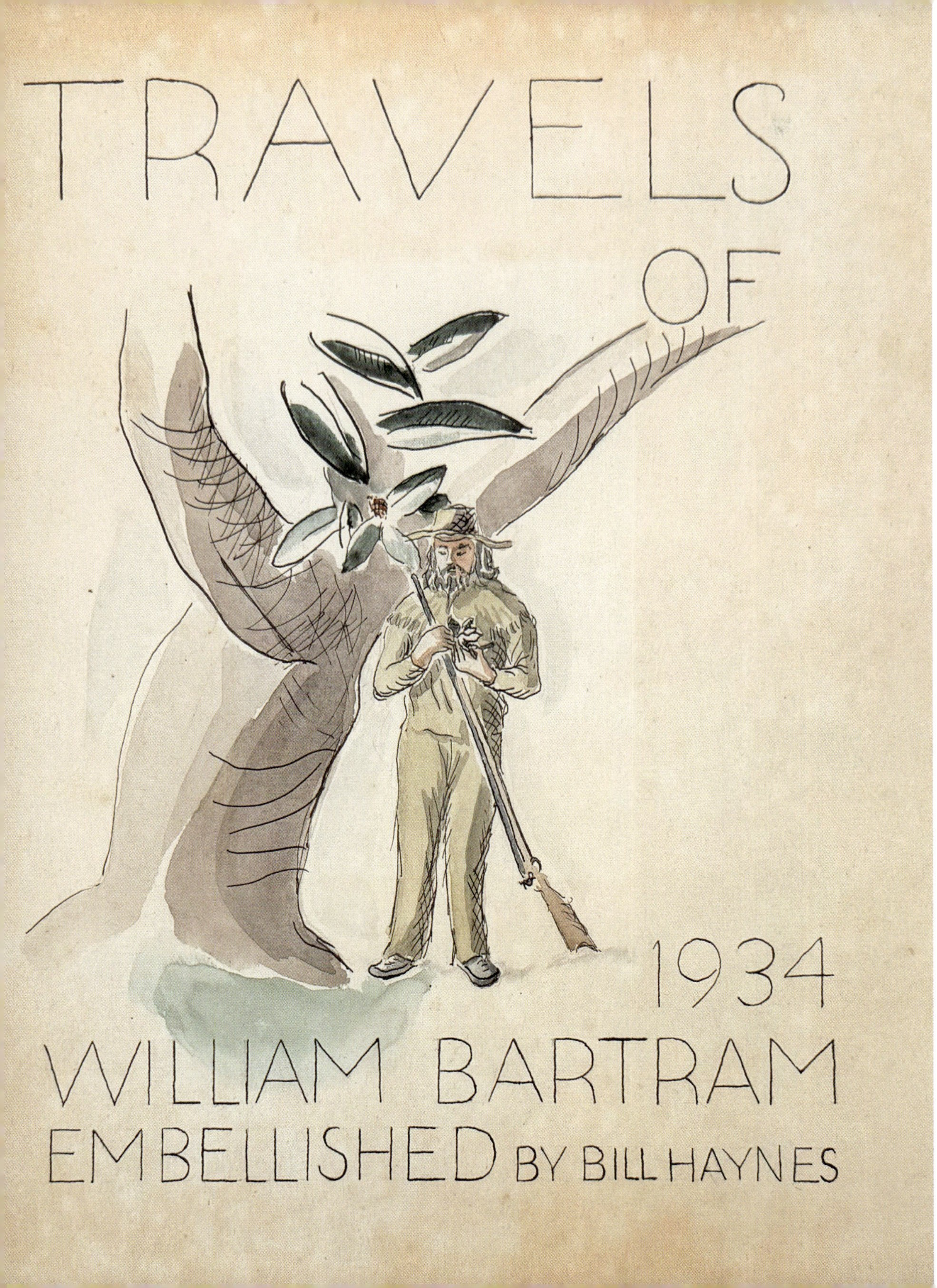

This title page, "*Travels of William Bartram—1934 Embellished by Bill Haynes*," borrows the concluding "Embellished with copper-plates" from Bartram's original title page. Bartram contemplates a magnolia flower beneath a great tree, his fusee at his side.

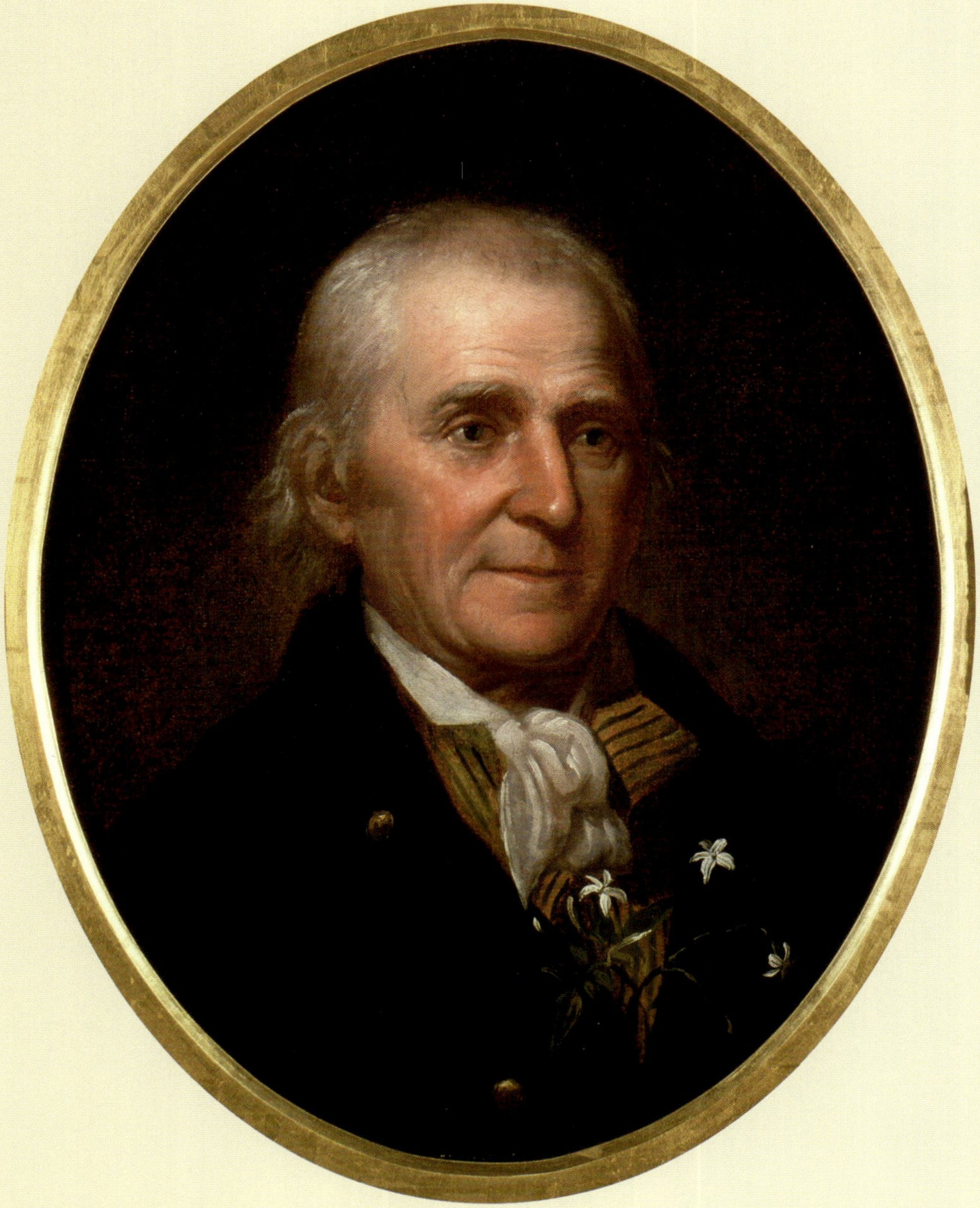

Charles Willson Peale (American, 1741–1827), William Bartram, 1808. Independence National Historical Park, Philadelphia.

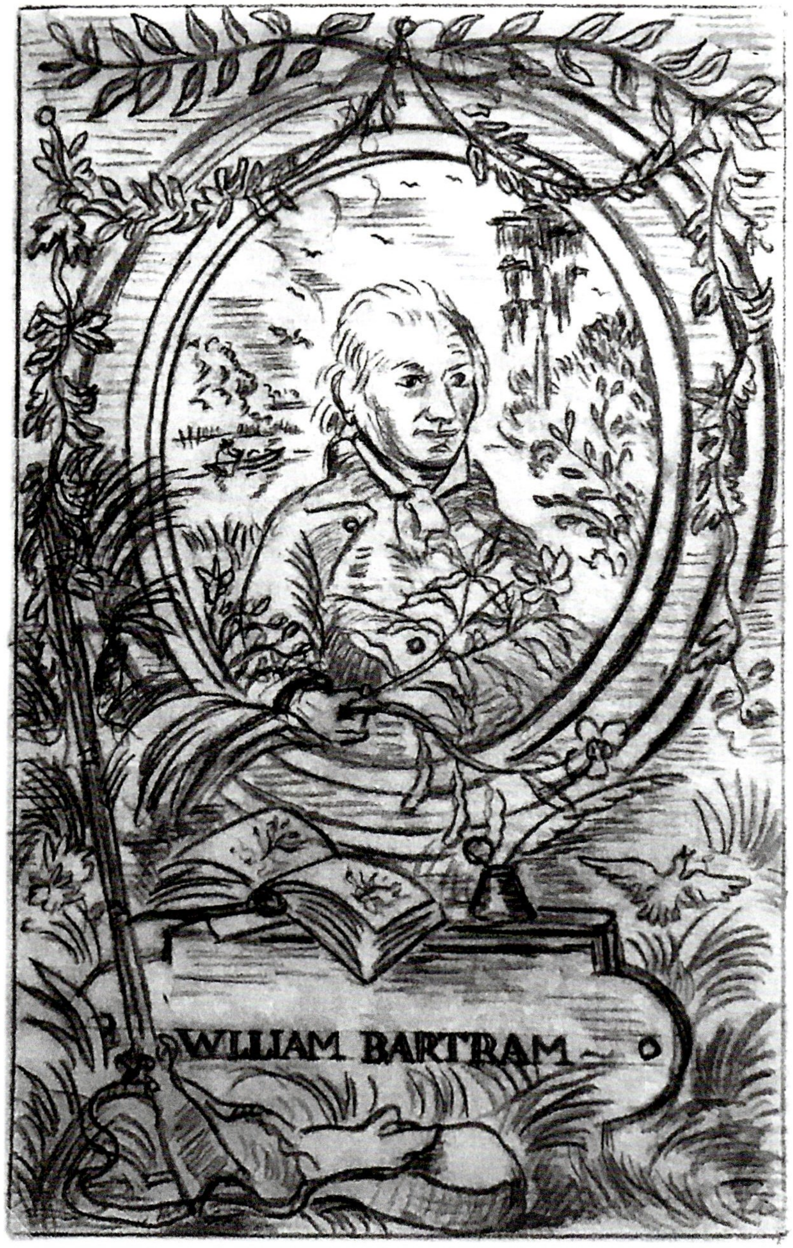

Unlike the rest of the illustrations, which are watercolors, Haynes included a small pencil sketch of Bartram based on the Charles Willson Peale portrait, the only known portrait of William Bartram, which was painted when Bartram was seventy years old. This portrait hung in the Long Room of Peale's museum in Philadelphia in the top section above his natural history specimens. Peale called this his "Gallery of Great Men," suggesting that male *Homo sapiens* were located only below God and the angels in the Great Chain of Being, a conception of the nature of the universe in which Peale believed.

Note that in the Peale portrait, the only ornament Bartram wears is a sprig of poet's jasmine tucked into the top of his waistcoat—a fitting symbol of his love for plants. In contrast, Haynes's sketch overflows with plants of all types and sizes. Using a similar "porthole" framing of his subject, Haynes nearly envelops Bartram in flowers and vines twining around the portrait's perimeter. Behind Bartram is a river landscape with a man in a boat approaching a cypress. Outside the oval, a botany book lies open beside an inkwell. In the foreground stands a gun and a shoulder bag ready for fieldwork. Again, the flying bird motif makes several appearances here.

➤ In this pair of watercolors, Haynes painted the figure of Bartram on the left as a neatly groomed older man in formal dress writing at his desk while visualizing the experiences of his youth. The watercolor on the right, helpfully labeled "William Bartram," illustrates him as a much younger man in the midst of his fieldwork on a river bordered with cypress and palms and featuring an alligator approaching the shore. Beneath the trees stands a Seminole gesturing either in welcome to Bartram or trying to wave the alligator away.

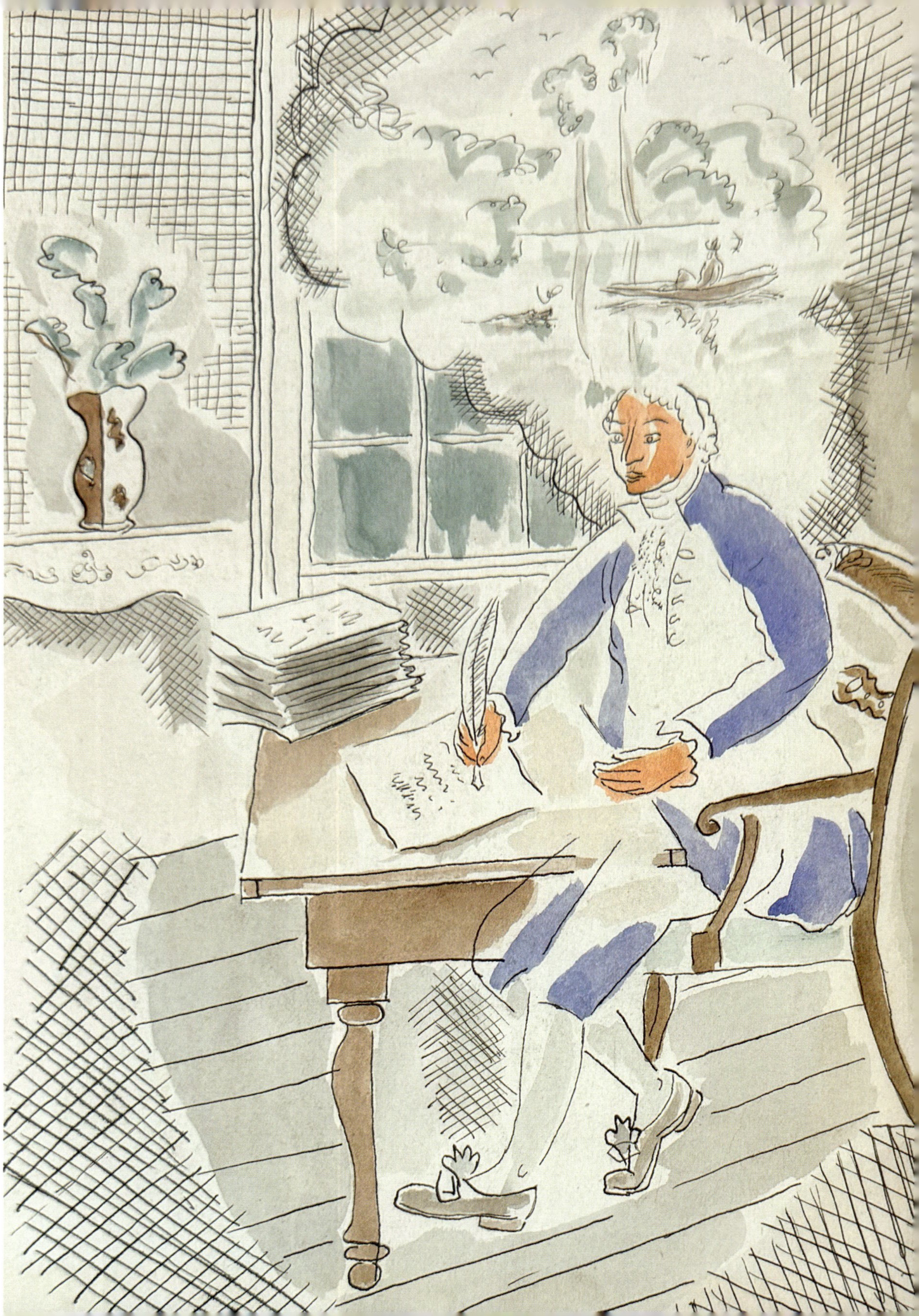

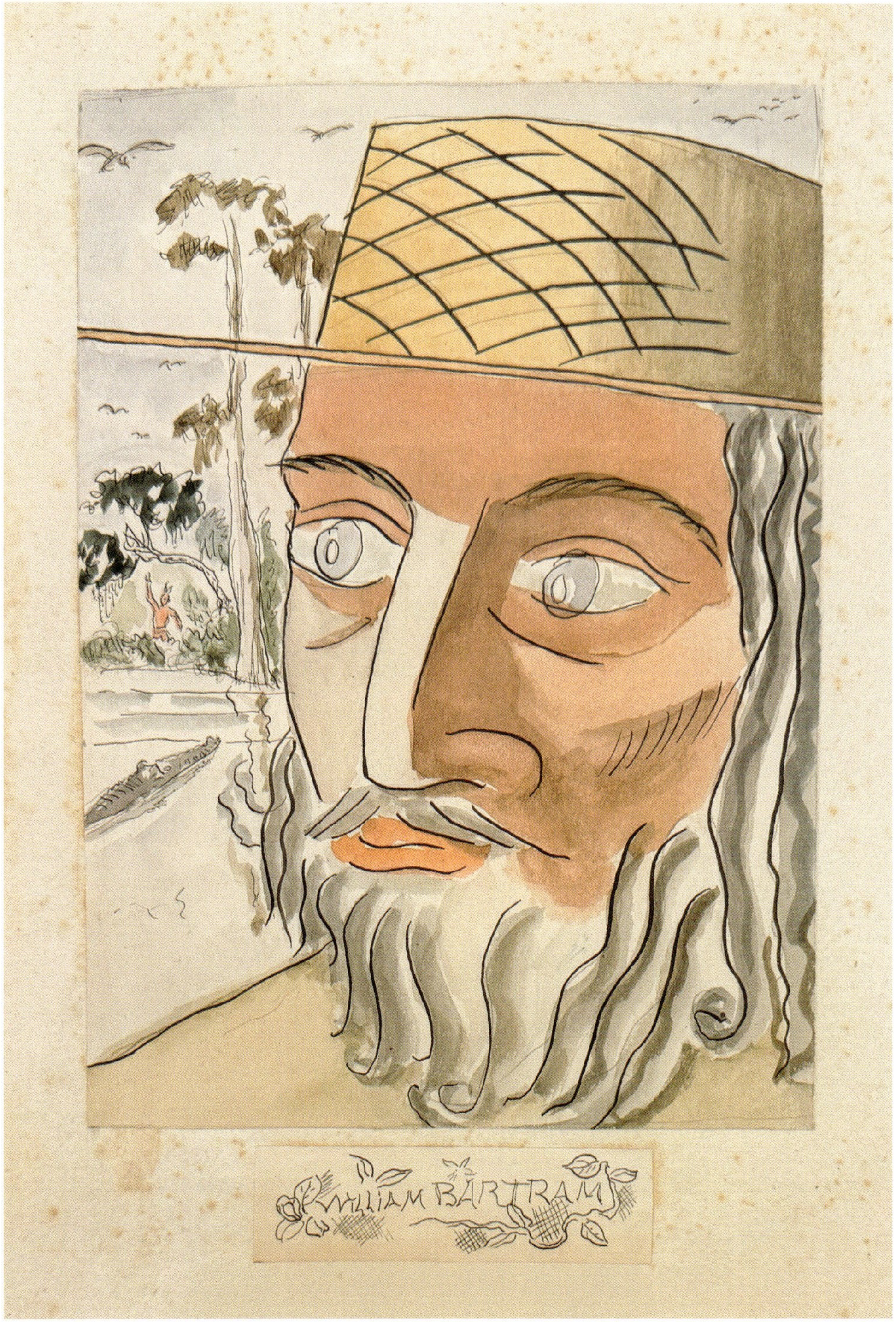

While paging through the images collected here, remember that Bartram was Haynes's muse. Similarly, this pair of watercolors poses a reciprocal visual dialogue that runs between the younger Bartram contemplating his future and the elder Bartram, with pen in hand, reflecting on his experiences in the South years before.

➤ The smaller images adorning the map title page are organized around a dividing wall similar in design to the historic Spanish colonial architecture in St. Augustine, Florida (see St. Augustine illustration on page 128). Moving clockwise from the upper left, the watercolor features an Indian couple (tribe unknown) calmly gazing at the viewer; the man holds a bow and the woman reclines, as a bird flies over this Edenic scene. The sailing ship in the upper right leads the eye to a bending palm surrounded by low plants; more birds fly into the scene near the palm.

Rounding out the watercolor is a pineapple, *Bromelia ananas*. Pineapples were a well-known symbol of hospitality in eighteenth-century colonial Europe, especially among British plantation owners. Although pineapples are not native anywhere in North America, they did grow in the British possessions in the Caribbean. One can imagine what a statement it made for a golden, ripe pineapple to take pride of place at an elegant dinner in England, not to mention for the guests to enjoy a taste of such a delicious, exotic fruit.

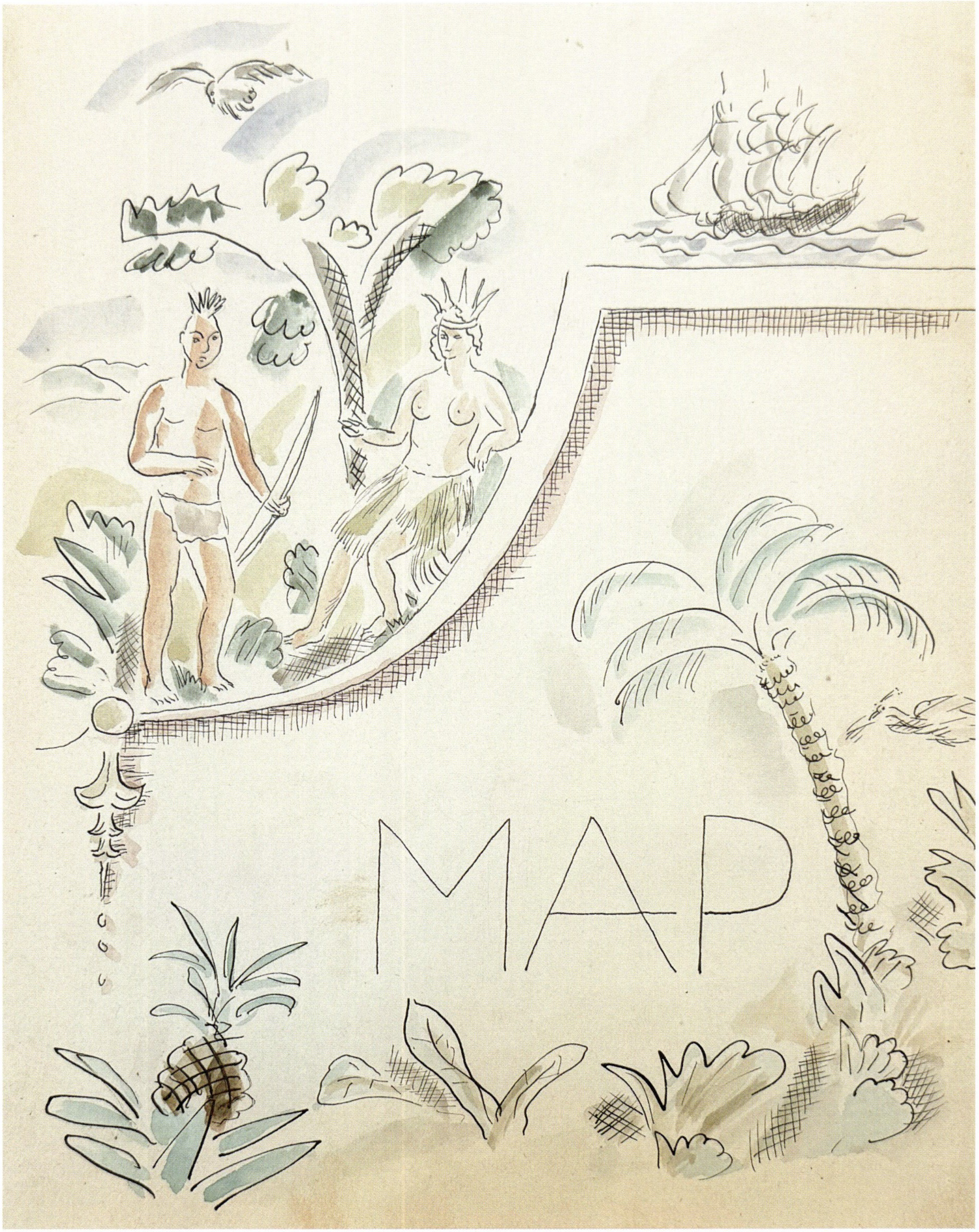

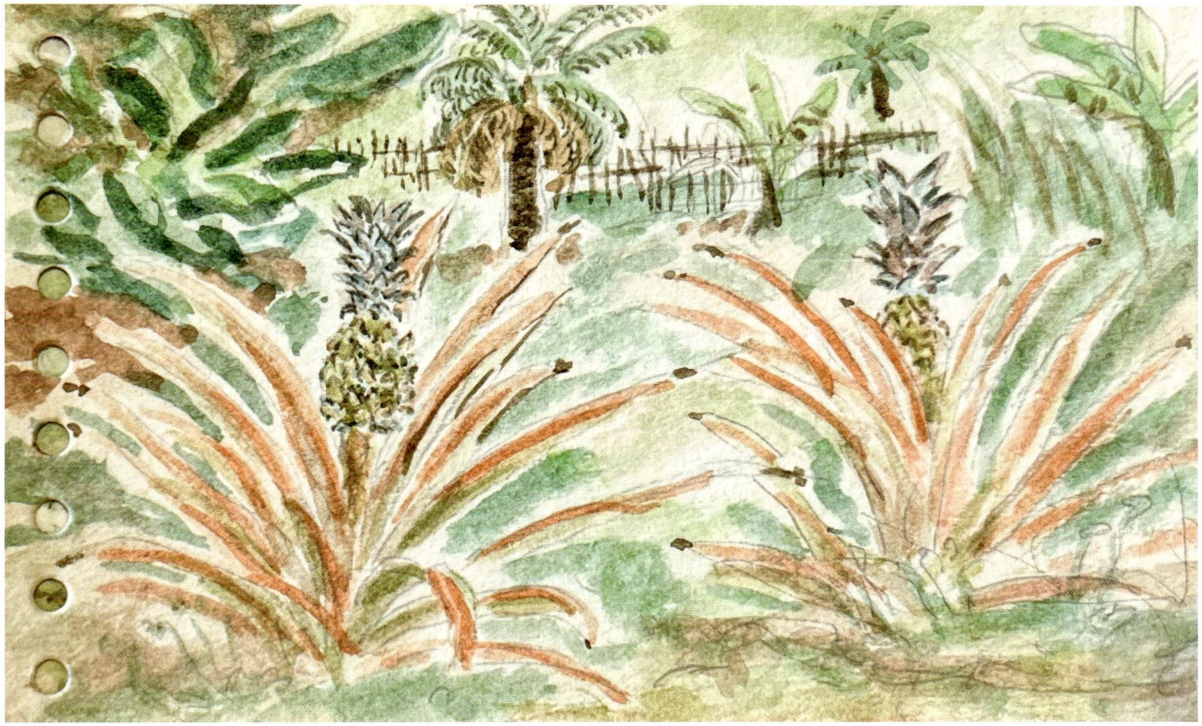

➤ When Bill Haynes was stationed in New Guinea during World War II, he had the opportunity to paint pineapples growing in a village field. With pineapples absent from Florida, William Bartram found a worthy artistic substitute, the cycad palm, as seen in the lower-left corner in Bartram's *The Great Alachua-Savana* (see page 40). The palm clearly mimics a pineapple and its intimation of the hospitality with which the Seminoles welcomed him.

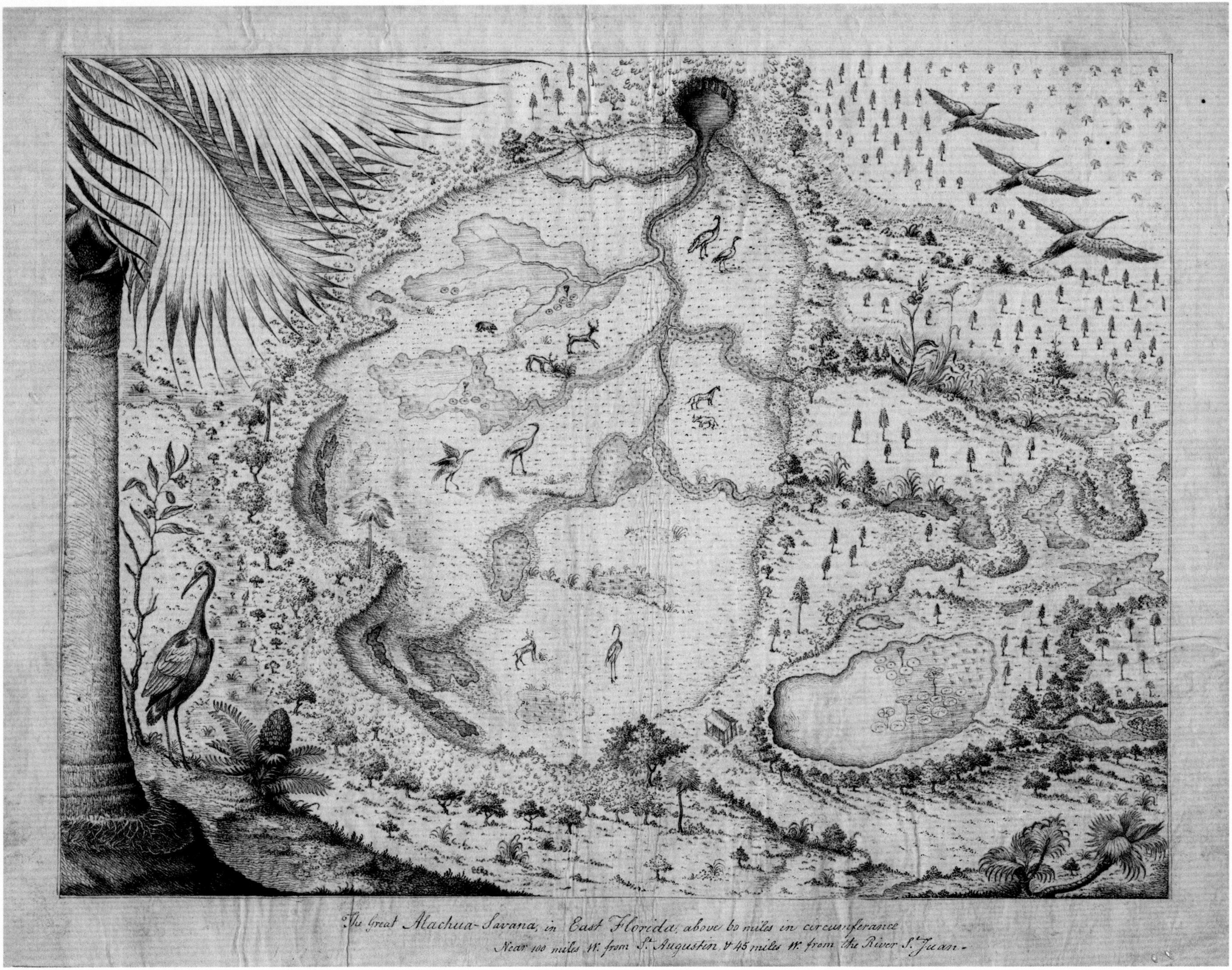

William Bartram (American, 1739–1823), *The Great Alachua-Savana*, East Florida, date unknown. Pen and ink, 15"x 12.25". Courtesy of the American Philosophical Society.

William Bartram did not produce many landscapes, but the ones we do have are stylized—approaching the fantastic—in viewpoint, perspective, and scale. His words as well as his landscape *The Great Alachua-Savana* epitomize the dream emerging from the draftsman's pen.

> *This little lake and surrounding meadows, would have been alone sufficient to surprise and delight the traveller, but being placed so near the great savanna, the attention is quickly drawn off, and wholly engaged in the contemplation of the unlimited, varied, and truly astonishing native wild scenes of landscape and perspective, there exhibited: how is the mind agitated and bewildered, at being thus, as it were, placed on the borders of a new world! On the first view of such an amazing display of the wisdom and power of the supreme author of nature, the mind for a moment seems suspended, and impressed with awe. (189)*

Despite the profound lack of topographic relief in this portion of central Florida, Bartram sets the viewer at the lip of a precipice, even hovering in midair, offering a palm trunk for a mooring mast, and a come-hither look on the face of a sandhill crane. The crane stands between a fruiting pawpaw and a blooming cycad.

Below, the wet grassland lies dissected by rivulets of water coursing toward and disappearing into its heart, the Great Sink. On the sun-swept floor of the savanna, all is movement. Between the watercourses, bucks prance and graze, a solo bear shuffles, while cranes and other large wading birds seem torn between cavorting and wariness. Like a Busby Berkeley musical, a trio of cranes arabesque toward the wings; even the palm tree seems to be sidling offstage.

Humans are offstage, too. Standing in for them are the Seminoles' beloved horse, a cow, and a small thatched structure representing the Indian town of Cuscowilla. The thatched hut manages to suggest both the rustic as well as the ordered geometry of a small Greek temple.

Accentuating all this vitality, scale is skewed. Lotus leaves dwarf deer, cranes tower over the horse, flowering plants and grasses sway five times the height of hardwoods. As Bartram biographer Thomas Slaughter suggests, this landscape represents not biological truths but "emotional truths discovered by a man of universal feeling. . . . The key biological metaphor is the heart, not the mind."[1]

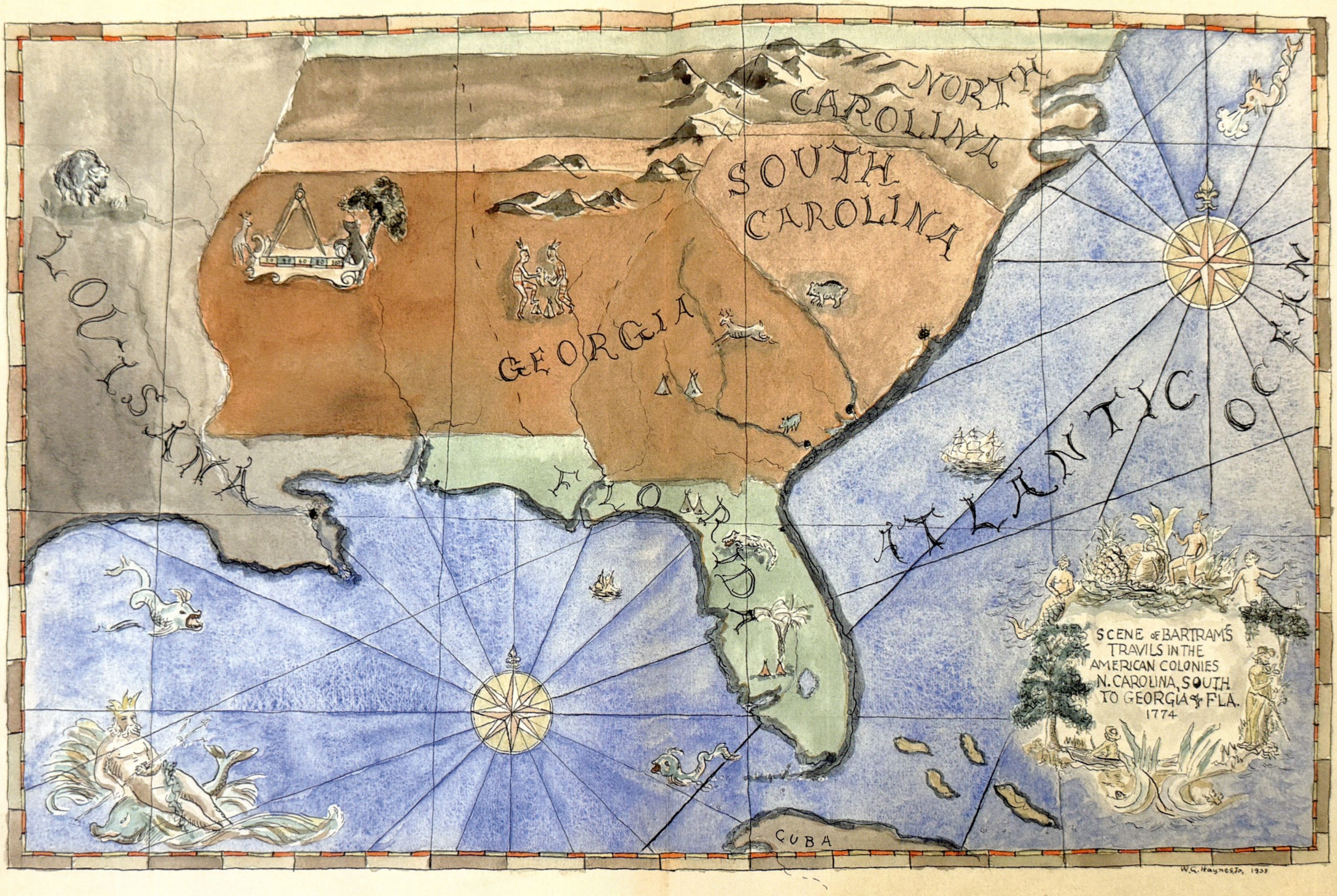
NORTH CAROLINA
SOUTH CAROLINA
GEORGIA
FLORIDA
LOUISANA
ATLANTIC OCEAN
CUBA
SCENE OF BARTRAM'S TRAVILS IN THE AMERICAN COLONIES N. CAROLINA, SOUTH TO GEORGIA & FLA. 1774

➢ Although Haynes illustrates only the portions of *Travels* covering Georgia, Florida, and western North Carolina, this overview map reinforces the wide geographic range Bartram covered from 1773 to 1777. Clearly, Haynes's map style is based on historic cartographic designs for portraying the New World. It features not one but two overlapping compass roses. The alternating dark-and-light border or graticulation usually represents a bar scale where the bar length equals some measured distance. With that information missing here, its function is decorative only.

➢ A bison appears in the map's northwestern corner. While early colonists reported bison in the Southeast, by the time Bartram arrived, they were no longer seen. However, Bartram mentioned them seven times in *Travels*, especially early in the text as he accompanied the survey party delineating the boundaries of the New Purchase in August 1773. Their stop at the "Great Buffalo Lick" in Oglethorpe County, Georgia, gave him the opportunity to test firsthand the palatability of the clay that formerly attracted bison as well as other wild animals and free-ranging livestock.

> *After four days moderate and pleasant travelling, we arrived in the evening at the Buffalo Lick. This extraordinary place occupies several acres of ground, at the foot of the S.E. promontory of the Great Ridge, which, as before observed, divides the rivers Savanna and Alatamaha. A large cane swamp and meadows, forming an immense plain, lies S.E. from it; in this swamp I believe the head branches of the great Ogeeche river take their rise. The place called the Lick contains three or four acres, is nearly level, and lies between the head of the cane swamp and the ascent of the Ridge. The earth, from the superficies to an unknown depth, is an almost white or cinerious coloured tenacious fattish clay, which all kinds of cattle lick into great caves, pursuing the delicious vein. It is the common opinion of the inhabitants, that this clay is impregnated with saline vapours, arising from fossile salts deep in the earth; but I could discover nothing saline in its taste, but I imagined an insipid sweetness. Horned cattle, horses, and deer, are immoderately fond of it, insomuch, that their excrement, which almost totally*

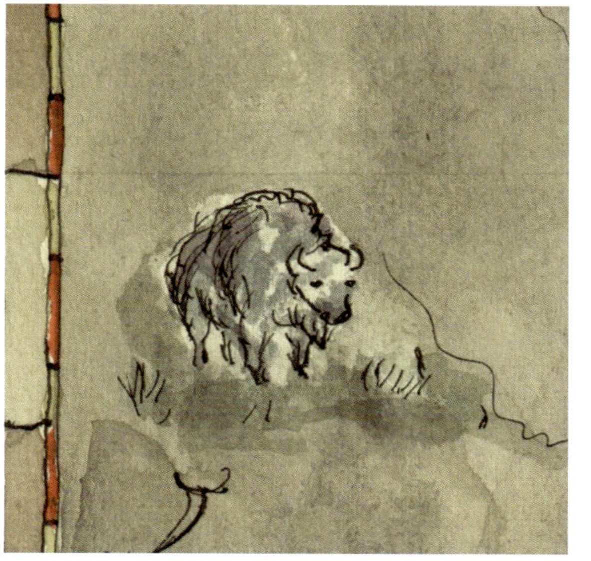

> *covers the earth to some distance round this place, appears to be perfect clay; which, when dried by the sun and air, is almost as hard as brick. (39)*

> *The buffalo (Urus) once so very numerous, is not at this day to be seen in this part of the country; a few elk, and those only in the Apalachian mountains. (46)*

> *. . . heaps of white, gnawed bones of the ancient buffaloe, elk and deer, indiscriminately mixed with those of men, half grown over with moss, altogether, exhibit scenes of uncultivated nature, on reflection, perhaps, rather disagreeable to a mind of delicate feelings and sensibility, since some of these objects recognize past transactions and events, perhaps not altogether reconcilable to justice and humanity. (322)*

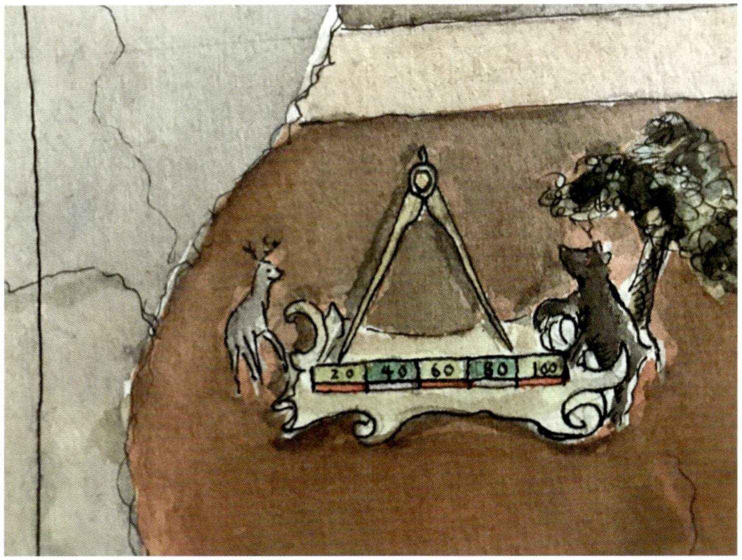

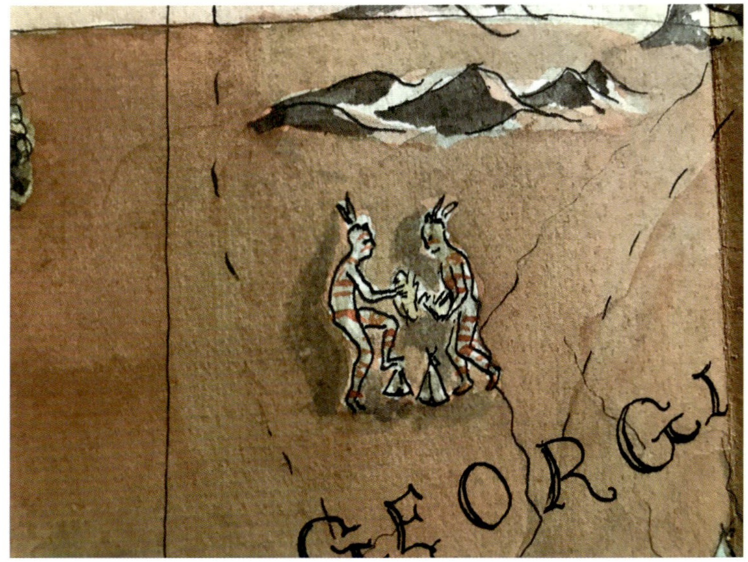

Although the map's border may be decorative only, Haynes does provide a bar-graph scale ornamented with a drawing compass and flanked by a deer and a bear by a tree.

In northwest Georgia, painted Indians (perhaps Creeks, given the location) are shown dancing, with teepees in the background. Elsewhere on the map, more teepees are scattered in southeast Georgia and into Florida, along with deer and feral swine.

Either Haynes believed popular portrayals of Indians living in teepees or chose to use them because his twentieth-century viewers would recognize them as habitations. Although Bartram mentions "wigwams," he used it as an analogy to describe floating islands of the marsh plant *Pistia*, which is abundant in the St. Johns River. If undisturbed, *Pistia* aggregations are steadily colonized by larger and larger plants and even trees. A "wigwam" in the strict sense is a more permanent house used in colder climates—certainly not a conical teepee, which is easily portable.

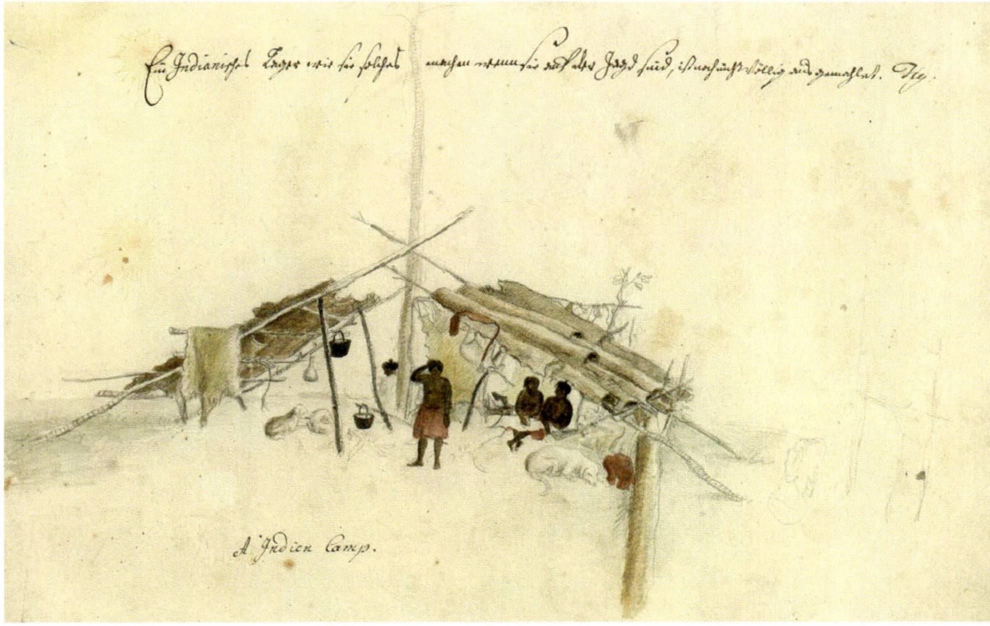

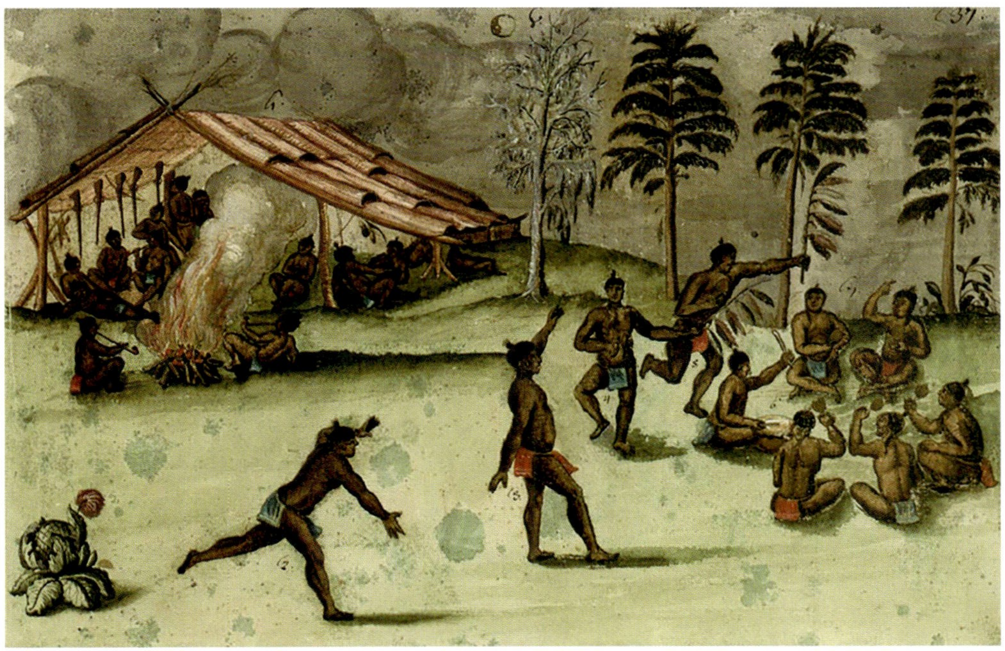

Images by Philip Georg Friedrich von Reck, courtesy of the National Library of Sweden, archive number NKS 565, 4'.

More accurate paintings of Indian habitations typical in Georgia and elsewhere appear in the 1736 journal of Philip Georg Friedrich von Reck, who assisted with the immigration of Salzburgers to the Georgia colony. His diary contains vivid descriptions of life in the nascent colony as well as detailed descriptions of relations between the colonists and the Indians. Fortunately, von Reck also was a skilled illustrator who was interested in everything from waterspouts at sea to common birds to edible plants. He was particularly interested in the coastal Indians who at that time had very cordial relationships with the settlers—nearly a matter of life and death for Europeans unaccustomed to the Georgia climate.

According to von Reck, when hunting, the Natives used tree materials available to them to construct temporary shelters of poles. In the first drawing, a temporary lean-to is topped on the right side with slabs of bark for shingles and drying deerskins draped on the other side.

That image is followed by von Reck's illustration of a "busk" or celebration with a larger and more substantial shelter for the participants. Daily quarters were even more snug, often made of stacked slabs of wood sealed with clay coatings inside and out and topped by wooden shingles. Bartram described the differences between building styles of the Creek and Cherokees this way:

> *The Cherokees construct their habitations on a different plan from the Creeks, that is but one oblong four square building, of one story high; the materials consisting of logs or trunks of trees, stripped*

of their bark, notched at their ends, fixed one upon another, and afterwards plaistered well, both inside and out, with clay well tempered with dry grass, and the whole covered or roofed with the bark of the Ches[t]nut tree or long broad shingles. This building is however partitioned transversely, forming three apartments, which communicate with each other by inside doors; each house or habitation has besides a little conical house, covered with dirt, which is called the winter or hot-house; this stands a few yards distance from the mansion-house, opposite the front door. (367)

Haynes clearly missed the mark on Native housing, but his portrayal of bodily adornment is closer to reality. Although body-painting and tattooing appear in many cultures, Europeans exploring North America paid particular attention to the Indians they encountered.

Sometime between 1585 and 1593, John White sketched this man he labeled as illustrating "The manner of their attire and painting them selves when they go to their general huntings or at theire Solemne feasts." Later, von Reck described how the local tribes temporarily painted their necks, faces, and bodies in stripes of favored shades of red and blue. Note that the ball players shown at the busk are wearing blue or red loincloths. General James Oglethorpe made sure to distribute red and blue cloth as highly sought-after presents. Red and black face paint was used only occasionally; as von Reck put it, "an indication that they have done injury or want to do it." Men were extensively tattooed, including the face; the women less so. Years later in *Travels*, Bartram also noted the significance of color to the Indians he encountered. Several times he refers in *Travels* to vibrantly "painted Seminoles" and later provides a more detailed discussion of Indian dress and bodily ornamentation in part IV, chapter III (501–505).

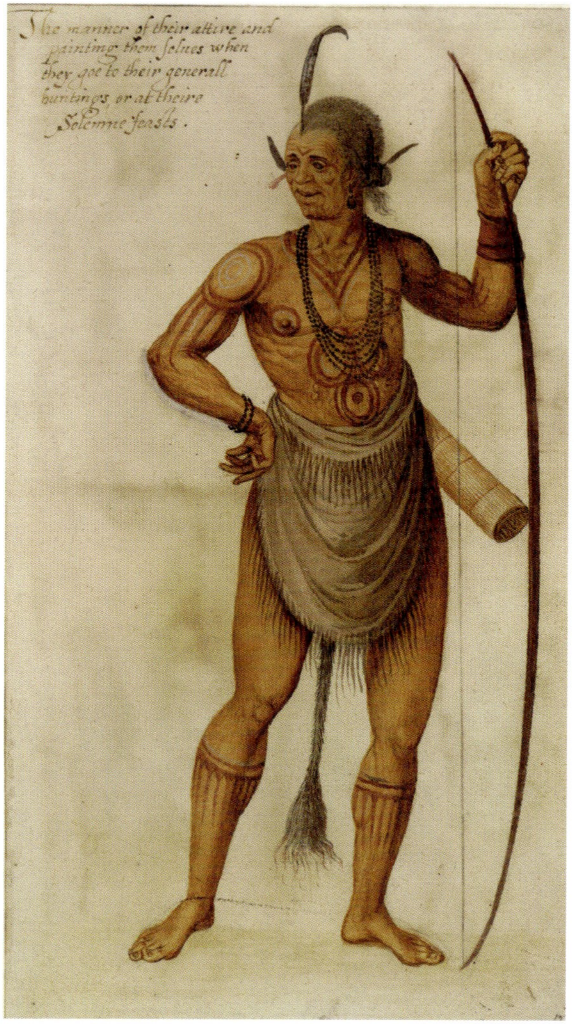

Image by John White, courtesy of the Trustees of the Natural History Museum, London.

➢ Although the outdoor theatrical drama *Unto These Hills* had yet to premiere in Cherokee, North Carolina, Haynes's 1934 illustration (page 44) looks remarkably similar to this vintage postcard view of the dancers' body paint from an early performance.

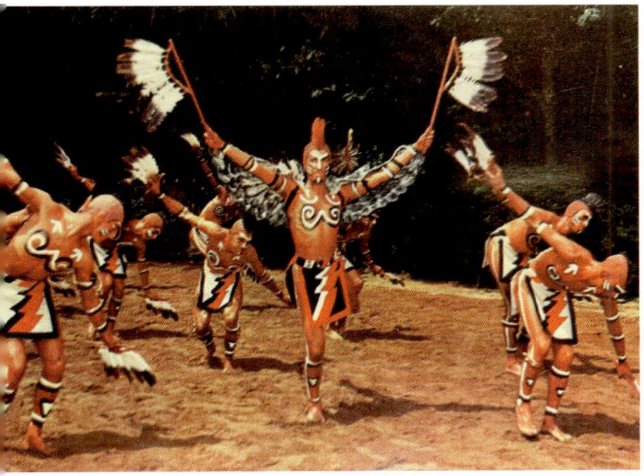

Postcard from private collection.

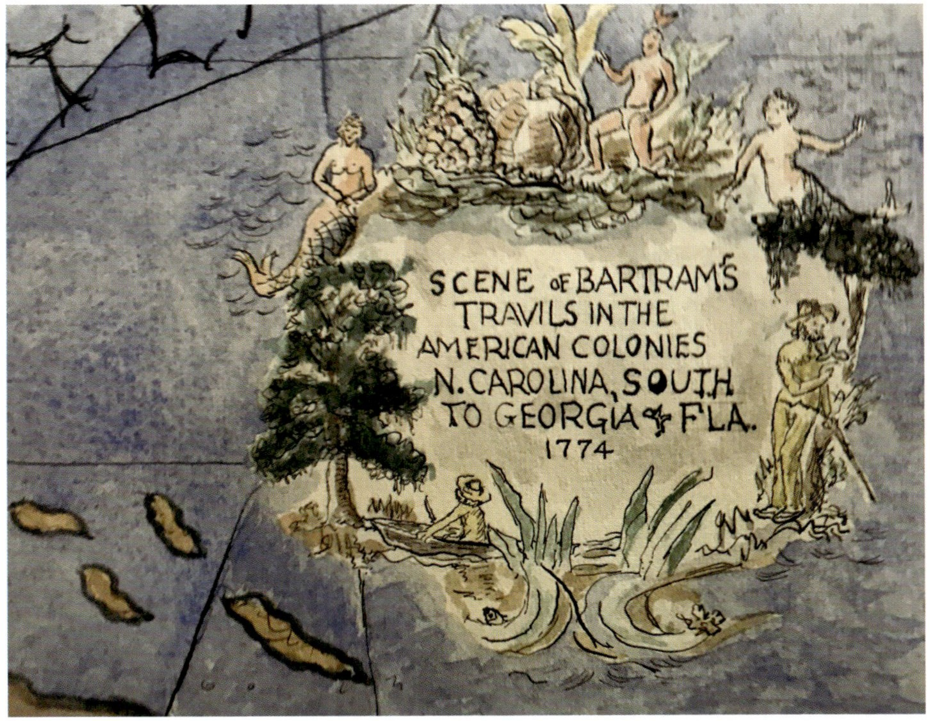

➢ The map's lower right features Haynes's homage to the elaborate cartouches found in early maps. Bartram appears at the lower left, watched by a fish as he lands his boat beneath a tree. On the right, Bartram takes time to smell a flower while a fallen flower floats away from him. At the top, mermaids flank a Native man who stands beside a pineapple, signifying hospitality, and a large pumpkin, emblematic of the bounty of crops grown by the Indians. As Bartram described it:

> *The fields surrounding the town and groves were plentifully stored with Corn, Citruels [a type of melon], Pumpkins, Squashes, Beans, Peas, Potatoes, Peaches, Figs, Oranges, &c. (304)*

Note that *Travels* is misspelled in Haynes's cartouche, a mistake that appears nowhere in Bartram's book. Also Haynes indicates to the viewer that his illustrations will encompass only Bartram's path in North Carolina, Georgia, and Florida.

For someone as interested in illustration as Haynes was, a cartouche provided the opportunity to add a more historic ambience and artwork to an otherwise austere map.

Some of the design elements could have been inspired by Bartram's own map from the 1791 edition of *Travels*, which showed only the east coast of Florida rather than his entire journey to the Mississippi. Bartram's map is more similar to a coastal nautical chart and even includes the site where he was shipwrecked and nearly drowned. Unlike the Haynes map, it includes only a few land animals and inland features. But Bartram's cartouche is equally symbolic. The map's title is encircled in a floral oval nestled in a rocky waterfall; a yucca's leaning bloom-stalk anchors the oval on its left margin. Although it may seem incongruous to show a flowing waterfall in Florida, Bartram visited the area now known as Ravine Gardens State Park, west of Palatka, where the limestone exposed in the steep sides of the ravine may be the inspiration for his cartouche.

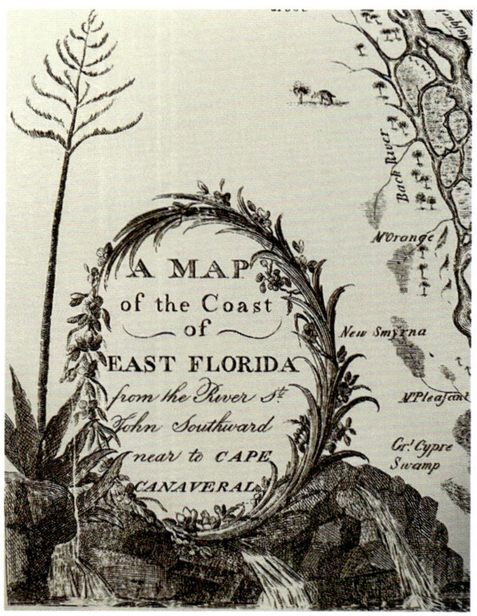

From Bartram's *Travels* at Documenting the American South.

In addition to his map cartouche, several of the Haynes watercolors illustrating Indians show them wearing headdresses adorned with many stiff feathers that rise vertically from a headband across the brow. Bartram did not describe or illustrate feathered headdresses constructed in this fashion among any of the Indians he encountered. His portrait of *Mico-chlucco, King of the Muscogulges or Criks, call'd the Long Warrior* underwent several transformations over time. The frontispiece to the first edition of *Travels* in 1791 was corrected to show the Long Warrior's affiliation with the Seminoles.

The 1791 frontispiece featured the headband with plumes, tonsure, ear ornaments, gorget, feather-and-fur cloaks or drapes, "scepter," and a pipe tomahawk.

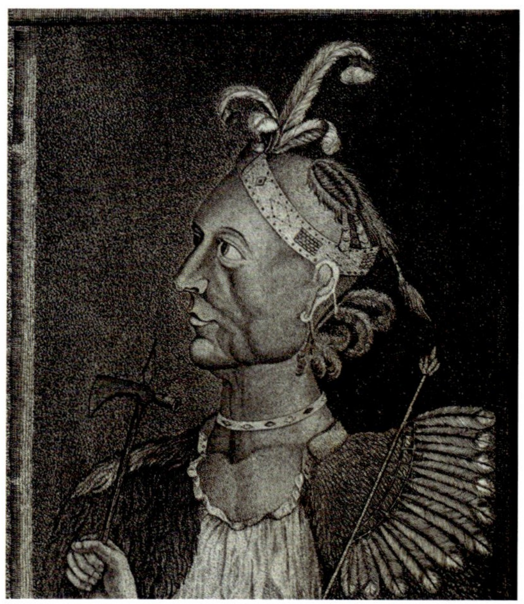

1791—First edition frontispiece, from Bartram's *Travels* at Documenting the American South.

The 1792 edition presents a more refined portrait, while still retaining the details from the original sketch.

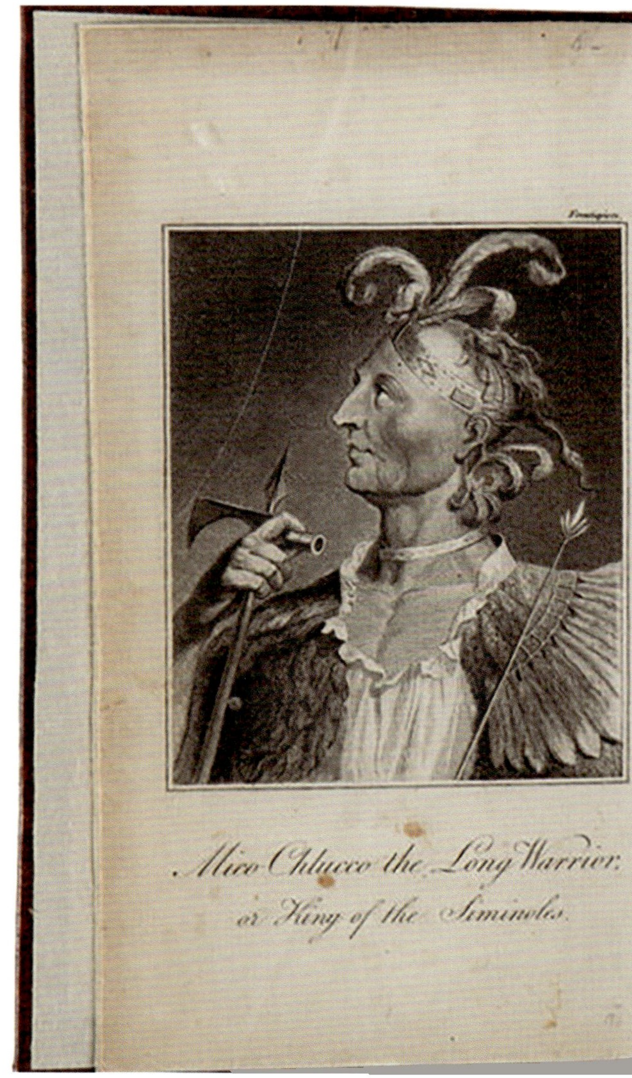

Courtesy of the Trustees of the Natural History Museum, London.

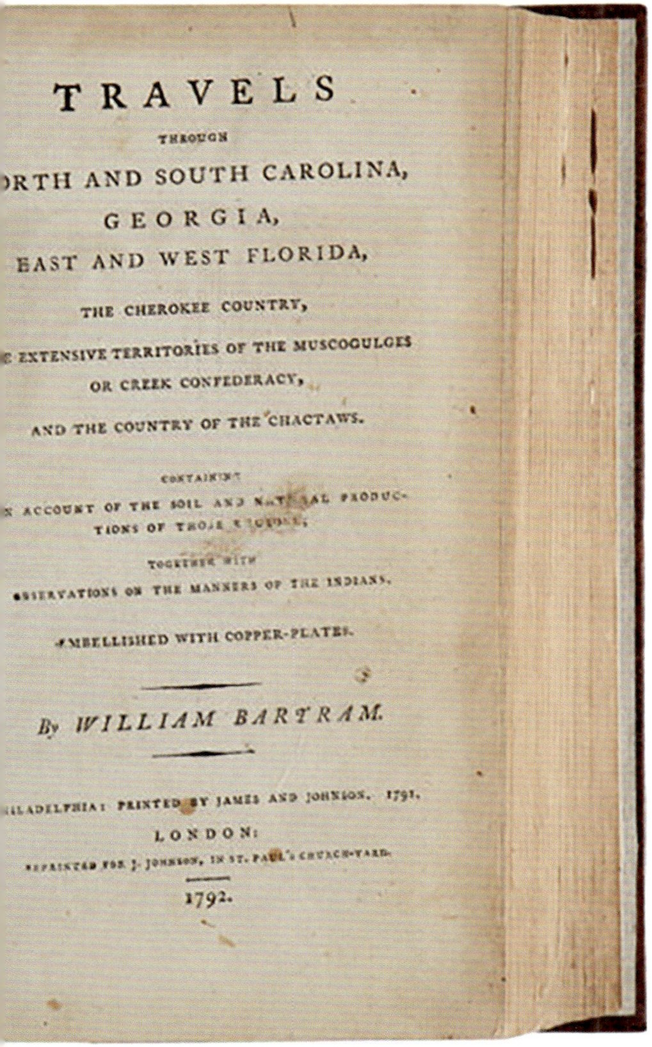

TRAVELS
THROUGH
RTH AND SOUTH CAROLINA,
GEORGIA,
EAST AND WEST FLORIDA,
THE CHEROKEE COUNTRY,
E EXTENSIVE TERRITORIES OF THE MUSCOGULGES
OR CREEK CONFEDERACY,
AND THE COUNTRY OF THE CHACTAWS.
CONTAINING
N ACCOUNT OF THE SOIL AND NATURAL PRODUC-
TIONS OF THOSE REGIONS;
TOGETHER WITH
OBSERVATIONS ON THE MANNERS OF THE INDIANS.
EMBELLISHED WITH COPPER-PLATES.
By WILLIAM BARTRAM.
ILADELPHIA: PRINTED BY JAMES AND JOHNSON. 1791.
LONDON:
REPRINTED FOR J. JOHNSON, IN ST. PAUL'S CHURCH-YARD.
1792.

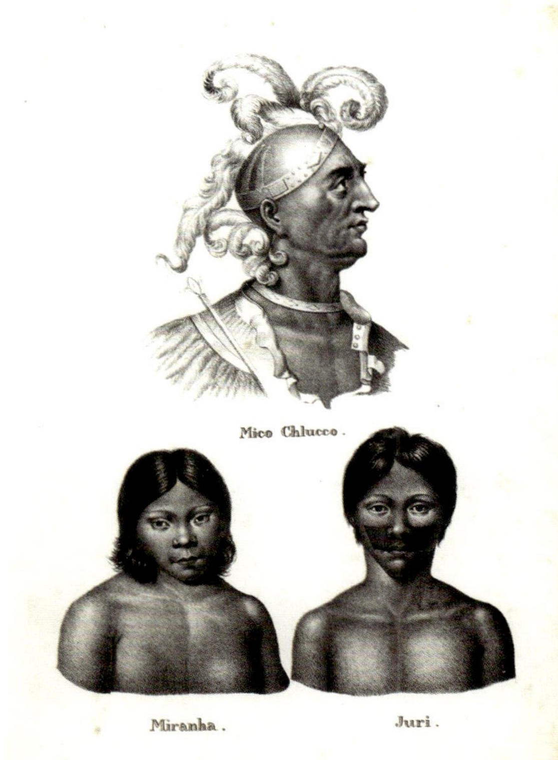

Mico Chlucco, the Long Warrior, King of the Seminole Nation of Florida in Feather Headdress and Coat, lithograph by Karl Joseph Brodtmann from Heinrich Rudolf Schinz's *Illustrated Natural History of Men and Animals*, 1836. Album / Florilegius / Album Archivo. Courtesy of Bridgeman Images.

➤ Once *Travels* began to be published in Europe, presentation of the frontispiece art often simplified the detail Bartram included in his original. By 1836, the image of the Long Warrior no longer was even connected directly with *Travels*, much less to the rich symbolism of Seminole life Bartram had described. In Heinrich Rudolf Schinz's *Illustrated Natural History of Men and Animals* (1836), the Long Warrior's profile is unmistakable. But gone are his pipe tomahawk, gorget, earrings, and fur cloak—important signals of his status.

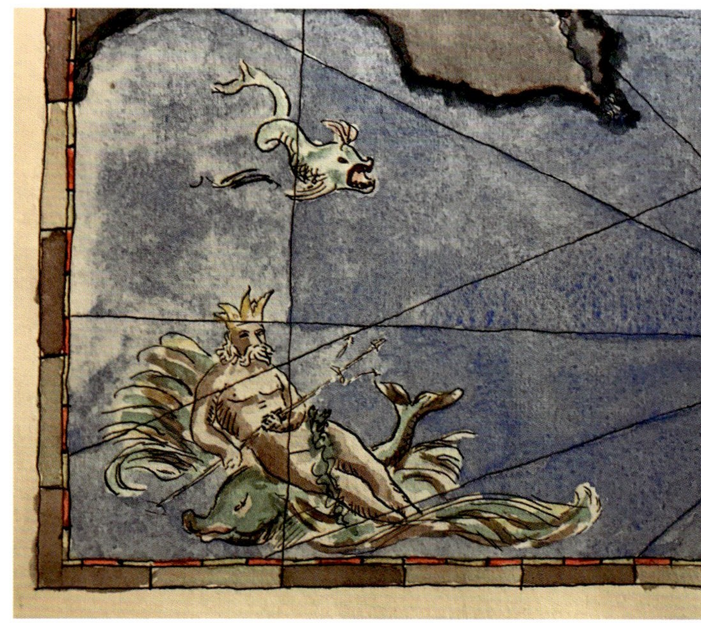

➤ Finally, no map showing the ocean would be complete without the requisite sailing ship, and here, a spouting sea monster attending Neptune with his trident as he lounges on a dolphin atop the waves.

The double-page index once again features the Spanish colonial architecture of St. Augustine as a backdrop, this time topped by a pineapple. Two Natives examine their quarry, a dead deer; at the wall's base rests an alert cottontail.

On the facing page, the viewer is given a list of the subjects Haynes will address in his paintings: flora, fauna, Indians, reptiles. A Native man rests in the shade of trees adorned with Spanish moss, while Bartram stands contemplating what appears to be the Alachua Savanna in northern Florida. Once again, a bird flies overhead.

Wherever he traveled, Bartram noted the fauna he encountered, edible or not. He was the first person to scientifically describe the cottontail:

> *The rabbit (lepus minor, cauda abrupta, pupillis atris) are pretty common, and no ways differing from those of Pennsylvania and the northern states. (284)*

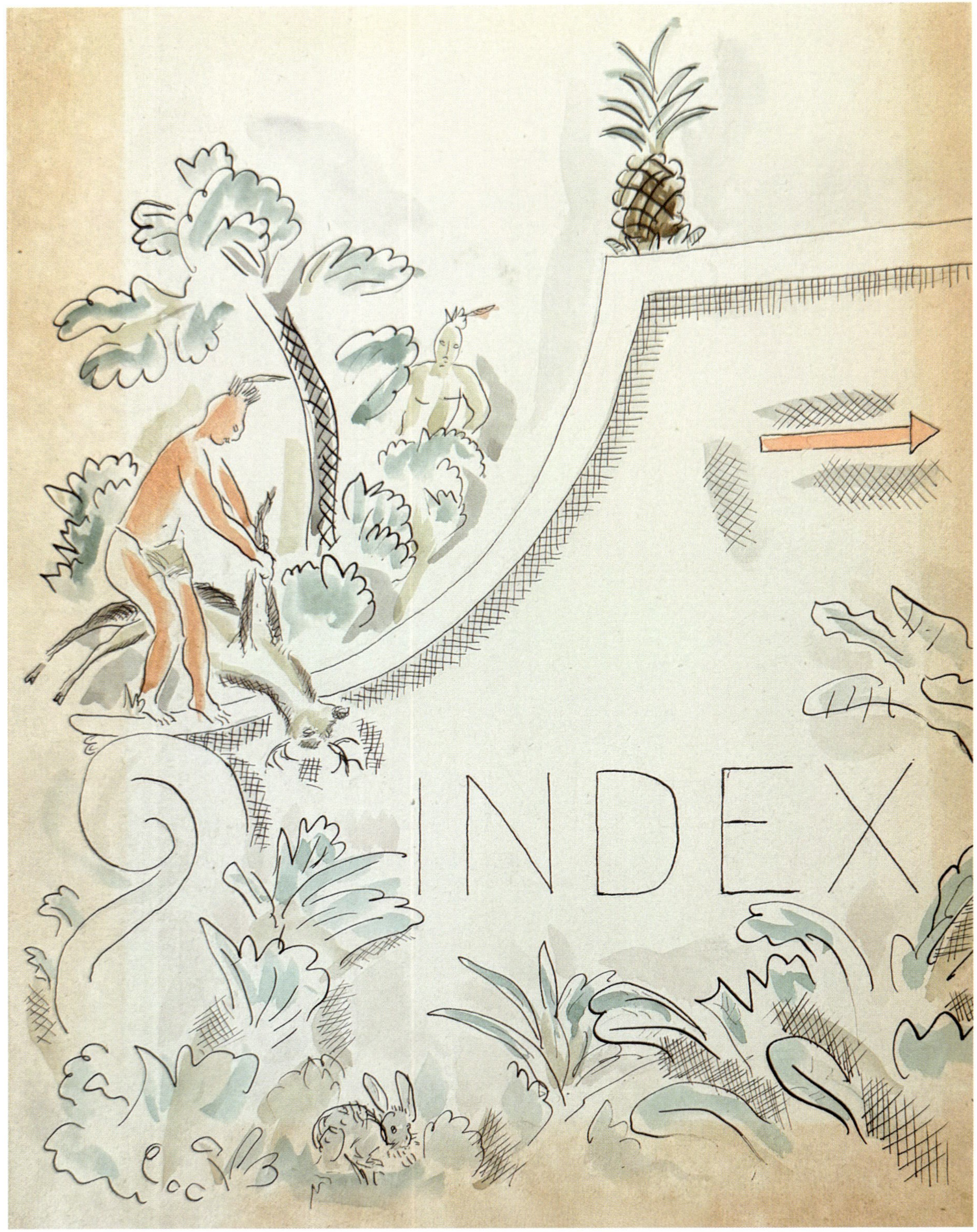

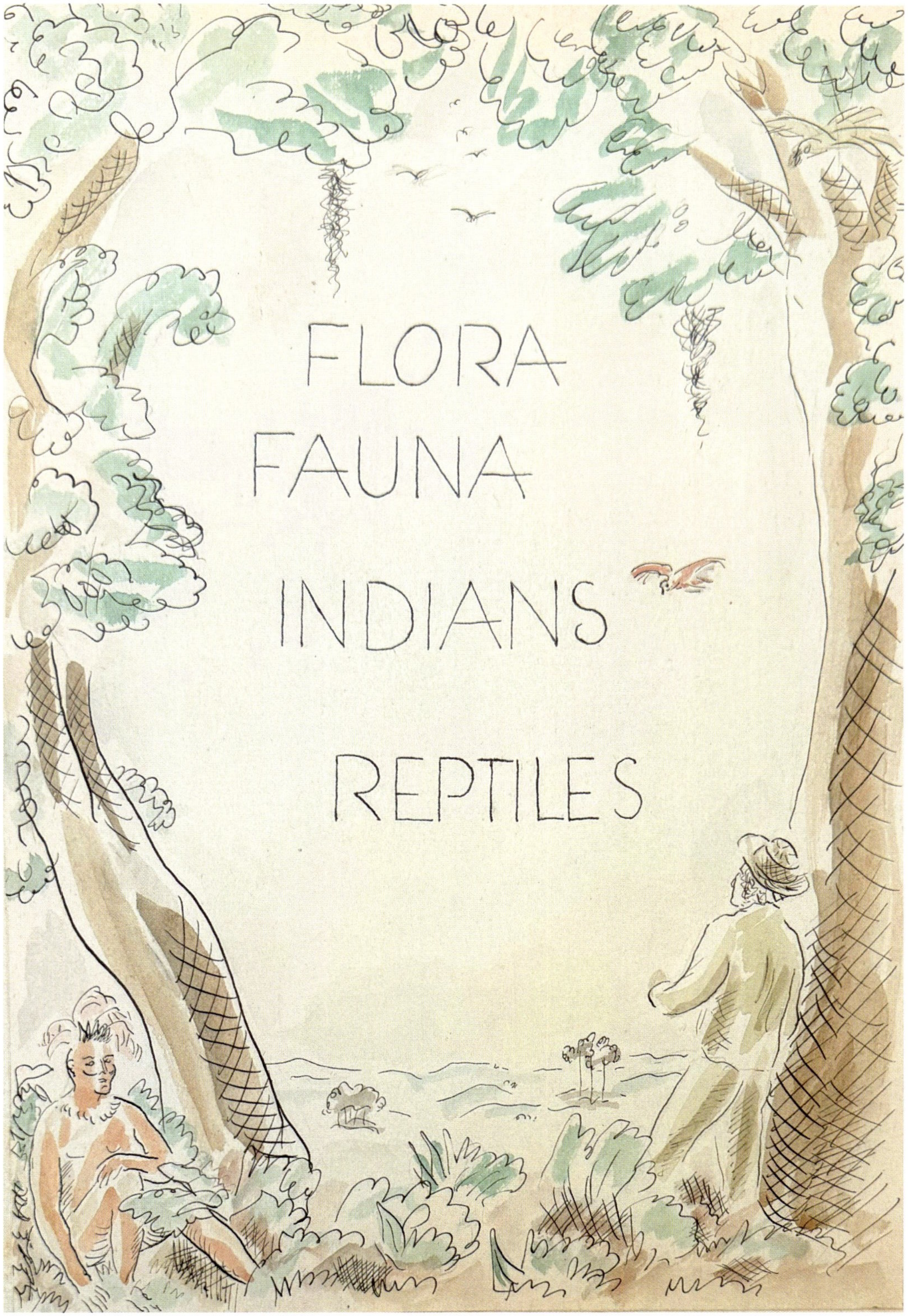

At the Georgia coast near Sunbury, he described the panoply of large and small mammals in the region.

> *The roebuck, or deer, are numerous on this island; the tyger, wolf, and bear, hold yet some possession; as also raccoons, foxes, hares, squirrels, rats and mice, but I think no moles; there is a large ground-rat, more than twice the size of the common Norway rat. In the night time, it throws out the earth, forming little mounds, or hillocks. Opposoms are here in abundance, as also pole-cats, wild-cats, rattle-snakes, glass-snake, coach-whip snake, and a variety of other serpents. (7)*

Later, Bill Haynes would illustrate Bartram's cottontail in the small pamphlet *Gulla Tales*, a collection of Gullah-Geechee folktales told by Albert H. Stoddard and printed by the Ashantilly Press. See pages 16–17.

Bartram, clad in head-to-toe buckskin, contemplates the Darien waterfront from the bow of a bateau paddled by a Black man. Many of Darien's historic buildings, which Haynes would have known well, still stand along the Altamaha.

> *The north channel, or entrance, glides by the heights of Darien, on the east bank, about ten miles above the bar, and, running from thence with several turnings, enters the ocean between Sapello and Wolf islands. The south channel, which is esteemed the largest and deepest, after its separation from the north, descends gently, winding by M'Intosh's and Broughton islands. (53)*

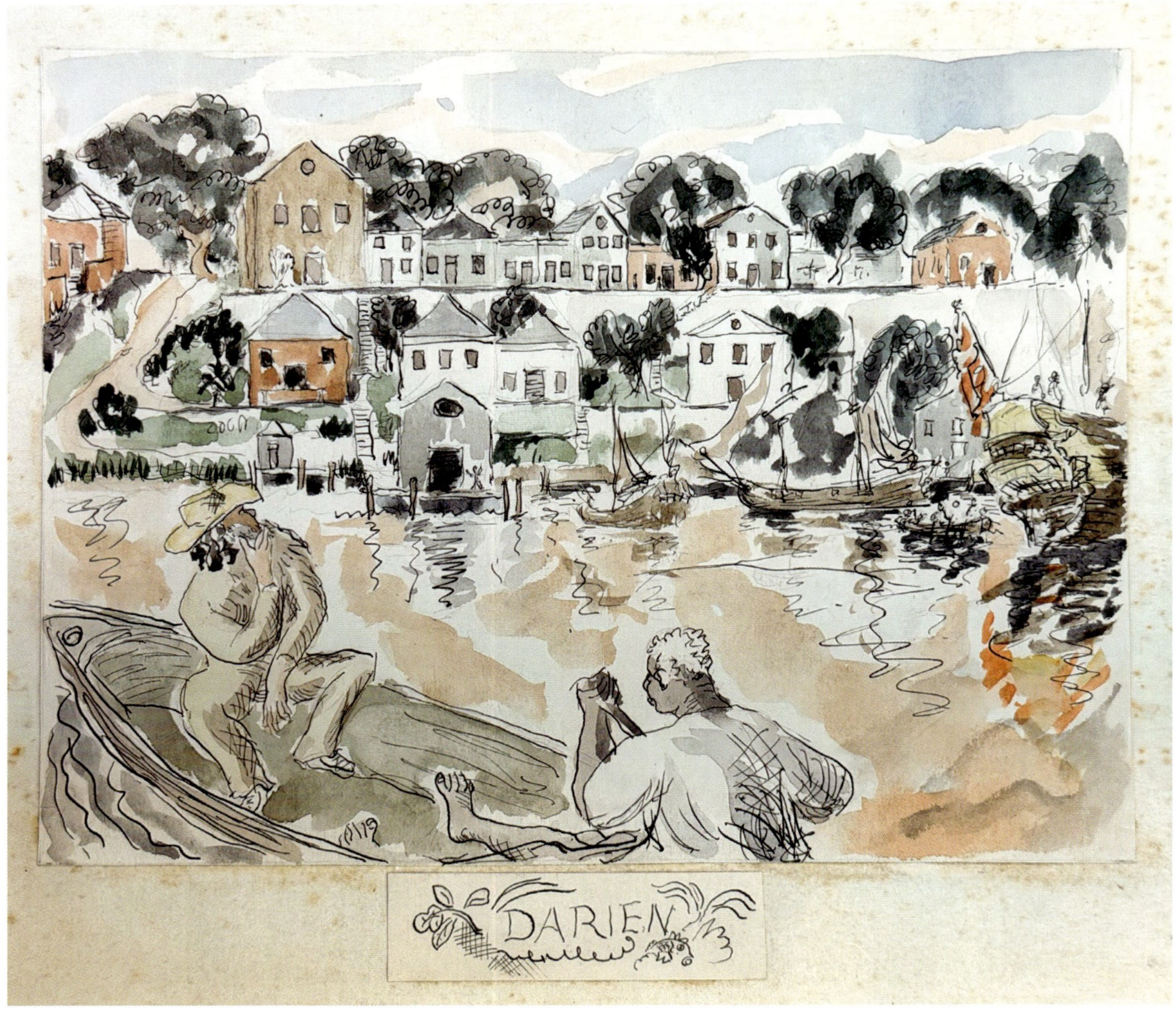

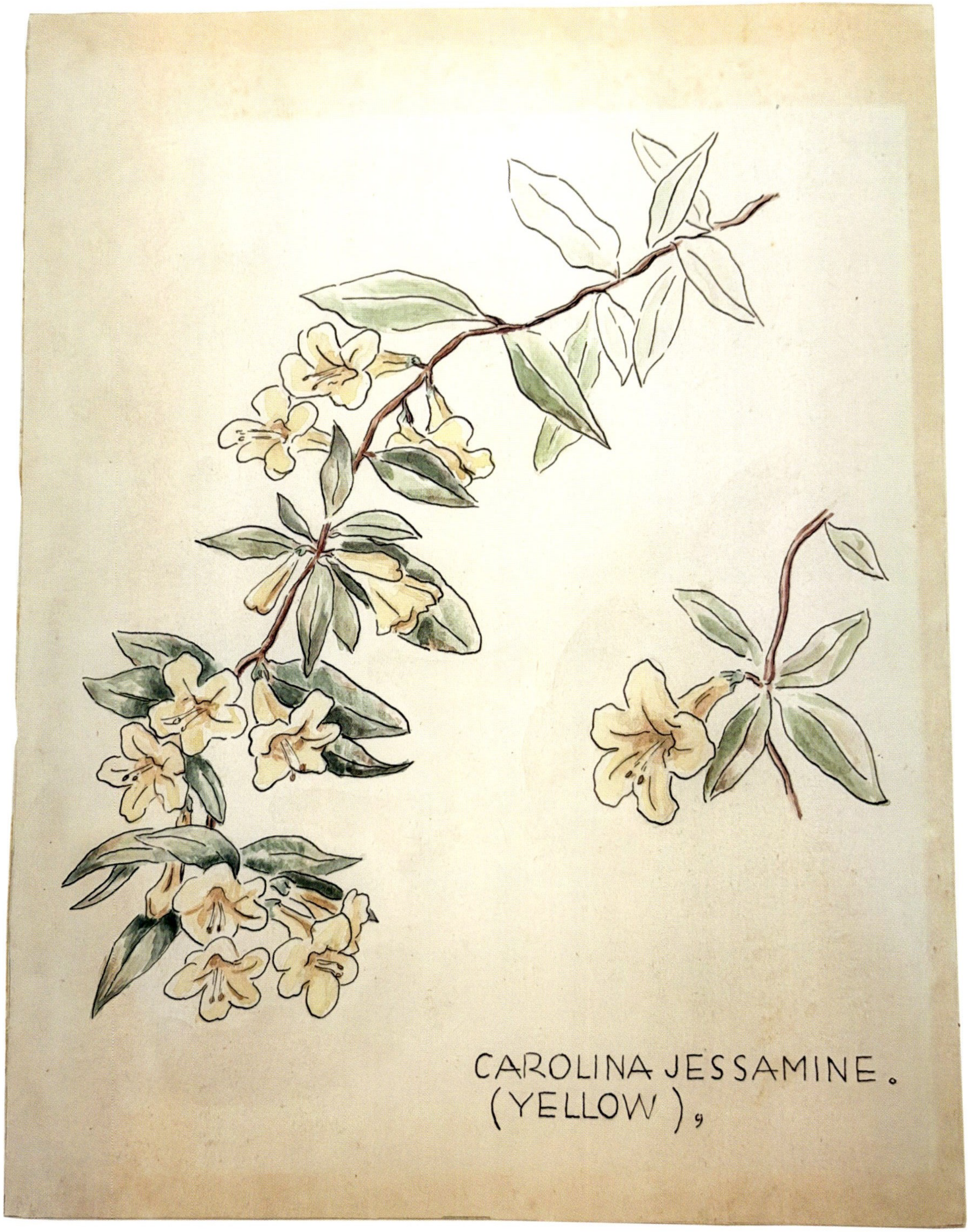

Unlike many of Haynes's flower paintings, this one is so carefully illustrated that it would not be mistaken for any other flowering vine, even absent his label. Although Bartram was familiar with this plant that tolerates the Pennsylvania winters, he was delighted to see it coexisting with what he called "Canadian vegetables" and lending its fragrance to the mountain valleys.

> *. . . but what seems remarkable, the yellow Jessamine, (Bignonia sempervirens) which is killed by a very slight frost in the open air in Pennsylvania, here on the summits of the Cherokee mountains associates with the Canadian vegetables, and appears roving with them in perfect bloom and gaiety. (337)*
>
> *. . . companies of young, innocent Cherokee virgins, some busily gathering the rich fragrant fruit, others having already filled their baskets, lay reclined under the shade of floriferous and fragrant native bowers of Magnolia, Azalea, Philadelphus, perfumed Calycanthus, sweet Yellow Jessamine. (357)*

Despite being based in an active war zone in tropical New Guinea, Haynes took the opportunity to illustrate its native plants and animals in addition to Allied military activities. In Haynes's wartime sketchbooks, his landscapes frequently feature the brightly colored flowering trees and shrubs at Milne Bay. He was particularly taken with their cadmium-red hues so different from his home in McIntosh County. No doubt Bartram would have enjoyed them as well. In New Guinea, Haynes also was able to observe and paint its colorful wild parrot species, especially the small flocks absorbed in feeding on flower nectar and pollen. In a sense, the soaring Carolina parakeets Haynes featured in many of his 1934 Bartram watercolors came to life before his own eyes half a world away from his Georgia home.

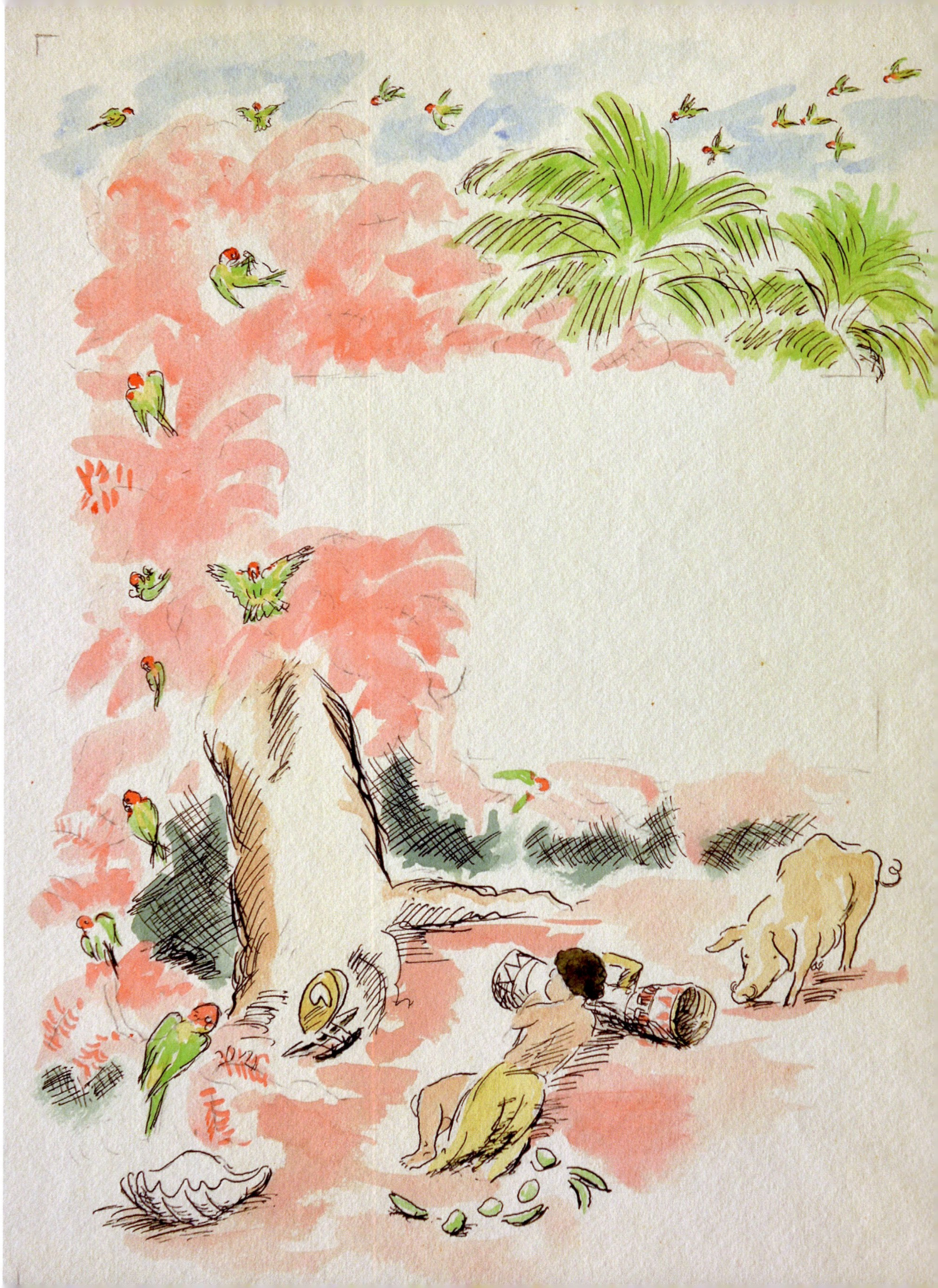

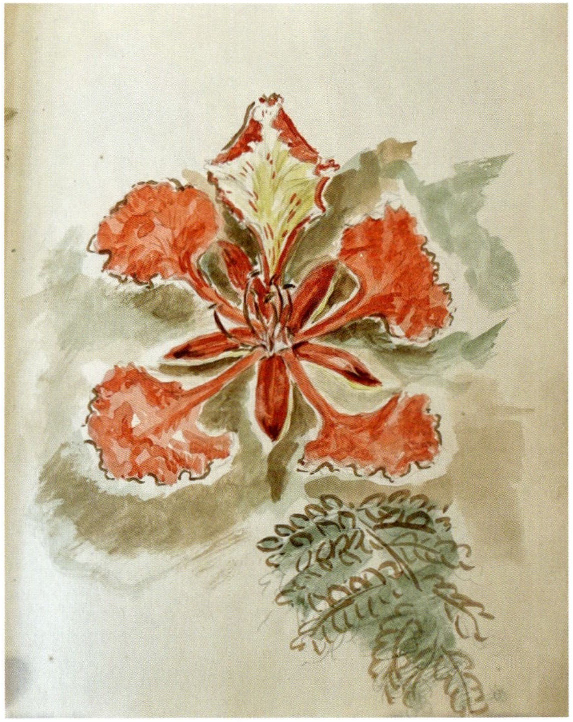

Royal poinciana (*Delonix regia*)

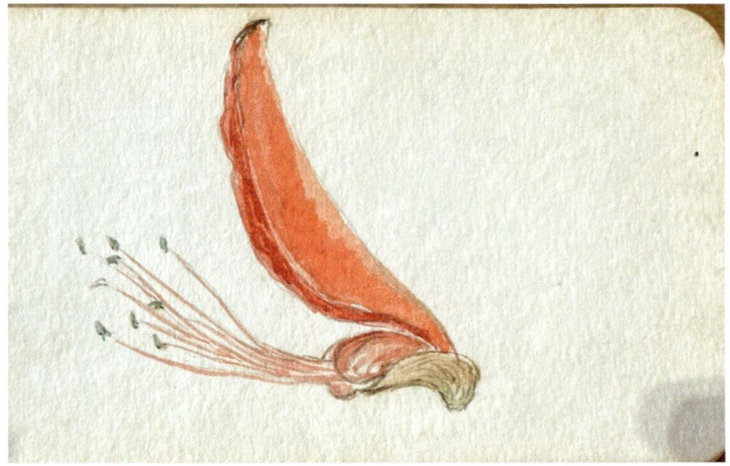

Tiger's claw (*Erythrina variegata*)

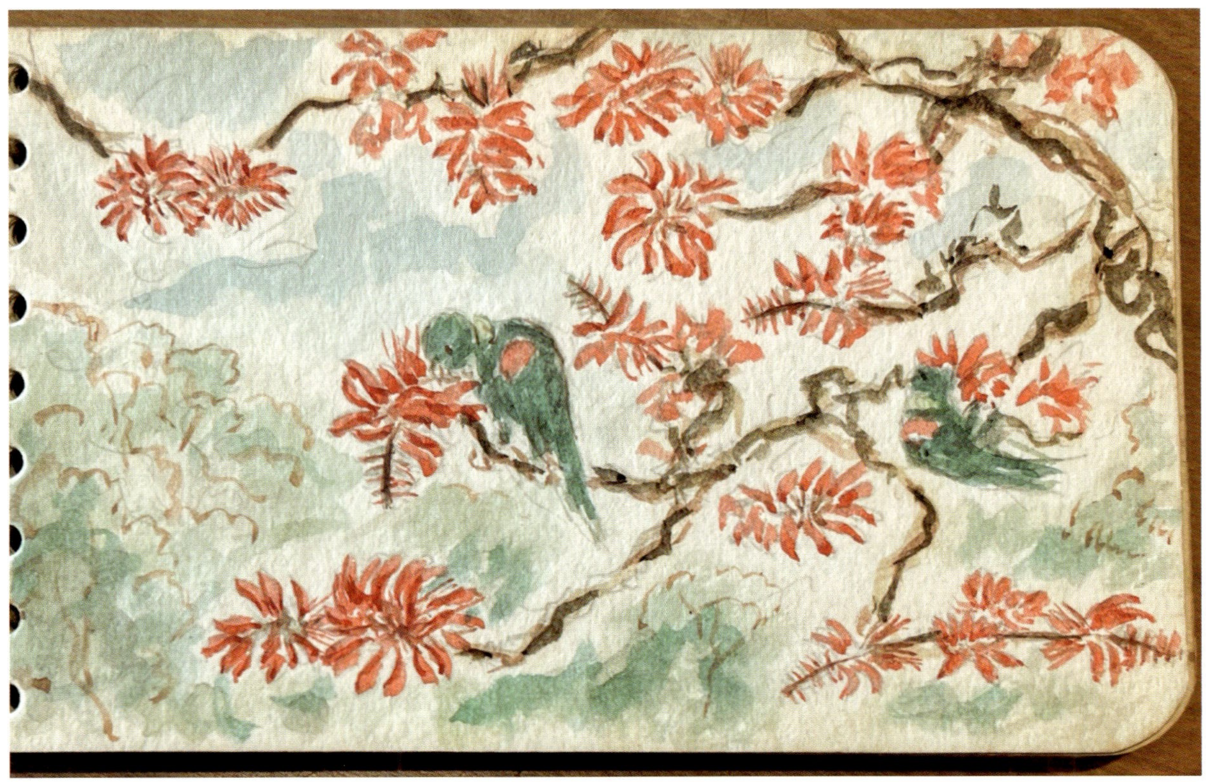

Parrots feeding on tiger's claw blossoms

After sailing to Frederica on St. Simons Island, Georgia (as shown in the watercolor of the boat under sail), one of Bartram's most interesting encounters is with the unnamed "man on a bear-skin rug," whom he met at the island's southern end. In these paintings and the quoted excerpt, Haynes skillfully illustrates a charming story of generosity and hospitality. Note in the large painting Haynes's inclusion of the beehives, honeyed water, jug of brandy, a signature live oak avenue, and the contentment of his host.

> *This delightful habitation was situated in the midst of a spacious grove of Live Oaks and Palms, near the strand of the bay, commanding a view of the inlet. A cool area surrounded the low but convenient buildings, from whence, through the groves, was a spacious avenue into the island, terminated by a large savanna; each side of the avenue was lined with bee-hives, to the number of fifty or sixty; they seemed to be well peopled, and exhibited a lively image of a colony that has attained to a state of power and affluence, by the practice of virtue and industry.*
>
> *When I approached the house, the good man, who was reclining on a bear-skin, spread under the shade of a Live Oak, smoking his pipe, rose and saluted me: "Welcome, stranger, I am indulging the rational dictates of nature, taking a little rest, having just come in from the chace and fishing." After some conversation and rest, his servant brought a bowl of honey and water, a very refreshing and*

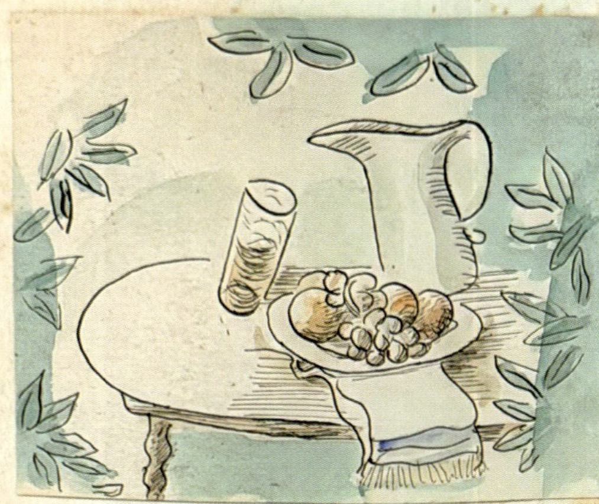

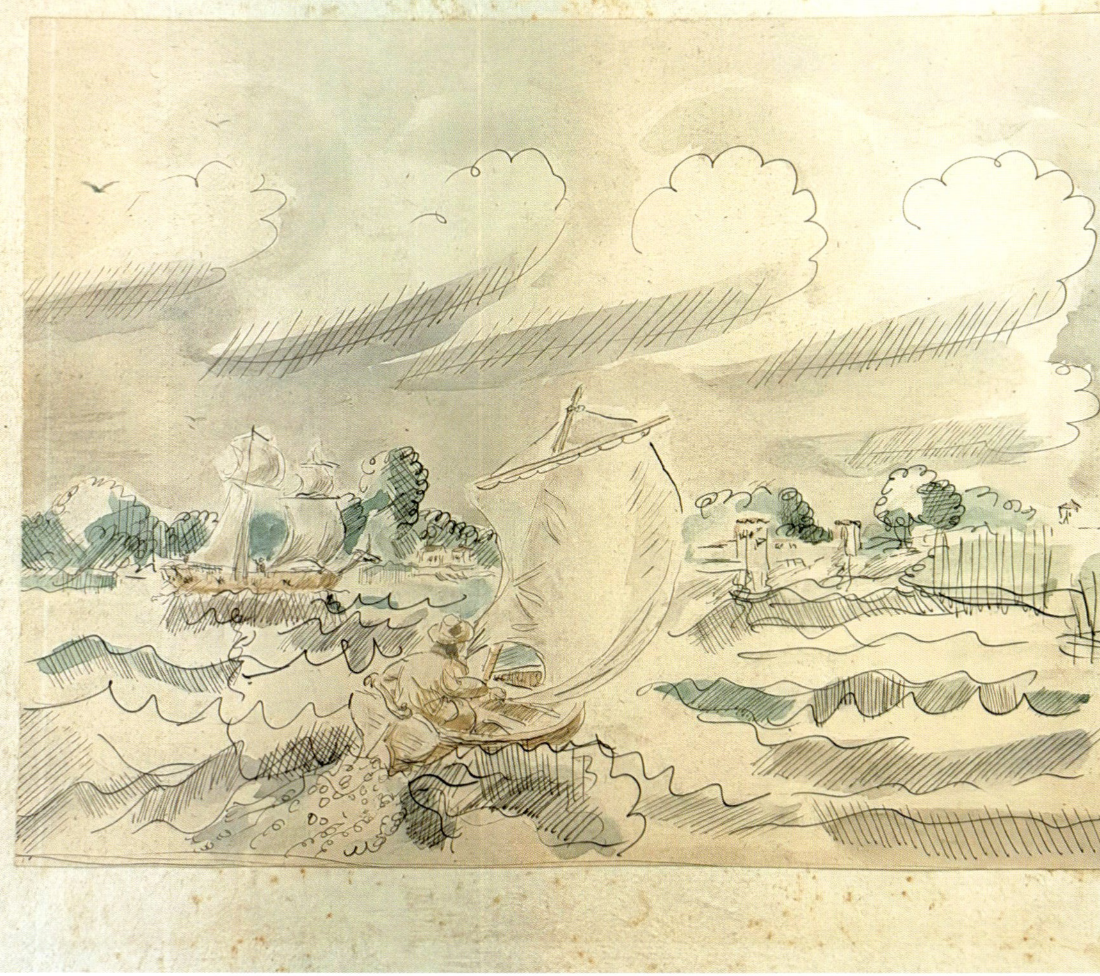

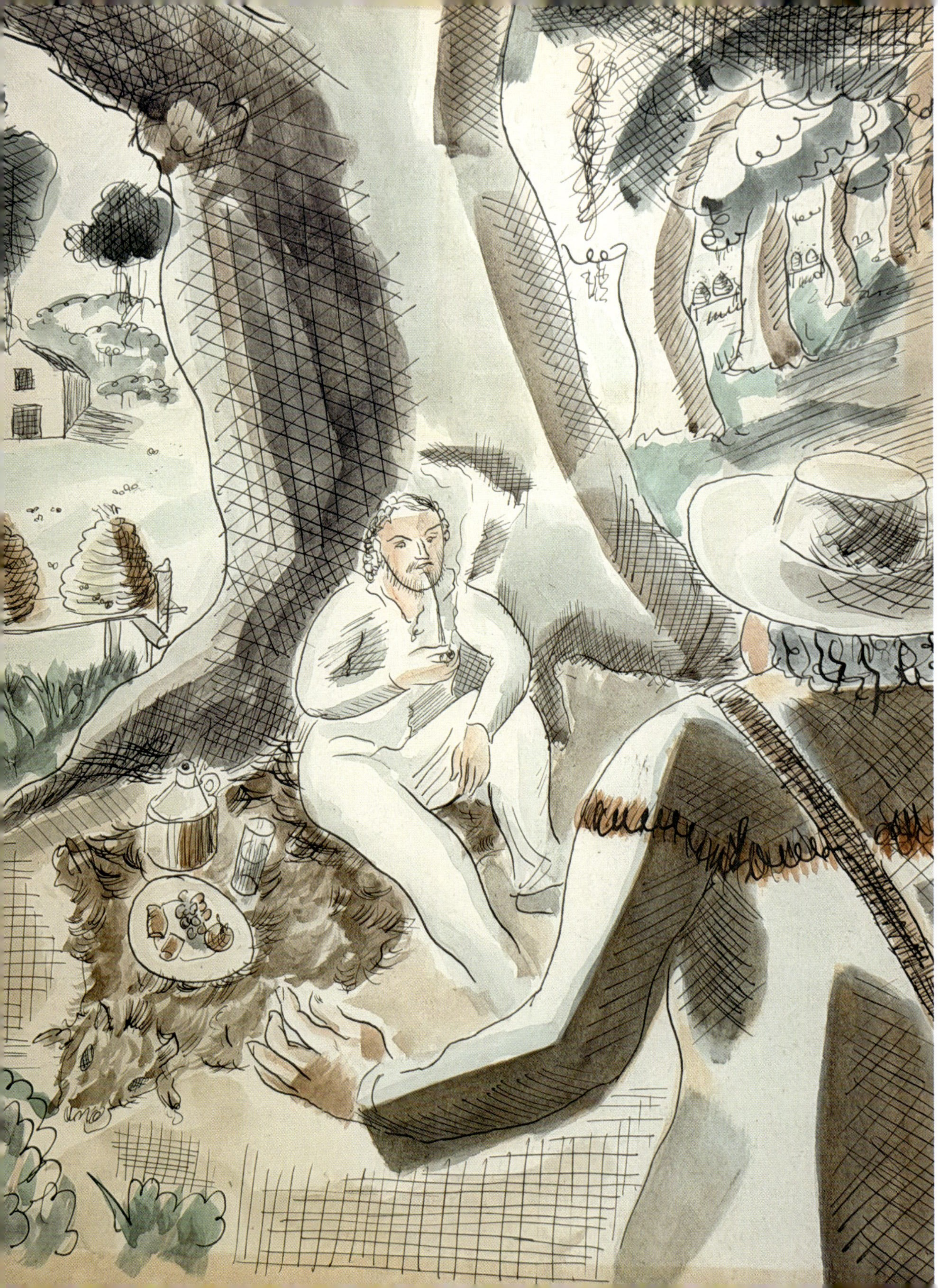

agreeable liquor, of which I drank. On rising to take my departure, he objected, and requested me to stay and dine with him; and on my pleading, for excuse, the necessity of my being at Frederica, "Yet, I pray you, stay a little, I will soon have some refreshment for you." Presently was laid before us a plentiful repast of venison, &c. our drink being honey and water, strengthened by the addition of brandy. Our rural table was spread under the shadow of Oaks, Palms, and Sweet Bays, fanned by the lively salubrious breezes wafted from the spicy groves. Our music was the responsive love-lays of the painted nonpareil, and the alert and gay mockbird; whilst the brilliant humming-bird darted through the flowery groves, suspended in air, and drank nectar from the flowers of the yellow Jasmine, Lonicera, Andromeda, and sweet Azalea. . . . Taking leave of my sylvan friend, I sat off on my return to the town. (60–61)

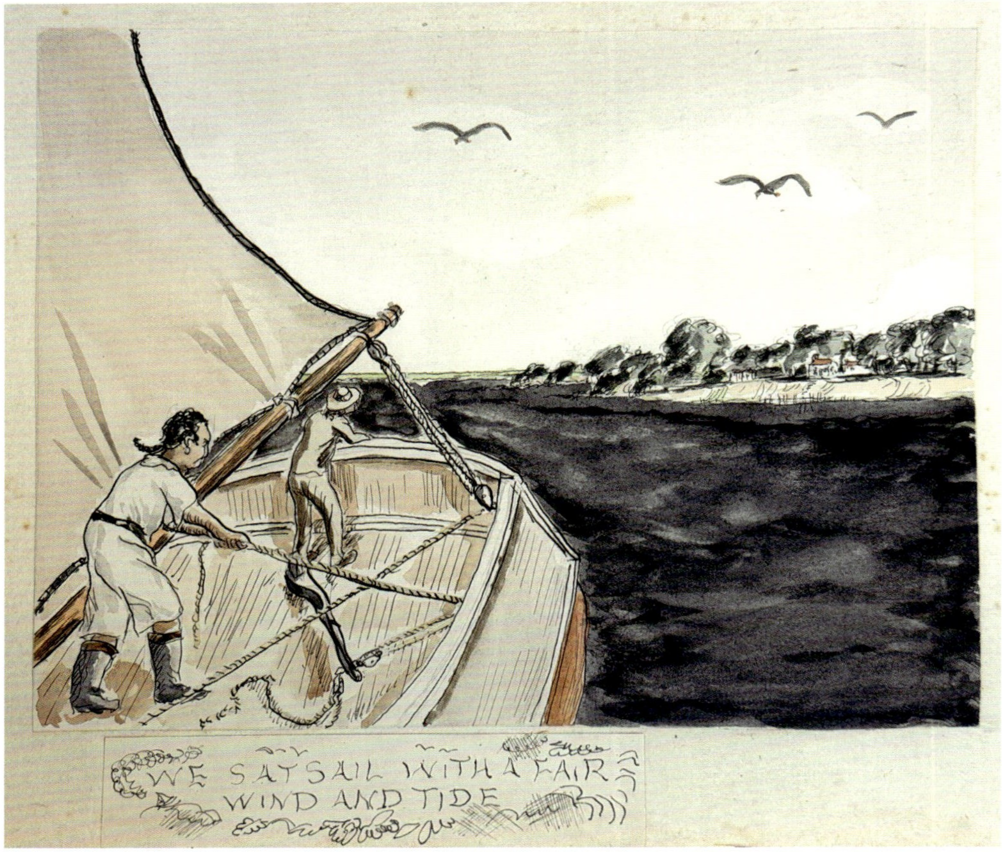

➢ Labeled "We sat sail with a fair wind and tide," this painting shows Bartram at the stern, gazing at the waterfront as he sails away from Frederica on the western shore of St. Simons Island. Note also that he is standing astride the rudder, which is being manipulated by a deckhand using ropes and pulleys. About this passage, Bartram wrote:

> *The vessel, in which I was to embark for East Florida, being now ready to pursue her voyage, we sat sail with a fair wind and tide. Our course was south, through the sound, betwixt a chain of sea-coast-islands, and the main. . . . Next morning early, we again got under way, running by Jekyl[l] and Cumberland Islands, large, beautiful and fertile, yet thinly inhabited, and consequently excellent haunts for deer, bears and other game. (63)*

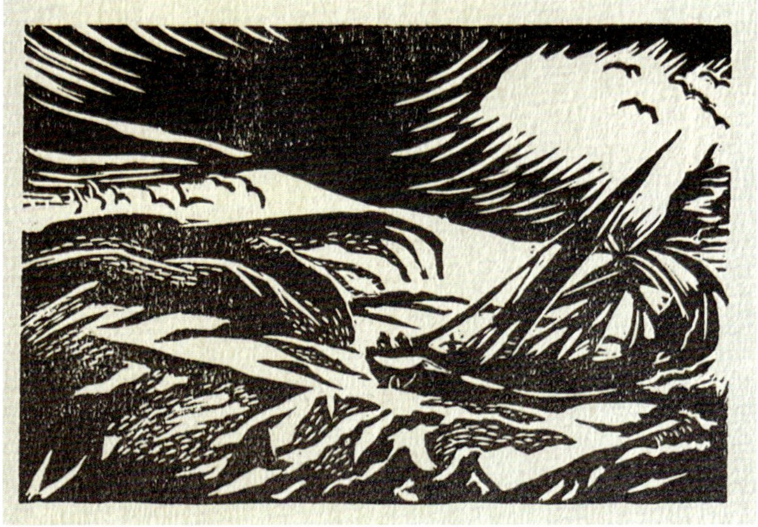

➢ Haynes would later illustrate Bartram's passage south from Frederica in this linoleum cut, emphasizing the captain's wise decision to shelter for the night in the lee of the south end of St. Simons Island.

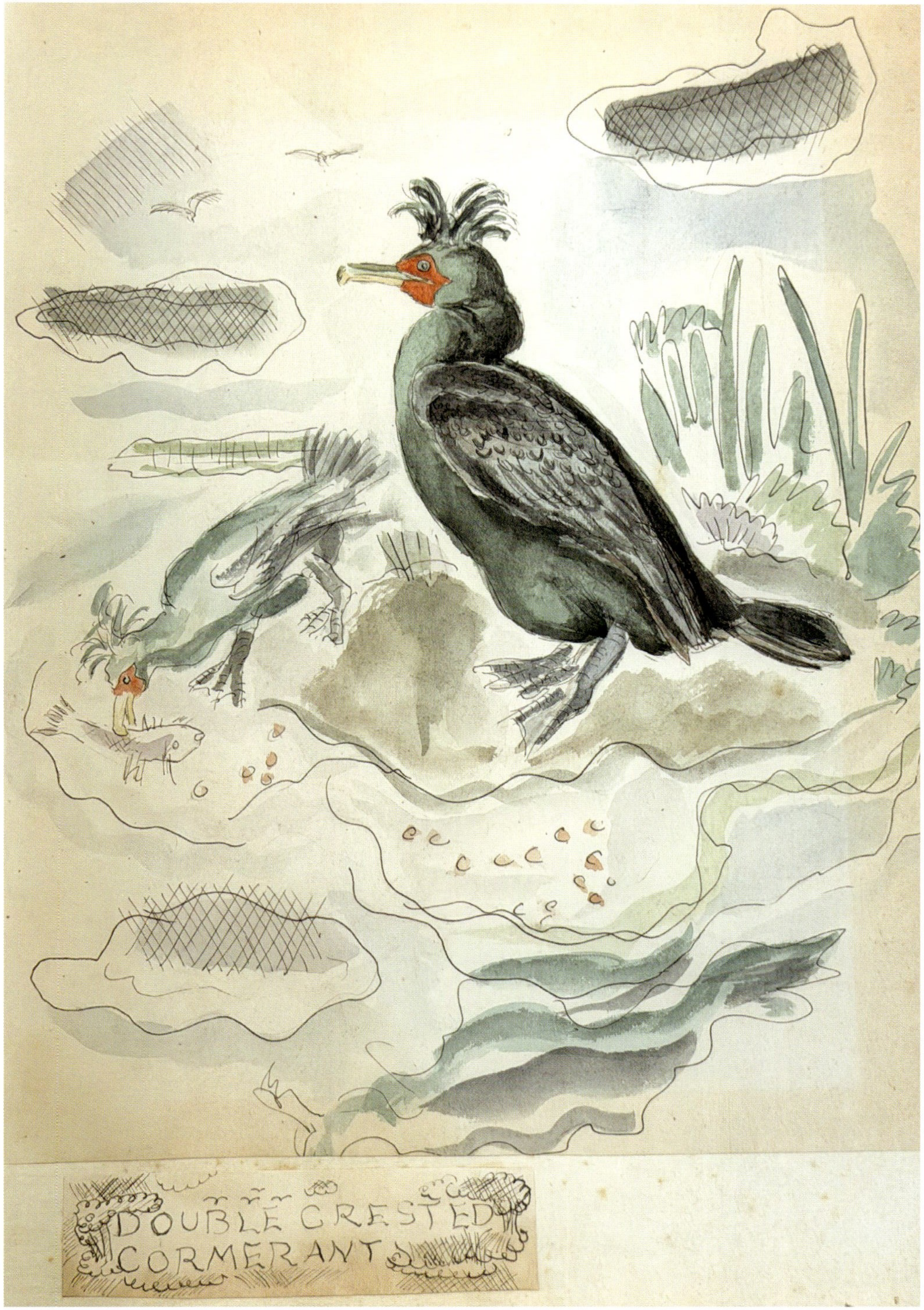

Haynes's illustration shows two double-crested cormorants. Although Bartram is credited as the first to describe the bird scientifically, only its name appears on his bird list in *Travels* (295). As with many of the birds Haynes sketched, there is no doubt that his cormorant painting was heavily influenced by Audubon's.

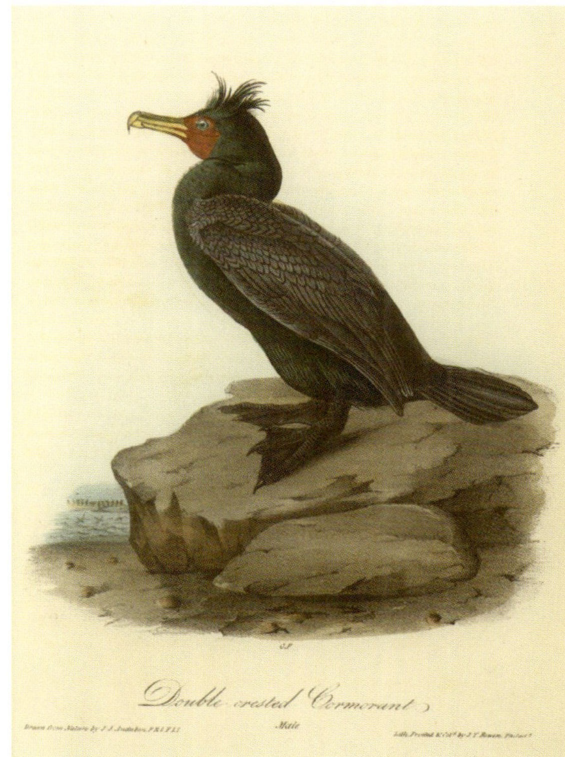

John James Audubon, *Cormorant*, New York Public Library.

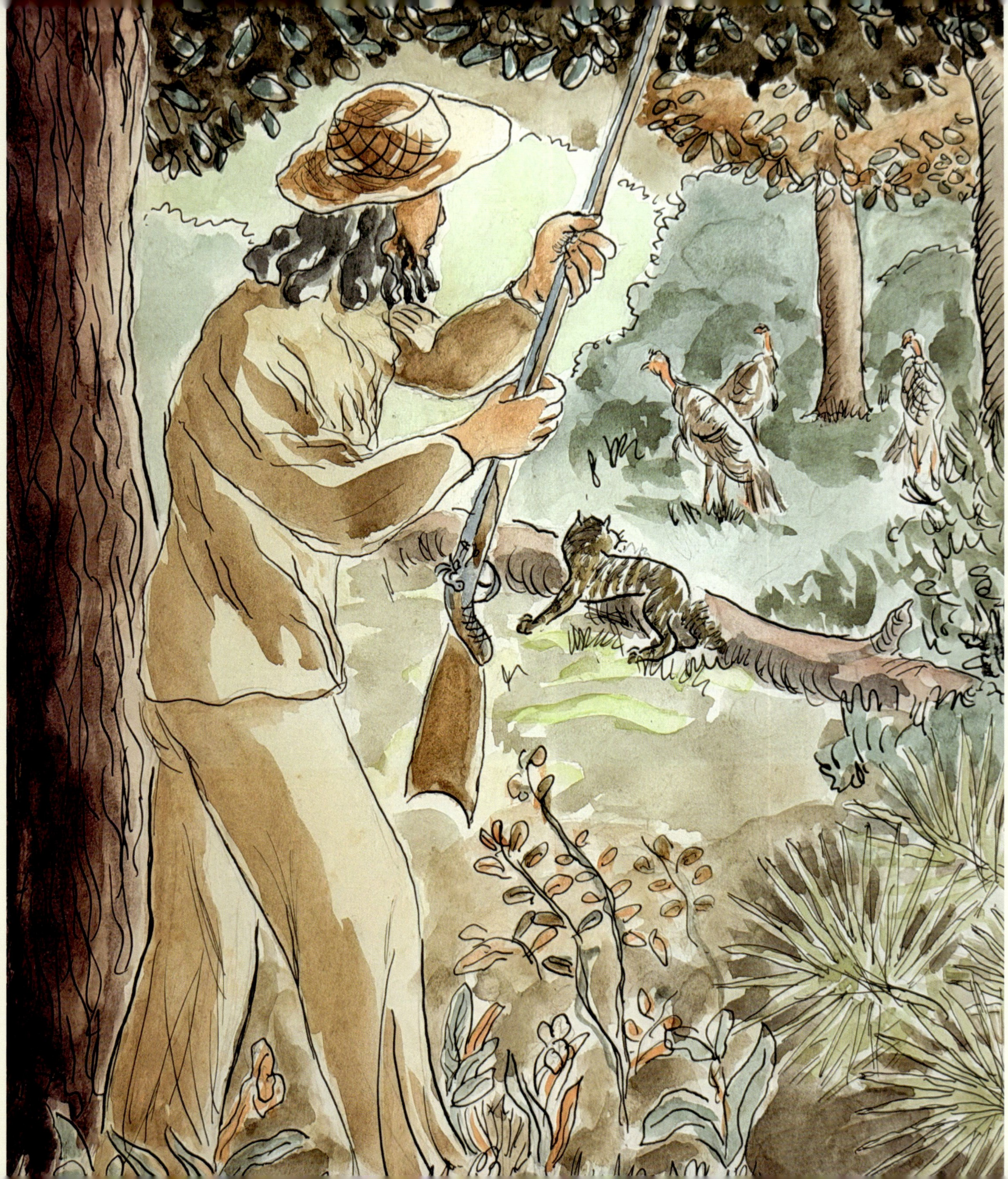

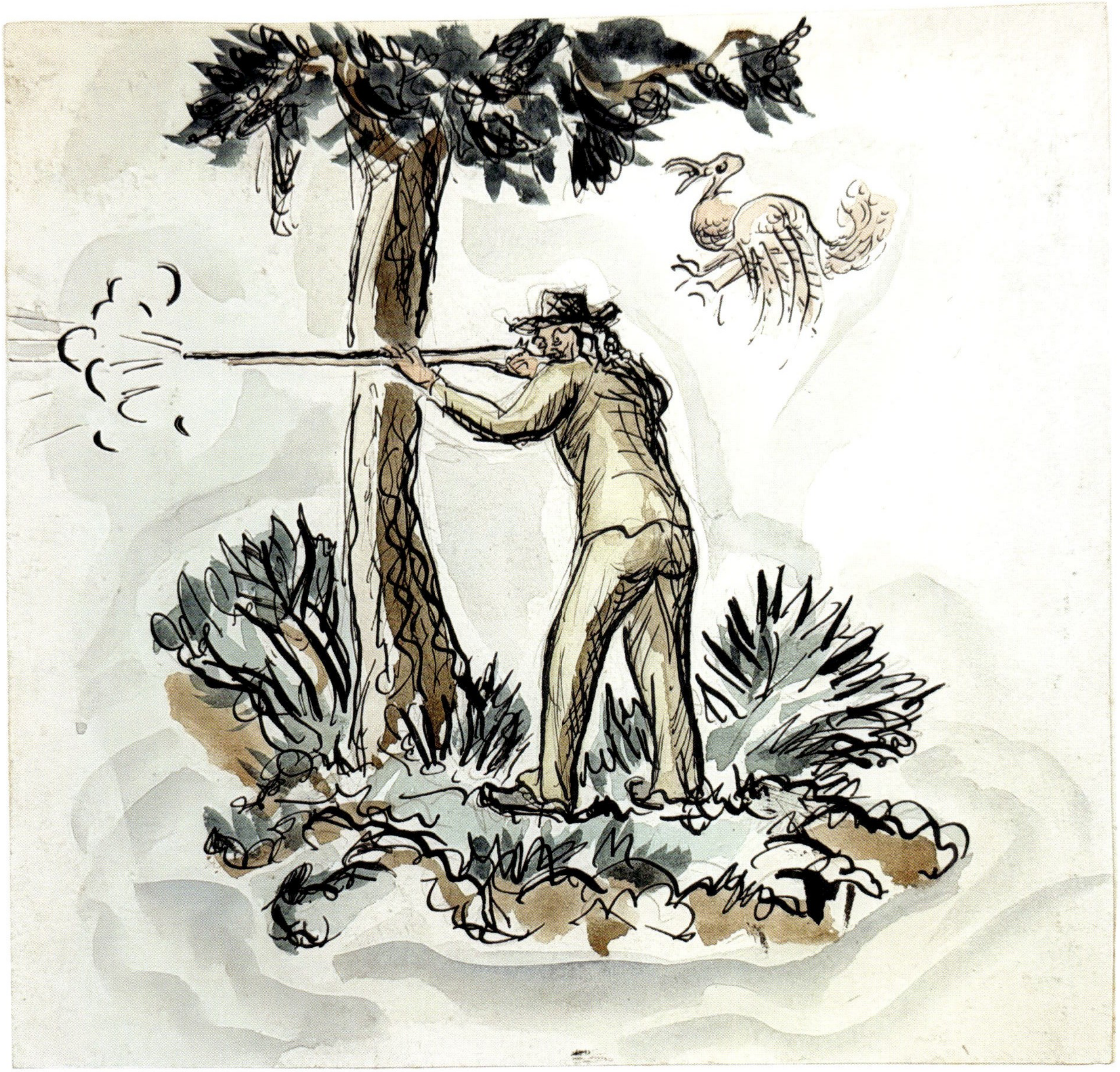

These two paintings illustrate Bartram's description of a turkey hunt gone awry.

> *My companion parting from me, in pursuit of the deer, one way, and I, observing a flock of turkeys at some distance, on the other, directed my steps towards them, and with great caution, got near them; when singling out a large cock, and being just on the point of firing, I observed that several young cocks were affrighted, and in their language, warned the rest to be on their guard, against an enemy, whom I plainly perceived was industriously making his subtile approaches towards them, behind the fallen trunk of a tree, about twenty yards from me. This cunning fellow hunter, was a large fat wild cat (lynx) he saw me, and at times seemed to watch my motions, as if determined to seize the delicious prey before me. Upon which I changed my object, and levelled my piece at him. At that instant, my companion, at a distance, also discharged his piece at the deer, the report of which alarmed the flock of turkeys, and my fellow hunter, the cat, sprang over the log and trotted off. The trader also missed his deer: thus we foiled each other. (110)*

The upper illustration is rather abstract, but we interpret it to be an American coot flushed from the marsh. Bartram did not draw the bird but only lists the species on page 296 as *Fulica floridana*, the great blue or slate-colored coot of Florida. However, he does include a rich description of their behavior in two excerpts: "the laughing coots with wings half spread were tripping over the little coves and hiding themselves in the tufts of grass" (118). Later, he refers to them as "the social pratling coot." (160)

The lower painting shows Bartram sketching from a boat in the marsh.

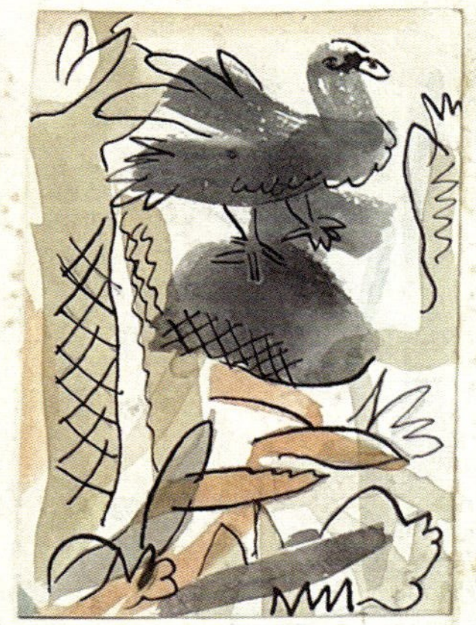

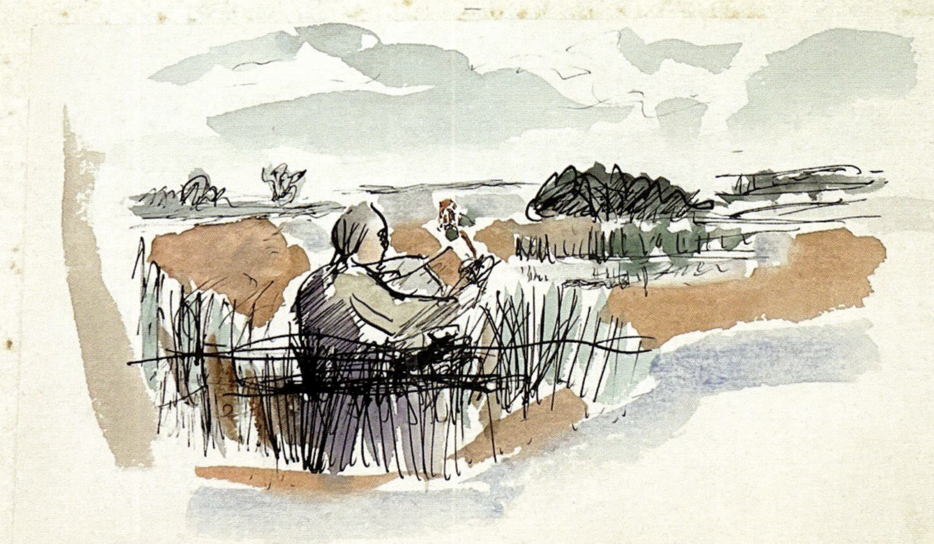

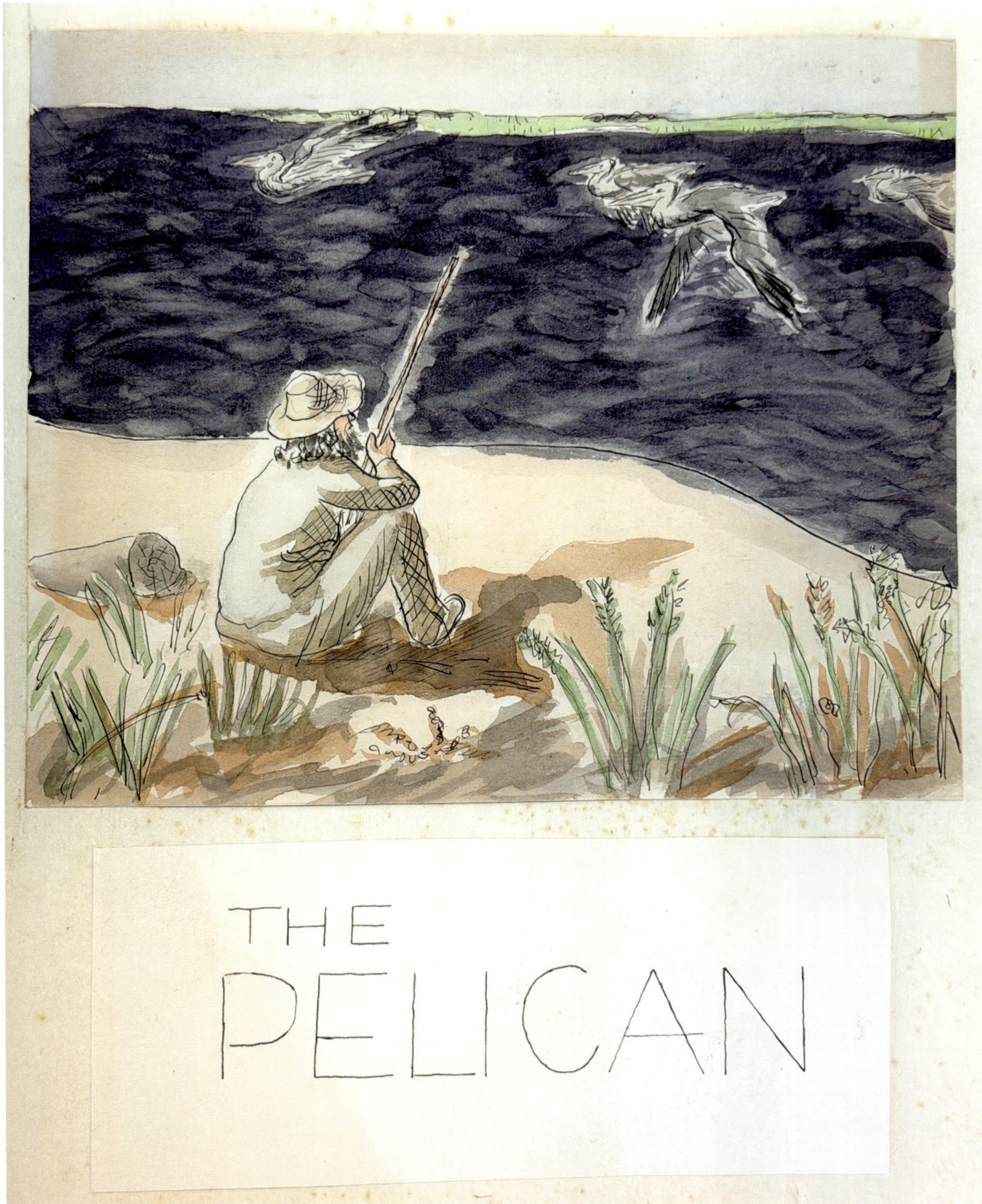

Haynes chose to illustrate Bartram taking aim at a pelican for scientific examination but sparing viewers images of the bird's bloody postmortem.

After passing Amelia Narrows, we had a pleasant run, across Fort George's sound, where, observing the pelicans fishing, Mr. Egan shot one of them, which we took into the boat. I was greatly surprised on observing the pouch or sack, which hangs under the bill: it is capable of being expanded to a prodigious size. One of the people on board, said, that he had seen more than half a bushel of bran, crammed into one of their pouches. The body is larger than that of a tame goose, the legs extremely short, the feet webbed, the bill of a great length, bent inwards like a scythe, the wings extend near seven feet from tip to tip, the tail is very short, the head, neck and breast, nearly white, the body of a light bluish grey, except the quill feathers of the wings, which are black. They seem to be of the gull kind, both in form and structure, as well as manner of fishing. (70)

Bartram was enthralled by the majestic sandhill cranes he encountered in great numbers in Florida, especially those in the Alachua Savanna (see page 40 for Bartram's Alachua Savanna image). Haynes paints a crane about to seize a frog.

> *Induced by the beautiful appearance of the green meadows, which open to the Eastward, I determined not to pass this Elisium without a visit. Behold the loud, sonorous, watchful savanna crane (grus pratensis) with musical clangor, in detached squadrons. They spread their light elastic sail; at first they move from the earth heavy and slow, they labour and beat the dense air; they form the line with wide extended wings, tip to tip, they all rise and fall together as one bird; now they mount aloft, gradually wheeling about, each squadron performs its evolution, incircling the expansive plains, observing each one their own orbit; then lowering sail, descend on the verge of some glittering lake; whilst other squadrons, ascending aloft in spiral circles, bound on interesting discoveries, wheel round and double the promontory, in the silvery regions of the clouded skies, where, far from the scope of eye, they carefully observe the verdant meadows on the borders of the East Lake; then contract their plumes and descend to the earth, where, resting awhile on some verdant eminence, near the flowery border of the lake, with dignified, yet slow, respectful steps, approach the kindred band; they confer and treat for habitation; the bounds and precincts being settled, they confederate and take possession. (146–147)*

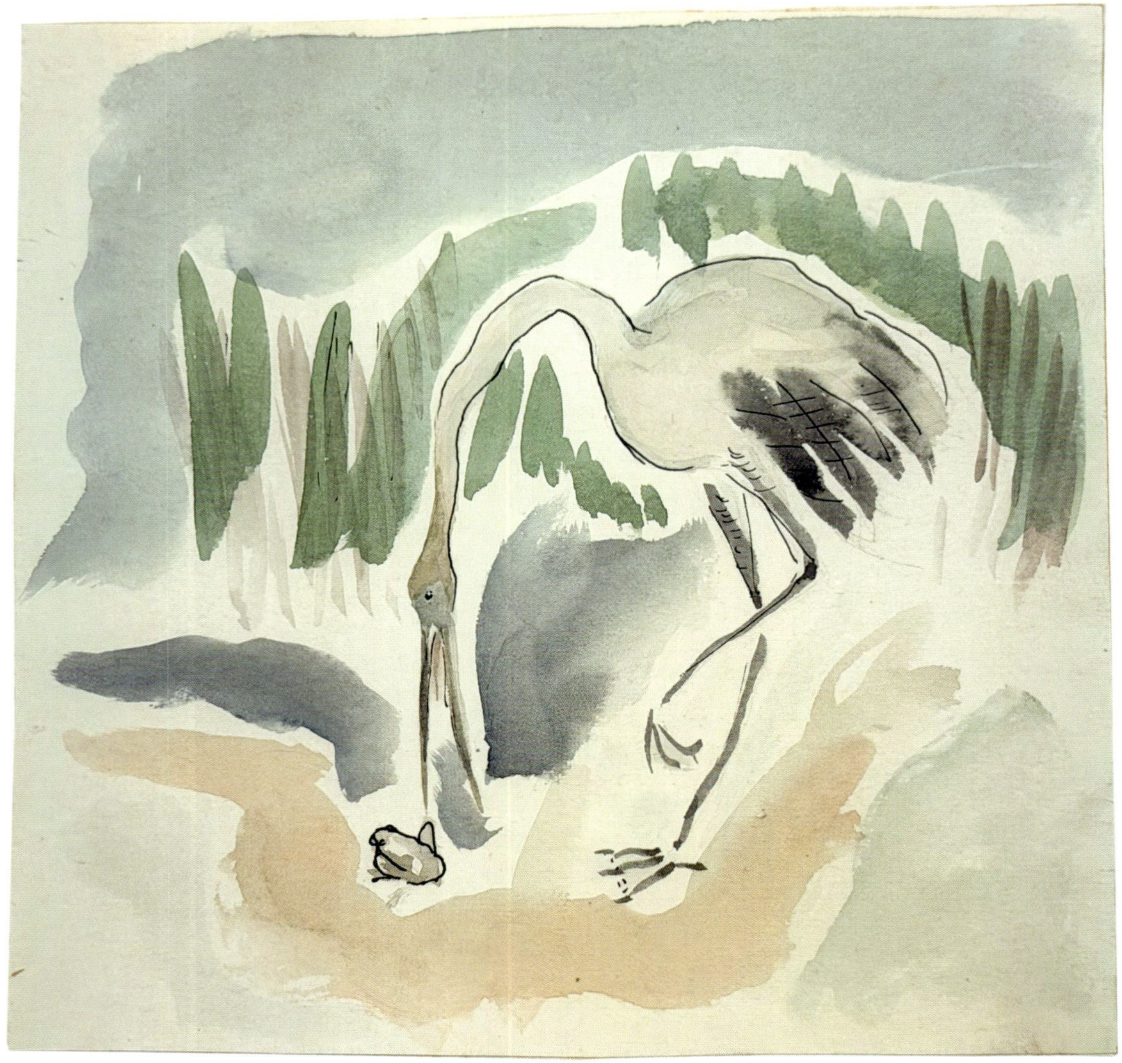

Bartram is credited with being the first person to scientifically describe the sandhill crane that had been shot by his hunting party. They then ate it. However, he did not preserve the skin or skeleton, and to this day, ornithologists complain about him having eaten the "type specimen" rather than sending it back for preservation.

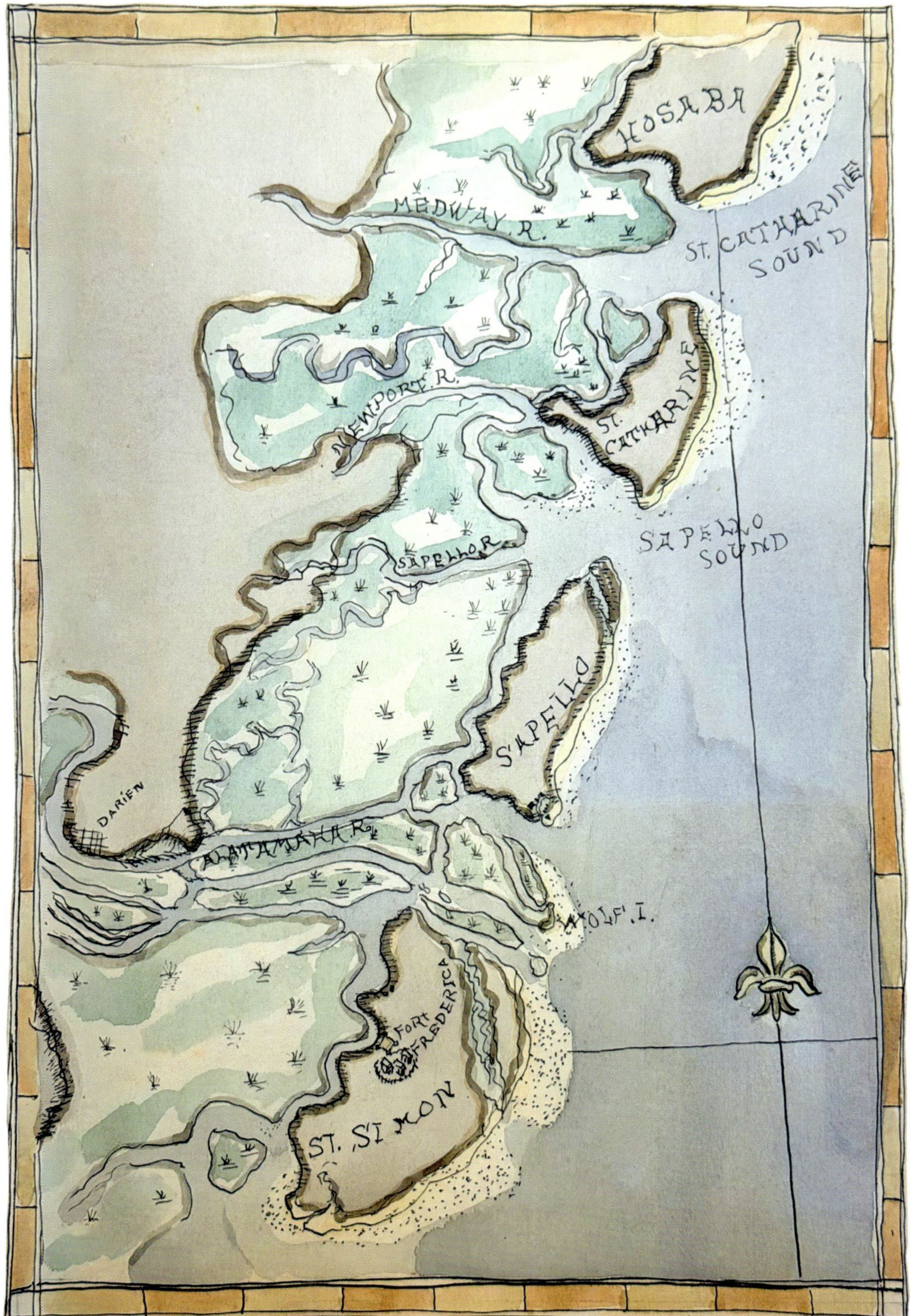

Similar to Bartram's map of the Florida coast (see page 48), Haynes turned his hand at making a map of a portion of the Georgia coast, centered on the places he knew best. The map extends from Ossabaw Island in the north to St. Simons Island in the south, in several cases using the older spelling of names or, as in the case of Ossabaw, the Native name Hosaba. Only two towns appear on the map: Darien, at the great bend in the Altamaha River, and Frederica, halfway down the western coast of St. Simons.

Haynes has left us with a quandary. While it is relatively easy to identify the live duck in hand as a blue-winged teal (only listed by Bartram on page 295), who is the man with the bird in his grasp? The person looks younger than Haynes's usual portrayal of Bartram. It may be John McIntosh, the teenage son of Lachlan McIntosh. The McIntosh family hosted Bartram numerous times when he was in the vicinity of Darien in addition to sending their son to accompany him.

> *I shall yet mention a remarkable instance of Mr. M'Intosh's friendship and respect for me; which was, recommending his eldest son, Mr. John M'Intosh, as a companion in my travels. He was a sensible virtuous youth, and a very agreeable companion through a long and toilsome journey of near a thousand miles. (15)*

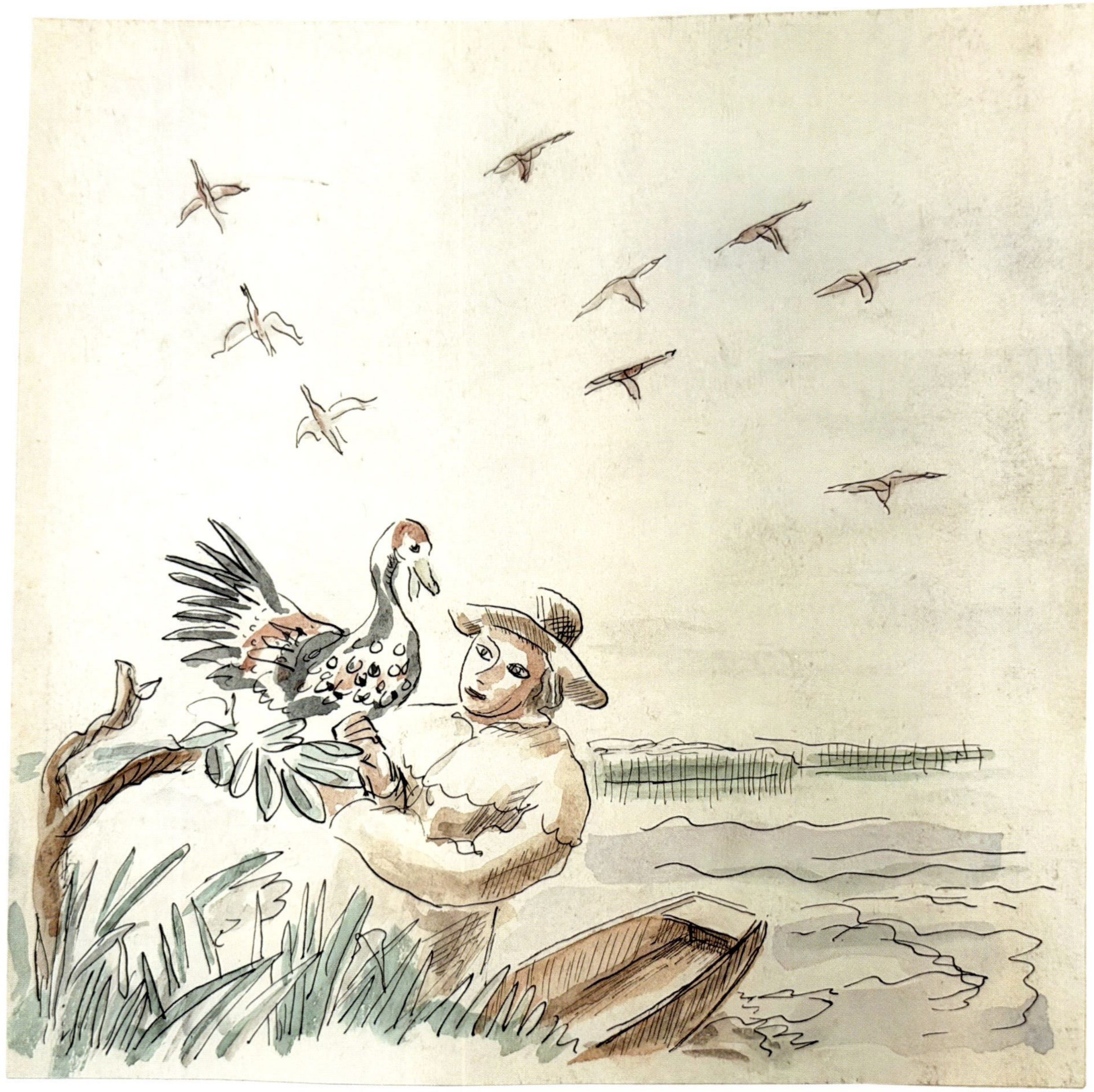

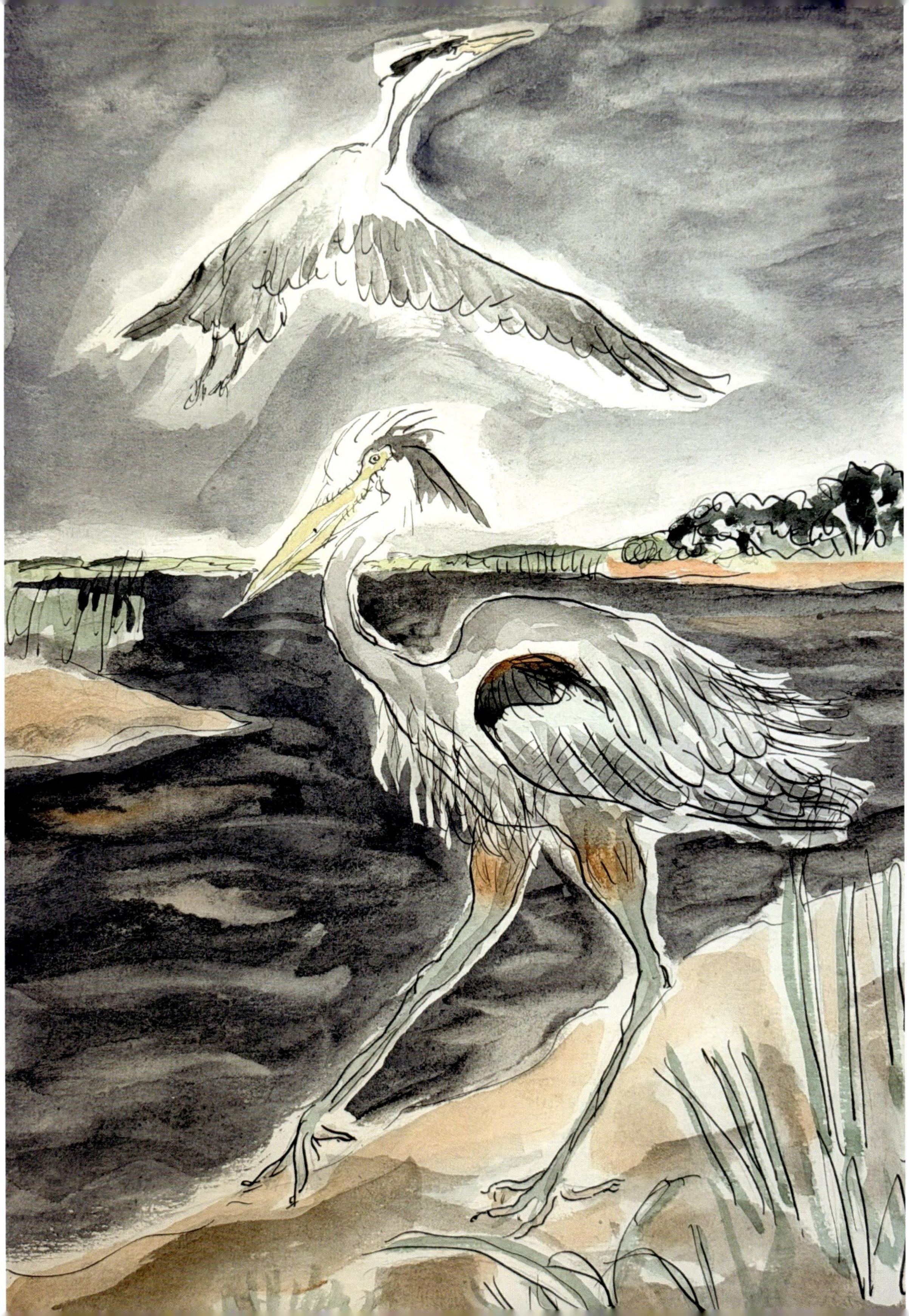

This is *Ardea herodias*, "the great bluish grey crested heron"—another bird not described in detail but only listed by Bartram (293). It is known commonly today as the great blue heron, a familiar sight wherever there is water and prey to be had. Unlike most of the other birds Bill Haynes painted, his heron shows no influence from the works of Bartram, his mentor George Edwards, or Audubon—all of whom posed only a single bird on a riverbank, lunging for a fish.

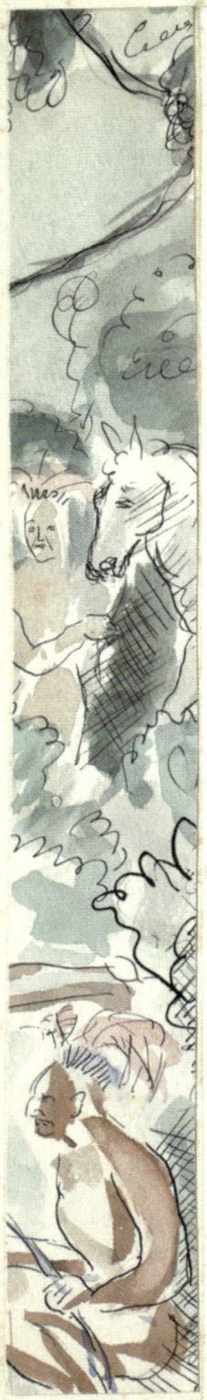

THE CHEROKEES THEMSELVES ARE IGNORANT AS WE ARE BY WHAT PEOPLE OR FOR WHAT PURPOSE THESE ARTIFICIAL HILLS WERE RAISED: BUT THEY HAVE A TRADITION THAT THEY FOUND THEM IN MUCH THE SAME CONDITION AS THEY NOW APPEAR WHEN THEIR FOREFATHERS ARRIVED FROM THE WEST, AND TOOK POSSESSION OF THE COUNTRY. THE FORMER POSSESSORS DELIVERING THE SAME STORY CONCERNING THEM

A. CHUNKEY YARD
B. ROTONDA, GREAT COUNCIL HOUSE
C. PUBLIC SQUARE
D. CHUNKEY POLE
E. SLAVE POST

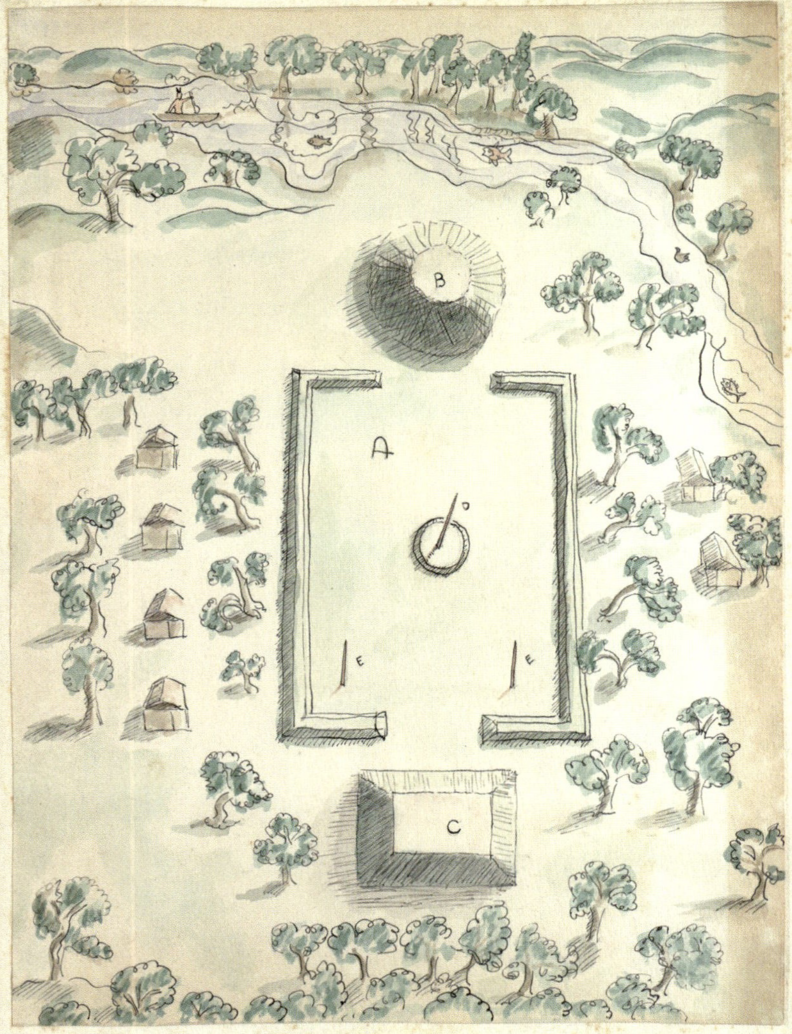

The first page contains a quote from Bartram regarding the Cherokee explanation for ancient mounds that existed prior to their arrival (367–368). At the bottom of that page is a legend for the diagram of a town typical of the Upper Creeks that appears on the facing page. This does not represent the whole town, just its central elements. Both pages have ornamentation to fill in the space. At the bottom of the first page is a landscape view of a town typical of the Upper Creek style showing a pyramidal mound with a ceremonial structure atop it. This page has a leafy border including a Native and horse. The facing page features a man in a dugout canoe and fish ascending shoals toward mountains.

Bartram's original drawing was included in a manuscript entitled "Observations," which Bartram never published. His original drawing has not been found and was likely destroyed; however, at least two other people made tracings of it before the original drawing and the manuscript vanished. As luck would have it, the original "Observations" manuscript was found in a box of books Josiah Nott had ordered from Philadelphia; the tracing and the manuscript had been used as miscellaneous packing materials for his book order! Fortunately, Nott recognized what it was and sent it to Samuel Morton in Philadelphia, where it eventually got into the hands of E. G. Squier, who used it in his own work and later published it (1853). Once again, the tracing disappeared from view until it was serendipitously rediscovered in 2003 by archaeologist Mark Williams in the Hargrett Rare Book and Manuscript Library. For more details on the chain of custody, see Mark Williams, "E. G. Squier's Manuscript Copy of William Bartram's *Observations on the Creek and Cherokee Indians*," in *Fields of Vision: Essays on the* Travels *of William Bartram*, ed. Katherine E. Holland Braund and Charlotte Porter, 169–179 (University of Alabama Press, 2010). According to Bartram:

> *The council or town-house is a large rotunda, capable of accom[m]odating several hundred people; it stands on the top of an ancient artificial mount of earth, of about twenty feet perpendicular, and the rotunda on the top of it being above thirty feet more, gives the whole fabric an elevation of about sixty feet from the common surface of the ground. But it may be proper to observe, that this mount on which the rotunda stands, is of a much ancienter date than the building, and perhaps was raised for another purpose. The Cherokees themselves are as ignorant as we are, by what people or for what purpose these artificial hills were raised; they have various stories concerning them, the best of which amounts to no more than mere conjecture, and leave us entirely in the dark; but they have a tradition common with the other nations of Indians, that they found them in much the same condition as they now appear, when their forefathers arrived from the West and possessed themselves of the country, after vanquishing the nations of red men who then inhabited it, who themselves found these mounts when they took possession of the country, the former possessors delivering the same story concerning them: perhaps they were designed and apropriated by the people who constructed them, to some religious purpose, as great altars and temples similar to the high places and sacred groves anciently amongst the Canaanites and other nations of Palestine and Judea.*
>
> *The rotunda is constructed after the following manner, they first fix in the ground a circular range of posts or trunks of trees, about six feet high, at equal distances, which are notched at top, to receive into them, from one to another, a range of beams or wall plates; within this is another circular order of very large and strong pillars, above twelve feet high, notched in like manner at top, to receive another range of wall plates, and within this is yet another or third range of stronger and higher pillars, but fewer in number, and standing at a greater distance from each other; and lastly, in the centre stands a very strong pillar, which forms the pinnacle of the building, and to which the rafters centre at top; these rafters are strengthened and bound together by cross beams and laths, which sustain the roof or covering, which is a layer of bark neatly placed, and tight enough to exclude the rain, and sometimes they cast a thin superficies of earth over all. There is but one large door, which serves at the same time to admit light from without and the smoak to escape when a fire is kindled; but as there is but a small fire kept, sufficient to give light at night, and that fed with dry small sound wood divested of its bark, there is but little smoak; all around the inside of the building, betwixt the second range of pillars and the wall, is a range of cabins or sophas, consisting of two or three steps, one above or behind the other, in theatrical order, where the assembly sit or lean down; these sophas are covered with matts or carpets, very curiously made of thin splints of Ash or Oak, woven or platted together; near the great pillar in the centre the fire is kindled for light, near which the musicians seat themselves, and round about this the performers exhibit their dances and other shews at public festivals, which happen almost every night throughout the year.* (367–369)

William Bartram, accompanied by a curious hound, greets Lachlan McIntosh at his home on General's Island, just across the Altamaha River from Darien.

Perhaps, to a grateful mind, there is no intellectual enjoyment, which regards human concerns, of a more excellent nature, than the remembrance of real acts of friendship. The heart expands at the pleasing recollection. When I came up to his door, the friendly man, smiling, and with a grace and dignity peculiar to himself, took me by the hand, and accosted me thus: "Friend Bartram, come under my roof, and I desire you to make my house your home, as long as convenient to your self; remember, from this moment, that you are a part of my family, and, on my part, I shall endeavour to make it agreeable," which was verified during my continuance in, and about, the southern territories of Georgia and Florida; for I found here sincerity in union with all the virtues, under the influence of religion. . . . Having been greatly refreshed, by continuing a few days with this kind and agreeable family, I prepared to prosecute my journey southerly. (15)

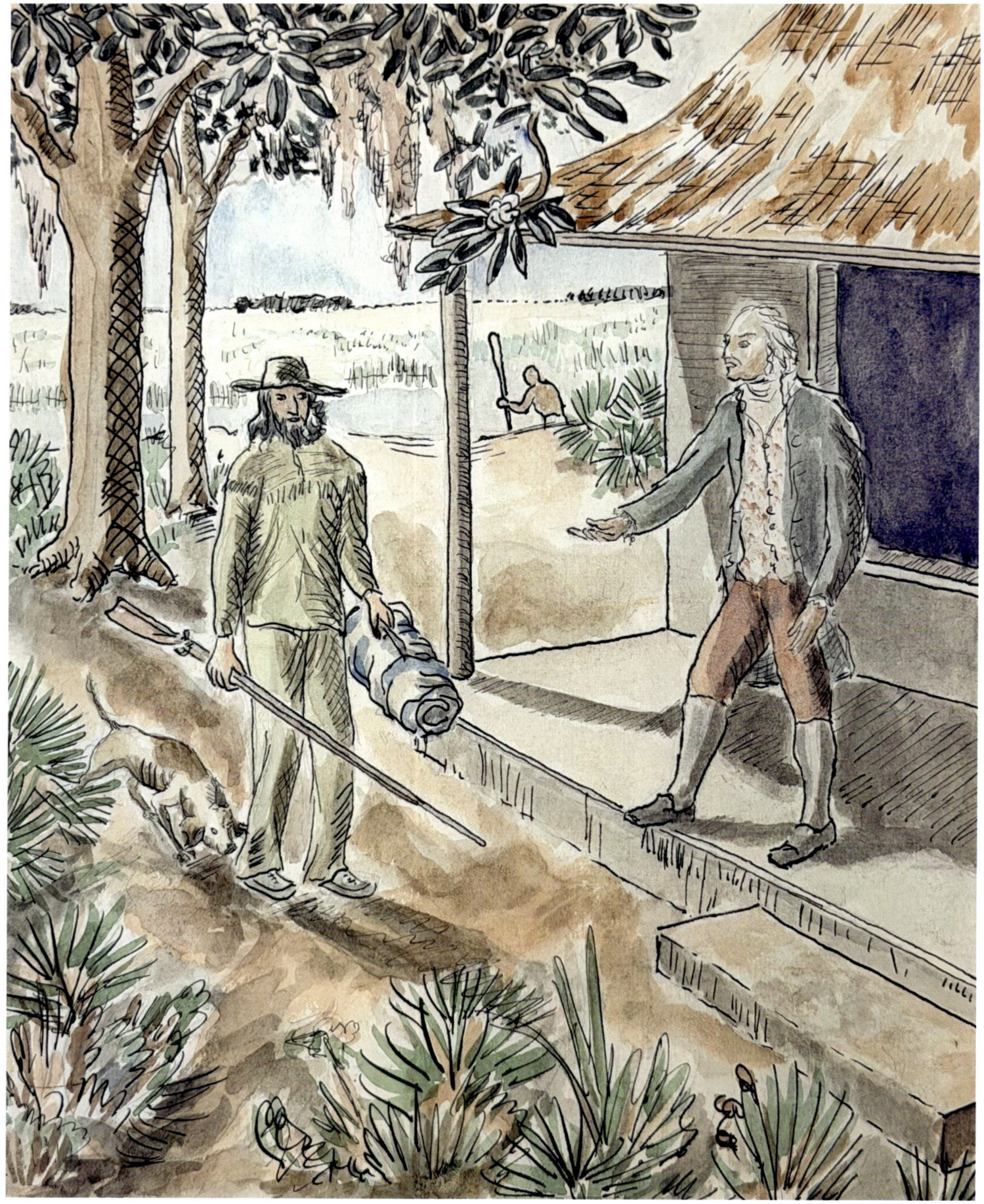

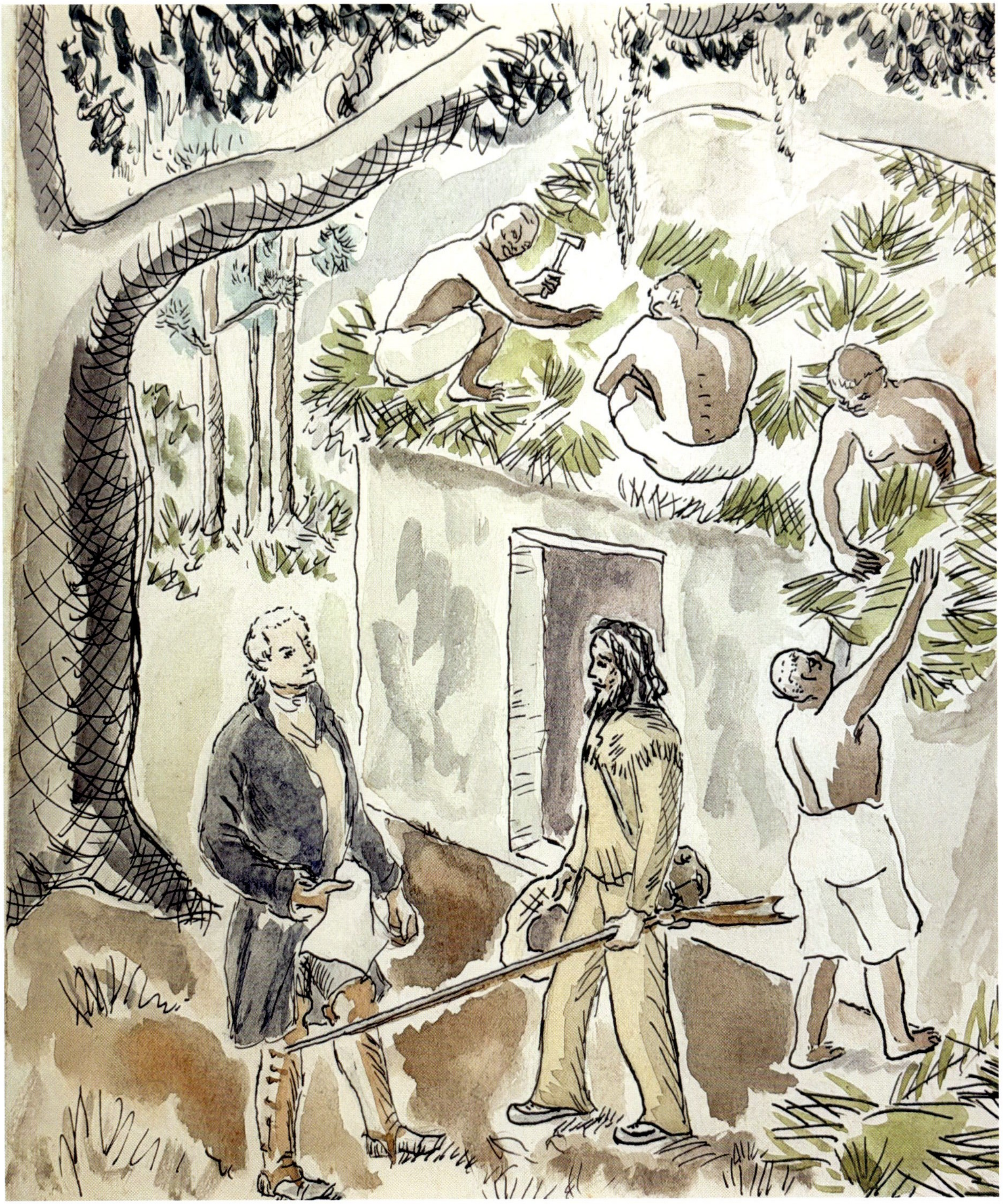

Another instance of generous hospitality is this first encounter between Bartram and Mr. Marshall, whose indigo plantation was located near the Cowford, now known as Jacksonville, Florida. Hearing that Bartram's boat needed repair, Marshall diverted his carpenters from their work on a new building to repair the damage. On his return to the vicinity, as promised, Bartram stopped by Mr. Marshall's to visit with him.

I had not left sight of my encampment, following a winding path through a grove of Live Oak, Laurel (Magn. grandiflora) and Sapindus, before an Indian stepped out of a thicket and crossed the path just before me, having a large turkey cock, slung across his shoulders, he saw me and stepping up and smiling, spoke to me in English, bidding me good-morning. I saluted him with "It's well brother," led him to my camp, and treated him with a dram. This friendly Indian informed me that he lived at the next plantation, employed as a hunter, I asked him how far it was to the house; he answered about half a mile by land, and invited me to go there, telling me that his master was a very good, kind man, and would be glad to see me. I replied, that I would, if my boat and effects in the mean time could be safe, he said that he would immediately return to the house, and acquaint his master of it, who would send trusty Negroes to bring my vessel round the point, to the landing, I thanked him for his civility, and not willing to be troublesome, I told him I would leave my boat, and follow after him; so taking my fusee on my shoulder, and after dragging my bark as high up on shore as I could, I followed the Indian, and soon reached the house.

The gentleman received me, in the most polite manner, and after hearing my situation, he requested me to make my abode with him, a few days, to rest and refresh myself. I thanked him and told him I would stay a day. He immediately sent slaves who brought my boat round, and having carpenters at work, on a new building, he sat them about repairing my vessel, which by night was completely refitted.

I spent the day in the most agreeable manner, in the society of this man of singular worth, he led me over his extensive improvements, and we returned in company with several of his neighbours. In the afternoon the most sultry time of the day, we retired to the fragrant shades of an Orange grove. The house was situated on an eminence, about one hundred and fifty yards, from the river. On the right hand was the Orangery, consisting of many hundred trees, natives of the place, and left standing, when the ground about it was cleared. These trees were large, flourishing and in perfect bloom, and loaded with their ripe golden fruit. On the other side was a spacious garden, occupying a regular slope of ground, down to the water; and a pleasent lawn lay between. Here were large plantations of the Indigo plant, which appeared in a very thriving condition: it was then about five or six inches high, growing in streight parallel rows, about eighteen inches apart. The Corn (Zea) and Potatoes (Convolv. batata) were greatly advanced in growth, and promised a plentiful crop. The Indigo made in East Florida is esteemed almost equal to the best Spanish, especially that sort, which they call Flora. Mr. Marshall presented me, with a specimen of his own manufacture, at this plantation: it was very little, if any inferior; to the best Prussian blue. (75–77)

. . . we sat sail in a neat little schooner for Frederica in Georgia, about the last of September. We had a pleasant and prosperous voyage down the grand river St. Juans, frequently visiting the plantations on the banks of the river, especially at such times as opposed by contrary winds, and according to promise did not neglect calling on the generous and friendly Mr. Marshall, who received me so politely, and treated me with such unparalleled friendship and hospitality, when ascending the river alone, last spring. (306)

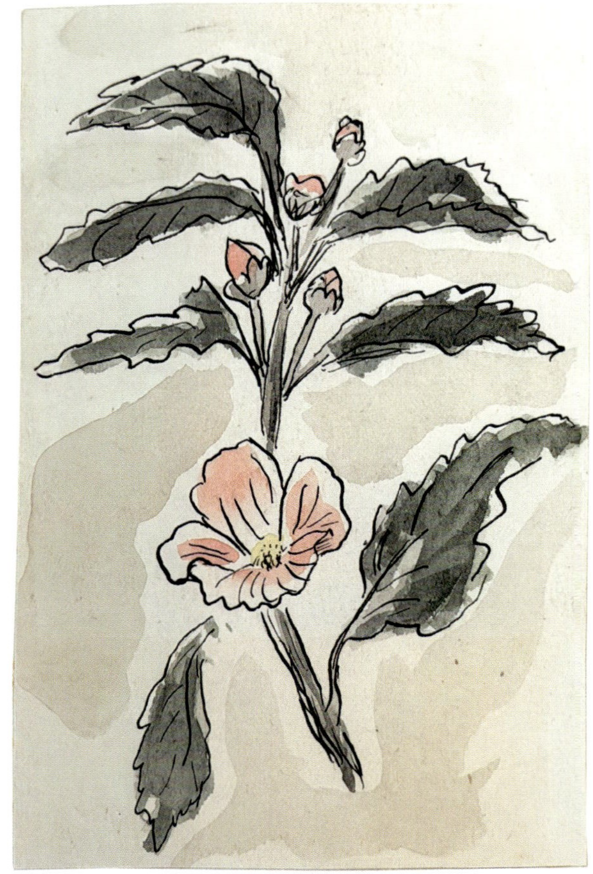

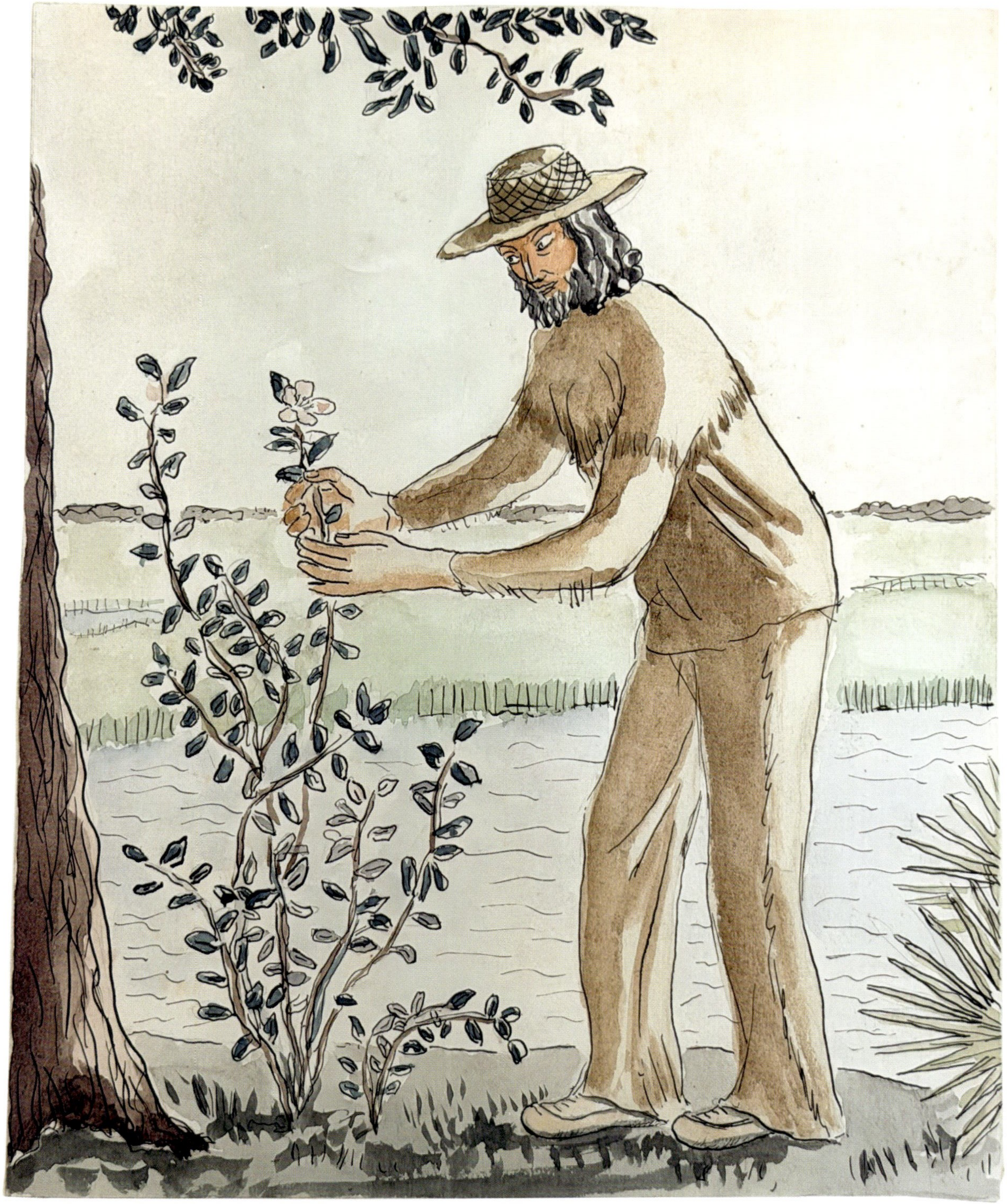

Bartram discovered a giant yellow evening primrose in Alabama on his return trip. Haynes's small painting, however, shows the more common pink variety introduced widely into the Southeast from its native range in America's central grasslands. On this page, Haynes painted Bartram carefully examining what could be a new flowering plant to add to his botanical list.

Passing through "splendid fields of the golden Oenothera," Bartram described his delight at the discovery:

> *Early one morning, passing along by some old uncultivated fields, a few miles above Taensa, I was struck with surprise at the appearance of a blooming plant, gilded with the richest golden yellow, stepping on shore, I discovered it to be a new species of the Oenothera (Oenothera grandiflora) . . . perhaps the most pompous and brilliant herbaceous plant yet known to exist. . . . There is a daily profuse succession for many weeks, and one single plant at the same instant presents to view many hundred flowers. I have measured these flowers above five inches in diameter, they have an agreeable scent. (406–407)*

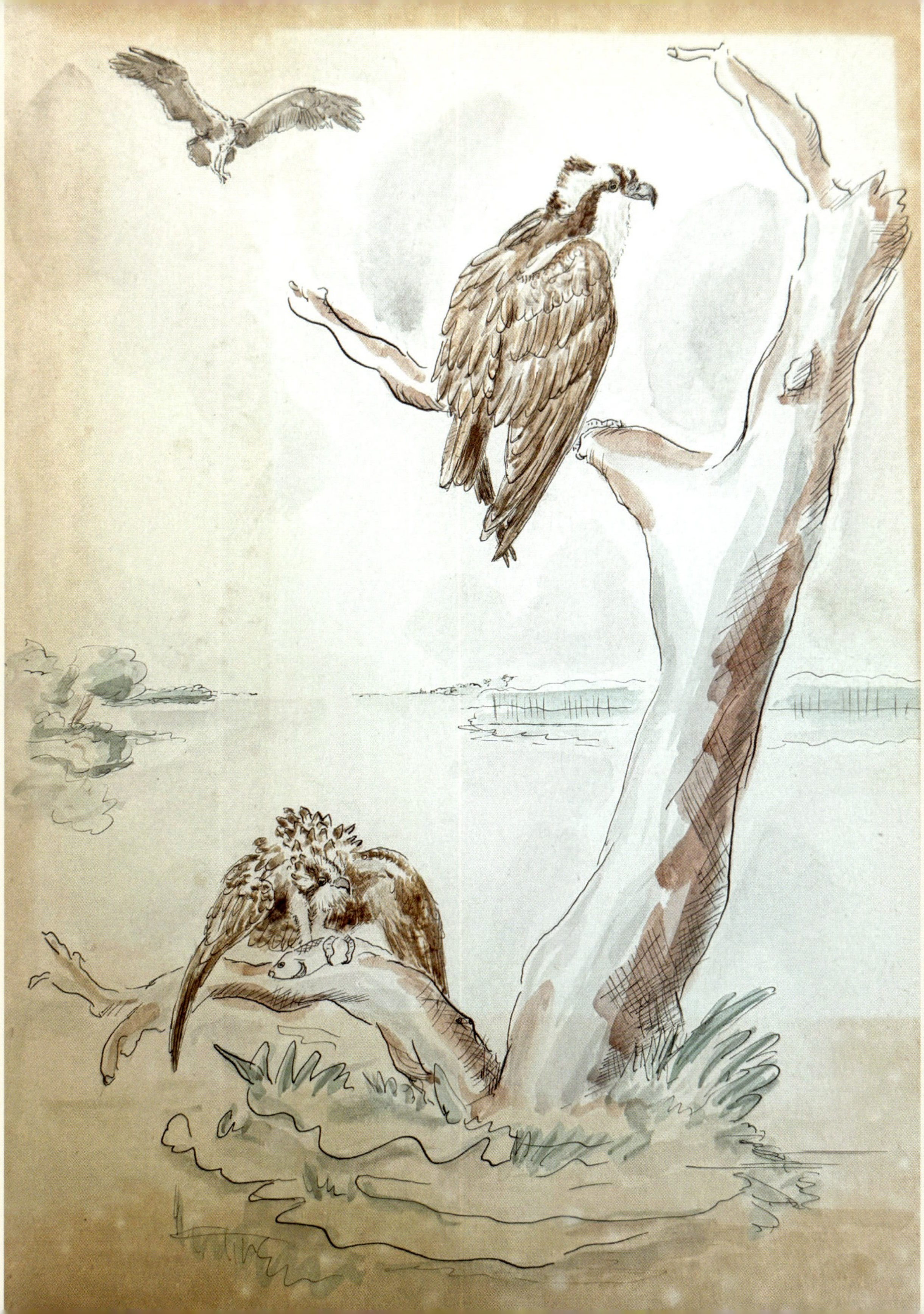

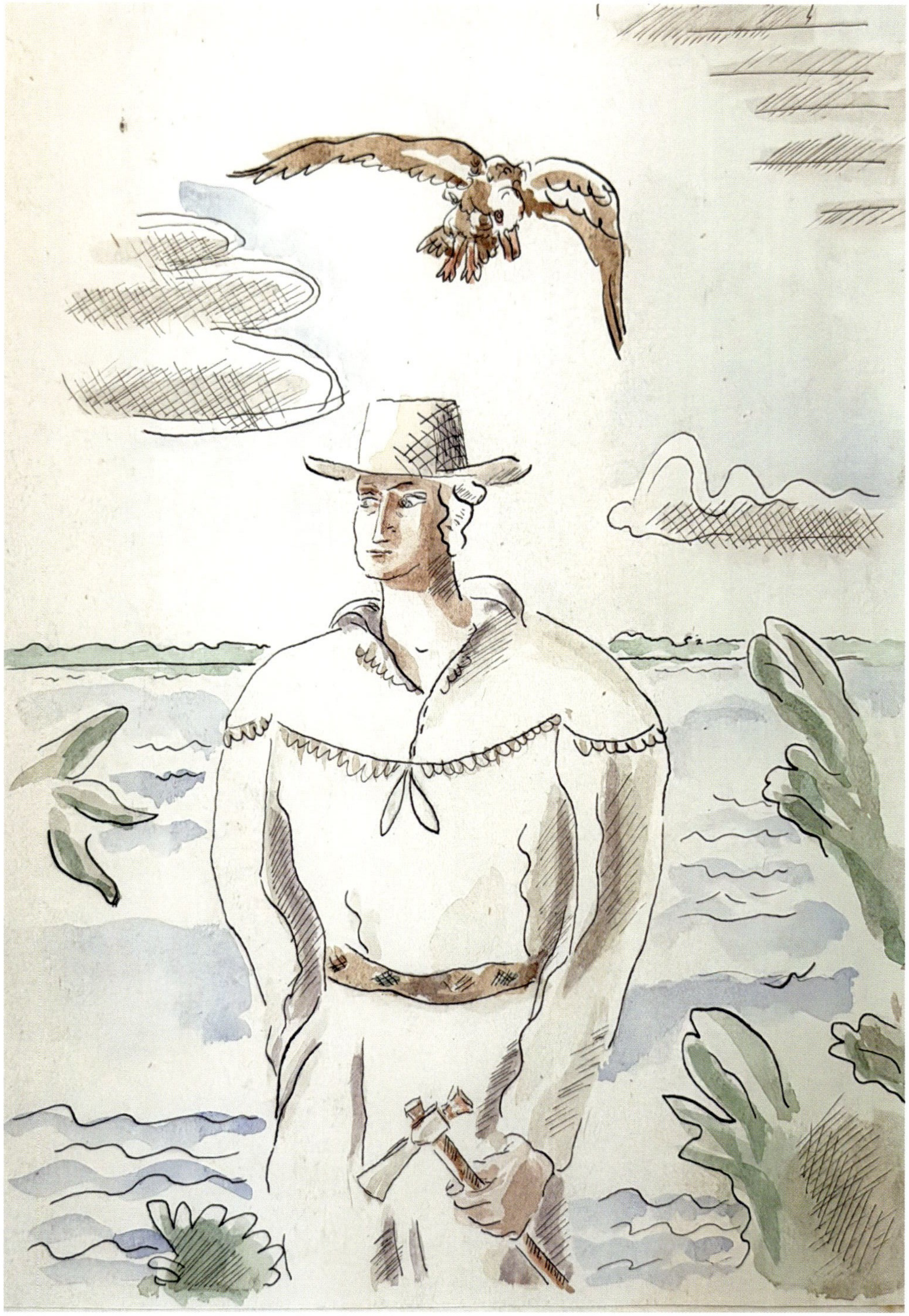

A broad-shouldered, clean-shaven man stands in immaculate buckskin with a pipe tomahawk in hand while an osprey hovers overhead. This figure differs greatly from Haynes's other representations of Bartram. Perhaps it represents Bartram having returned from his fieldwork, well scrubbed and clean-shaven for a change. Perhaps it is John McIntosh. Or perhaps even Bill Haynes imagining himself as Bartram.

Haynes presents a wonderfully detailed painting of ospreys, or what Bartram called *Falco piscatorius*, the fishing hawk, a familiar sight to all who visit the Georgia coast. Bartram not only described the bird itself but also its behavior.

> *The last of this race I shall mention is the falco piscatorius, or fishing-hawk: this is a large bird, of high and rapid flight; his wings are very long and pointed, and he spreads a vast sail, in proportion to the volume of his body. This princely bird subsists entirely on fish, which he takes himself, scorning to live and grow fat on the dear-earned labours of another; he also contributes liberally to the support of the bald eagle. (8)*

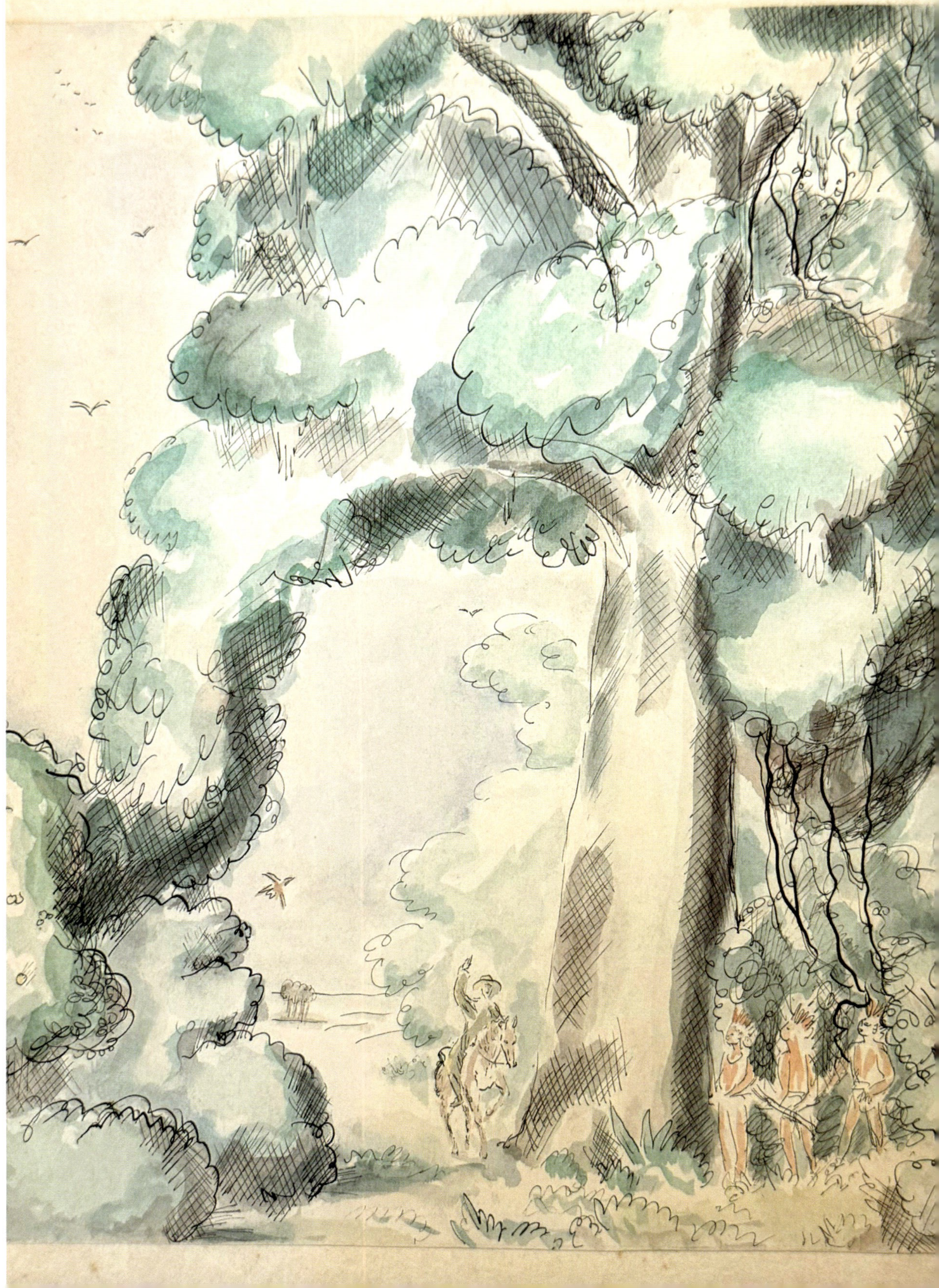

On horseback, William Bartram hails three Native men under a huge tree. Note again the bird flying overhead to Bartram's left. Bartram describes this scene as part of a hunt on the Alachua Savanna.

> *The morning cool and pleasant, and the skies serene, we decamped, pursuing our progress round the Alachua savanna. Three of our companions separating from us, went a-head and we soon lost sight of them: they again parting on different excursions, in quest of game and in search of their horses; some enter the surrounding groves and forests, others strike off into the green plains.* (196)

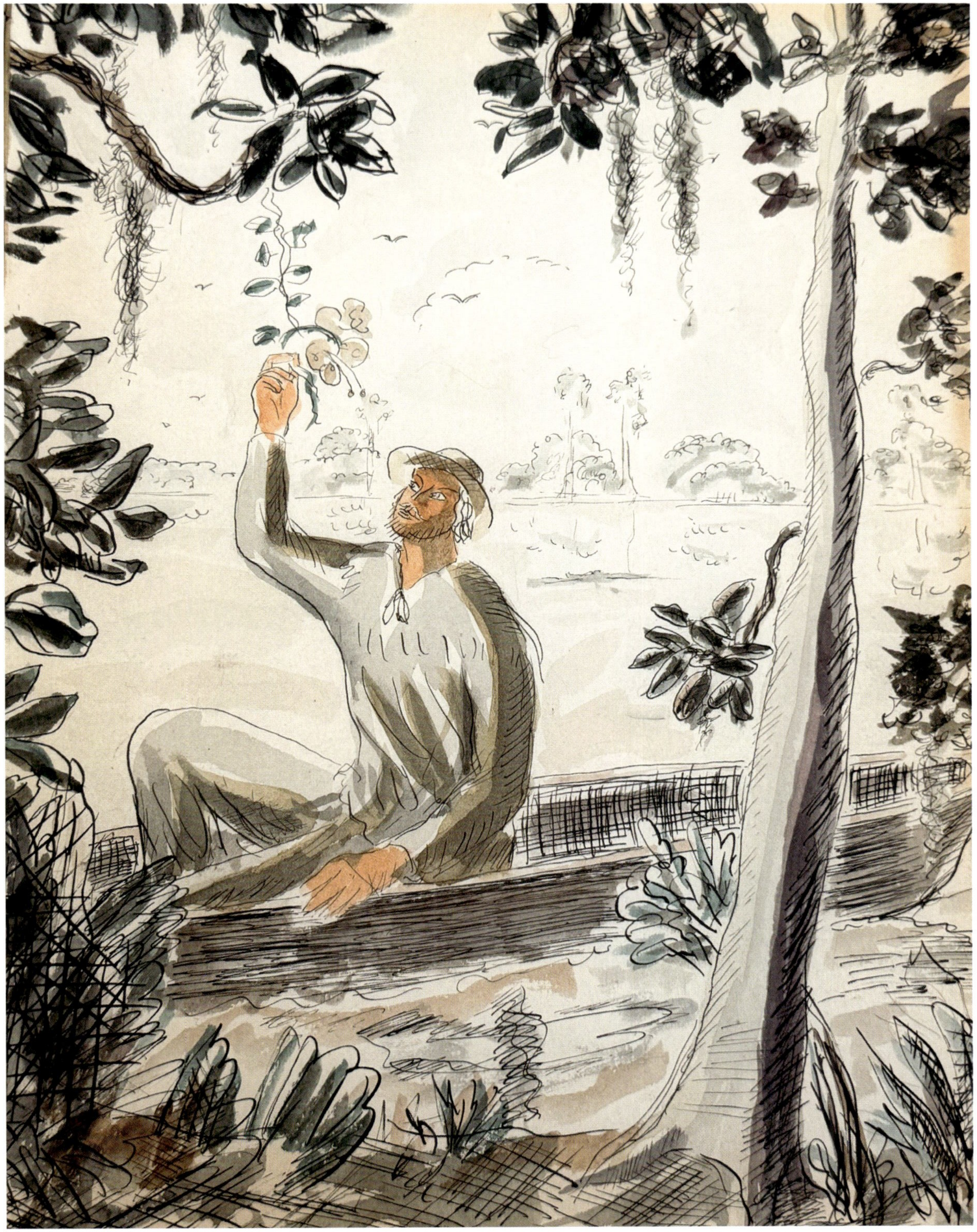

From his dugout, Bartram admires a flowering vine hanging from a magnolia or bay tree festooned with Spanish moss. The pink flowers suggest this may be one of two different species of *Bignonia*, commonly called trumpet vine or crossvine.

The Grape vines with the Rhamnus volubilis, Bignonia radicans, Bignonia crucigera, and another rambling shrubby vine, which seems allied to the Rhamnus, perhaps Zizyphus scandens, seem to tie the trees together, with garlands and festoons, and form enchanting shades. (87)

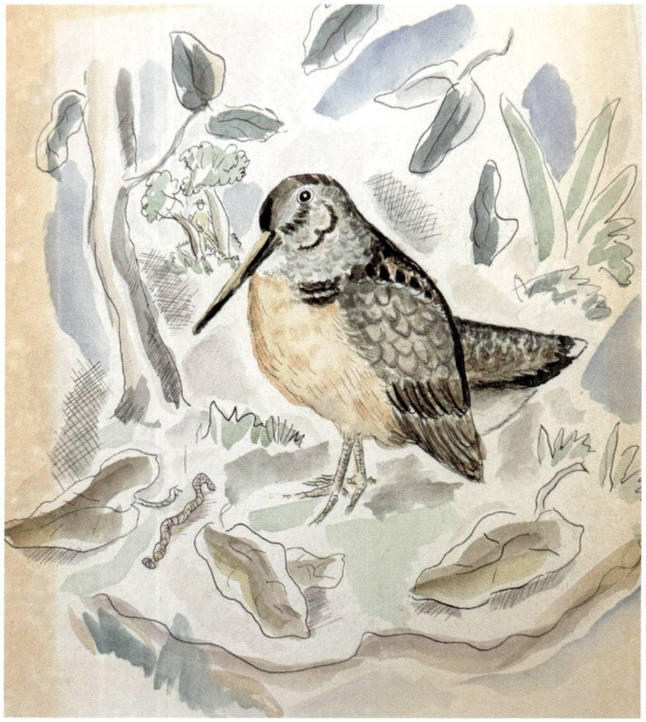

A woodcock regards a worm on the ground in front of it. A different kind of hunter stands among the trees in the background. Among his remarks on birdlife, Bartram only lists the woodcock's presence, without offering further details of its behavior or appearance.

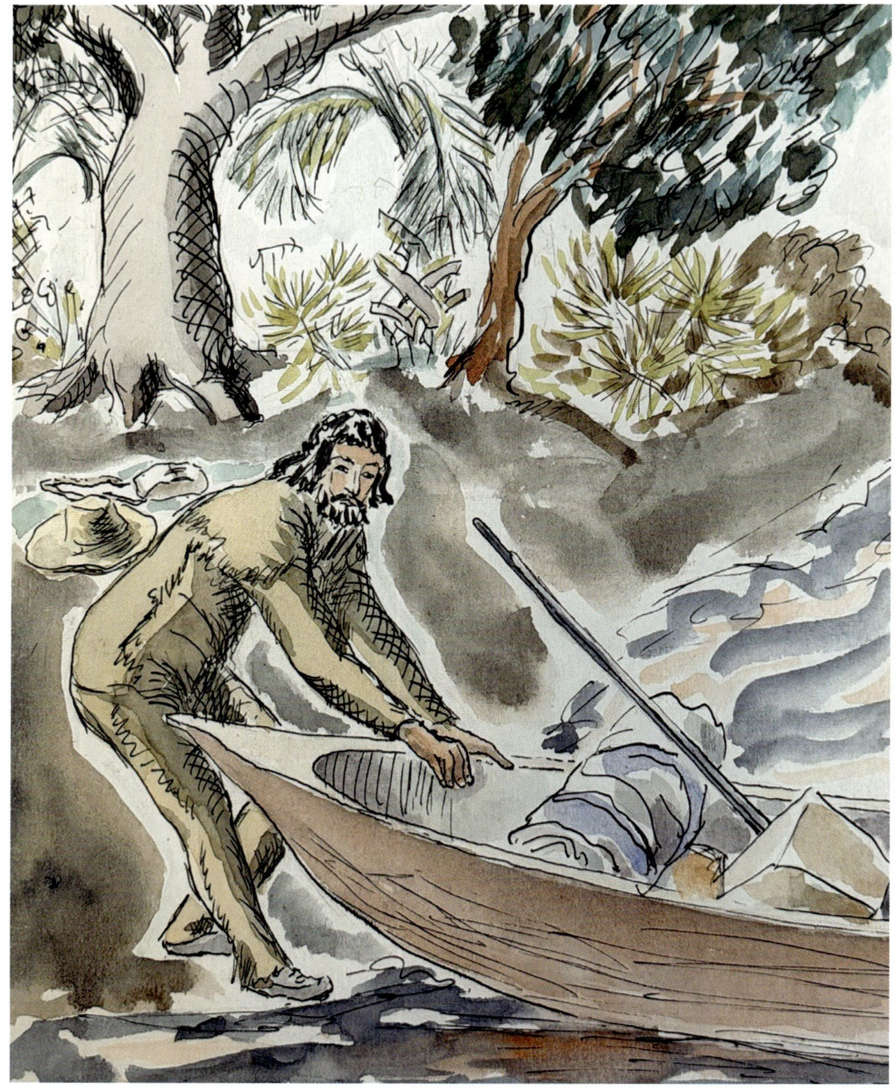

Whether traveling by dugout canoe alone or with others, Bartram had to ensure his watercraft was safely pulled onshore for the night, especially where there was a significant rise and fall in the tidal level and/or alligators.

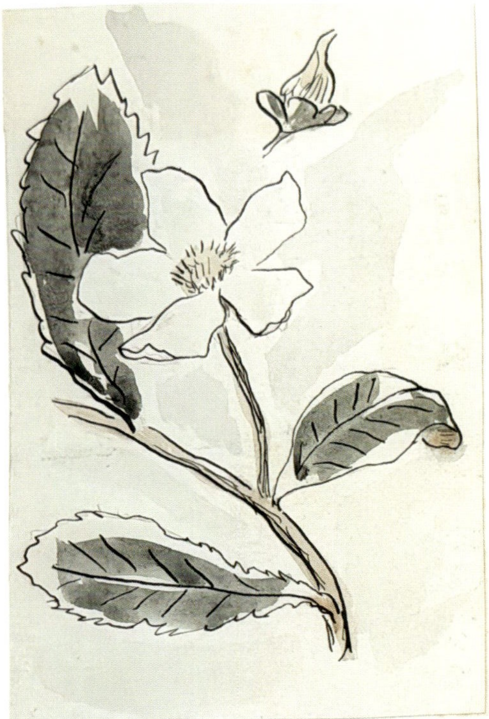

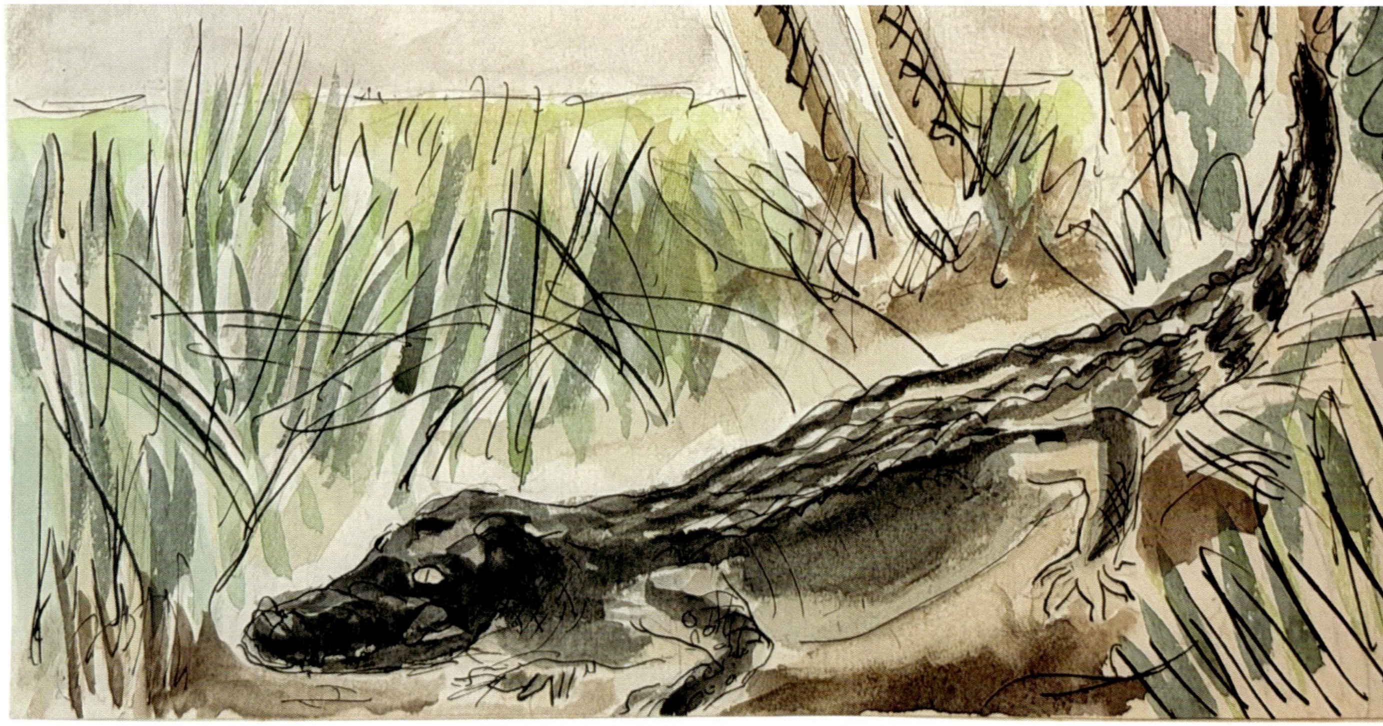

➢ The white flower may be that of the loblolly bay, *Gordonia lasianthus*, commonly found in freshwater swamps along the southeastern coast.

➢ However, there is no mistaking the alligator, often the bane of Bartram's existence, especially in Florida. Haynes illustrated the animal he also knew well from his boyhood in Darien. Haynes's painting shows an alligator among the reeds high up on a riverbank.

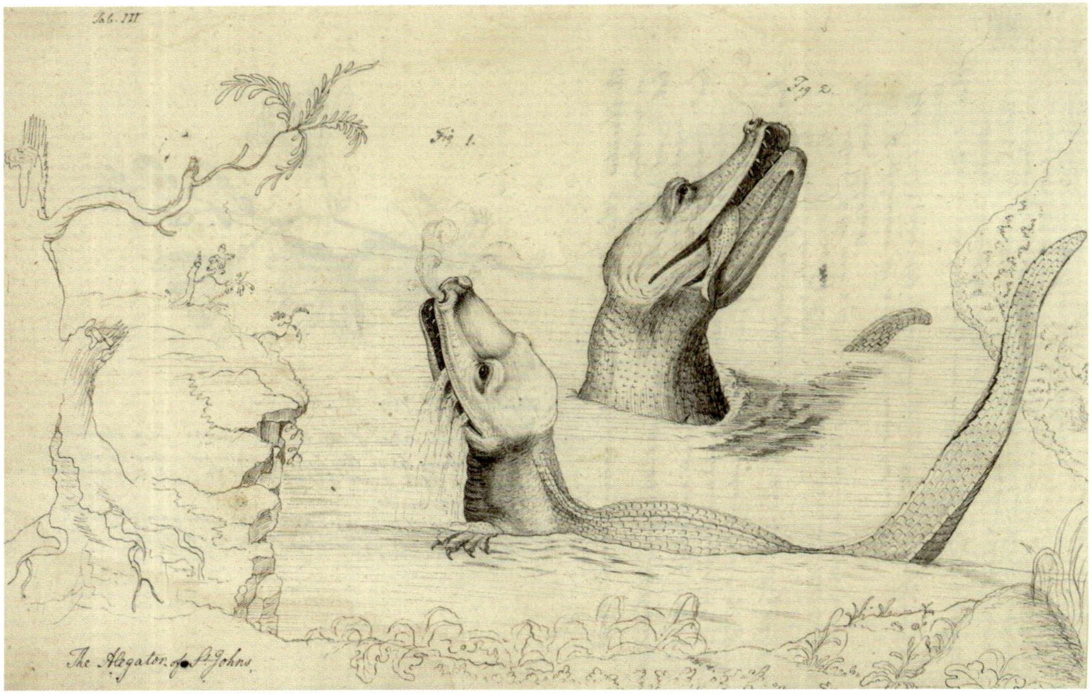

Image courtesy of the Trustees of the Natural History Museum, London.

In contrast, Bartram chose to situate two alligators on a nearly bare stage, depicting them almost dragonlike with smoke from their exhaled breath, thereby converting them into creatures embodying the sublimity and awe he felt in their presence.

> *The subtle, greedy alligator. Behold him rushing forth from the flags and reeds. His enormous body swells. His plaited tail brandished high, floats upon the lake. The waters like a cataract descend from his opening jaws. Clouds of smoke issue from his dilated nostrils. The earth trembles with his thunder. When immediately from the opposite coast of the lagoon, emerges from the deep his rival champion. They suddenly dart upon each other. The boiling surface of the lake marks their rapid course, and a terrific conflict commences. They now sink to the bottom folded together in horrid wreaths. The water becomes thick and discoloured. Again they rise, their jaws clap together, re-echoing through the deep surrounding forests. Again they sink, when the contest ends at the muddy bottom of the lake, and the vanquished makes a hazardous escape, hiding himself in the muddy turbulent waters and sedge on a distant shore. The proud victor exulting returns to the place of action. The shores and forests resound his dreadful roar, together with the triumphing shouts of the plaited tribes around, witnesses of the horrid combat. (118)*

In this second painting, Haynes's watercolor differs markedly from Bartram's stately alligator portrait. Always wary of the reptiles, Bartram now has turned from awe to desperately fending them away from his catch of small fish lying on the shoreline.

> *My apprehensions were highly alarmed after being a spectator of so dreadful a battle; it was obvious that every delay would but tend to encrease my dangers and difficulties, as the sun was near setting, and the alligators gathered around my harbour from all quarters; from these considerations I concluded to be expeditious in my trip to the lagoon, in order to take some fish. Not thinking it prudent to take my fusee with me, lest I might lose it overboard in case of a battle, which I had every reason to dread before my return, I therefore furnished myself with a club for my defence, went on board, and penetrating the first line of those which surrounded my harbour, they gave way; but being pursued by several very large ones, I kept strictly on the watch, and paddled with all my might towards the entrance of the lagoon, hoping to be sheltered there from the multitude of my assailants; but ere I had half-way reached the place, I was attacked on all sides, several endeavouring to overset the canoe. My situation now became precarious to the last degree: two very large ones attacked me closely, at the same instant, rushing up with their heads and part of their bodies above the water, roaring terribly and belching floods of water over me. They struck their jaws together so close to my ears, as*

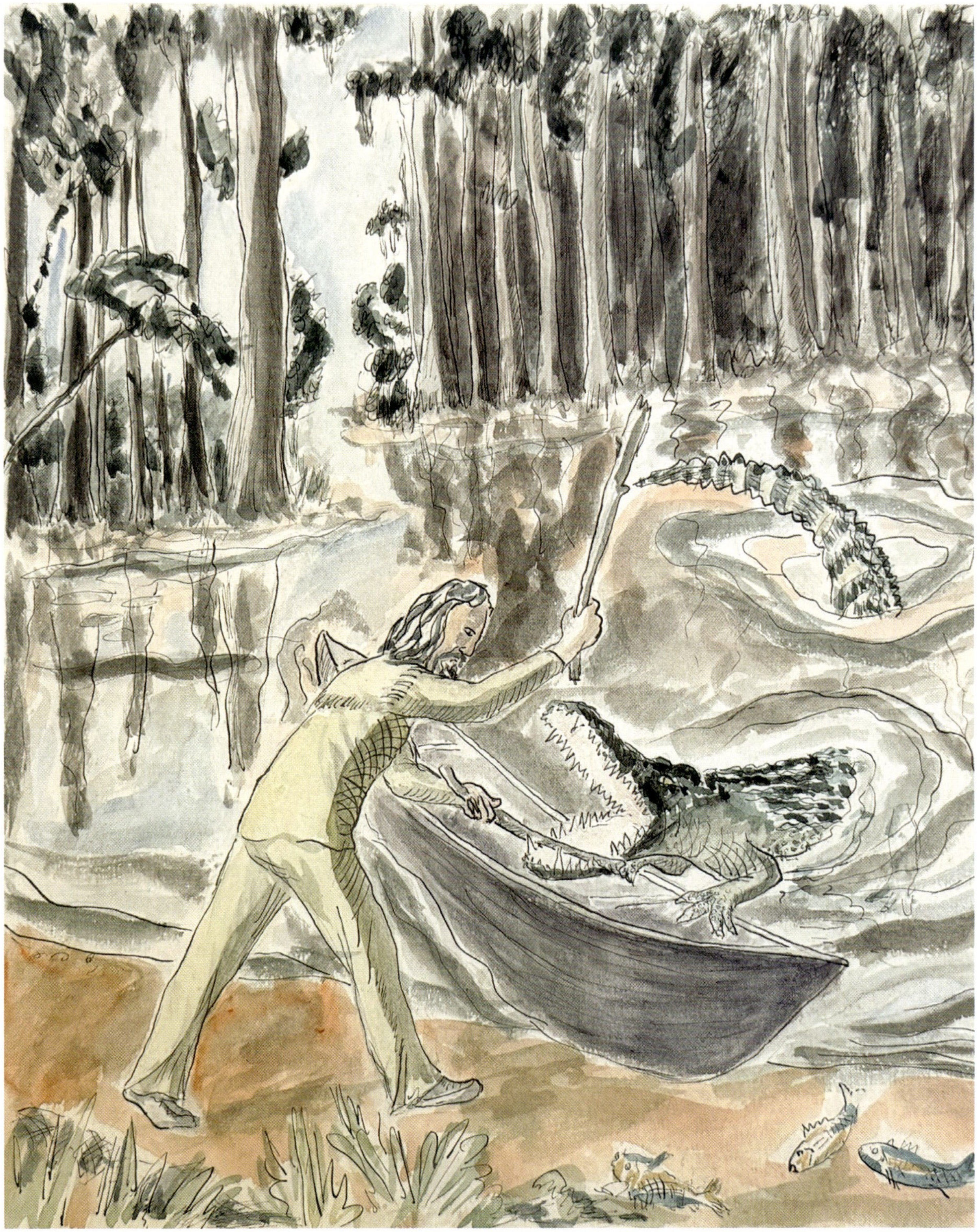

almost to stun me, and I expected every moment to be dragged out of the boat and instantly devoured, but I applied my weapons so effectually about me, though at random, that I was so successful as to beat them off a little; when, finding that they designed to renew the battle, I made for the shore, as the only means left me for my preservation, for, by keeping close to it, I should have my enemies on one side of me only, whereas I was before surrounded by them, and there was a probability, if pushed to the last extremity, of saving myself, by jumping out of the canoe on shore, as it is easy to outwalk them on land, although comparatively as swift as lightning in the water. I found this last expedient alone could fully answer my expectations, for as soon as I gained the shore they drew off and kept aloof. This was a happy relief, as my confidence was, in some degree, recovered by it. (119–120)

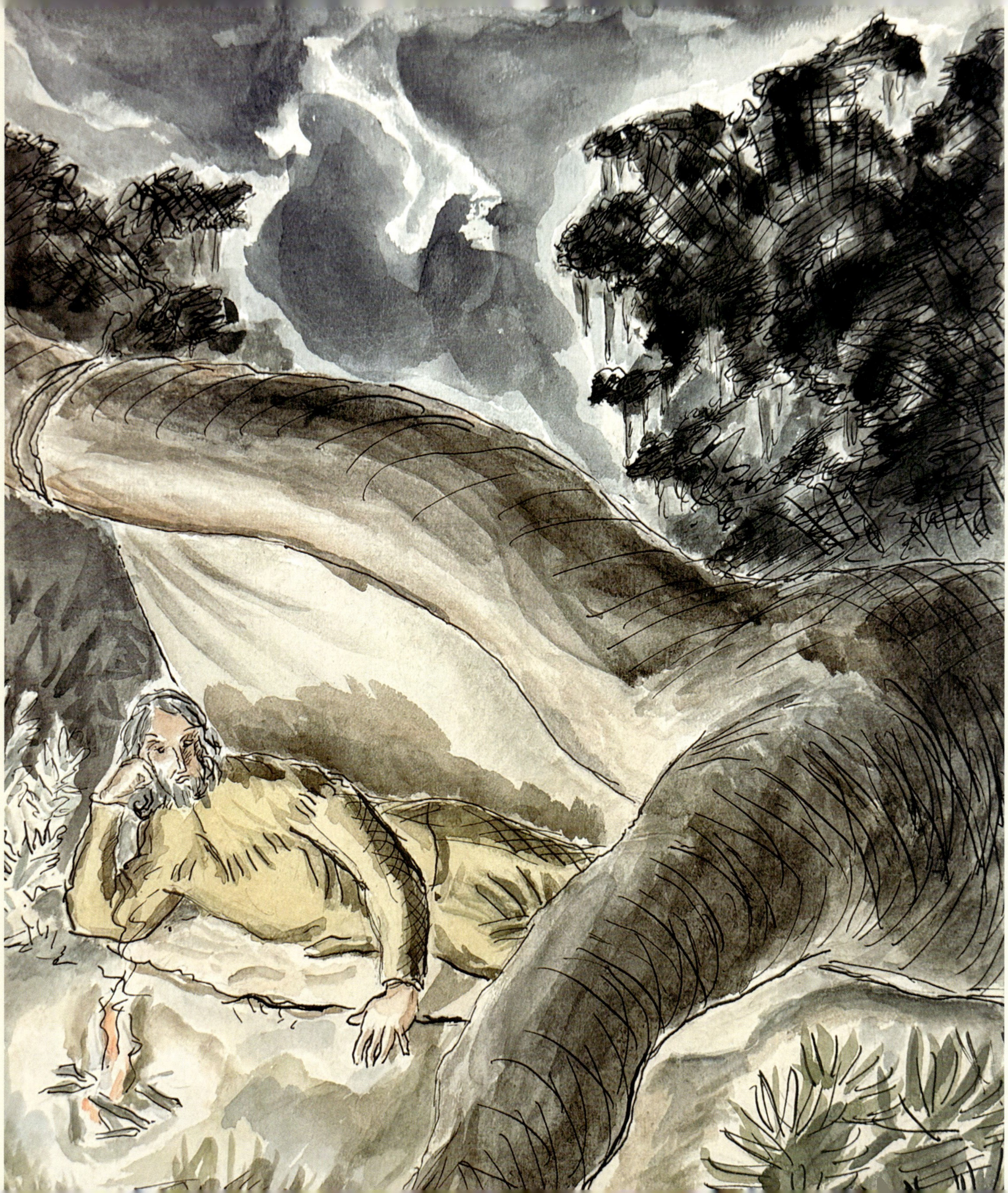

Bartram makes his bed for the night under cover of huge downed oak, with a small fire for light and warmth.

> *It beginning to thunder, I was sufficiently warned to prepare against a wet night, and observing a very large Oak tree, which had been thrown down, by a hurricane and offered me a convenient shelter, as its enormous limbs bore up the trunk, a sufficient height from the earth, to admit me to sit or lie down under it, I spread my sail, slanting from the trunk of the tree, to the ground, on the windward side; and having collected a quantity of wood, sufficient to keep up a fire, during the night, I struck one up in front, and spreading skins on the ground, and upon these placing a blanket, one half I laid down upon, turning the other over me for a covering.* (74–75)

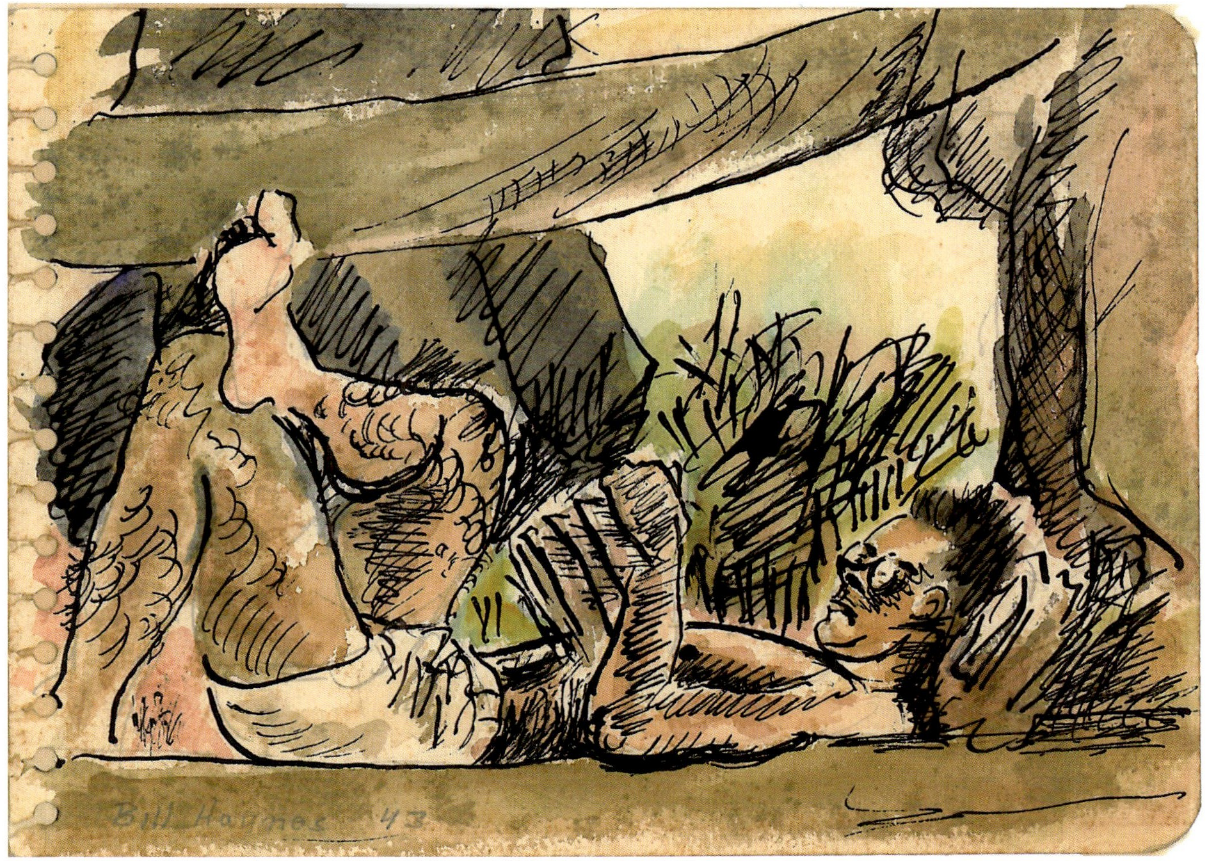

Ashantilly Center Archives.

Note the similarity of this self-portrait Bill Haynes painted years later while serving in New Guinea during World War II.

Haynes pairs a pelican with a small, five-petaled white flower we interpret to be black mangrove (*Avicennia germinans*, the *Rhizophora conjugata* of Bartram). Although a tree, the plant only attains the size of a small shrub at its northernmost limit near St. Augustine, Florida. Nevertheless, its small flowers are a highly sought-after nectar source for honeybees and butterflies. Bartram wrote:

> *The broad leaved sweet Myrtus, Erythrina corrallodendrum, Cactus cochenellifer, Cacalia suffruticosa, and particularly, Rhizophora conjugata, which stood close to, and in the salt water of the river, were in full bloom, with beautiful white sweet scented flowers, which attracted to them, two or three species of very beautiful butterflies, one of which was black, the upper pair of its wings very long and narrow, marked with transverse stripes of pale yellow, with some spots of a crimson colour near the body. Another species remarkable for splendor, was of a larger size, the wings were undulated and obtusely crenated round their ends, the nether pair terminating near the body, with a long narrow forked tail; the ground light yellow, striped oblique-transversely, with stripes of pale celestial blue, the ends of them adorned with little eyes encircled with the finest blue and crimson, which represented a very brilliant rosary. But those which were the most numerous were as white as snow, their wings large, their ends lightly crenated and ciliated, forming a fringed border, faintly marked with little black crescents, their points downward, with a cluster of little brilliant orbs of blue and crimson, on the nether wings near the body; the numbers were incredible, and there seemed to be scarcely a flower for each fly, multitudinous as they were, besides clouds of them hovering over the mellifluous groves. (xxviii–xxix)*

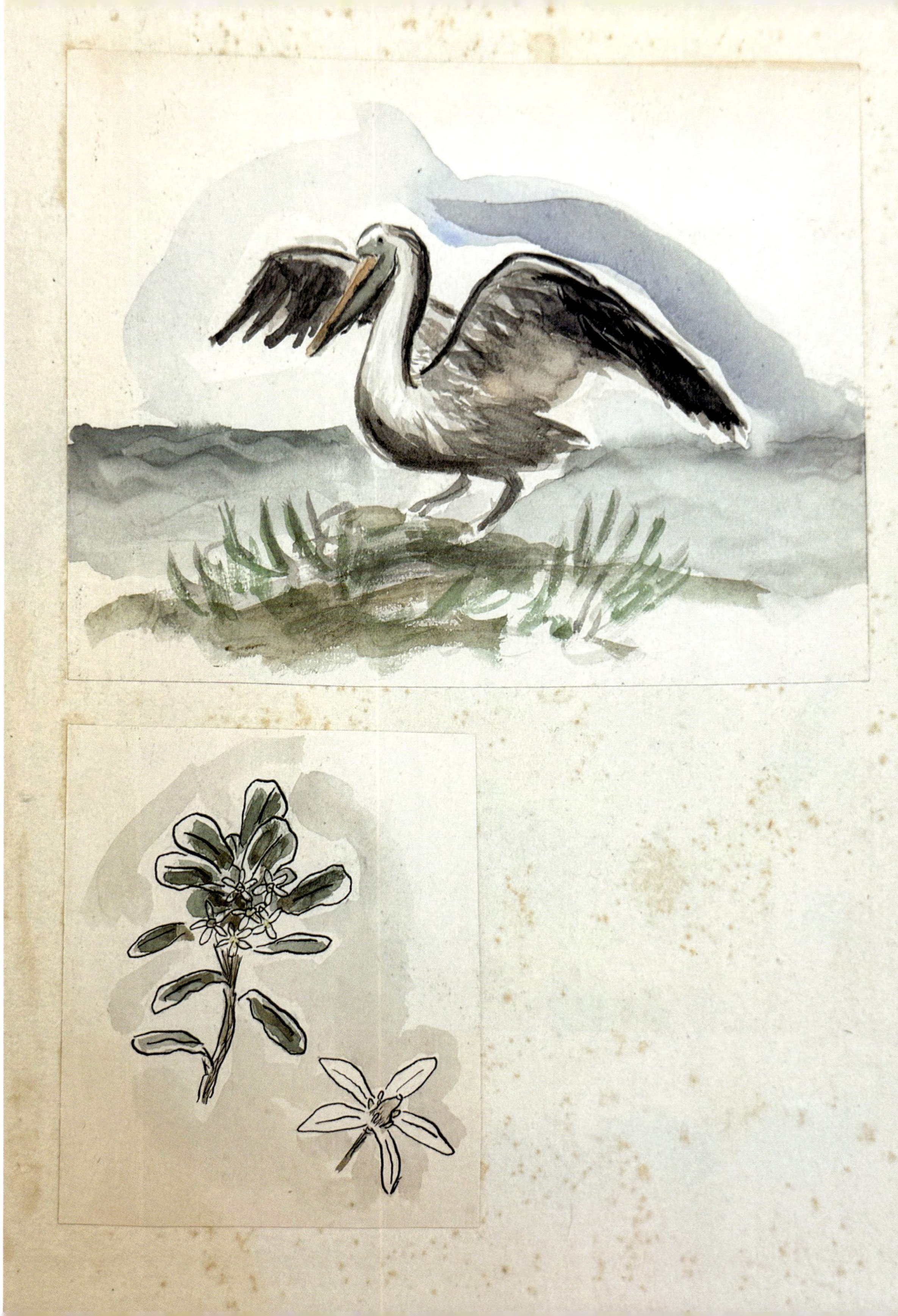

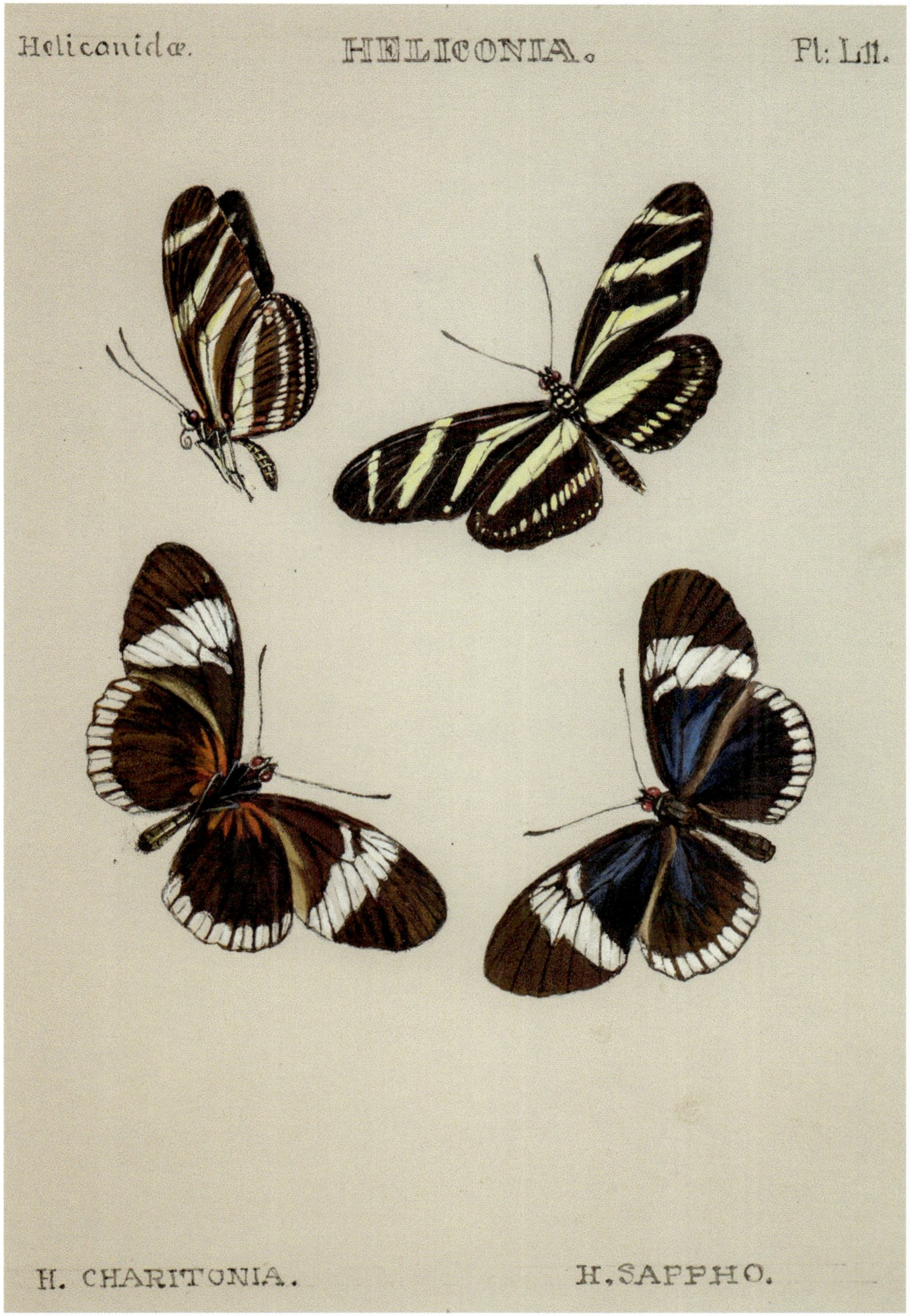

Titian Ramsay Peale II, zebra butterfly, at top of plate. Courtesy of the American Museum of Natural History, New York.

➤ The butterflies described by Bartram are the (black and yellow) zebra butterfly *Heliconius charithonia*; (blue long-tailed) zebra swallowtail *Protographium* (formerly *Papilio marcellus*); and the great southern white, *Ascia monuste*, commonly seen year-round in Florida salt marshes. See Francis Harper, ed., *The Travels of William Bartram*, naturalist edition, (1958; University of Georgia Press, 1998), 459n19.

Titian Ramsay Peale II (1799–1885), youngest son of Bartram portraitist Charles Willson Peale, was a protégé of William Bartram. Even in his teens he was a highly sought-after illustrator and naturalist. In 1817 he joined an expedition of Philadelphia scientists from the newly incorporated American Philosophical Society in retracing Bartram's path in Georgia and northern Florida. The group, led by geologist William Maclure, included entomologist Thomas Say and ornithologist George Ord. See Charlotte M. Porter, "Following Bartram's 'Track': Titian Ramsay Peale's Florida Journey," *Florida Historical Quarterly* 61, no. 4 (April 1983): 431–444. Peale's later travels encompassed western North America, South America, plus the South Seas and the Antarctic as part of the U.S. Exploring Expedition. He spent the last fifty years of his life preparing the descriptions and plates for his monumental *The Butterflies of North America*. One hundred thirty years after his death, it was finally published in 2015 by the American Museum of Natural History.

Bartram served as a mentor across the centuries to William Haynes during his youth, so it seems only fitting that examples of Peale's work should accompany his mentor's description, which, in turn, inspired Haynes's small sketch of one of the nectar sources. Plates from *The Butterflies of North America: Titian Peale's Lost Manuscript* (2015), zebra butterfly, top of plate, page 86; zebra swallowtail, page 31; great southern white, page 65.

In addition to his illustrations of the colorful flowers of New Guinea, Haynes took a particular interest in its striking butterflies and moths, as shown on the facing page.

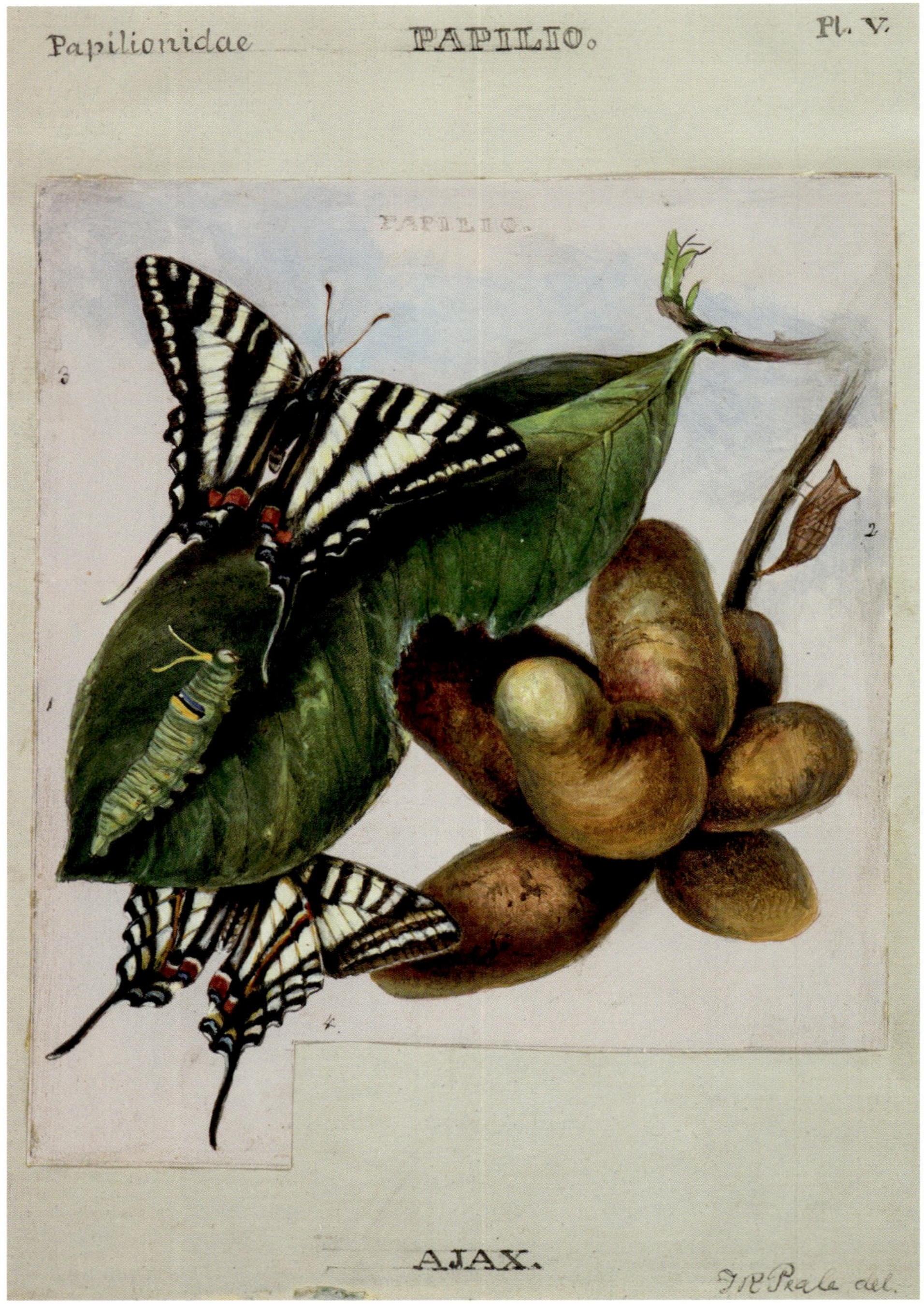

Titian Ramsay Peale II, zebra swallowtail, caterpillar, and chrysalis on pawpaw. Courtesy of the American Museum of Natural History, New York.

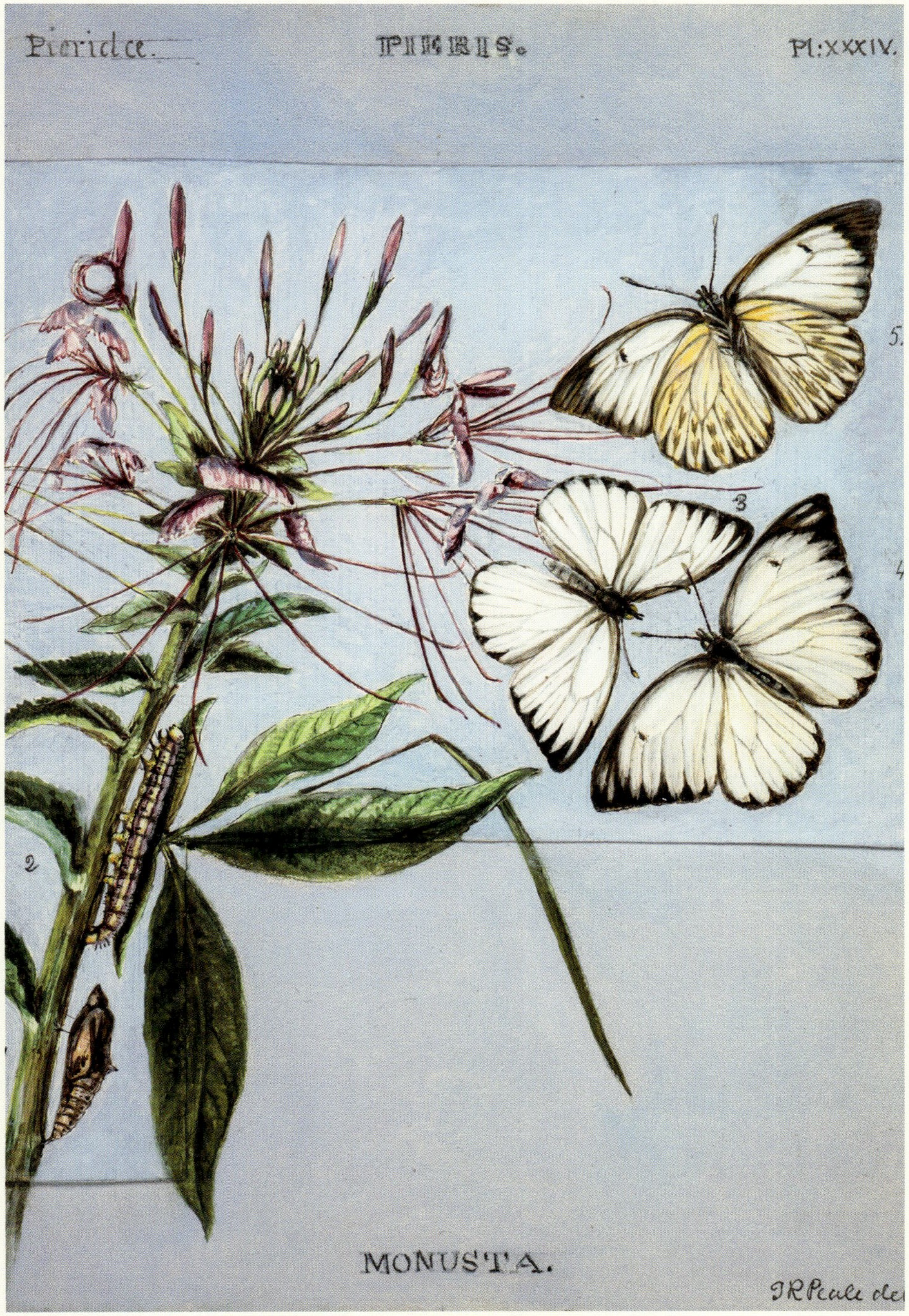

Titian Ramsay Peale II, great southern white butterfly. Courtesy of the American Museum of Natural History, New York.

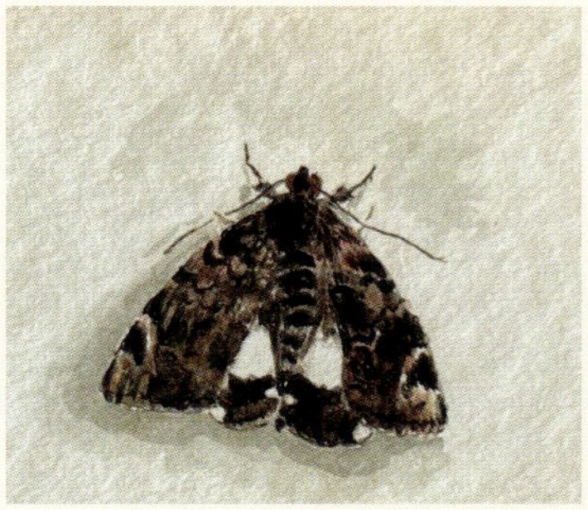

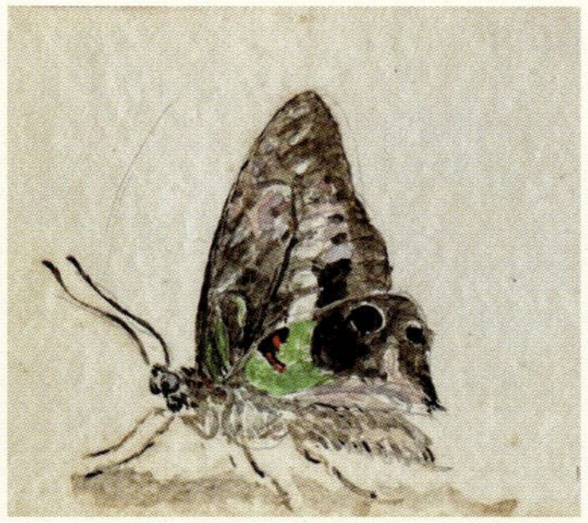

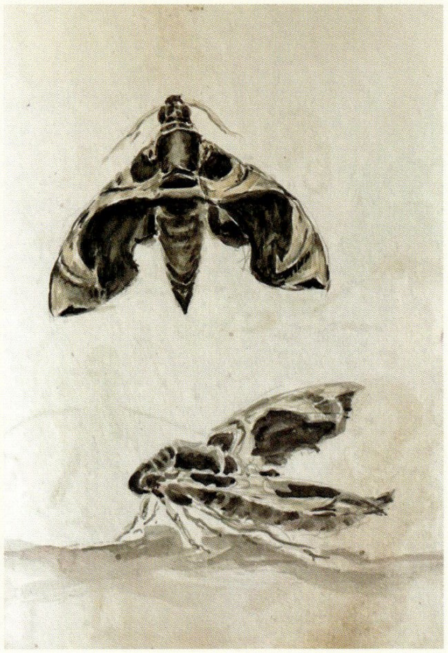

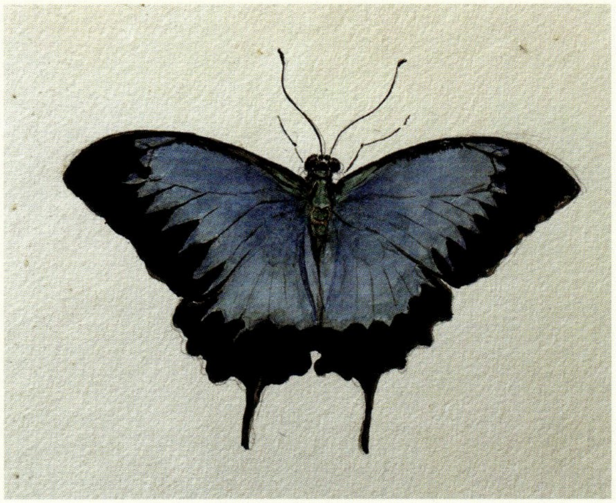

The flowering branch in the upper left is sweet bay *Persea borbonia* (Bartram's *Laurus borbonia*), a common tree that thrives along the coast in consistently moist soils. That Bartram mentions this tree species in *Travels* may have had particular meaning for Bill Haynes, for Bartram described its presence on St. Simons Island during his visit with James Spalding, a historic owner of the Ashantilly property (see page 5).

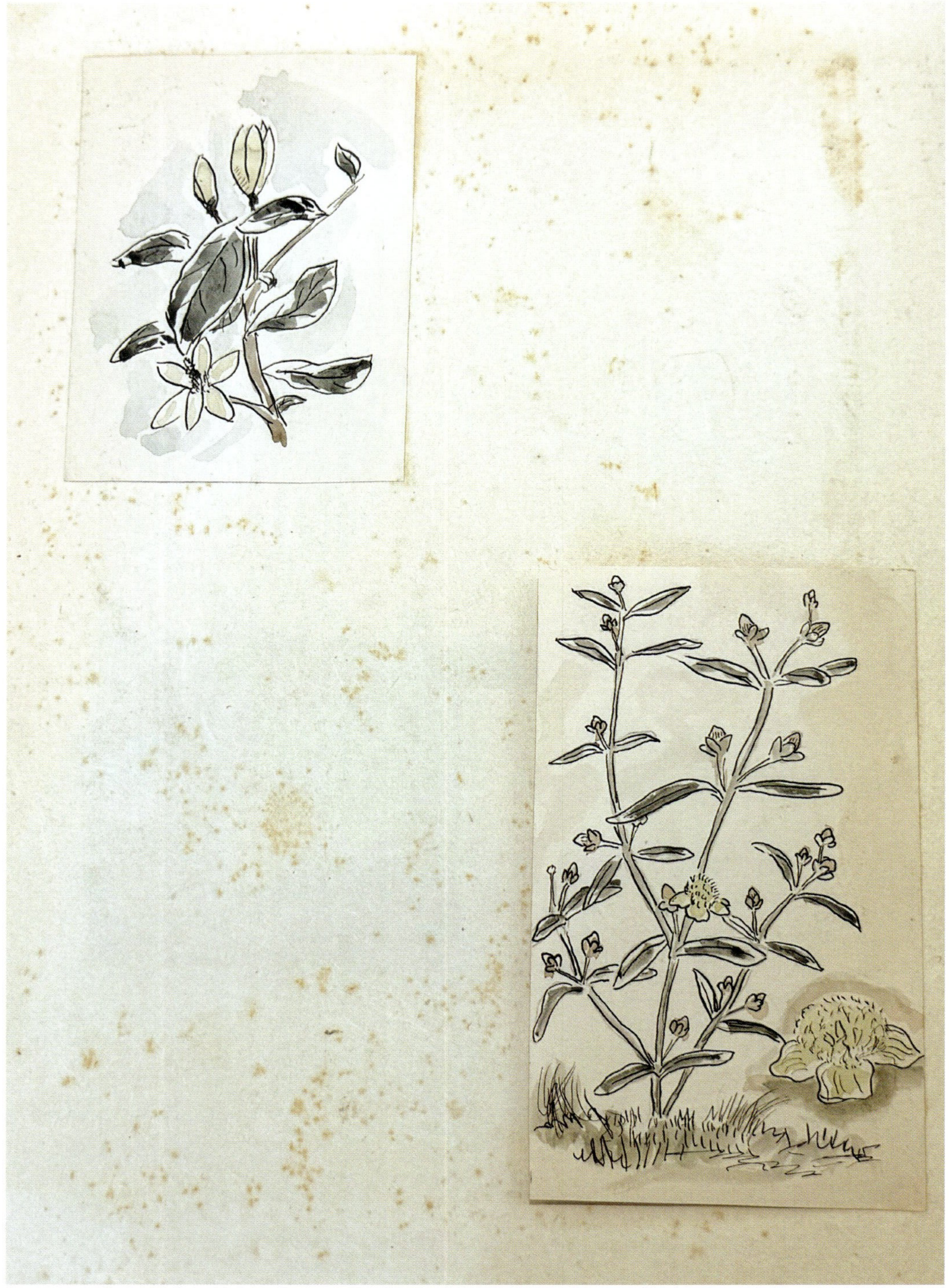

> *I arrived at Frederica, on the island of St. Simon, where I was well received and entertained by James Spalding, Esq; this gentleman carrying on a very considerable trade, and having extensive connections with the Indian tribes of East Florida, furnished me with letters to his agents residing at his trading houses, ordering them to furnish me with horses, guides, and every other convenient assistance.*
>
> *Before the vessel was ready to sail again for St. Johns, I had time to explore the island. In the cool of the morning early, I rode out of the town, directing my course to the south end of the island. After penetrating a thick grove of oaks, which almost surrounded the town on the land side, suddenly a very extensive and beautiful green savanna opened to view, in length nearly two miles, and in breadth near a mile, well stocked with horned cattle, horses, sheep, and deer. Following an old highway, now out of repair, across the Savanna, I ascended the sloping green bank, and entered a noble forest of lofty pines, and then a venerable grove of Live Oaks, under whose shady spreading boughs opened a spacious avenue, leading to the former seat of General Oglethorp[e], but now the property of Capt. Raimond Demere. After leaving this town,*

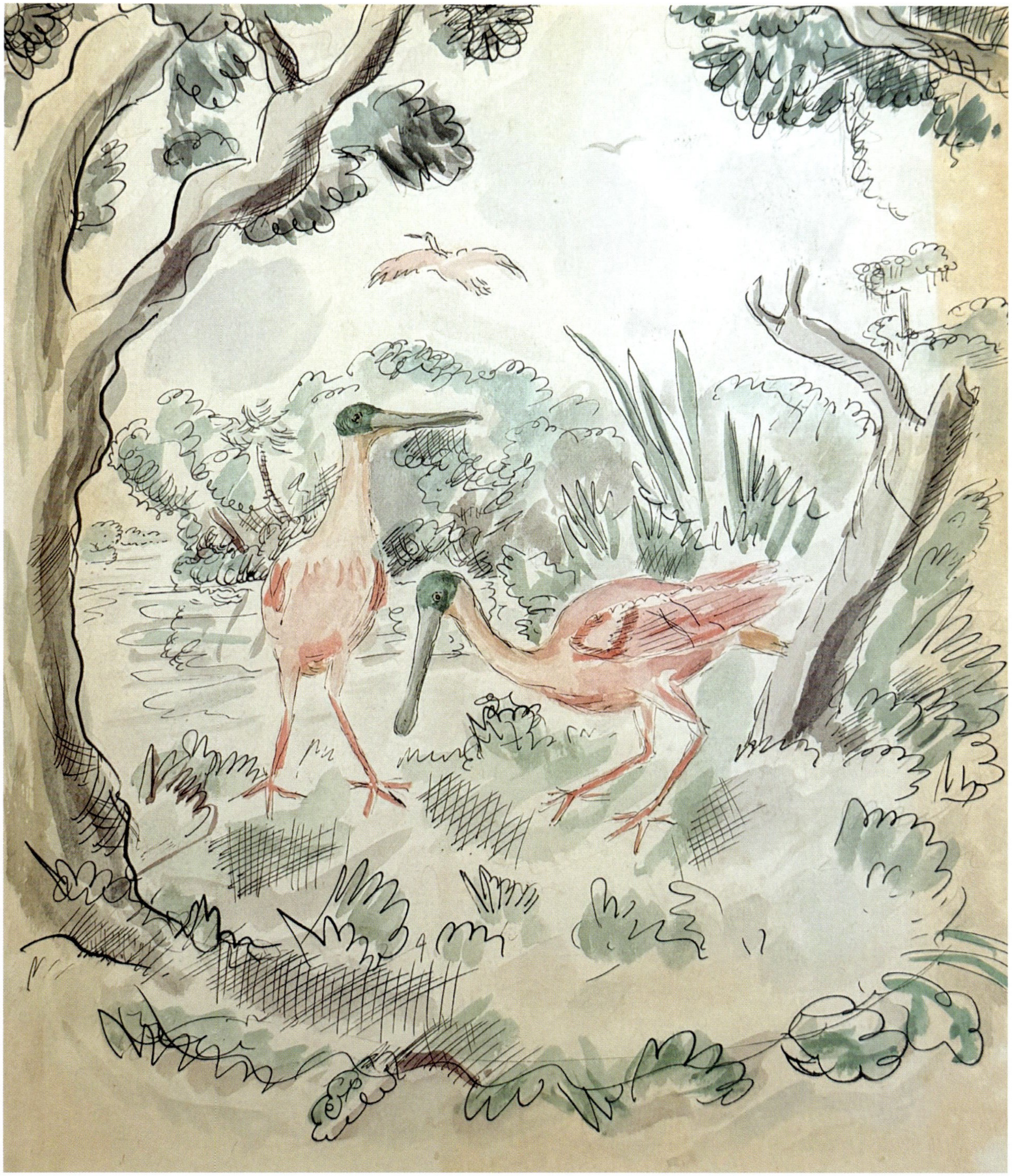

I was led into a high pine forest; the trees were tall, and generally of the species called Broom-pine (P. palustris Linn.) the surface of the ground covered with grass, herbage, and some shrubbery: I continued through this forest nearly in a direct line towards the sea coast, five or six miles, when the land became uneven, with ridges of sand-hills, mixed with sea shells, and covered by almost impenetrable thickets, consisting of Live Oaks, Sweet-bay (L. Borbonia) . . . and other species. (57–59)

At the lower right of the facing page is *Hypericum frondosum* (Bartram's *Hypericum aureum*), a hardy but short-lived shrub native to sunny, well-drained soils from southern Indiana south to Georgia and Texas (see the Lady Bird Johnson Wildflower Center website at www.wildflower.org/plants/result.php?id_plant+HYFR). Captivated by its golden flowers, Bartram wrote,

It grows erect, three or four feet high, forming a globular top, representing a perfect little tree; the leaves are large, oblong, firm of texture, smooth and shining; the flowers are very large, their petals broad and conspicuous, which, with their tufts of golden filaments, give the little bushes a very splendid appearance. (383)

While some of Haynes's flowering plants are difficult to identify, there's no mistaking roseate spoonbills. In *Travels*, Bartram makes no mention of them other than to list them among the other birds on page 293.

With the bird flying above him, Bartram stands contemplating a flower among orange trees, palmettos, and other taller trees.

I crossed the river to a high promontory of woodland, on the west shore, and being struck with the magnificence of a venerable grove of Live Oak, Palms and Laurel (Magnolia grandiflora) I stepped on shore to take a view of the place. Orange trees were in full bloom, and filled the air with fragrance. (74)

These high forest trees surrounding the bason, by their great height and spread, so effectually shade the waters, that coming suddenly from the open plains, we seem at once shut up in darkness, and the waters appear black, yet are clear; when we ascend the top of the hills, we perceive the ground to be uneven, by round swelling points and corresponding hollows, overspread with gloomy shade, occasioned by the tall and spreading trees, such as Live Oak, Morus rubra, Zanthoxilon, Sapindus, Liquid-amber, Tilia, Laurus Borbonia, Quercus dentata, Juglans cinerea, and others, together with Orange trees of remarkable magnitude and very fruitful. (204)

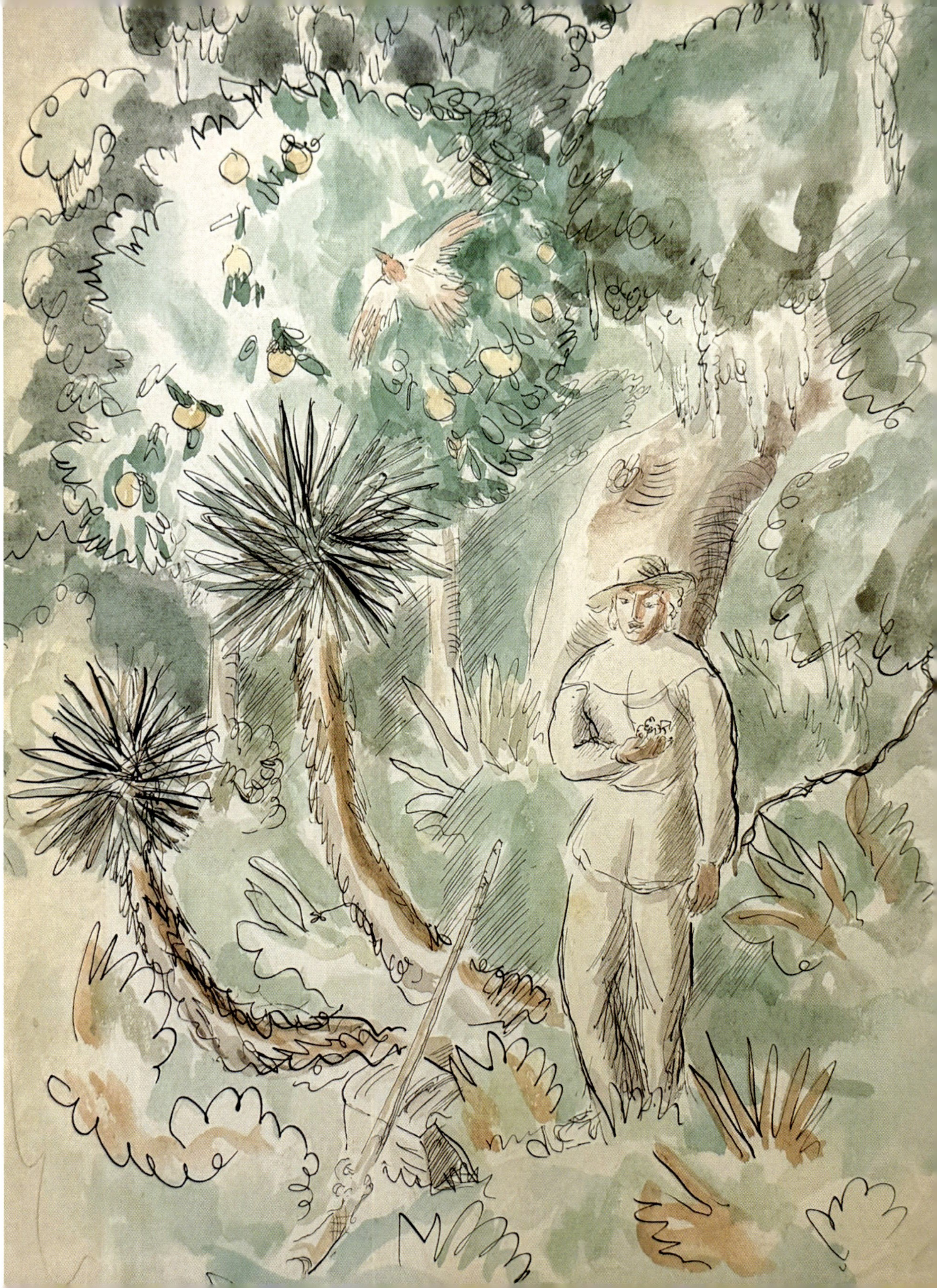

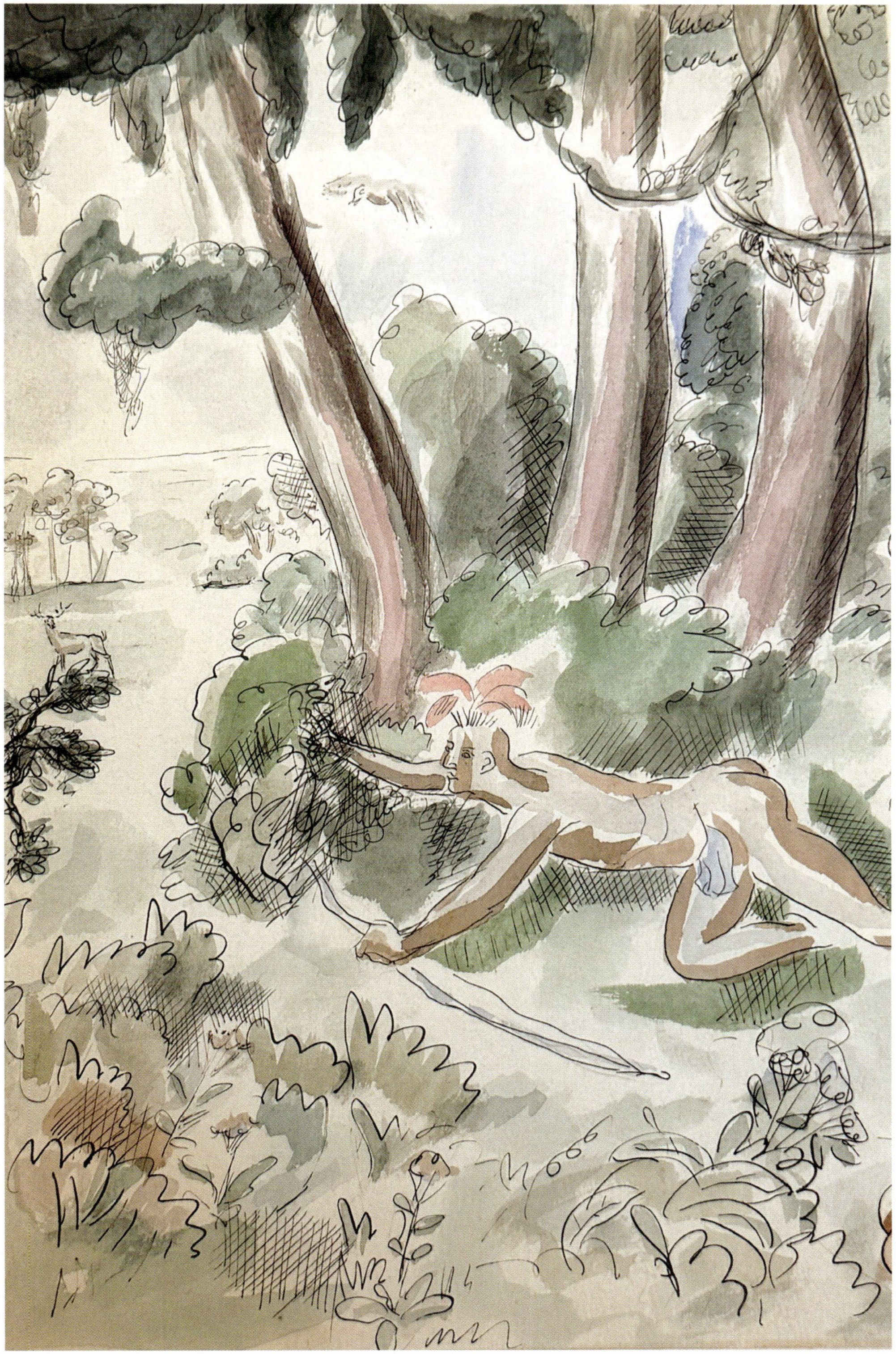

Haynes portrays a Seminole armed with his bow, stalking deer at the Alachua Savanna. Again, a hovering bird looks on. The red feathers adorning the Seminole's head add a splash of color, Haynes's artistic license, as the Seminoles preferred either black or black-and-white feathers in their headdress.

Herds of deer were feeding in the green meadows before us; flocks of turkeys, walking in the groves around us; and myriads of fish, of the greatest variety and delicacy, sporting in the chrystaline floods before our eyes. (179)

This painting may represent the Seminole named Cowkeeper, smelling a large, white, five-petaled flower, perhaps from a fragrant pawpaw or moonvine. Cowkeeper was the Seminole who named Bartram "Puc Puggy"—the Flower Hunter.

> *. . . the chief trader informed the Cowkeeper; in the presence of his council or attendants, the purport of our business, with which he expressed his satisfaction. He was then informed what the nature of my errand was, and he received me with complaisance; giving me unlimited permission to travel over the country for the purpose of collecting flowers, medicinal plants, &c. saluting me by the name of Puc Puggy or the Flower hunter, recommending me to the friendship and protection of his people.* (185)

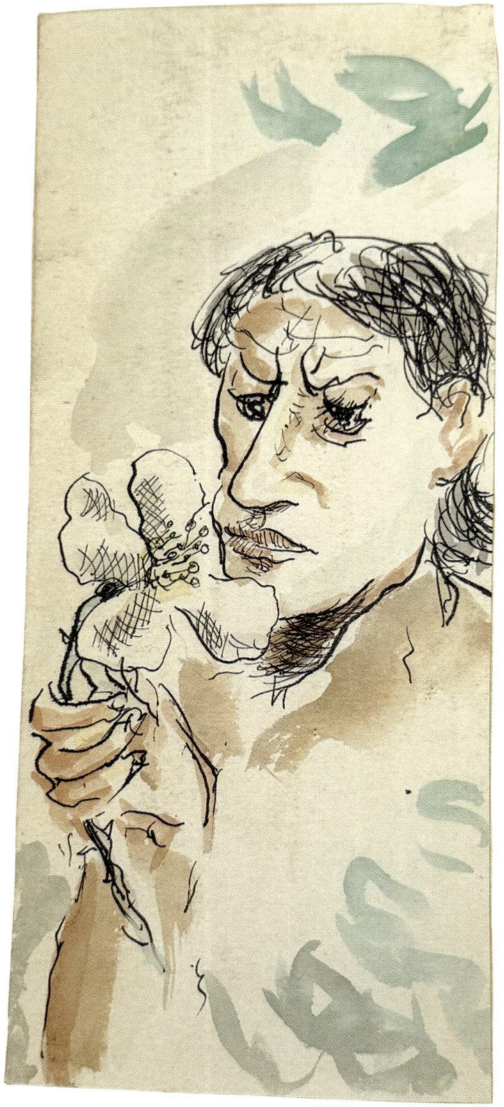

Bill Haynes painted a familiar coastal bird, two *Anhingas* perched and one characteristically nearly submerged in the water. William Bartram glides downriver in a dugout, attracting the notice of an alligator.

> *Here is in this river and in the waters all over Florida, a very curious and handsome bird, the people call them Snake Birds, I think I have seen paintings of them on the Chinese screens and other India pictures: they seem to be a species of cormorant or loon (Colymbus cauda elongata) but far more beautiful and delicately formed than any other species that I have ever seen. The head and neck of this bird are extremely small and slender, the latter very long indeed, almost out of all proportion, the bill long, strait and slender, tapering from its ball to a sharp point, all the upper side, the abdomen and thighs, are as black and glossy as a raven's, covered with feathers so firm and elastic, that they in some degree resemble fish-scales, the breast and upper part of the belly are covered with feathers of a cream colour, the tail is very long, of a deep black, and tipped with a silvery white, and when spread, represents an unfurled fan. They delight to sit in little peaceable communities, on the dry limbs of trees, hanging over the still waters, with their wings and tails expanded, I suppose to cool and air themselves, when at the same time they behold their images in the watery mirror: at such times, when we approach them, they drop off the limbs into the water as if dead, and for a minute or two are not to be seen; when on a sudden at a vast distance, their long slender head and neck*

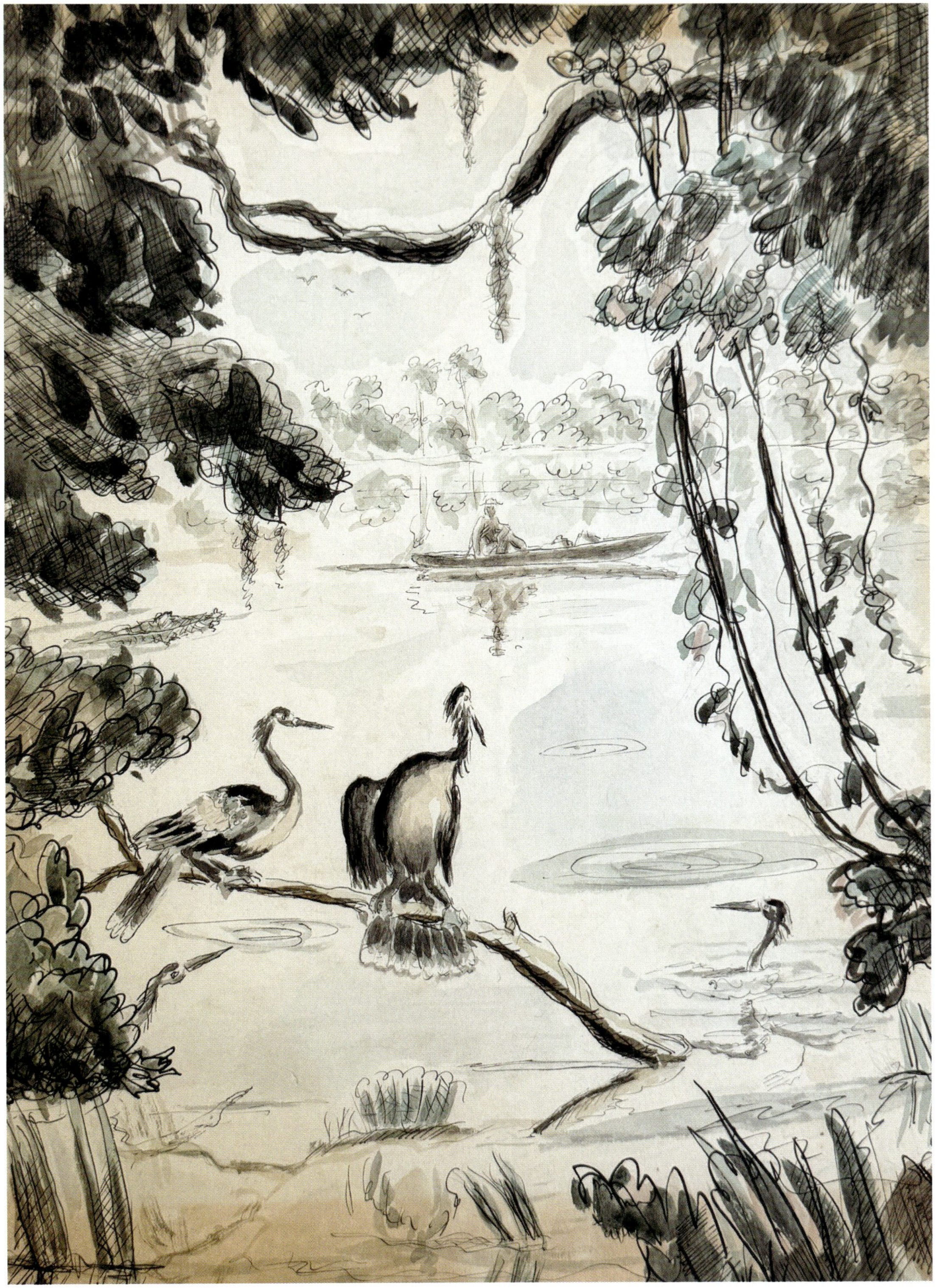

only appear, and have very much the appearance of a snake, and no other part of them are to be seen when swimming in the water, except some the tip end of their tail. In the heat of the day they are seen in great numbers, sailing very high in the air, over lakes and rivers.

I doubt not but if this bird had been an inhabitant of the Tiber in Ovid's days, it would have furnished him with a subject, for some beautiful and entertaining metamorphoses. I believe they feed intirely on fish, for their flesh smells and tastes intolerably strong of it, it is scarcely to be eaten unless constrained by insufferable hunger. (132–133)

At low tide, a trio of wood storks feed along a tidal creek. Bartram describes their solemn appearance.

> *[H]e stands alone on the topmost limb of tall dead Cypress trees, his neck contracted or drawn in upon his shoulders, and beak resting like a long scythe upon his breast: in this pensive posture and solitary situation, they look extremely grave, sorrowful and melancholy, as if in the deepest thought. They are never seen on the salt sea coast, and yet are never found at a great distance from it. (149)*

The wood stork feeding in the background definitely was influenced by Audubon's painting.

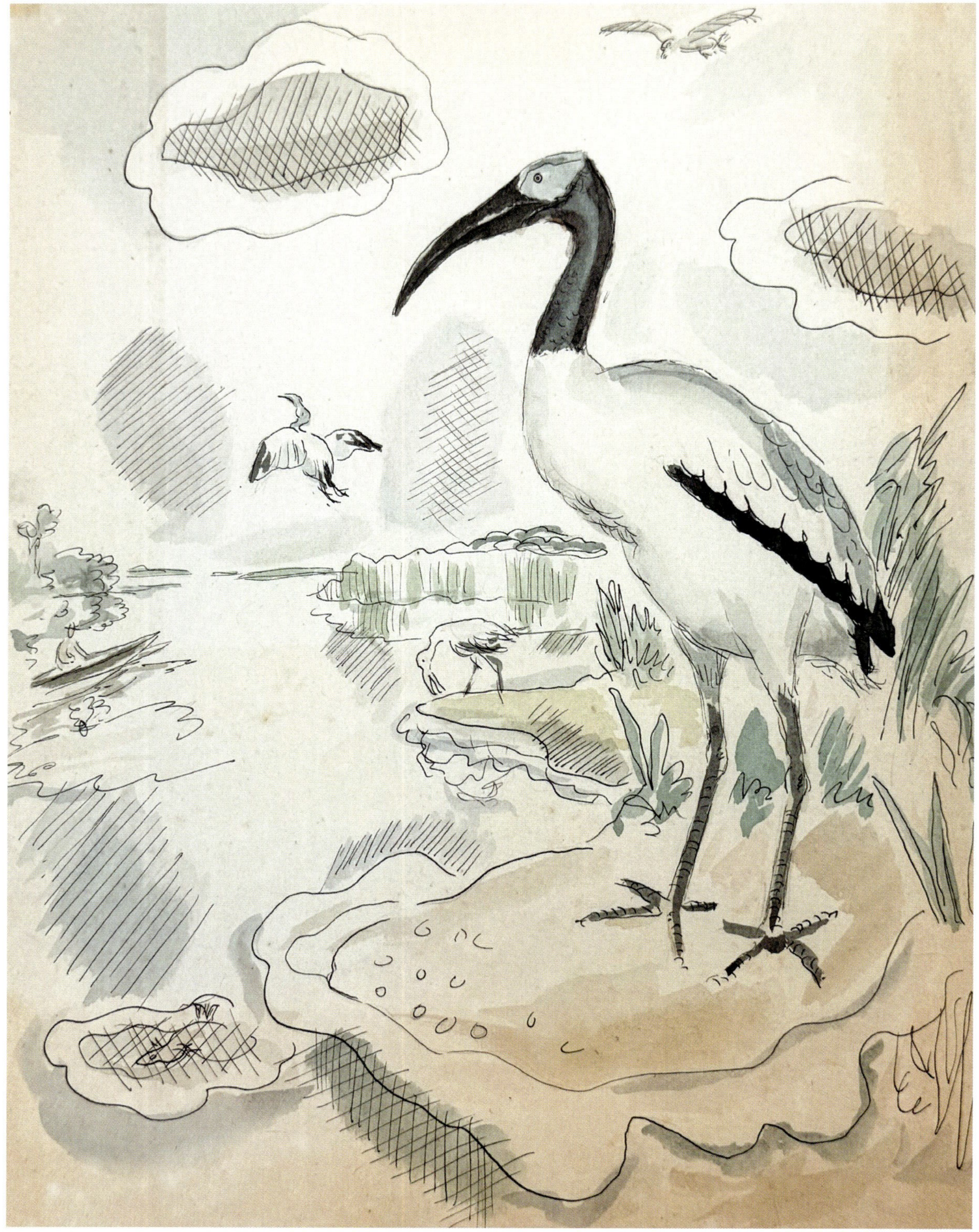

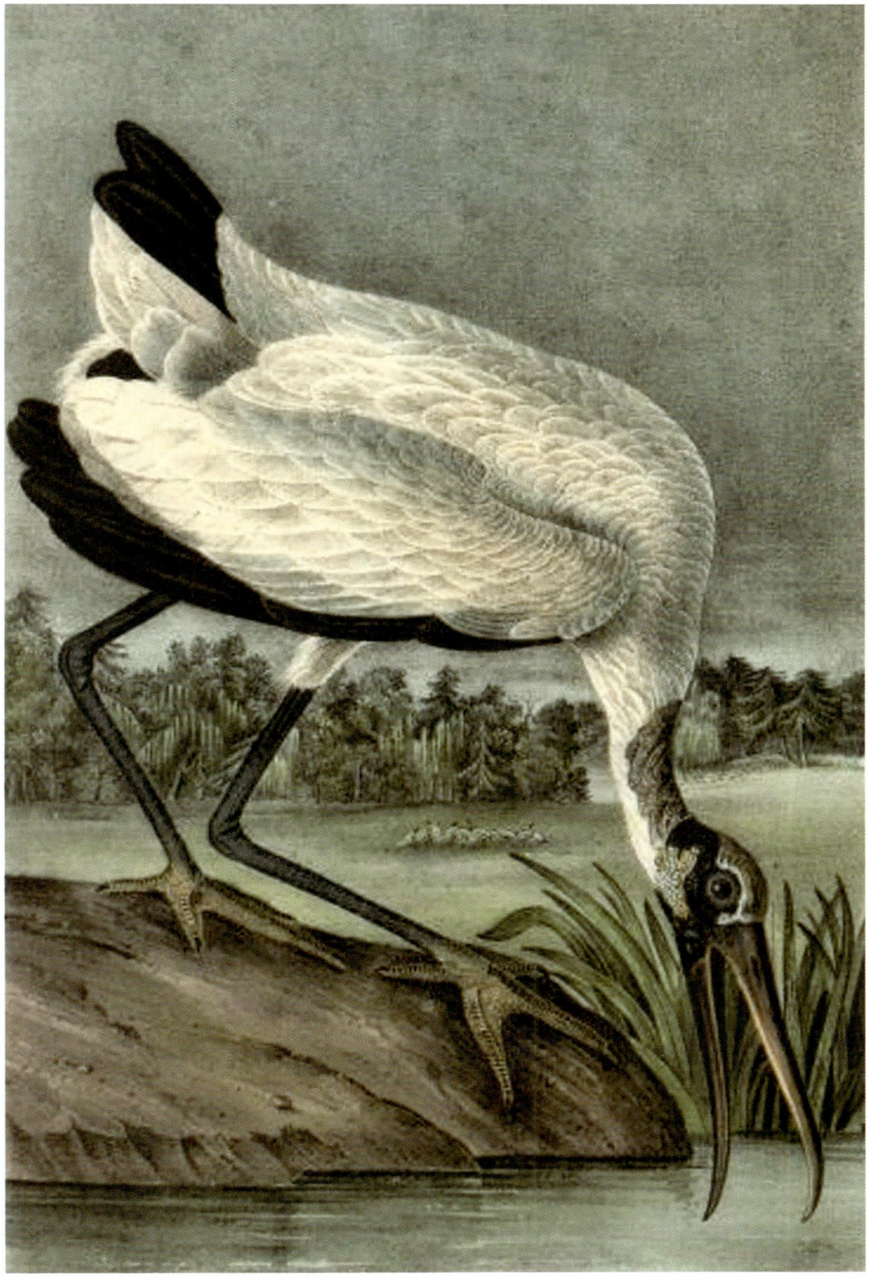

John James Audubon, *Wood Stork*, courtesy of New York Public Library.

This detail and shading of a hand holding an unidentified white tubular flower may reflect the influence of Marguerite Zorach on Haynes's painting technique. The women pictured on page 110 show similar shading. Note the bird flying overhead once more.

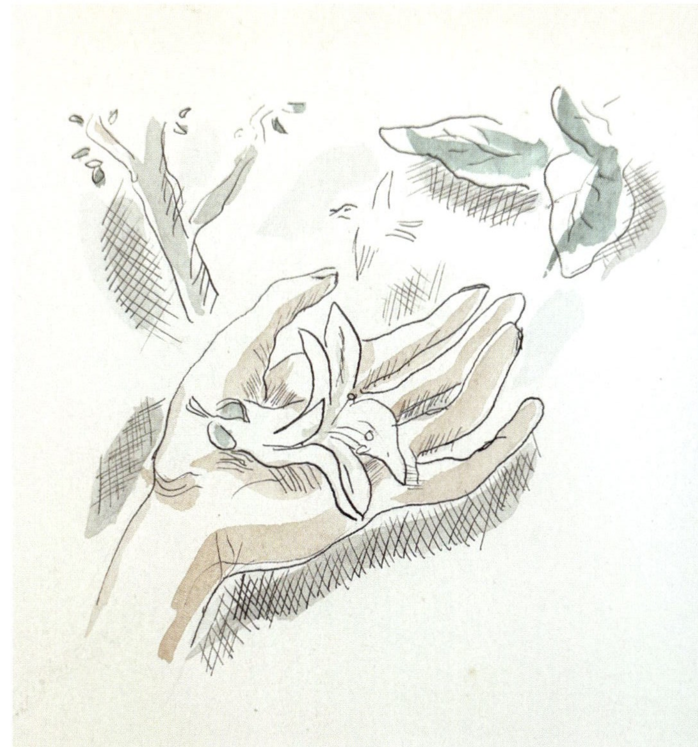

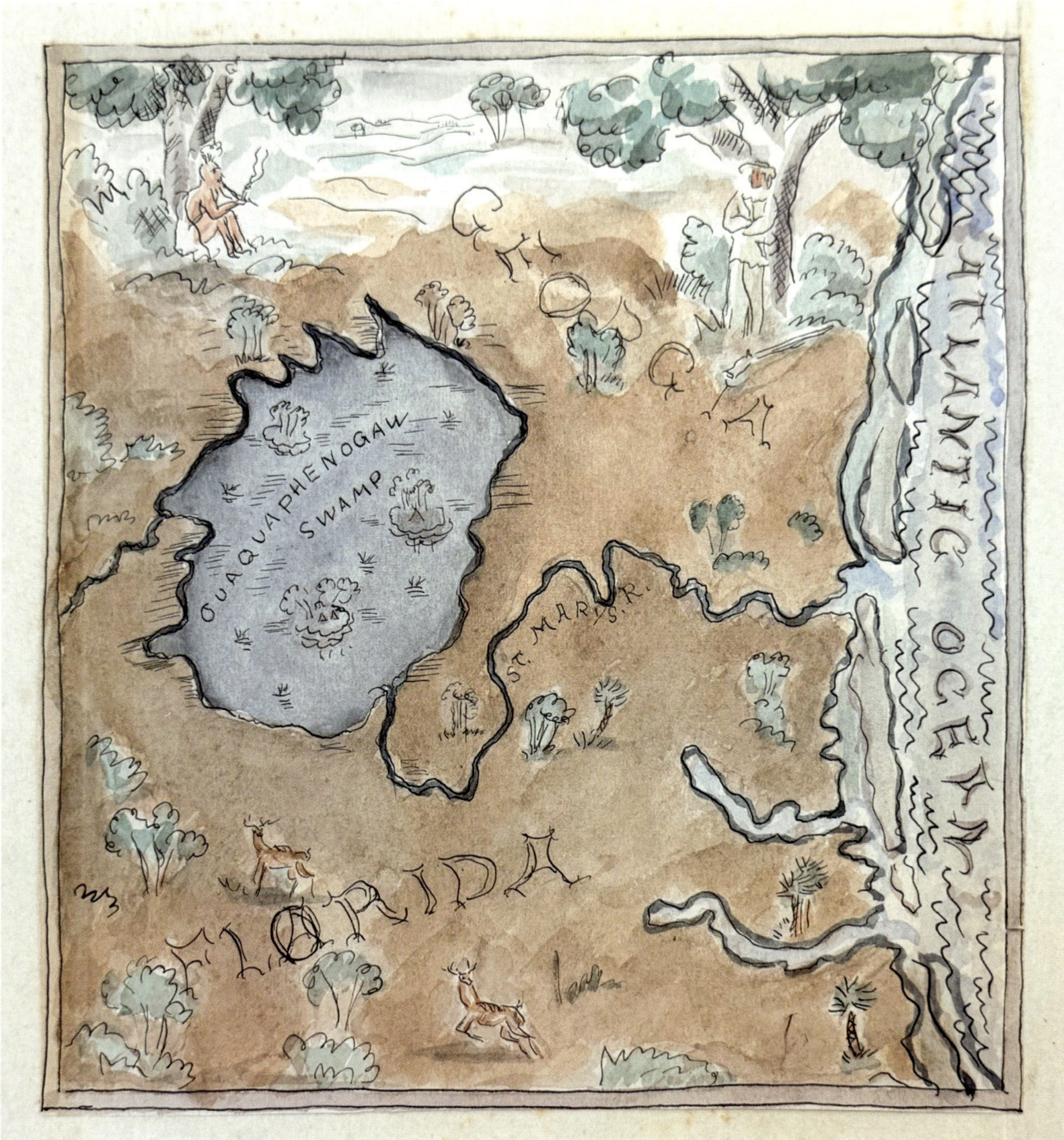

Haynes expanded his mapmaking with this detail of the region surrounding the Okefenokee Swamp. "Okefenokee" is said to translate as "Land of the Trembling Earth." Its waters are often dotted with floating islands hosting very large trees. Despite that extensive root mass, the "ground" surface undulates underfoot. In the upper-right corner, Bartram observes the scene, with prancing deer and an Indian smoking a pipe in the shade.

The [Little St. Juan] river at the town is about two hundred yards over, and fifteen or twenty feet in depth. The great swamp and lake Oaquaphenogaw is said to be its source, which is about one hundred miles by land North of this place, which would give the river a course of near two hundred miles from its source to the sea, to follow its meanders; as in general our rivers, that run any considerable distance through the country to the sea, by their windings and roaving about to find a passage through the ridges and heights, at least double their distance. (224)

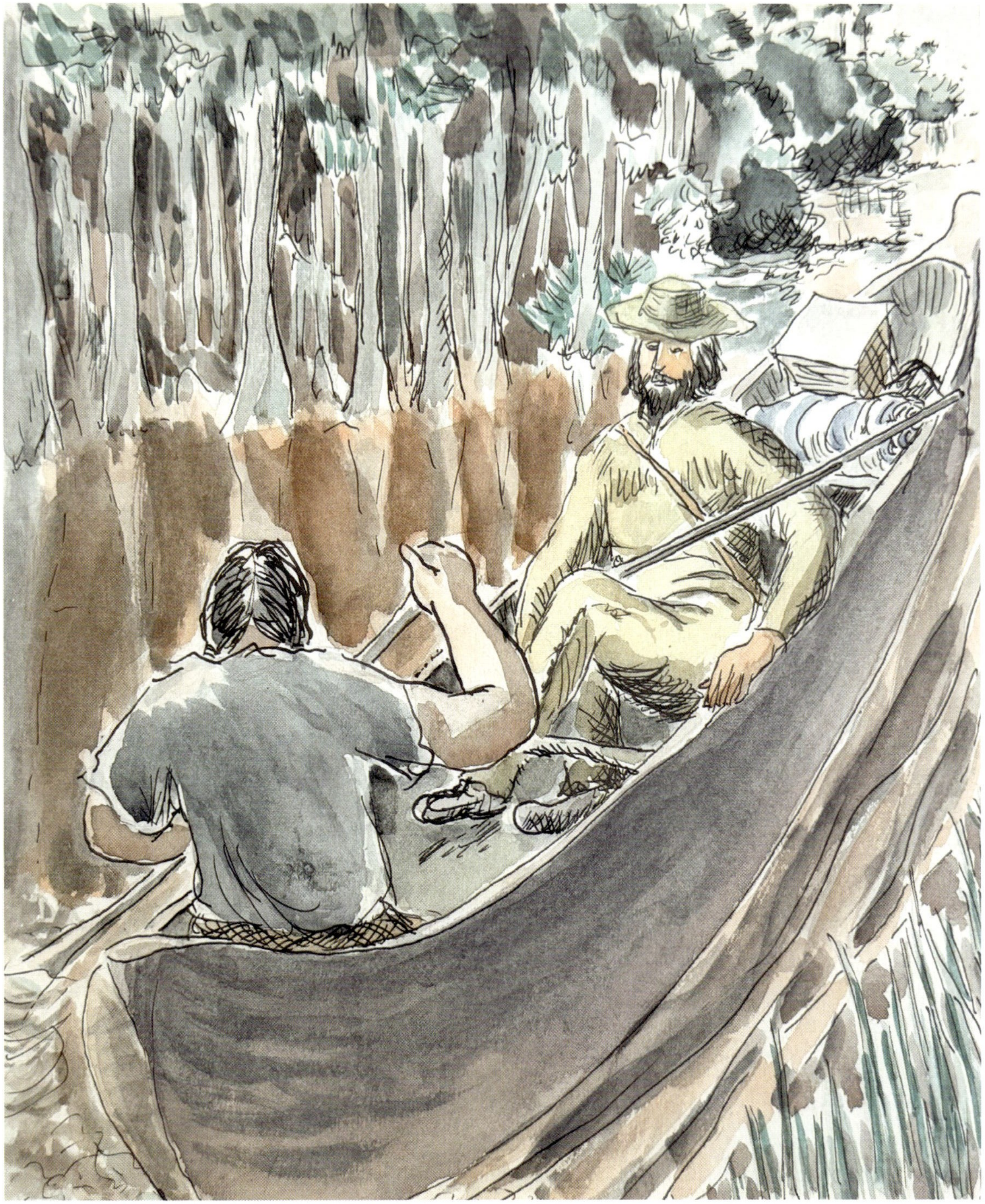

Bartram and his interpreter pass through a narrow opening in a stand of cypress.

. . . the young interpreter, my companion, who was obliging to me and whom our chief previously recommended to me as an associate; proposed to me another little voyage down the river; this was agreeable to me, being desirous of increasing my observations during our continuance at Talahasochte; as when the White King should return to town (which was expected every hour) we intended after audience and treaty to leave them and encamp in the forests, about fifteen miles distance and nearer the range of their horses.

Having supplied ourselves with am[m]unition and provision, we set off in the cool of the morning, and descended pleasantly, riding on the chrystal flood, which flows down with an east, gentle, yet active current, rolling over its silvery bed; how abundantly are the waters replenished with inhabitants! the stream almost as transparent as the air we breathe; there is nothing done in secret except on its green flowery verges, where nature at the command of the Supreme Creator, hath spread a mantle, as a covering and retreat at suitable and convenient times, but by no means a secure refuge from the voracious enemy and pursuer. (229)

On my doubling a long point of land, the river appeared surprisingly widened, forming a large bay, of an oval form, and several miles in extent. On the West side it was bordered round with low marshes, and invested with a swamp of Cypress, the trees so lofty, as to preclude the sight of the high-land forests, beyond them; and these trees, having flat tops, and all of equal height, seemed to be a green plain, lifted up and supported upon columns in the air, round the West side of the bay. (90)

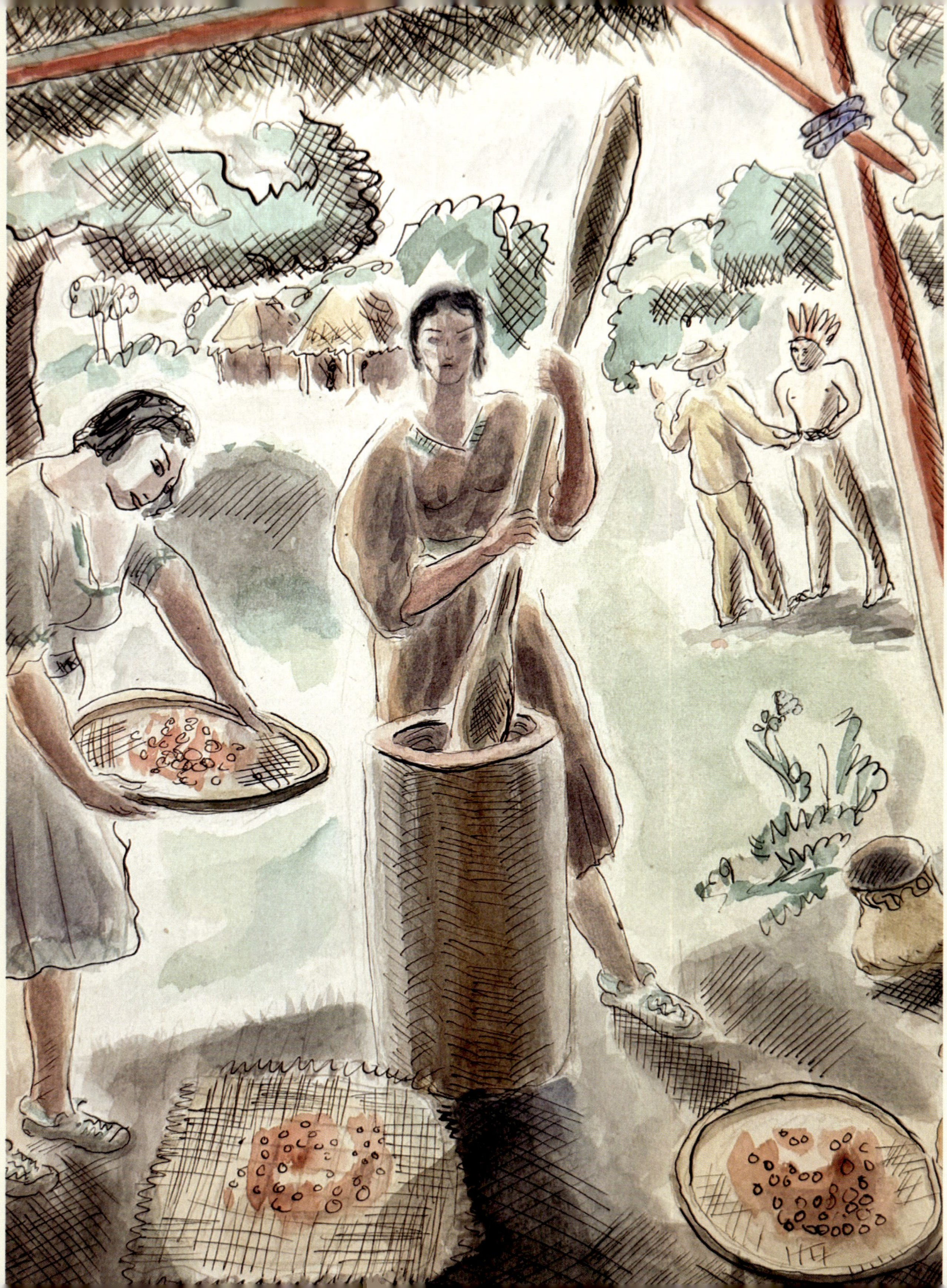

Creek women crack hickory nuts in a mortar to produce "hickory milk" while Bartram confers with a Creek man in the background. Bartram greatly admired the Indians' ability to cultivate native plants in their fields and to collect all sorts of edible fruits, vegetables, and nuts.

> *I observed, in the antient cultivated fields, 1. Diospyros [persimmon], 2. Gleditsia triacanthos [honey locust], 3. Prunus Chicasaw [plum],* 4. Callicarpa [beauty-berry], 5. Morus rubra [red mulberry], 6. Juglans exaltata [shell-bark hickory], 7. Juglans nigra [black walnut], which inform us, that these trees were cultivated by the ancients, on account of their fruit, as being wholesome and nourishing food. Tho' these are natives of the forest, yet they thrive better, and are more fruitful, in cultivated plantations, and the fruit is in great estimation with the present generation of Indians, particularly Juglans exaltata* commonly called shell-barked hiccory; the Creeks store up the latter in their towns. I have seen above an hundred bushels of these nuts belonging to one family. They pound them to pieces, and then cast them into boiling water, which, after passing through fine strainers, preserves the most oily part of the liquid: this they call by a name which signifies Hiccory milk; it is as sweet and rich as fresh cream, and is an ingredient in most of their cookery, especially homony and corn cakes.*
>
> **The Chicasaw plumb I think must be excepted, for though certainly a native of America, yet I never saw it wild in the forests, but always in old deserted Indian plantations: I suppose it to have been brought from the S.W. beyond the Missis[s]ippi, by the Chicasaws. (38–39)*

In the summer of 1773 Bartram set out, with John McIntosh in tow, to participate in the survey of lands conveyed by the Creeks and Cherokees to the British crown under the Treaty of Augusta. Because of a disagreement about the direction of the line being surveyed, the chief and his men staged a sit-down strike. Note, on the next page, the compass rose above the survey party. Also note the look of disdain on the seated chief, who ignores the compass offered to him.

> *We were detained at this place one day, in adjusting and planning the several branches of the survey. A circumstance occurred during this time, which was a remarkable instance of Indian sagacity, and had nearly disconcerted all our plans, and put an end to the business. The surveyor having fixed his compass on the staff, and about to ascertain the course from our place of departure, which was to strike Savanna river at the confluence of a certain river, about seventy miles distance from us; just as he had determined upon the point, the Indian Chief came up, and observing the course he had fixed upon, spoke, and said it was not right; but that the course to the place was so and so, holding up his hand, and pointing. The surveyor replied, that he himself was certainly right, adding, that that little instrument (pointing to the compass) told him so, which, he said, could not err. The Indian answered, he knew better, and that the*

little wicked instrument was a liar; and he would not acquiesce in its decisions, since it would wrong the Indians out of their land. This mistake (the surveyor proving to be in the wrong) displeased the Indians; the dispute arose to that height, that the Chief and his party had determined to break up the business, and return the shortest way home, and forbad the surveyors to proceed any farther: however, after some delay, the complaisance and prudent conduct of the Colonel made them change their resolution; the Chief became reconciled, upon condition that the compass should be discarded, and rendered incapable of serving on this business; that the Chief himself should lead the survey; and, moreover, receive an order for a very considerable quantity of goods.

Matters being now amicably settled, under this new regulation, the Colonel having detached two companies on separate routes, Mr. M'Intosh and myself attaching ourselves to the Colonel's party, whose excursion was likely to be the most extensive and varied, we sat off from the Buffalo Lick, and the Indian Chief, heading the party, conducted us on a straight line, as appeared by collateral observation, to the desired place. (39–40)

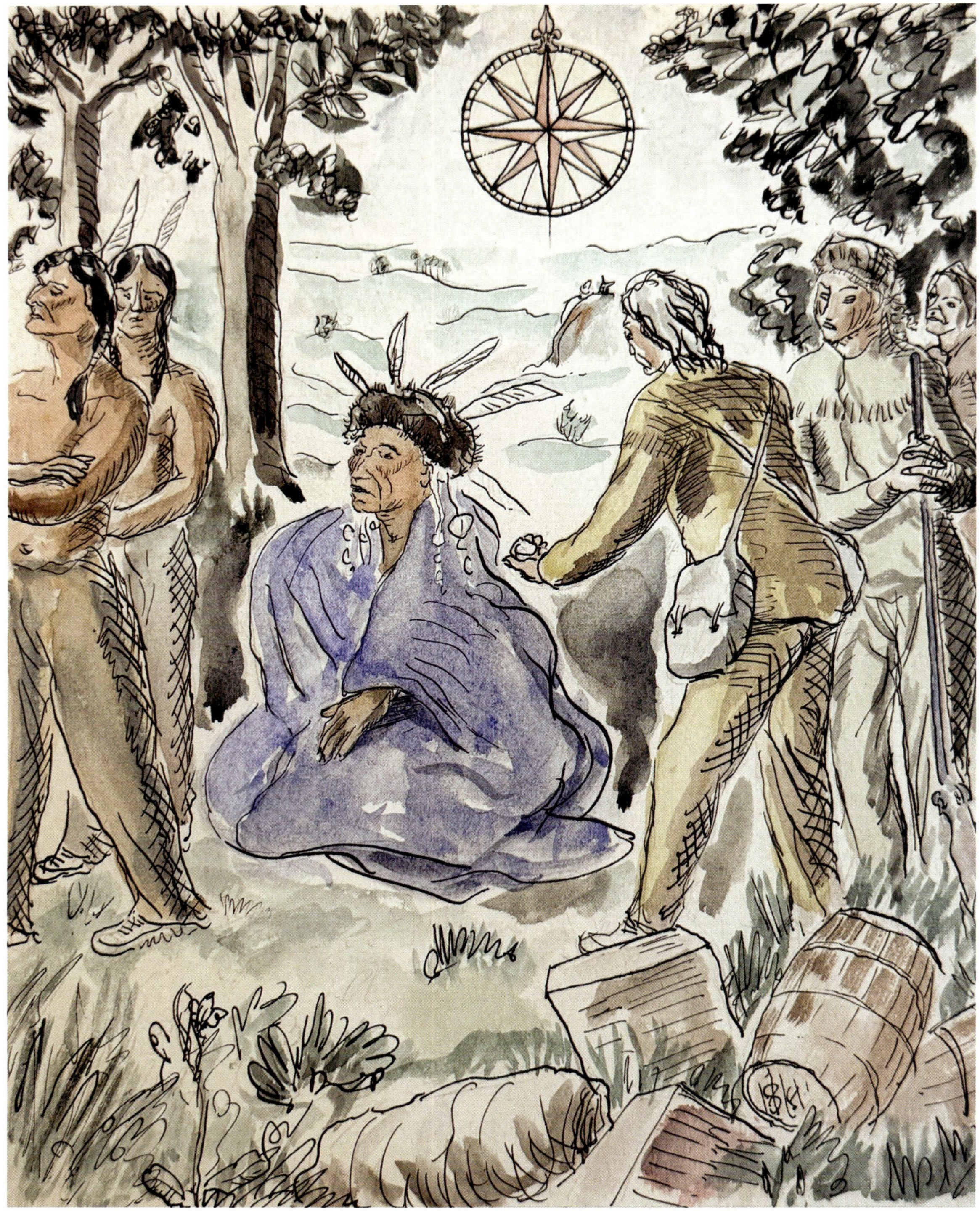

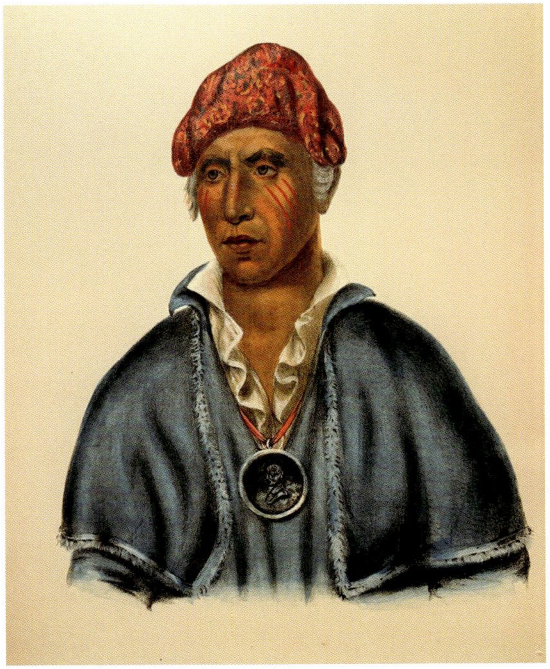

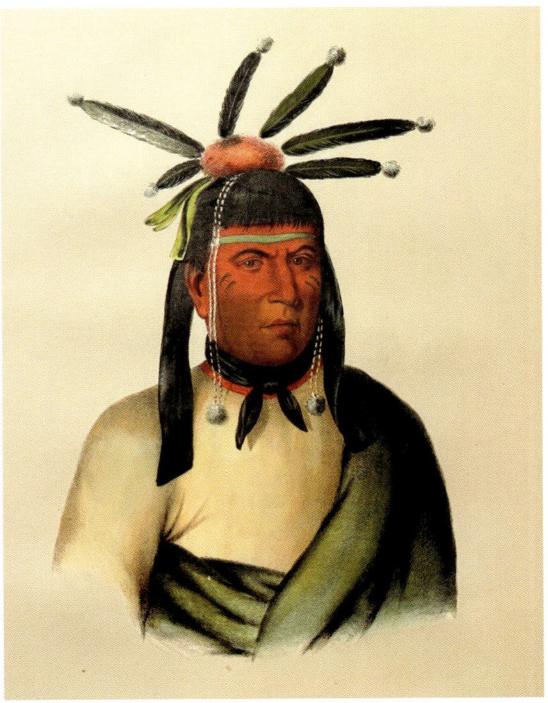

Private collection.

Although Bartram left copious written details about all aspects of Indian life, he chose to illustrate only the Long Warrior in *Travels*. Consequently, in painting this incident, Haynes had little visual guidance from Bartram. Instead, Haynes may have relied on one of the books held by the New York Public Library: Thomas L. McKenney and James Hall's *History of the Indian Tribes of North America*, published in a series of folio editions from 1836 to 1844. The full folio set contains 128 colored lithographs, with 120 devoted to individual portraits. A longtime superintendent of Indian affairs, McKenney wanted to capture portraits of tribal leaders and tribe members before they were extirpated from their homelands. The original paintings were destroyed in a fire at the Smithsonian where they were housed. However, they lived on in colored engravings, which are still highly sought at auction. For an extensive history of the project as well as the complete set of engravings, see James D. Horan, *The McKenney-Hall Portrait Gallery of American Indians* (Crown, 1972; reprinted by Bramhall House, 1986).

During his art studies in New York, Haynes worked at the New York City Library shelving books. The three-volume McKenney-Hall portrait set appears in the library's catalog, although there is no information about when the volumes entered the library's possession after they were published in the 1840s. However, due to the popularity of the work, it probably became part of this major library's collection soon after it was published. Many of Haynes's Indian sketches make it nearly certain that he was inspired by these portraits painted by Charles Bird King.

Haynes may have borrowed the design for the chief's blue mantle from the McKenney and Hall portrait of a Shawnee chief Quatawapea (Horan, 162) and the feathered headdress from their portrait of Amiskquew, a Menominee chief (Horan, 350).

With the sit-down strike concluded to the chief's satisfaction, at last the survey party reached the Cherokee Corner, whose "marked tree" would serve as the turning point for the northernmost sweep. Haynes's mural portrays a similar group in search of boundary lines coming upon a marked tree. However, that mural panel is entitled "The Coming of the French," obviously illustrating a site somewhere other than northeast Georgia. As noted on page 10, this is one of the six mural panels held in the Ashantilly Center Archives suggesting that the Mississippi River and the opening of the West were the subject matter for a class project either at the Grand Central School of Art or the Art Students League.

If situated in the correct place, the black oak *Quercus vellutina* often was used to mark corners of land parcels. In the old-growth forests of the Georgia frontier, black oaks often grew to gargantuan size and were very long-lived. Bartram wrote:

> *I think I can assert that many of the black oaks measured eight, nine, ten, and eleven feet diameter five feet above the ground, as we measured several that were above thirty feet girt. (37)*

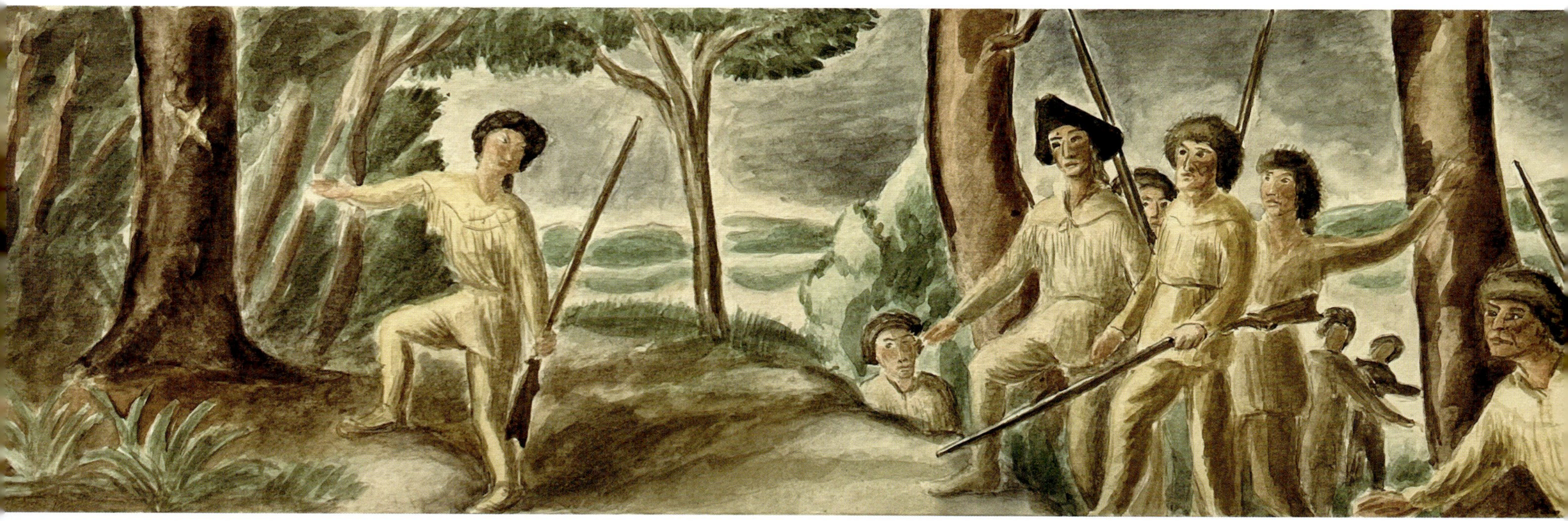

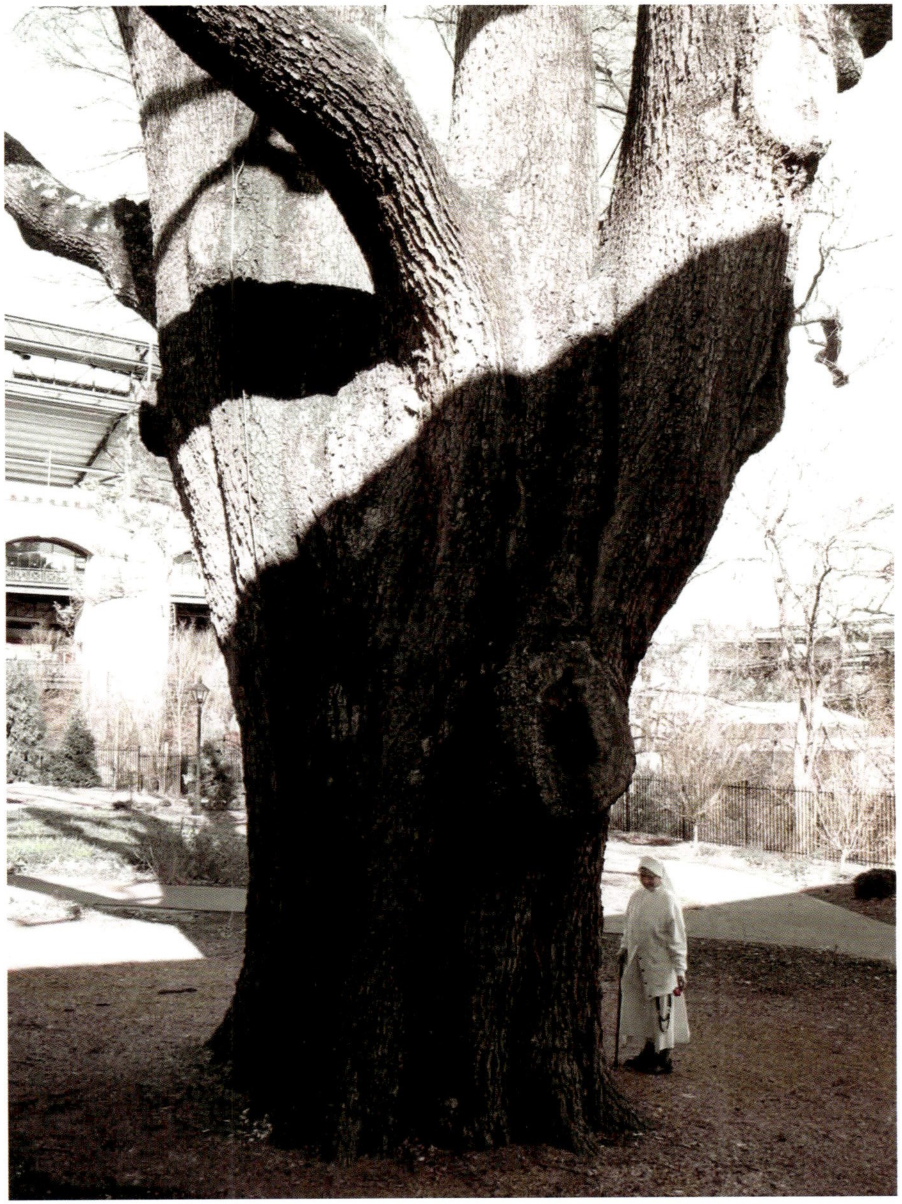

Courtesy of the Georgia Forestry Commission.

This photograph shows one current "champion" black oak found in Georgia. Measured by trained foresters, this specimen is 276 inches (20.5 feet) in circumference, or approximately 6.5 feet in diameter. It has been estimated to be three hundred years old. Surprisingly, it grows in downtown Atlanta, protected within the grounds of a Catholic hospice.

With the passage of time, Bartram's marked tree east of today's Athens, Georgia, is long gone, but its importance to the Bartram story is memorialized by the Bartram Trail marker beside the Mossy Creek picnic area, a low stone marker to the east and, beyond that, the fellowship of the Cherokee Corner Church.

Haynes's standing portrait of a Native man apparently was inspired by the portrait (at right) of Tachee (Tatsi), a Cherokee painted by Charles Bird King that appears in the *McKenney-Hall Portrait Gallery of American Indians* (see earlier discussion at page 101). Haynes's standing figure wears a calico print cloak, silver double gorget, red plumes and turban, a bandolier pouch, high-necked shirt with black ascot, and carries a long-handled tomahawk. While Haynes's version of Tachee sports more regalia than King's (simply a knife tucked into the sash), the wardrobe and accessories are typical of Southeastern tribes during the colonial era.

Tachee was a popular subject with many artists. Also in the collection of the New York Public Library is artist George Catlin's *Souvenir of the N. American Indians: As They Were in the Nineteenth Century* (1850). He posed Tachee for multiple pencil sketches in the field. Catlin wrote:

> *Tuch-ee, called "Dutch," Chief of a Band of the Cherokees, a very distinguished man. This man led 1500 of his tribe west of the Mississippi River, a distance of 1200 miles, to evade the advance of civilization, and then desperately and successfully maintained his position against the continued assaults of the Osages, on whose hunting grounds he had located. (https://digitalcollections.nypl.org/items/66491d30-c647-012f-5d8c-58d385a7bc34, accessed Nov. 23, 2023)*

For more of Catlin's sketches of Tachee, see Emma Lila Fundaburk, ed., *Southeastern Indians, Life Portraits: A Catalogue of Pictures, 1564–1935*, images 224, 248, 261, 269, and 280 (University of Alabama Press, 1958). Catlin also painted a delicate watercolor miniature of Tachee (now held in the collection of the Gilcrease Museum, Tulsa, Oklahoma) and a later oil portrait that shows Tachee with a much darker complexion (now held in the Virginia Museum of Fine Arts, Richmond, Virginia).

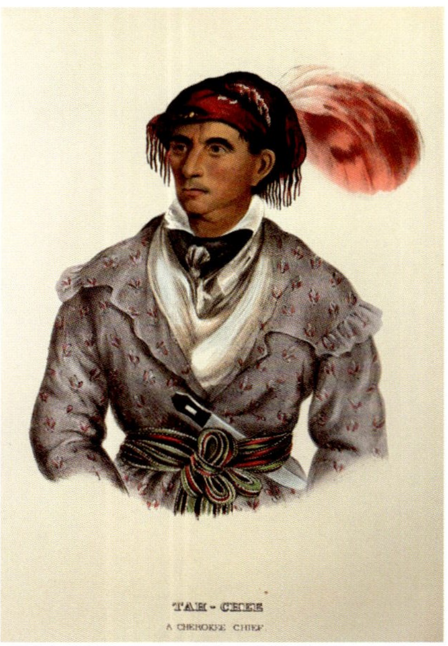

Portrait from *McKenney-Hall Portrait Gallery.*

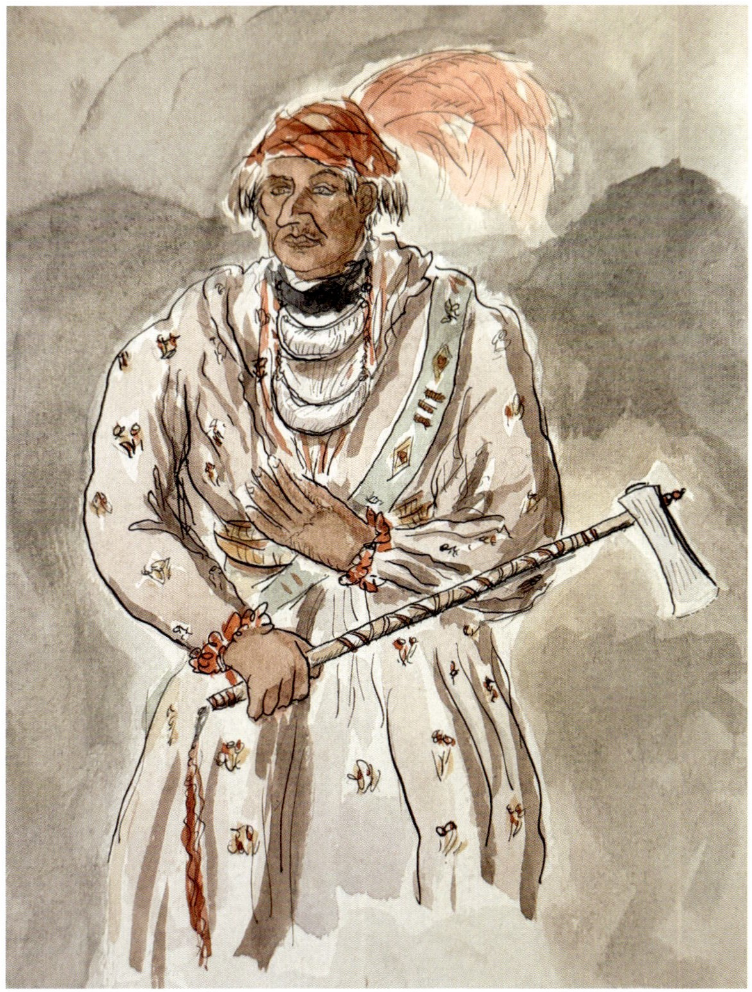

Bartram swaps trout for bream with two Seminoles. Note that both parties are traveling in dugouts.

> *Observing a fishing canoe of Indians turning a point below and coming towards us, who hailing us, we waited their coming up; they were cheerful merry fellows, and insisted on our accepting of part of their fish, they having a greater quantity and variety, especially of the bream my favourite fish; we exchanged some of our trout with them. (228)*

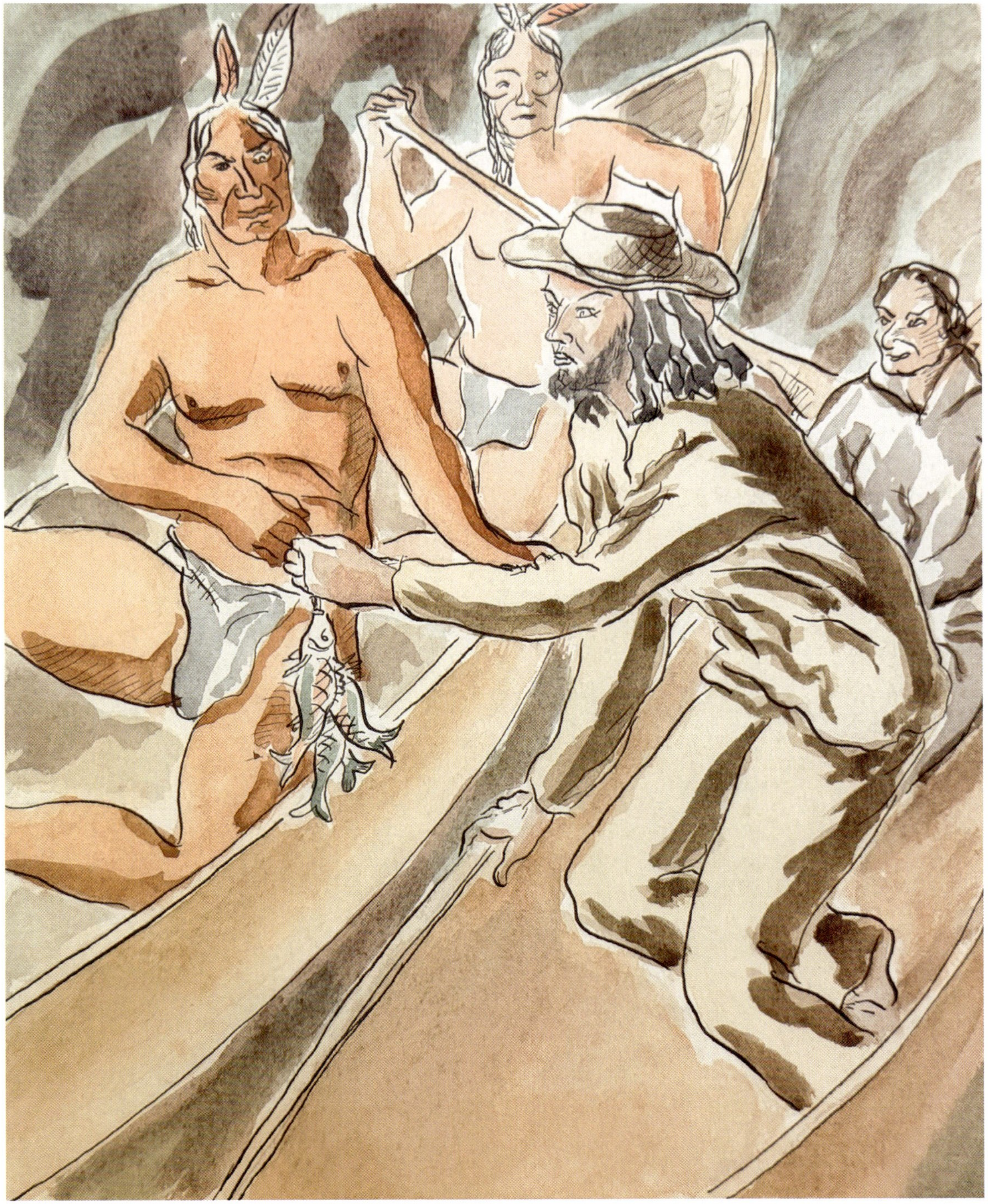

➤ The willet commonly is seen patrolling the tideline for food.

We pitched our tent under the shelter of a forest of Live Oaks, Palms and Sweet Bays; and having in the course of the day, procured plenty of sea fowl, such as curlews, willets, snipes, sand birds and others; we had them dressed for supper, and seasoned with excellent oysters, which lay in heaps in the water, close to our landing place. (70)

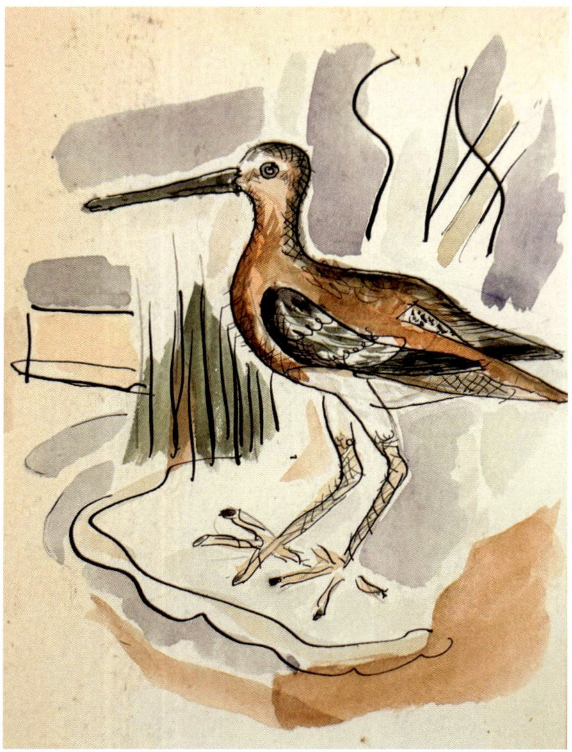

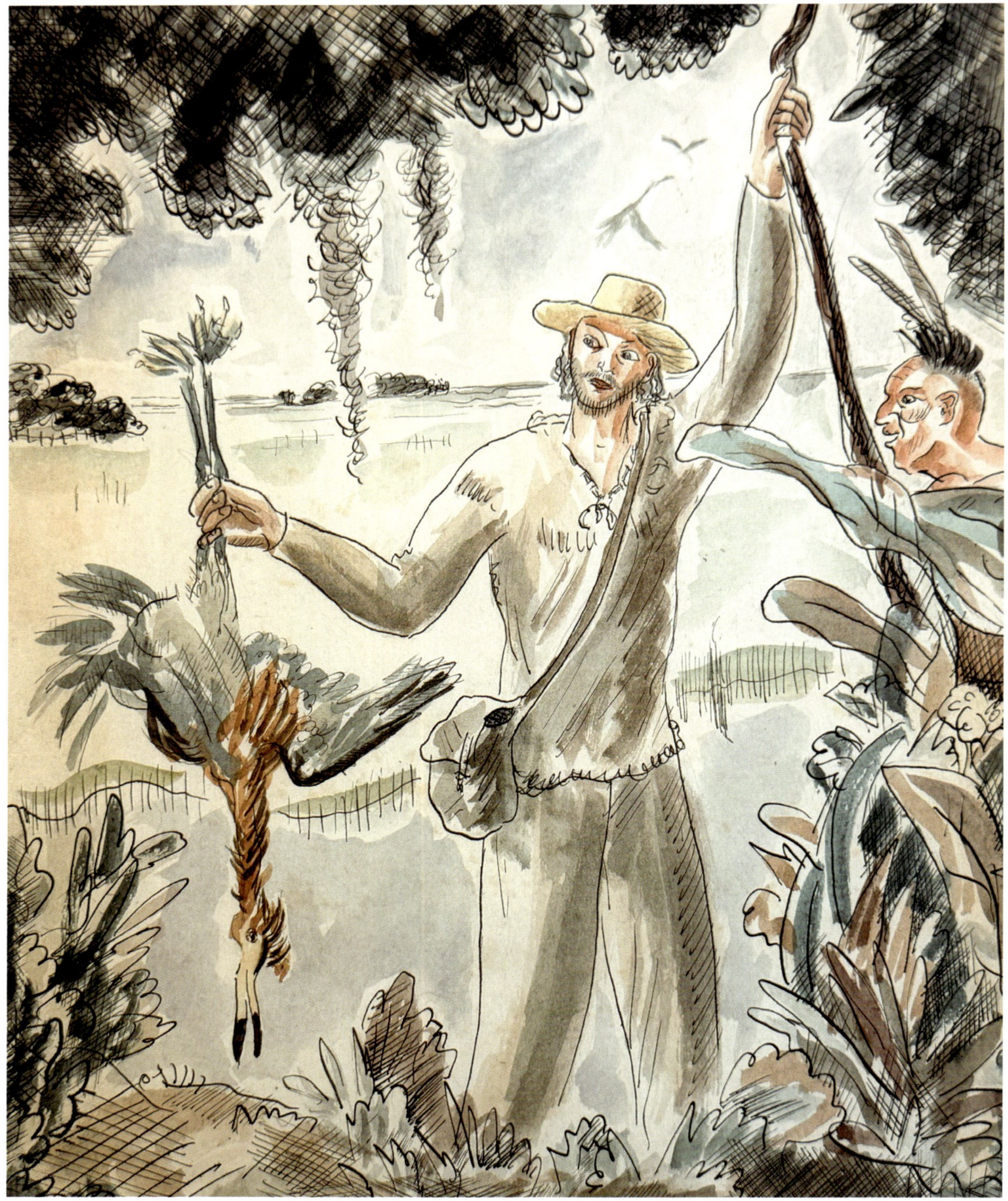

➢ With a Seminole looking on, Bartram hoists a dead rufous egret. However, Bartram discovered that nearly all the fish-eating birds were quite unpalatable, writing "most of them, except the bitterns and tantali, were so excessively fishy in taste and smell, I could not relish them" (249).

Although dead, the bird in Haynes's painting shows clear similarities to the coloration of Audubon's rufous egret posing in the marsh.

➢ Haynes knew Georgia's marsh birds so well that he included this painting of the seldom-seen sora. It is included on Bartram's bird list as "Rallus aquaticus minor," the little dark-blue water rail (296).

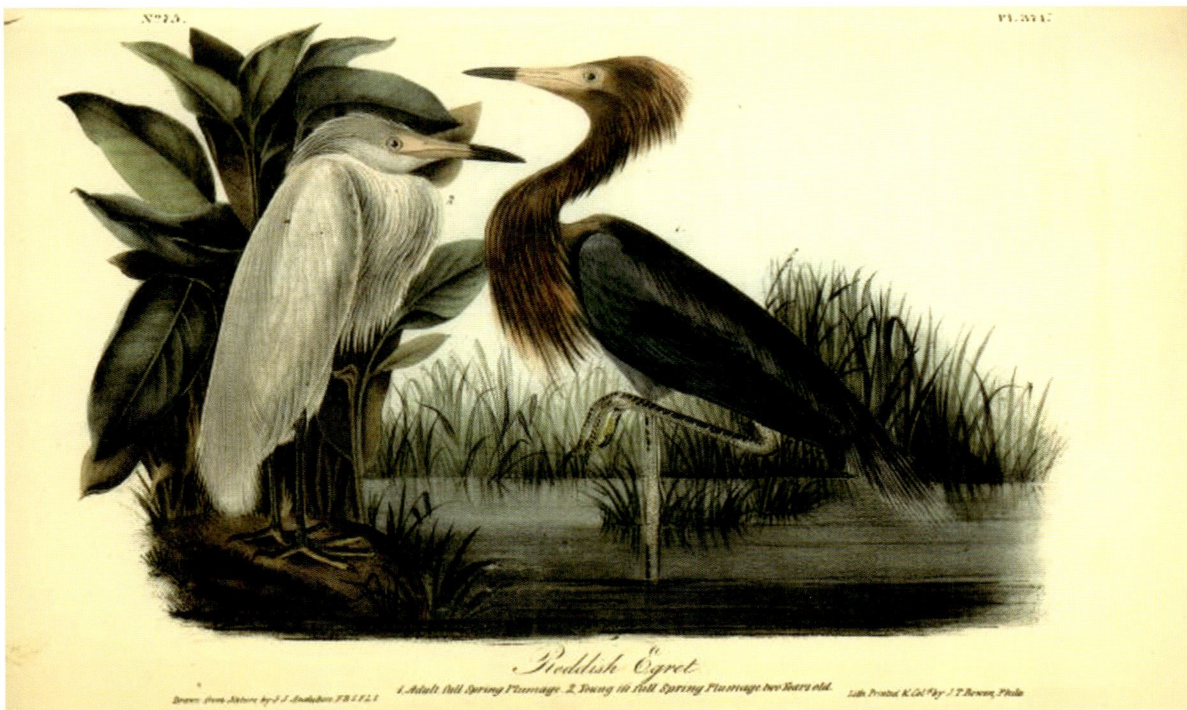

John James Audubon, *Rufous Egret*, courtesy of New York Public Library.

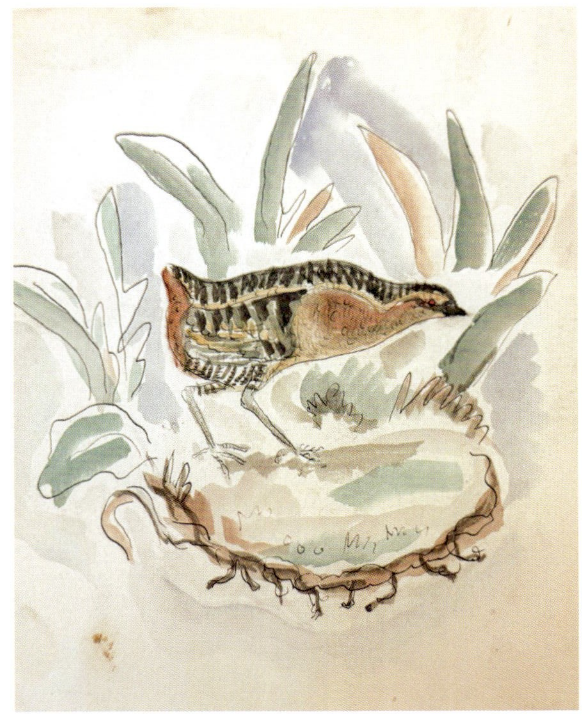

Once on a collecting excursion, John and William Bartram were surprised by a rattlesnake. Although he killed it, William had lifelong regrets. Later, he often confronted rattlesnakes throughout the South. At the Georgia coast on Sapelo Island, a huge rattlesnake lay next to a path to a spring where he and his friends passed repeatedly during the night. None of them knew it was there, and the snake made no attempt to alert them by rattling or striking at them. The next morning when they discovered it, Bartram insisted that they let it live in peace (268–270).

On the other hand, Bartram once had to put his feelings aside to come to the aid of the Seminoles. They feared rattlesnakes but had a tradition of leaving them alone. However, one was in the village upsetting daily life. Because Bartram was not bound by their beliefs, he could kill the rattlesnake for them. This is the scene set for Haynes's painting.

An occurrence happened this day, by which I had an opportunity of observing their extraordinary veneration or dread of the rattle snake; I was in the forenoon busy in my apartment in the council-house, drawing some curious flowers; when, on a sudden, my attention was taken off by a tumult without, at the Indian camp; I stepped to the door opening to the piazza, where I met my friend the old interpreter, who informed me that there was a very large rattle snake in the Indian camp, which had taken possession of it, having driven the men, women and children out, and he heard them saying that they would send for Puc-Puggy (for that was the name which they had given me, signifying the

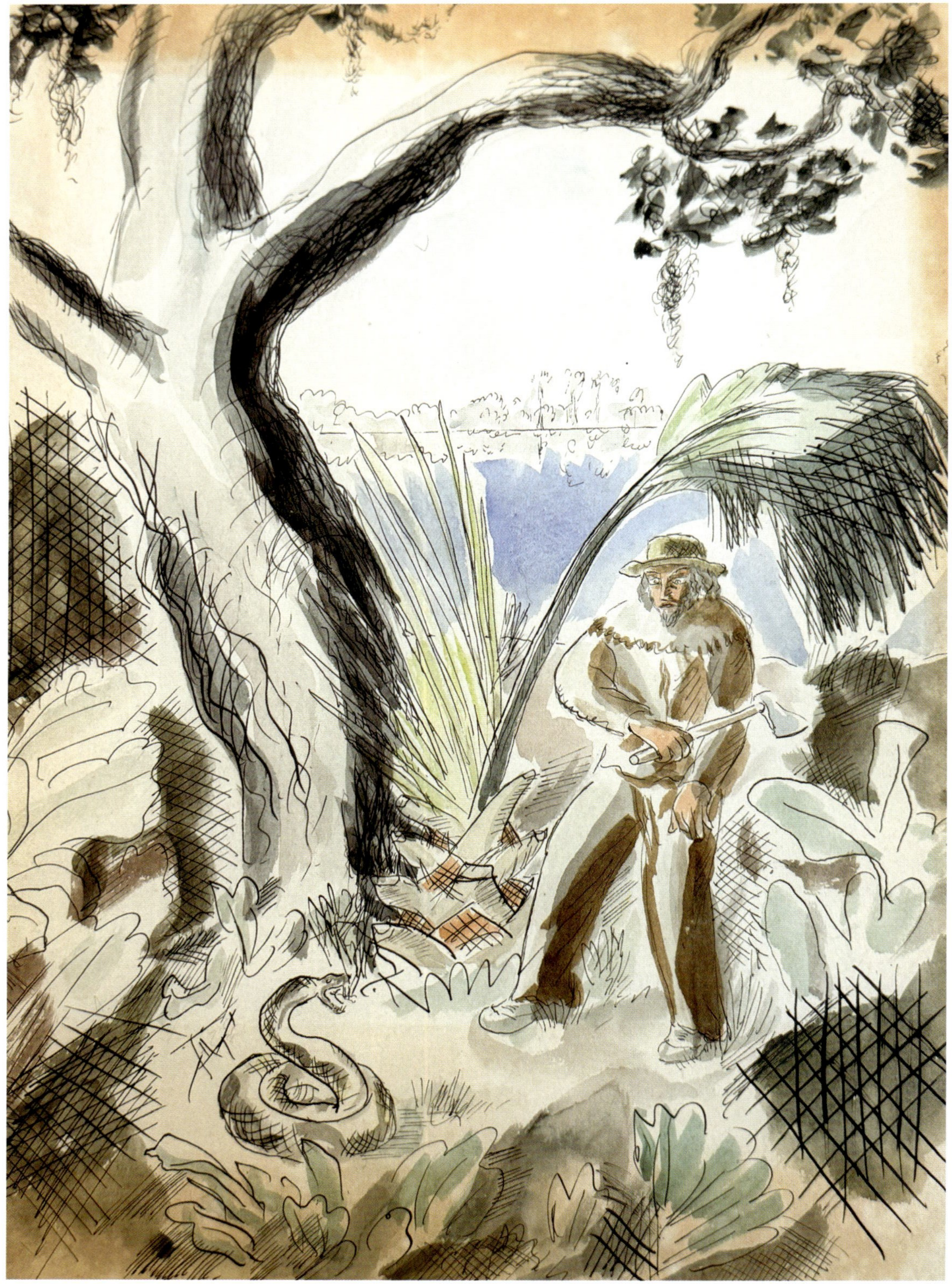

Flower Hunter) to kill him or take him out of their camp; I answered that I desired to have nothing to do with him, apprehending some disagreeable consequences, and desired that the Indians might be acquainted that I was engaged in business that required application and quiet, and was determined to avoid it if possible; my old friend turned about to carry my answer to the Indians, I presently heard them approaching and calling for Puc-Puggy; starting up to escape from their sight by a back door, a party consisting of three young fellows, richly dressed and ornamented, stepped in, and with a countenance and action of noble simplicity, amity and complaisance, requested me to accompany them to their encampment; I desired them to excuse me at this time; they plead and entreated me to go with them, in order to free them from a great rattle snake which had entered their camp, that none of them had freedom or courage to expel him, and understanding that it was my pleasure to collect all their animals and other natural productions of their land, desired that I would come with them and take him away, that I was welcome to him. I at length consented and attended on them to their encampment, where I beheld the Indians greatly disturbed indeed. The men with sticks and tomahawks, and the women and children collected together at a distance in affright and trepidation, whilst the dreaded and revered serpent leisurely traversed their camp, visiting the fire places from one to another, picking up fragments of their provisions and licking their platters. The men gathered around me, exciting me to remove him: being armed with a lightwood knot, I approached the reptile, who instantly collected himself in a vast coil (their attitude of defence). I cast my missile weapon at him, which luckily taking his head, dispatched him instantly, and laid him trembling at my feet; I took out my knife, severed his head from his body, then turning about, the Indians complimented me with every demonstration of satisfaction and approbation for my heroism, and friendship for them. I carried off the head of the serpent bleeding in my hand as a trophy of victory, and taking out the mortal fangs, deposited them carefully amongst my collection. I had not been long retired to my apartment before I was again roused from it by a tumult in the yard, and hearing Puc-Puggy called on, I started up, when instantly the old interpreter met me again, and told me the Indians were approaching in order to scratch me; I asked him for what; he answer[ed] for killing the rattle snake within their camp. Before I could make any reply or effect my escape, three young fellows singing, arm in arm, came up to me; I observed one of them there was a young prince who had, on my first interview with him, declared himself my friend and protector, when he told me that if ever occasion should offer in his presence, he would risk his life to defend mine or my property. This young champion stood by his two associates, one on each side of him, the two affecting a countenance and air of displeasure and importance, instantly presenting their scratching instruments, and flourishing them, spoke boldly, and said that I was too heroic and violent, that it would be good for me to loose some of my blood to make me more mild and tame, and for that purpose they were come to scratch me; they gave me no time to expostulate or reply, but attempted to lay hold on me, which I resisted, and my friend, the young prince, interposed and pushed them off, saying that

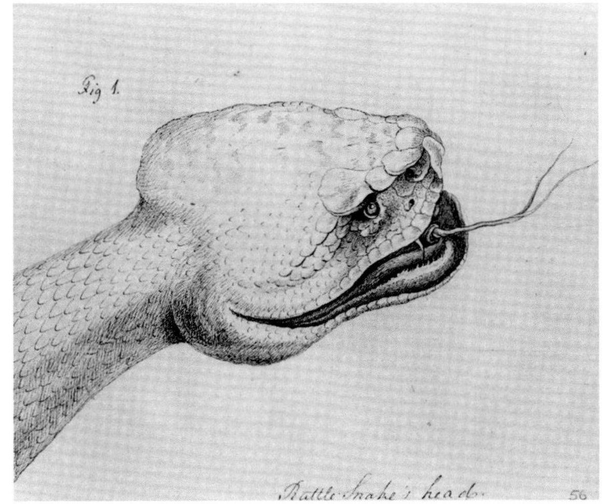

William Bartram's illustration of a rattlesnake, Trustees of the Natural History Museum, London.

I was a brave warrior and his friend, that they should not insult me, when instantly they altered their countenance and behaviour; they all whooped in chorus, took me friendly by the hand, clapped me on the shoulder and laid their hands on their breasts in token of sincere friendship, and laughing aloud, said I was a sincere friend to the Siminoles, a worthy and brave warrior, and that no one should hereafter attempt to injure me: they then all three joined arm in arm again and went off, shouting and proclaiming Puc-Puggy was their friend, &c. Thus it seemed that the whole was a ludicrous farce to satisfy their people and appease the manes of the slain rattlesnake.*

**These people never kill the rattle snake or any other serpent, saying if they do so, the spirit of the killed snake will excite or influence his living kindred or relatives to revenge the injury or violence done to him when alive. (260–263)*

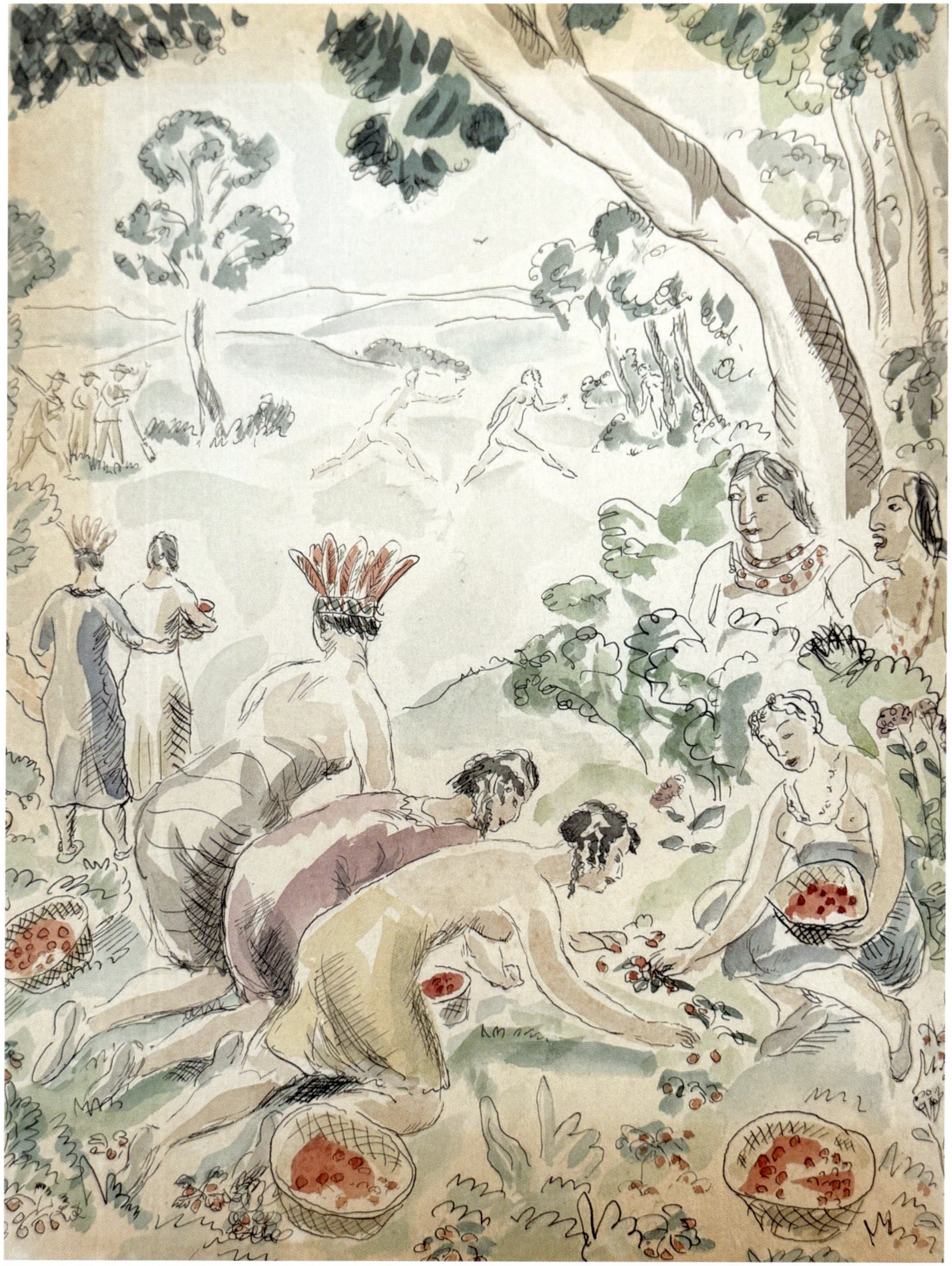

Sometimes botanizing offered more than enjoying the floral richness of western North Carolina. Haynes painted Bartram and two companions spying on young Cherokee women and their chaperones collecting wild strawberries.

> *Having paid our attention to this useful part of the creation, who, if they are under our dominion, have consequently a right to our protection and favour. We returned to our trusty servants that were regaling themselves in the exuberant sweet pastures and strawberry fields in sight, and mounted again; proceeding on our return to town, continued through part of this high forest skirting on the meadows; began to ascend the hills of a ridge which we were under the necessity of crossing, and having gained its summit, enjoyed a most enchanting view, a vast expanse of green meadows and strawberry fields; a meandering river gliding through, saluting in its various turnings the swelling, green, turfy knolls, embellished with parterres of flowers and fruitful strawberry beds; flocks of turkies strolling about them; herds of deer prancing in the meads or bounding over the hills; companies of young, innocent Cherokee virgins, some busily gathering the rich fragrant fruit, others having already filled their baskets, lay reclined under the shade of floriferous and fragrant native bowers of Magnolia, Azalea, Philadelphus, perfumed Calycanthus, sweet Yellow Jessamine and cerulian Glycine frutescens, disclosing their beauties to the fluttering breeze, and bathing their limbs in the cool fleeting streams; whilst other parties, more gay and libertine, were yet Collecting strawberries or wantonly chasing their companions, tantalising them, staining their lips and cheeks with the rich fruit.*

This sylvan scene of primitive innocence was enchanting, and perhaps too enticing for hearty young men long to continue idle spectators.

In fine, nature prevailing over reason, we wished at least to have a more active part in their delicious sports. Thus precipitately resolving, we cautiously made our approaches, yet undiscovered, almost to the joyous scene of action. Now, although we meant no other than an innocent frolic with this gay assembly of hamadryades, we shall leave it to the person of feeling and sensibility to form an idea to what lengths our passions might have hurried us, thus warmed and excited, had it not been for the vigilance and care of some envious matrons who lay in ambush, and espying us gave the alarm, time enough for the nymphs to rally and assemble together; we however pursued and gained ground on a group of them, who had incautiously strolled to a greater distance from their guardians, and finding their retreat now like to be cut off, took shelter under cover of a little grove, but on perceiving themselves to be discovered by us, kept their station, peeping through the bushes; when observing our approaches, they confidently discovered themselves and decently advanced to meet us, half unveiling their blooming faces, incarnated with the modest maiden blush, and with native innocence and cheerfulness presented their little baskets, merrily telling us their fruit was ripe and sound.

We accepted a basket, sat down and regaled ourselves on the delicious fruit, encircled by the whole assembly of the innocently jocose sylvan nymphs; by this time the several parties under the conduct of the elder matrons, had disposed themselves in companies on the green, turfy banks.

My young companion, the trader, by concessions and suitable apologies for the bold intrusion, having compromised the matter with them, engaged them to bring their collections to his house at a stipulated price, we parted friendly.

And now taking leave of these Elysian fields, we again mounted the hills, which we crossed, and traversing obliquely their flowery beds, arrived in town in the cool of the evening. (356–358)

Marguerite Thompson Zorach was one of the artists affiliated with the Grand Central School of Art while Haynes studied there. In her early work, her technique for shading the contours of the human body is similar to Haynes's shading of the strawberry pickers as well as the hand holding the white flower on page 95.

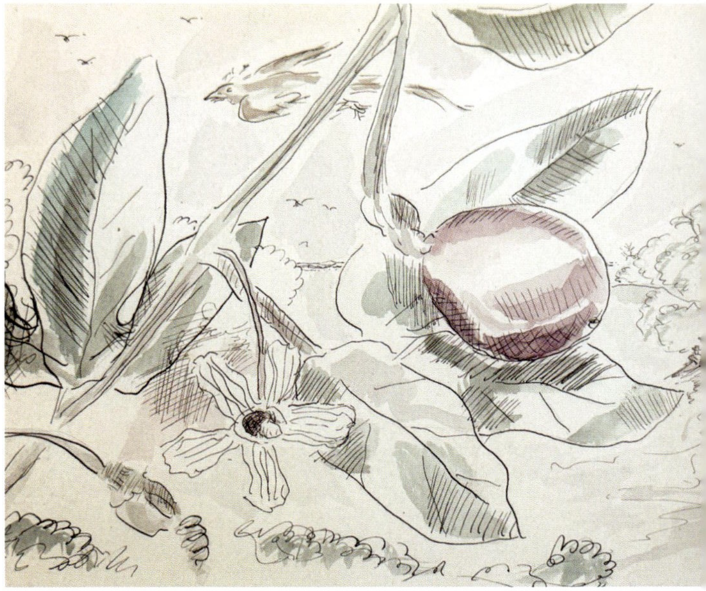

An eggplant (*Solanum melongena*) is shown with the Carolina parakeet flying overhead. The only *Solanum* species mentioned in *Travels* is *Solanum tuberosa*, the Irish potato. However, the eggplant was locally known as "Guinea squash," an attribution to its arrival in North America as part of the African slave trade.[2] Bartram only lists "squash," not differentiating among the many types of squash he encountered.

Of all people, he would have recognized this eggplant as a *Solanum*.

William Bartram and a Seminole stalk deer at the Alachua Savanna.

Leaving this delightful retreat, we soon came to the verge of the groves, when presented to view, a vast verdant bay of the savanna; we discovered a herd of deer feeding at a small distance, upon the sight of us they ran off, taking shelter in the groves on the opposite point or cape of this spacious meadow. My companions being old expert hunters, quickly concerted a plan for their destruction; one of our company immediately struck off, obliquely crossing the meadow for the opposite groves, in order to intercept them, if they should continue their course up the forest, to the main; and we crossed strait over to the point, if possible to keep them in sight, and watch their motions, knowing that they would make a stand thereabouts, before they would attempt their last escape: on drawing near the point, we slackened our gate, and cautiously entered the groves, when we beheld them thoughtless and secure, flouncing in a sparkling pond, in a green meadow or cove beyond the point; some were lying down on their sides in the cool waters, whilst others were prancing like young kids; the young bucks in playsome sport, with their sharp horns hooking and spurring the others, urging them to splash the water.

I endeavoured to plead for their lives, but my old friend though he was a sensible, rational and good sort of man, would not yield to my philosophy; he requested me to mind our horses, while he made his approaches, cautiously gaining ground on them, from tree to tree, when they all suddenly sprang up and herded together; a princely buck who headed the party, whistled and bounded off, his retinue followed, but unfortunately for their chief, he led them

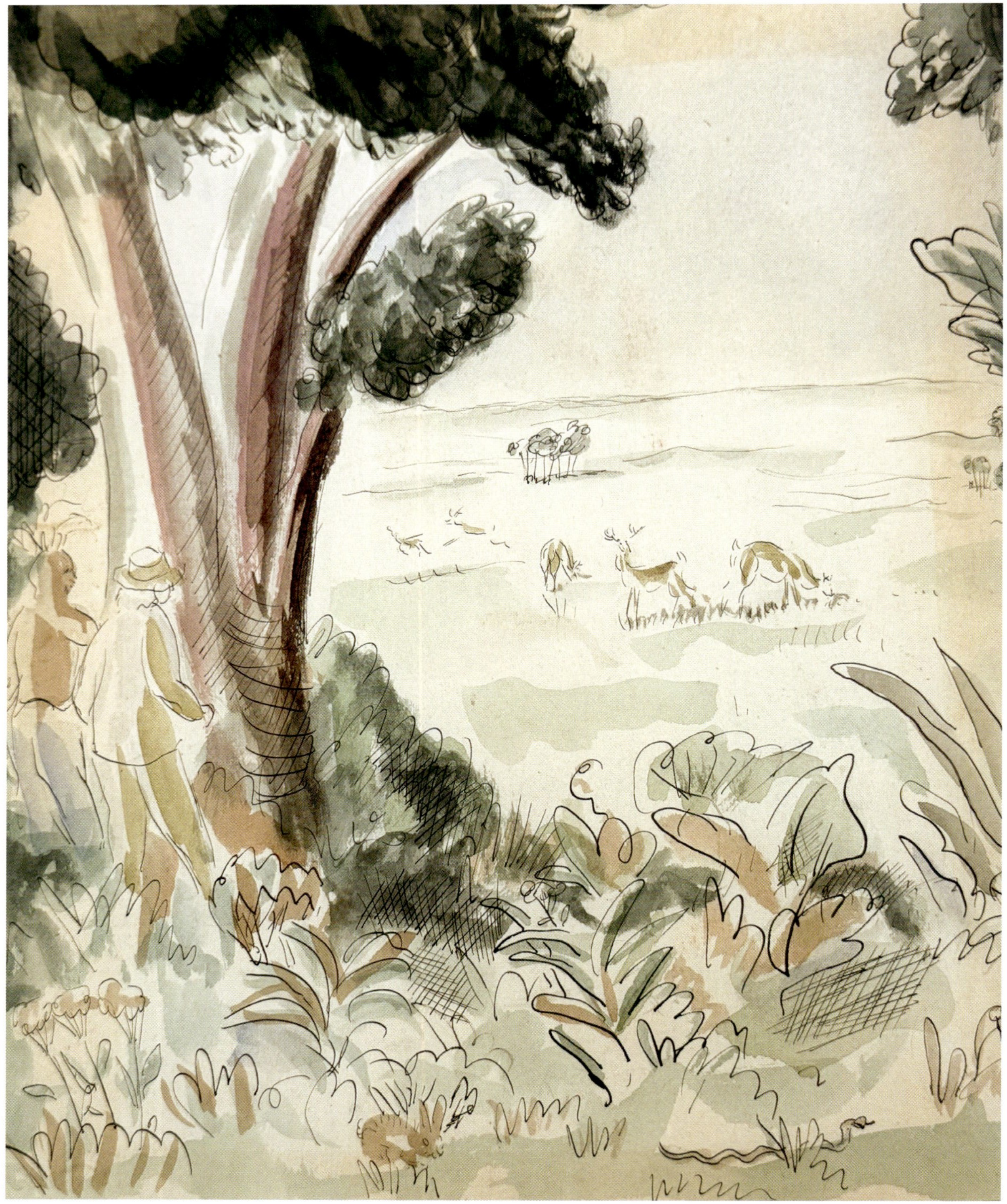

with prodigious speed out towards the savanna very near us, and when passing by, the lucky old hunter fired and laid him prostrate upon the green turf, but a few yards from us; his affrighted followers at the instant, sprang off in every direction, streaming away like meteors or phantoms, and we quickly lost sight of them: he opened his body, took out the entrails and placed the carcase in the fork of a tree, casting his frock or hunting shirt over to protect it from the vultures and crows, who follow the hunter as regularly as his own shade. (199–201)

➢ Facing the Alachua Savanna painting is a Seminole with a colorful sash (perhaps the strap for a bandolier bag), a red turban topped by light red feathers, and surrounded with foliage. This is a foretaste of the closing Bartram painting on page 143, which shows him shaking hands with a man dressed in similar fashion. Note that once again Haynes uses artistic license to adorn him with red feathers when the Seminole preferred black or black-and-white feathers.

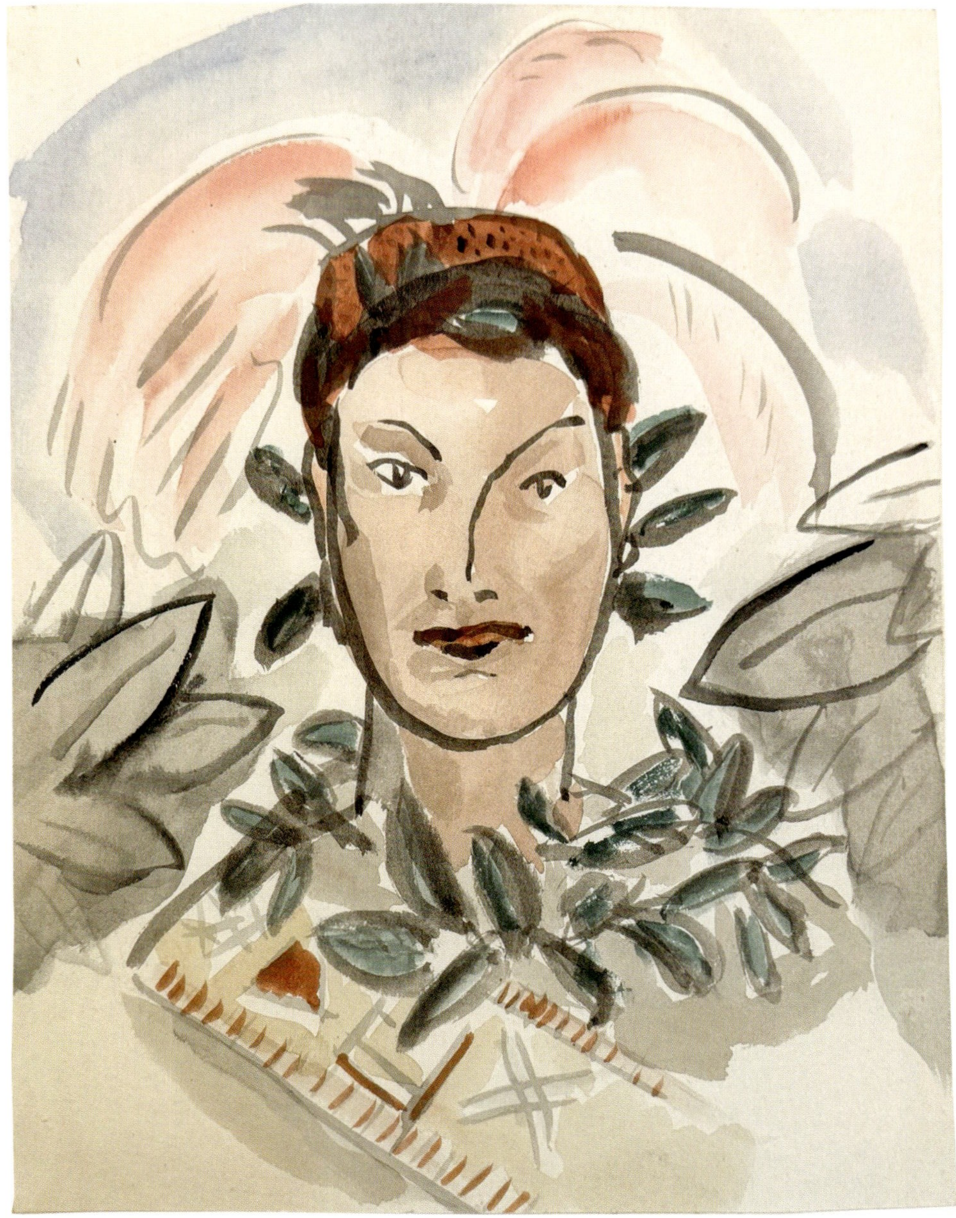

➤ Haynes painted this study of a man wearing a tan turban with red feathers, juxtaposed perfectly across from his rendition of Audubon's flamingo.

William Bartram wrote very detailed descriptions of the dress and ornamentation of the tribes he encountered.

> *The men shave their head, leaving only a narrow crest or comb, beginning at the crown of the head, where it is about two inches broad and about the same height, and stands frized upright; but this crest tending backwards, gradually widens, covering the hinder part of the head and back of the neck; this lank hair behind is ornamented with pendant silver quills, and then jointed or articulated silver plates, and usually the middle fascicle of hair, which being by far the longest, is wrapped in a large quill of silver, or the joint of a small reed, curiously sculptured and painted, the hair continuing through it terminates in a tail or tossil.*
>
> *Their ears are lacerated, separating the border or cartilagenous limb, which at first is bound round very close and tight with leather strings or thongs, and anointed with fresh bear's oil, until healed; the weight of the lead, extends this cartilage an incredible length, which afterwards being craped, or bound round in brass or silver wire, extends it semicircularly like a bow or crescent; and it is then very elastic, even so as to spring and bound about with the least motion or flexure of the body; this is decorated with soft white plumes of heron feathers.*
>
> *A very curious diadem or band, about four inches broad, and ingeniously wrought or woven, and curiously decorated with stones, beads, wampum, porcupine quills, &c. encircles their temples, the front peak of which is embellished with a high waving plume, of crane or heron feathers.* (501–502)

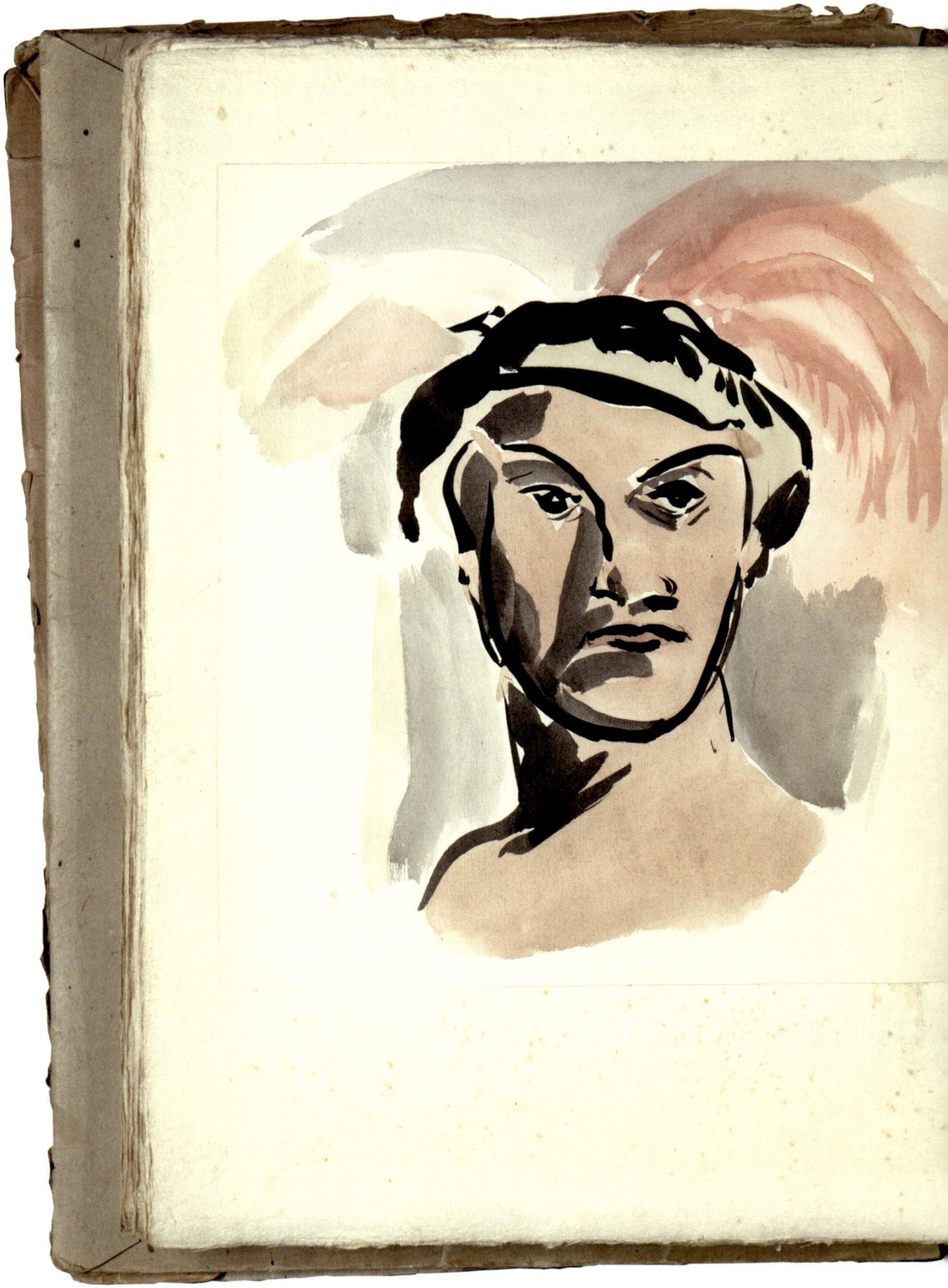

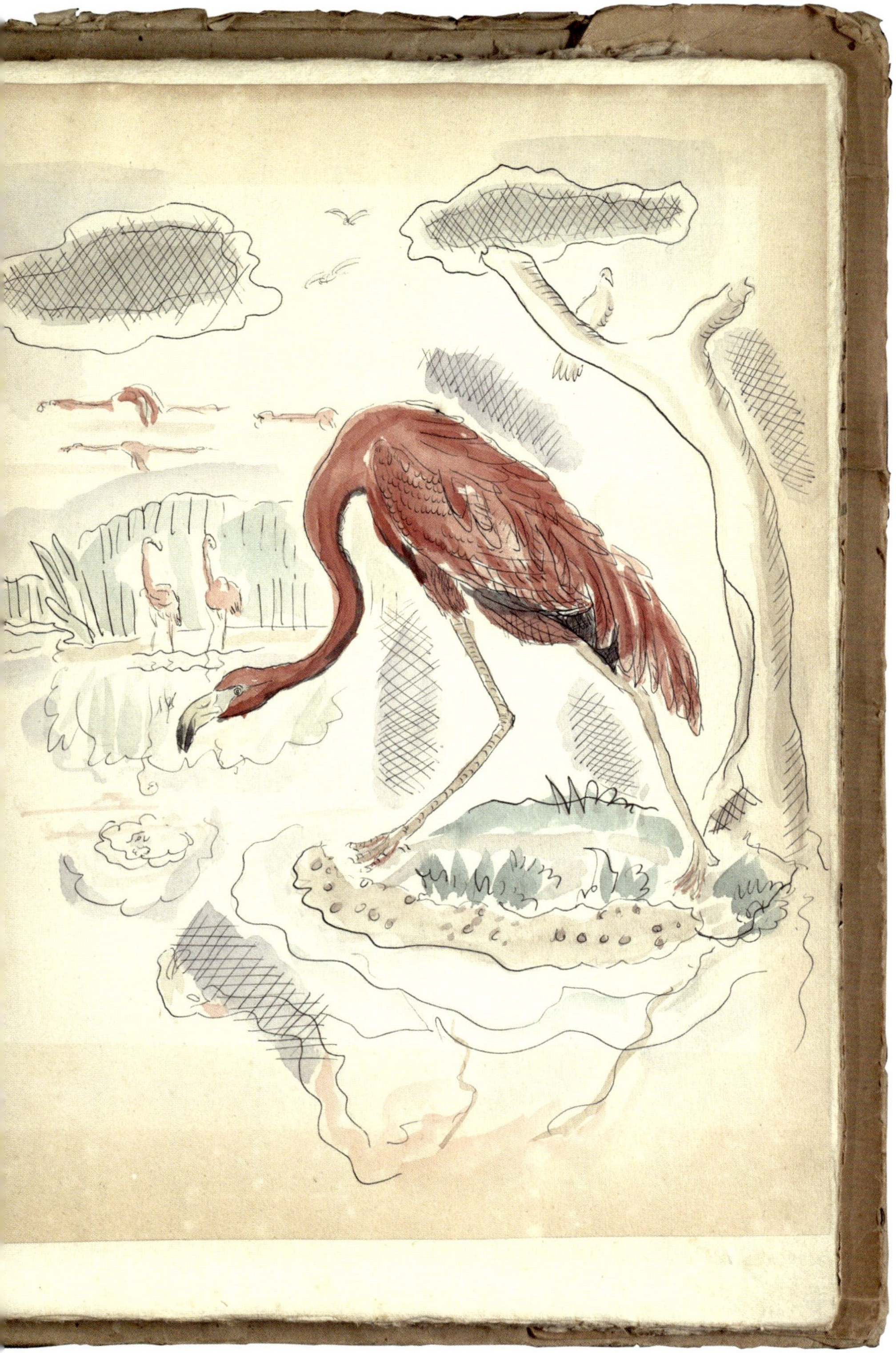

Most artists are challenged by fitting exceptionally tall flamingos on paper. Haynes posed his flamingo reminiscent of Audubon's portrayal, but did add their unmistakable shape in flight. Bartram stated that flamingos were seen as far north as St. Augustine but otherwise only listed them (296).

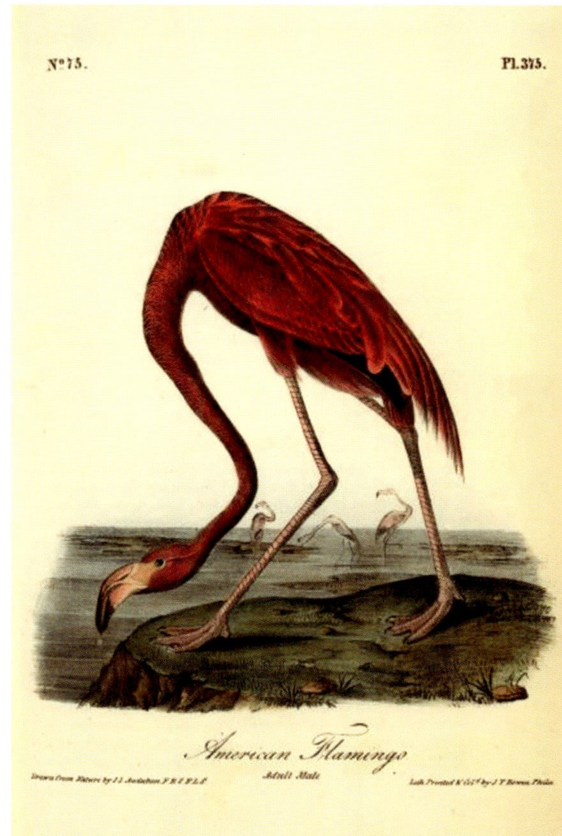

John James Audubon, *Flamingo*, courtesy of New York Public Library.

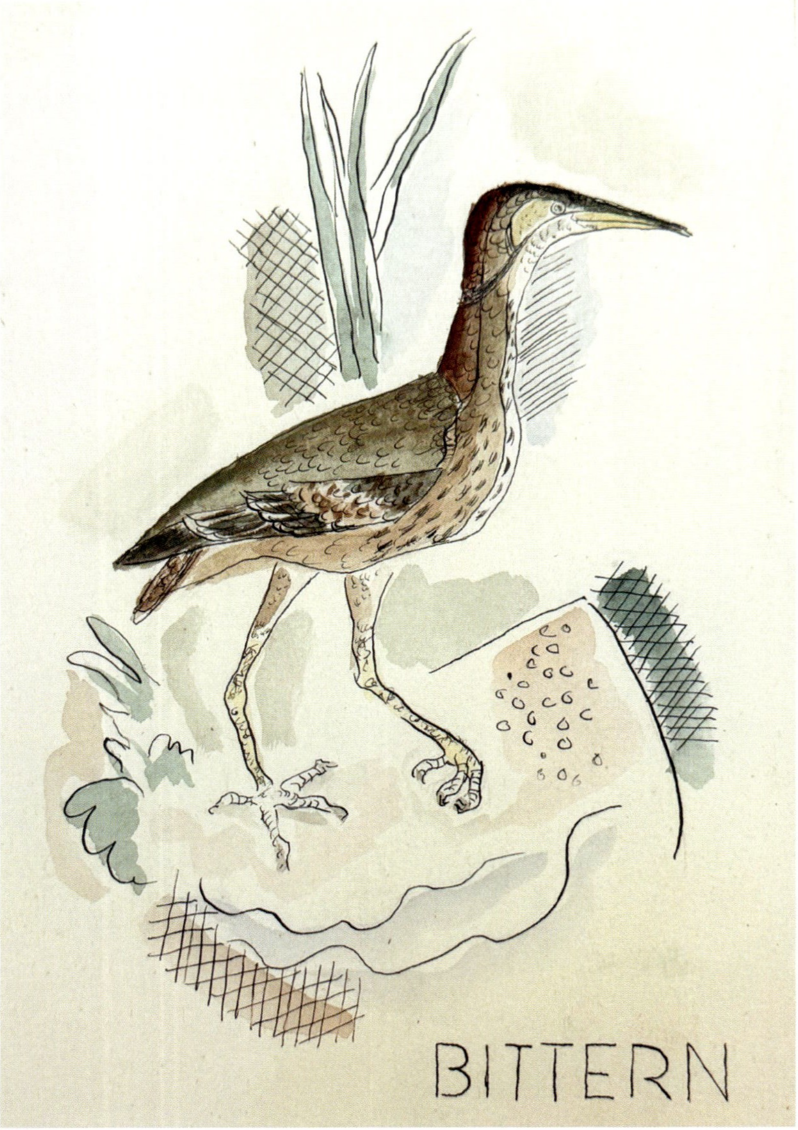

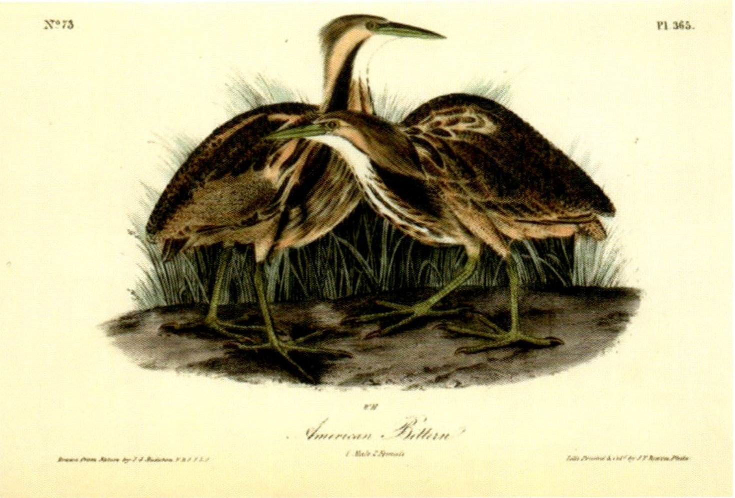

John James Audubon, *Bittern*, courtesy of New York Public Library.

Bartram mentioned bitterns in passing several times without elaborating much on them except for one unsettled night.

> *[Two bears] did not presume to return again, nor was I molested by any other creature, except being occasionally awakened by the whooping of owls, screaming of bitterns, or the wood-rats running amongst the leaves. (124)*

Haynes's rendition of the bittern clearly was inspired by Audubon's rendering of the bird.

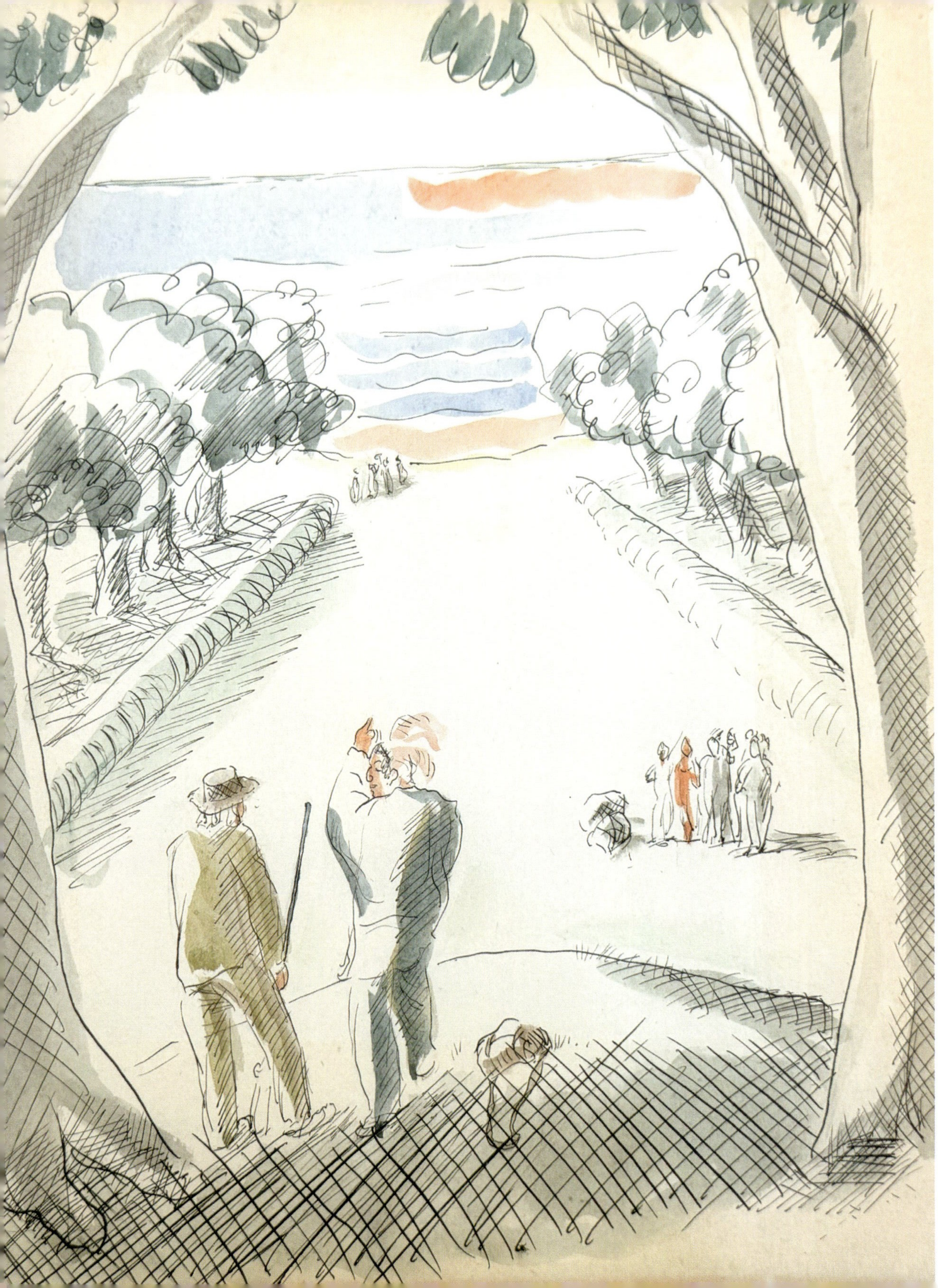

Bartram stands alongside a Seminole at Mount Royal, at the head of a spacious avenue leading to Lake George.

From this place we enjoyed a most enchanting prospect of the great Lake George, through a grand avenue, if I may so term this narrow reach of the river, which widens gradually for about two miles, towards its entrance into the lake, so as to elude the exact rules of perspective and appears of an equal width. (98–99)

These three paintings honor Bartram's effusive praise of the papaya, which he referred to as "the Carica papaya, supercilious with all the harmony of beauty and gracefulness" (xvii). Later in *Travels*, Bartram continued his paean to the papaya:

> *And now appeared in sight, a tree that claimed my whole attention: it was the Carica papaya, both male and female, which were in flower; and the latter both in flower and fruit, some of which were ripe, as large, and of the form of a pear, and of a most charming appearance.*
>
> *This admirable tree, is certainly the most beautiful of any vegetable production I know of; the towering Laurel Magnolia, and exalted Palm, indeed exceed it in grandeur and magnificence, but not in elegance, delicacy and gracefulness; it rises erect, with a perfectly strait tapering stem, to the height of fifteen or twenty feet, which is smooth and polished, of a bright ash colour, resembling leaf silver, curiously inscribed with the footsteps of the fallen leaves, and these vestiges, are placed in a very regular uniform imbricated order, which has a fine effect, as if the little column were elegantly carved all over. Its perfectly spherical top, is formed of very large lobe-sinuate leaves, supported on very long footstalks; the lower leaves are the largest as well as their petioles the longest, and make a graceful sweep or flourish, like the long S on the branches of a sconce candlestick. The ripe and green fruit are placed round about the stem or trunk, from the lowermost leaves, where the ripe fruit are, and upwards almost to the top; the heart or inmost pithy part of the trunks is in a manner hollow, or at best consists of very thin porous medullae or membranes; the tree very seldom branches or divides into limbs, I believe never unless the top is by accident broken off when very young: I saw one which had two tops or heads, the stem of which divided near the earth. It is always green, ornamented at the same time with flowers and fruit, which like figs come out singly from the trunk or stem. (131–132)*

How unfortunate it is for us that, because of their sensitivity to frost, papaya now grow only in the southern extremity of Florida.

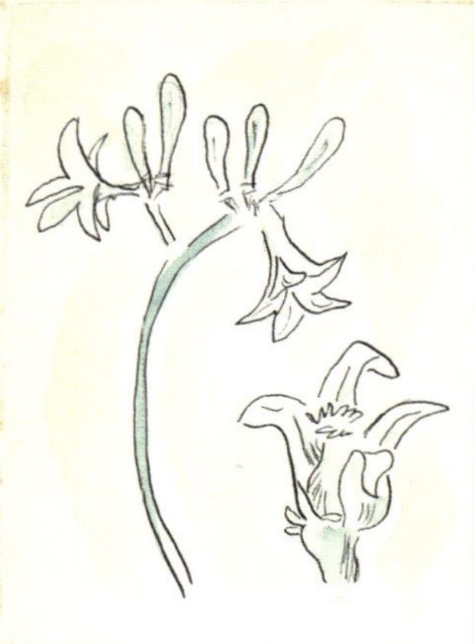

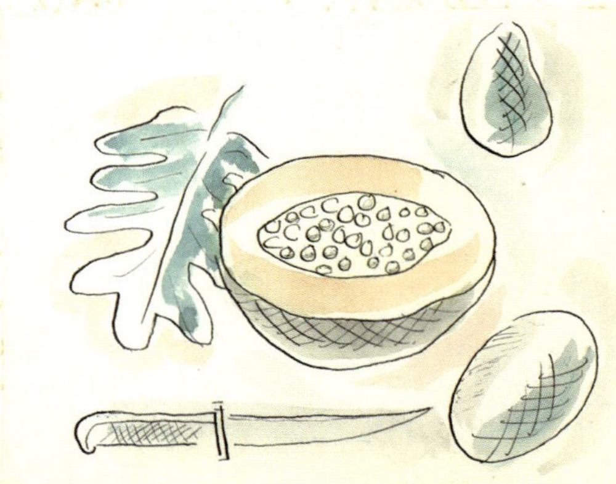

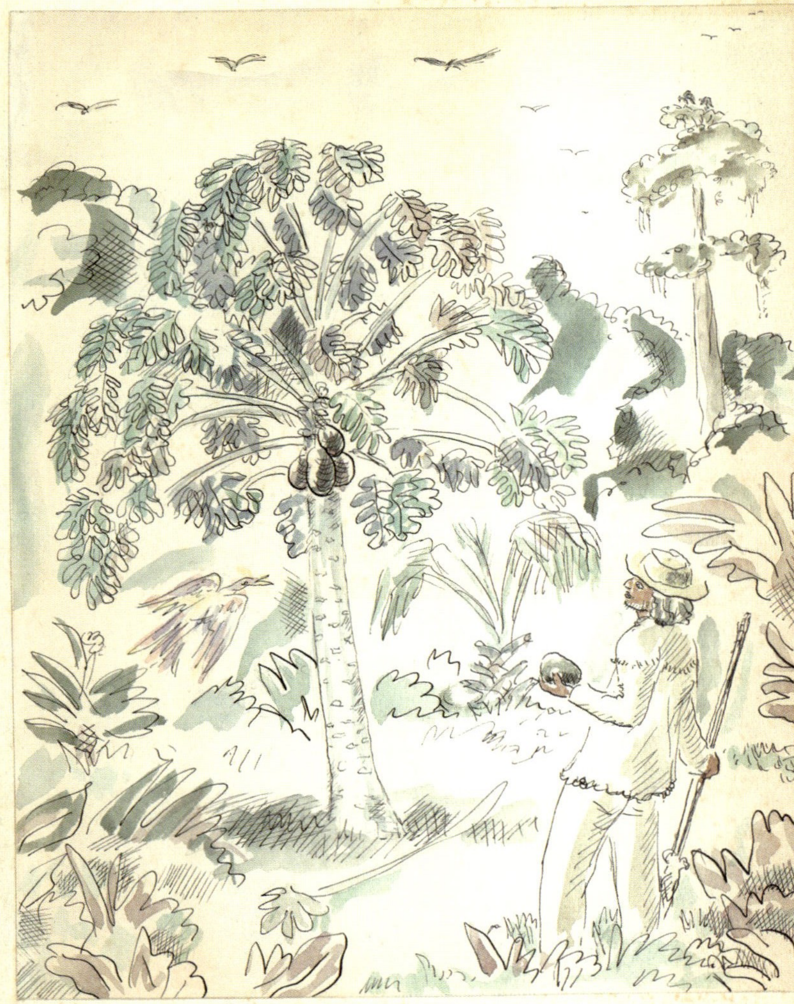

This black-and-white wading bird or shorebird may be a spotted sandpiper in winter plumage with a gull-billed tern, also in winter plumage, flying overhead. See Audubon's spotted sandpiper in winter plumage for comparison.

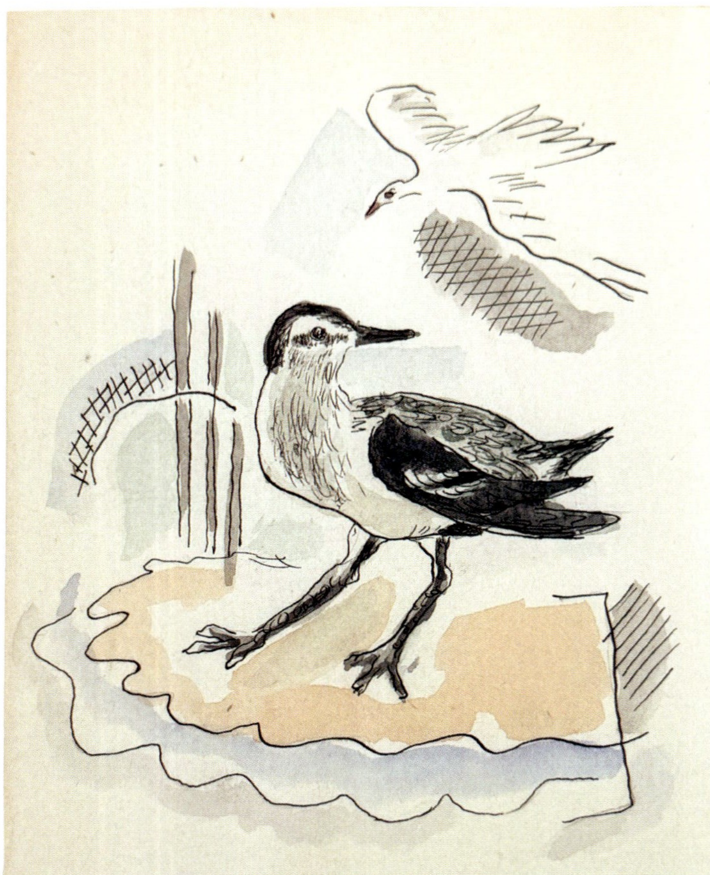

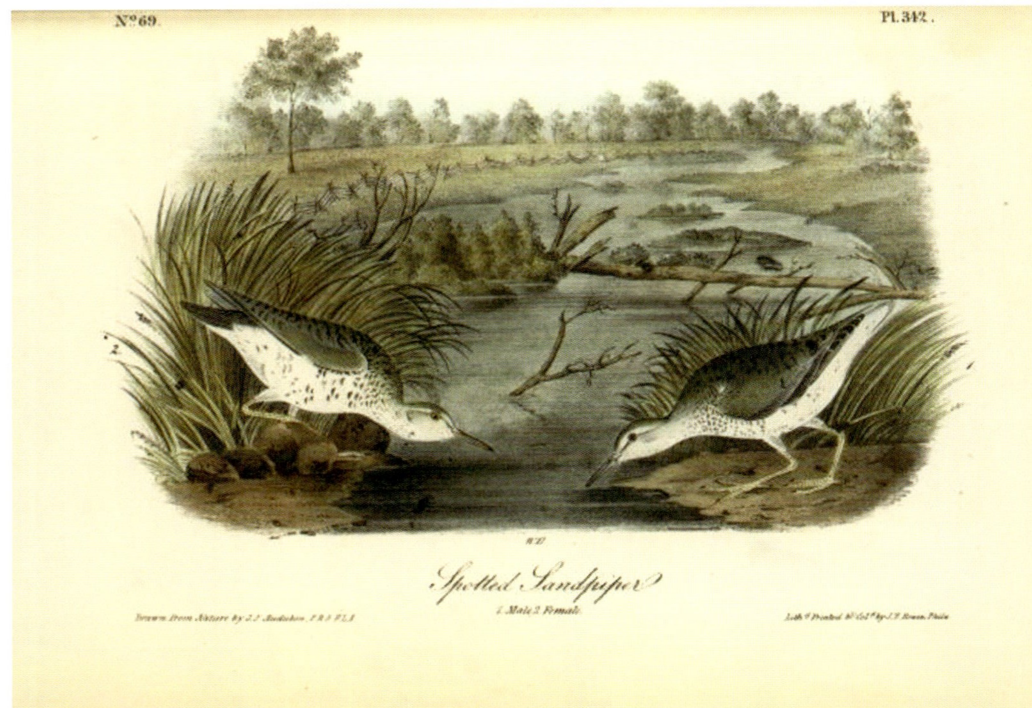

John James Audubon, *Spotted Sandpiper*, courtesy of New York Public Library.

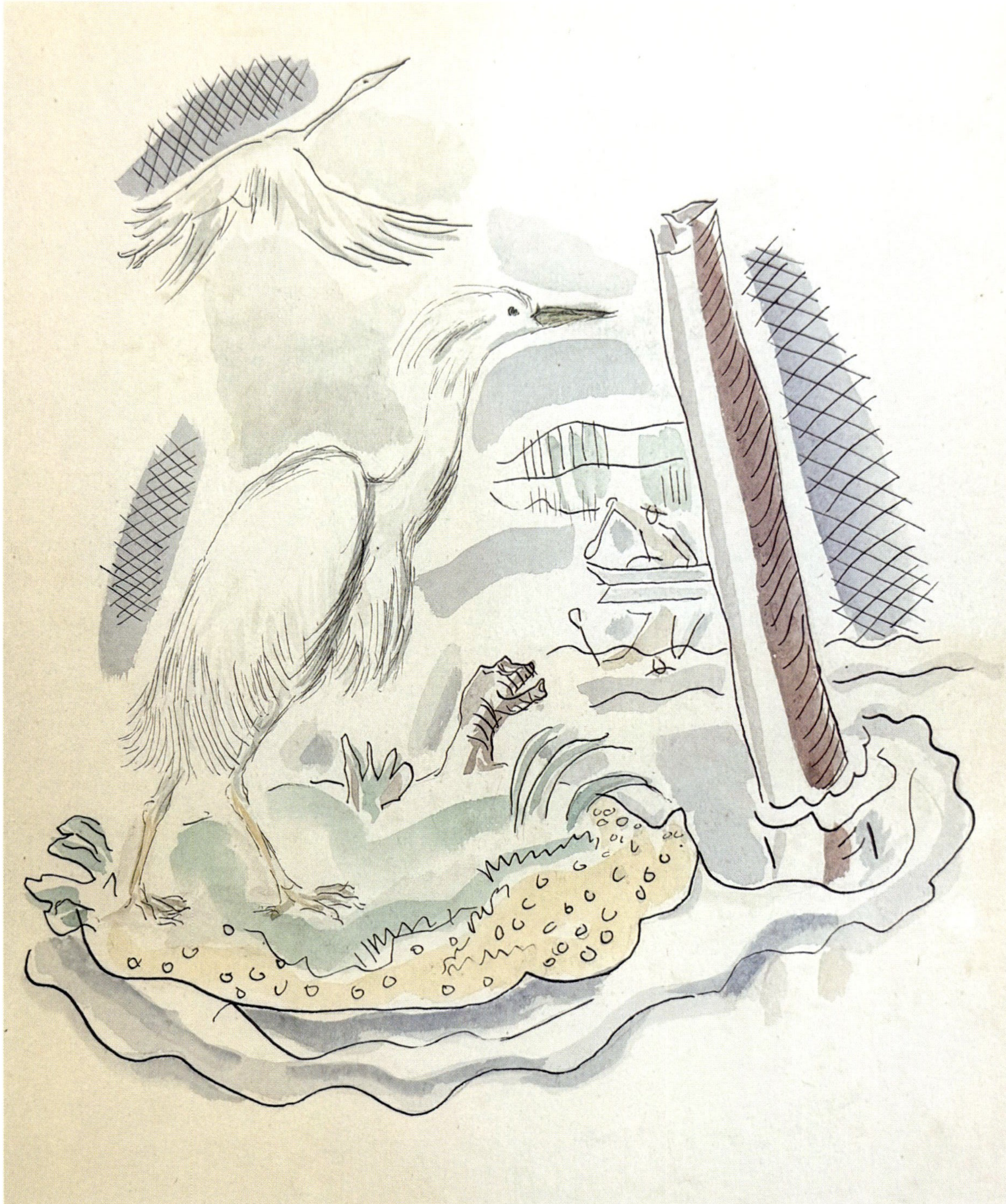

Haynes knew snowy egrets quite well from the Georgia marshes. In the background, it appears that a man in a canoe is attempting to help someone whose boat has capsized. Bartram doesn't describe such a mishap. He simply places the snowy egret among the rest of his bird list on page 293. Clearly, Haynes's egret was inspired by the pose of Audubon's bird. Both Bartram and Audubon grouped these birds with herons, as was common at the time, rather than egrets.

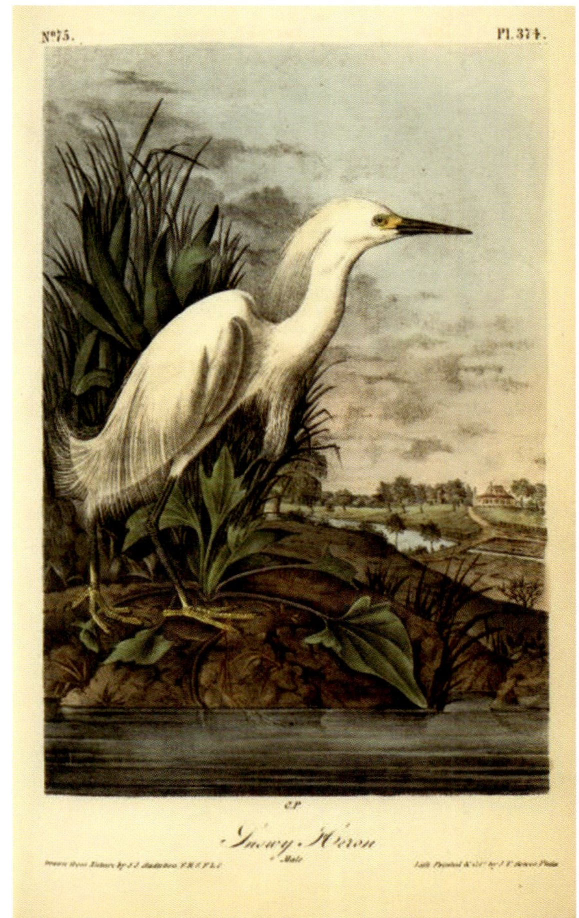

John James Audubon, *Snowy Egret*, courtesy of New York Public Library.

William Bartram sits in a boat at Blue Spring in Florida, admiring all the inhabitants—fish, alligator, eel, and shellfish—in its "absolutely diaphanous" waters.

> *Behold, for instance, a vast circular expanse before you, the waters of which are so extremely clear as to be absolutely diaphanous or transparent as the ether; the margin of the bason ornamented with a great variety of fruitful and floriferous trees, shrub and plants, the pendant golden Orange dancing on the surface of the pellucid waters, the balmy air vibrates the melody of the merry birds, tenants of the encircling aromatic grove.*
>
> *At the same instant innumerable bands of fish are seen, some cloathed in the most brilliant colours; the voracious crocodile stretched along at full length, as the great trunk of a tree in size, the devouring garfish, inimical trout, and all the varieties of gilded painted bream, the barbed catfish, dreaded sting-ray, skate and flounder, spotted bass, sheeps head and ominous drum; all in their seperate bands and communities, with free and unsuspicious intercourse performing their evolutions: there are no signs of enmity, no attempt to devour each other; the different bands seem peaceably and complaisantly to move a little aside, as it were to make room for others to pass by.*
>
> *But behold yet something far more admirable, see whole armies descending into an abyss, into the mouth of the bubbling fountain, they disappear! are they gone forever? is it real? I raise my eyes with terror and astonishment,—I look down again to the fountain with anxiety, when behold them as it were emerging from the blue ether of another world, apparently at a vast distance, at their first appearance, no bigger than flies or minnows, now gradually enlarging, their brilliant colours begin to paint the fluid.*
>
> *Now they come forward rapidly, and instantly emerge, with the elastic expanding column of chrystaline waters, into the circular bason or funnel, see now how gently they rise, some upright, others obliquely, or seem to lay as it were on their sides, suffering themselves to be gently lifted or born up, by the expanding fluid towards the surface, sailing or floating like butterflies in the cerulean ether: then again they as gently descend, diverge and move off; when they rally, form again and rejoin their kindred tribes.*
>
> *This amazing and delightful scene, though real, appears at first but as a piece of excellent painting; there seems no medium, you imagine the picture to be within a few inches of your eyes, and that you may without the least difficulty touch any one of the fish, or put your finger upon the crocodile's eye, when it really is twenty or thirty feet under water.*
>
> *And although this paradise of fish, may seem to exhibit a just representation of the peaceable and happy state of nature which existed before the fall, yet in reality it is a mere representation; for the nature of the fish is the same as if they were in lake George or the river; but here the water or element in which they live and move, is so perfectly clear and transparent, it places them all on an equality with regard to their ability to injure or escape from one another; (as all river fish of prey, or such as feed upon each other, as well as the unwieldy crocodile, take their prey by surprise; secreting themselves under covert or in ambush, until an opportunity offers, when they rush suddenly upon them:) but here is no covert, no ambush, here the trout freely passes by the very nose of the alligator and laughs in his face, and the bream by the trout.*
>
> *But what is really surprising, that the consciousness of each others safety or some other latent cause, should so absolutely alter their conduct, for here is not the least attempt made to injure or disturb one another. (166–168)*

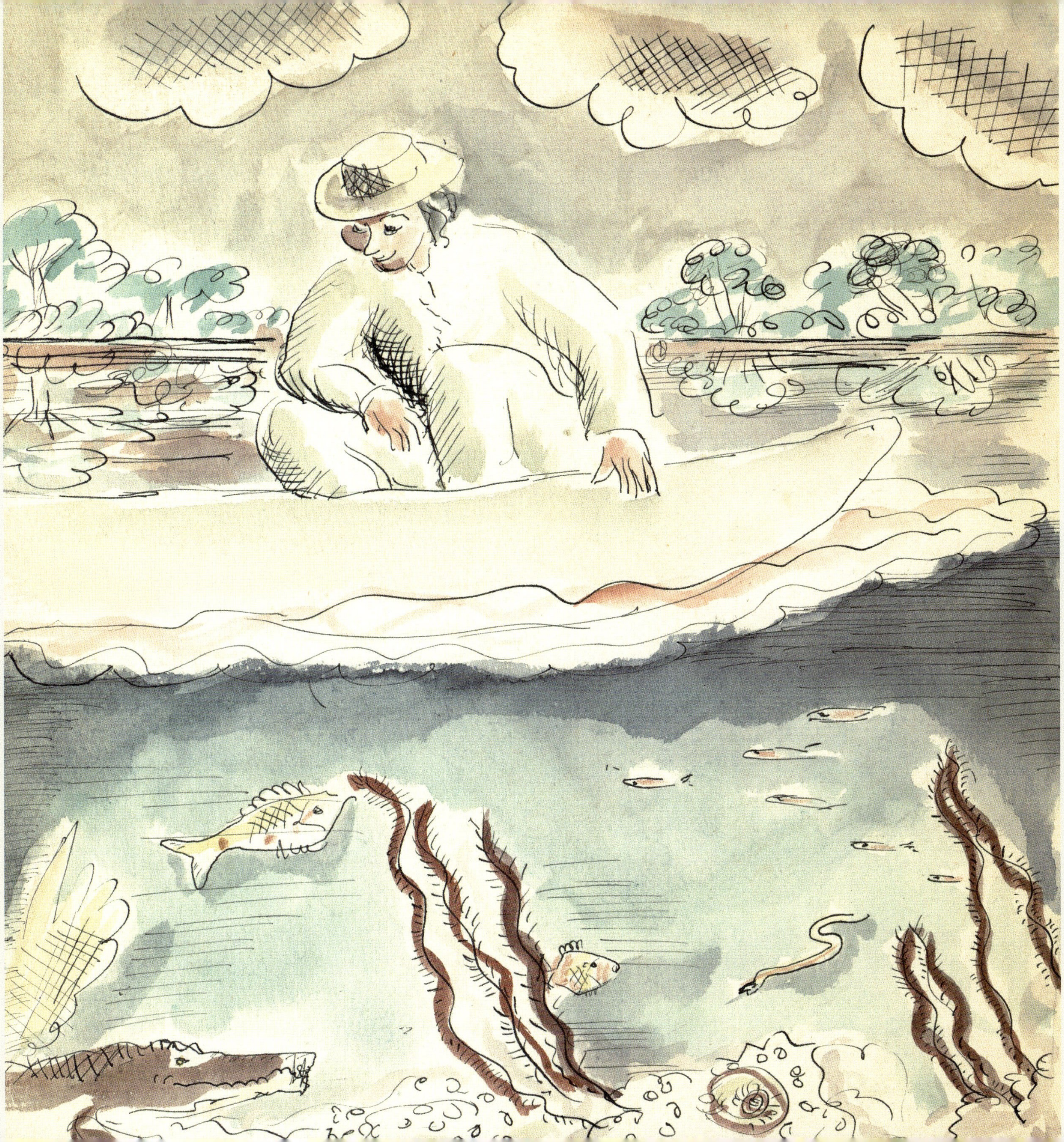

➢ Haynes was intimately familiar with fishing in tidal creeks and the Altamaha River itself. The following paintings come from the Ashantilly Center Archives.

➢ The Gullah-Geechee on neighboring Sapelo Island were famous for their handcrafted cast nets and seines. Here is one of Haynes's paintings from home showing an expert throwing a billowing cast net to haul in shrimp or baitfish. Note the fish seen just under the surface.

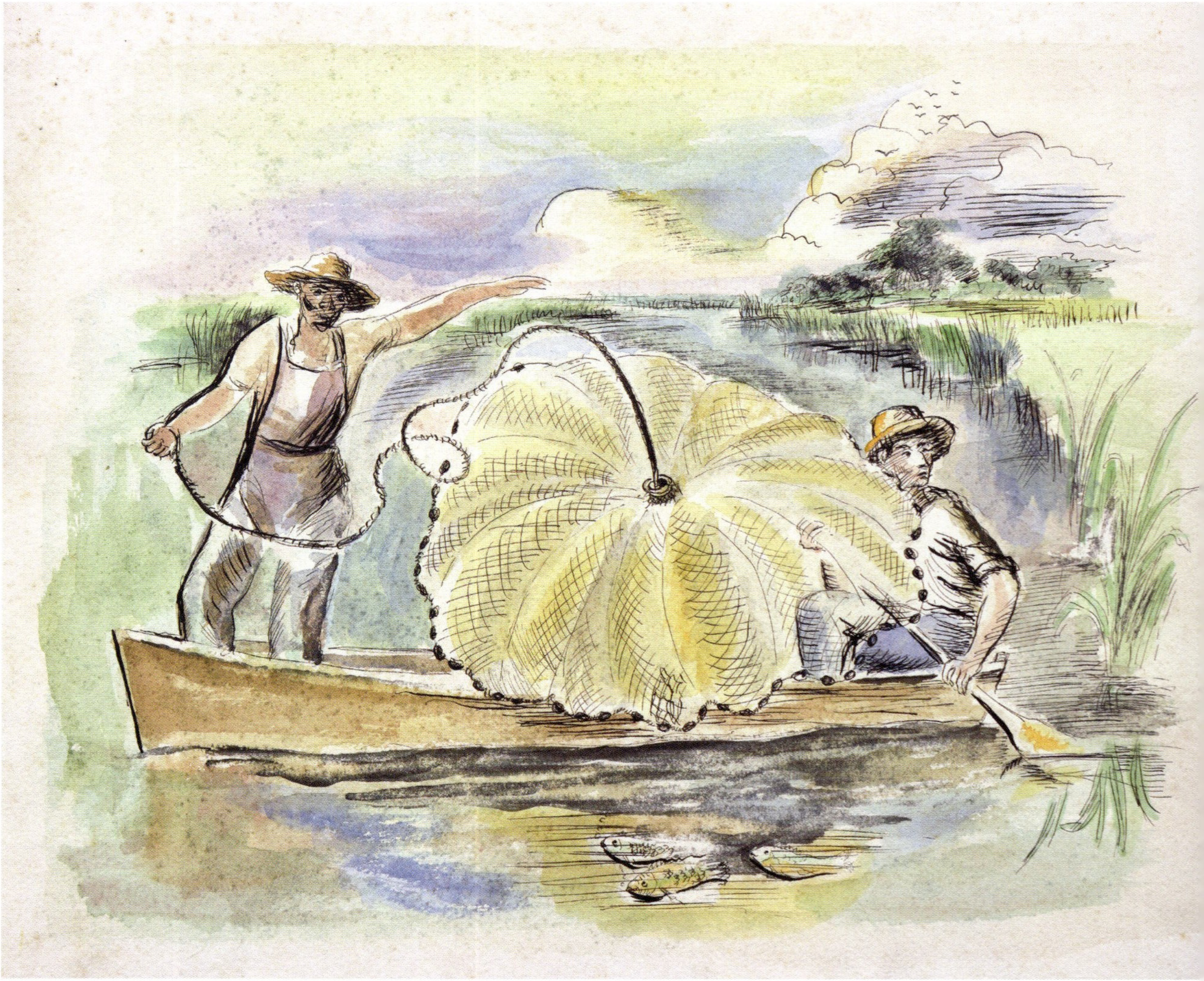

Ashantilly Center Archives.

Fishing was not an all-male enterprise. Here is Haynes's painting of three women working their crab traps.

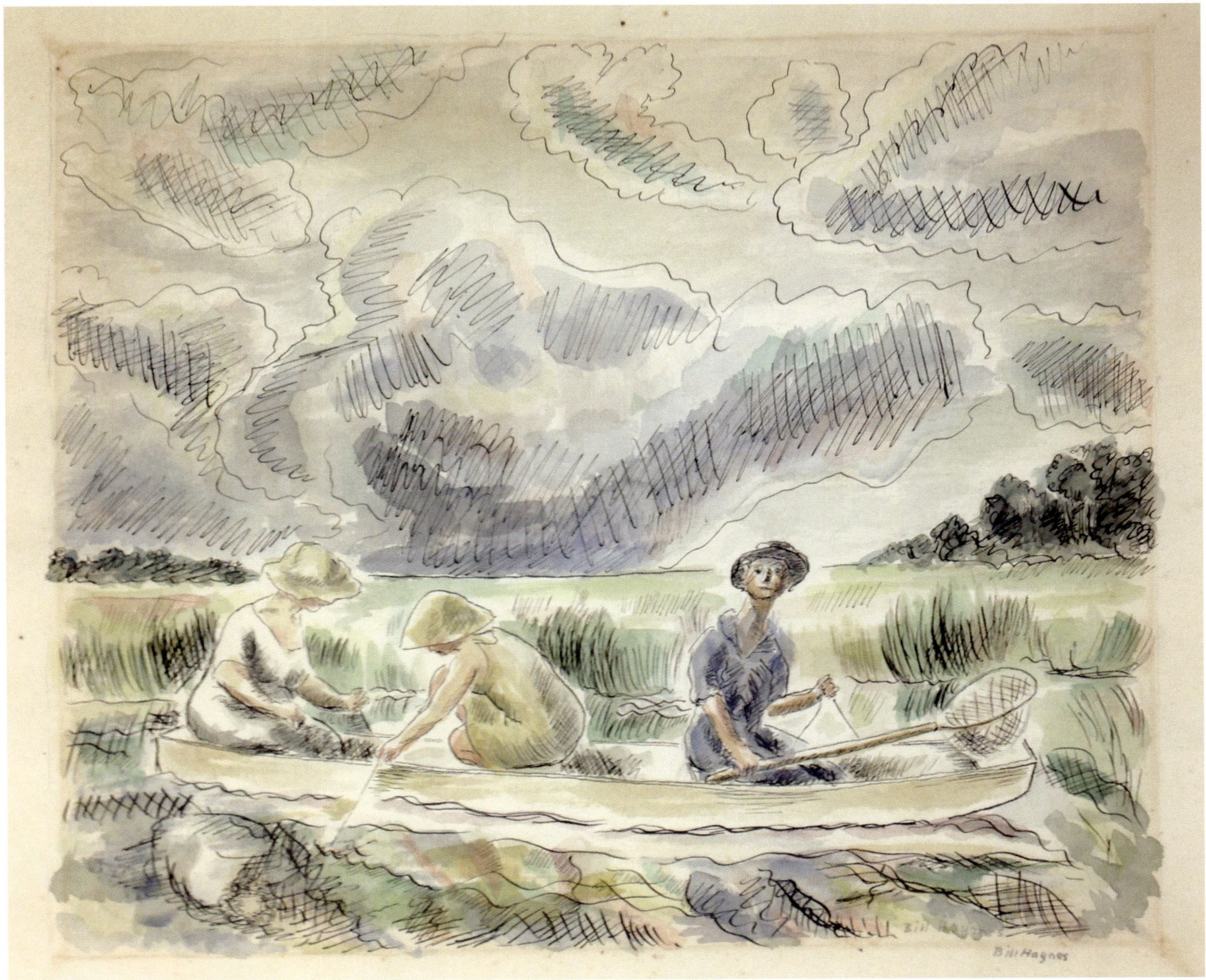

Ashantilly Center Archives.

Then there was fishing for mullet. The mouth of a mullet is so small that they are difficult to catch with a hook, so they often are caught in gill nets. Another method is to go out in a boat at night in the appropriate season and tide. Bring a lantern, but do not light it until you are in the "right" place. Once you are there, light the lantern and stand by. Finding the light irresistible, mullet will leap high out of the water and flop into the boat.

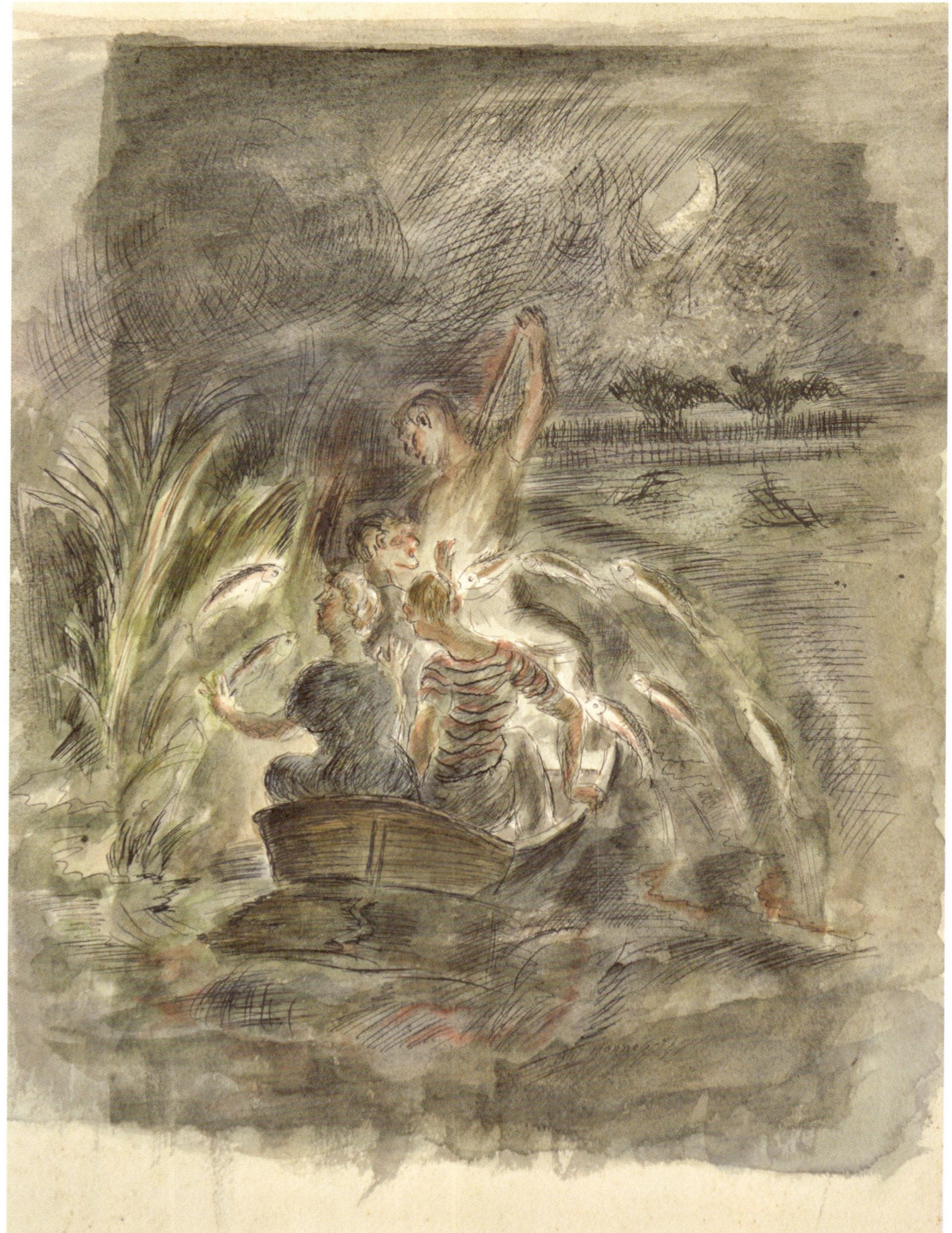

Ashantilly Center Archives.

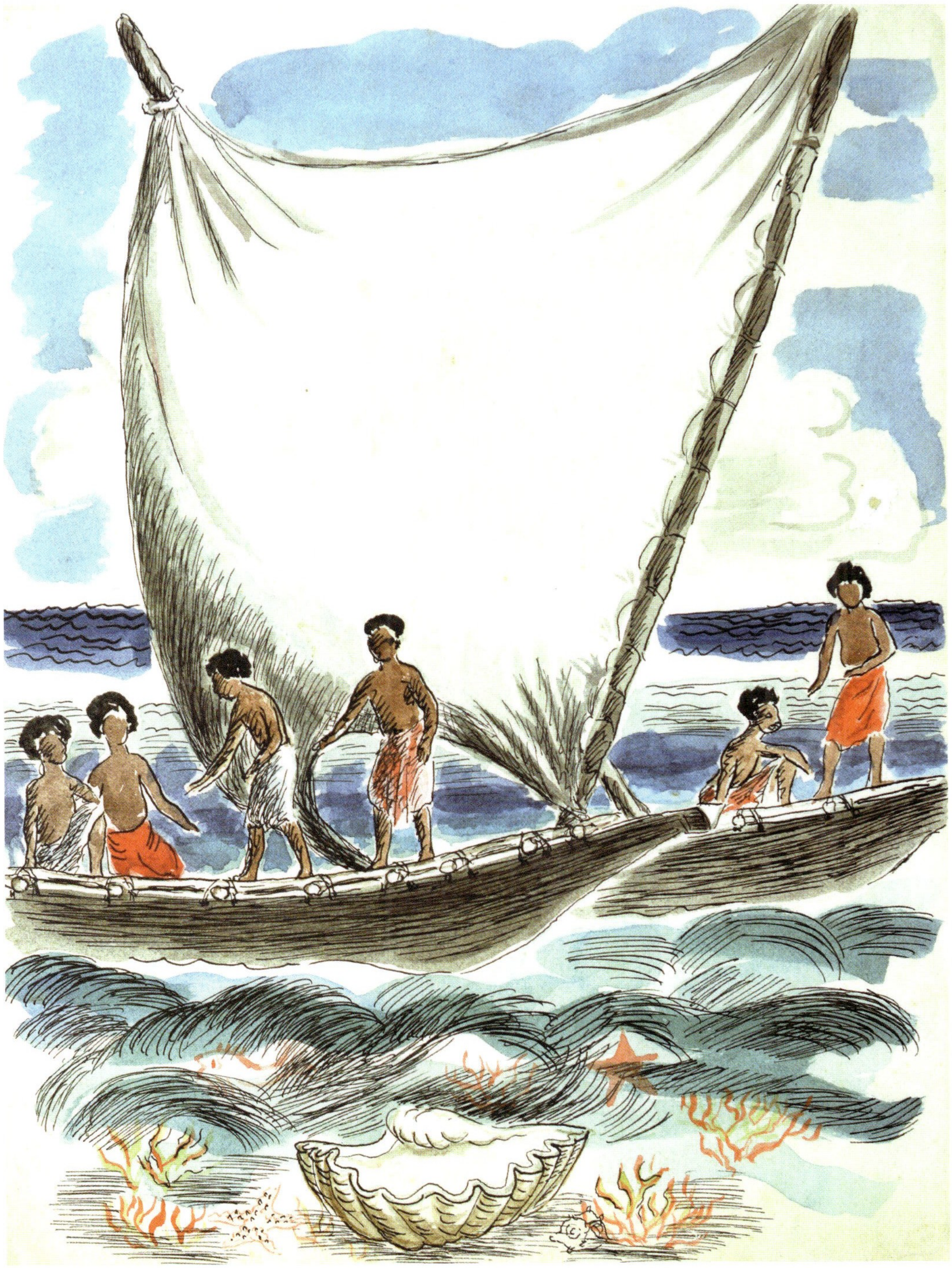

Unlike Bartram's rapturous descriptions of Florida springs, Haynes's home waters were hardly "diaphanous." So, he made the most of being stationed in New Guinea with its clear tropical sea to realize the dream he had of being able to see what was going on under the surface. At Milne Bay, he could witness the vitality Bartram saw in Florida's springs half a world away.

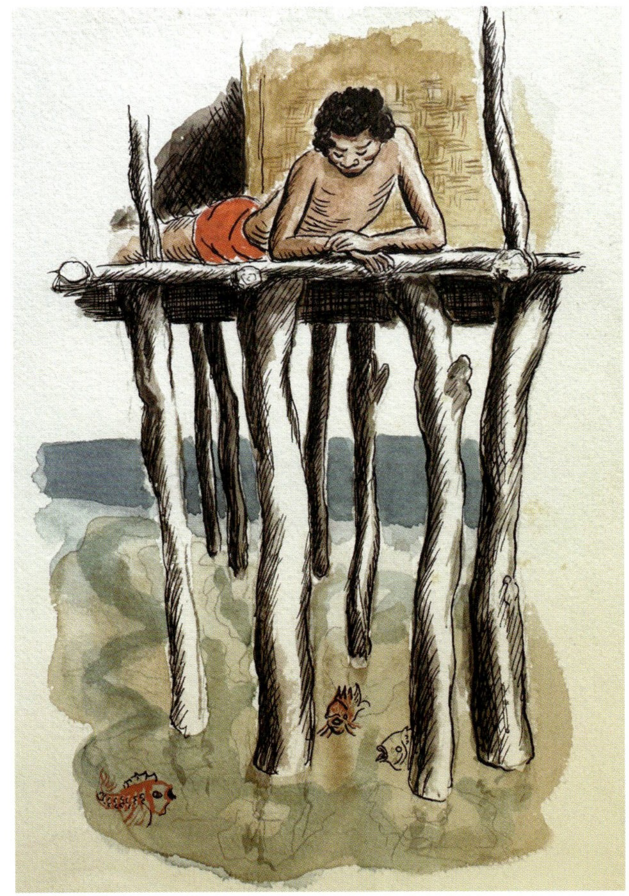

Ashantilly Center Archives.

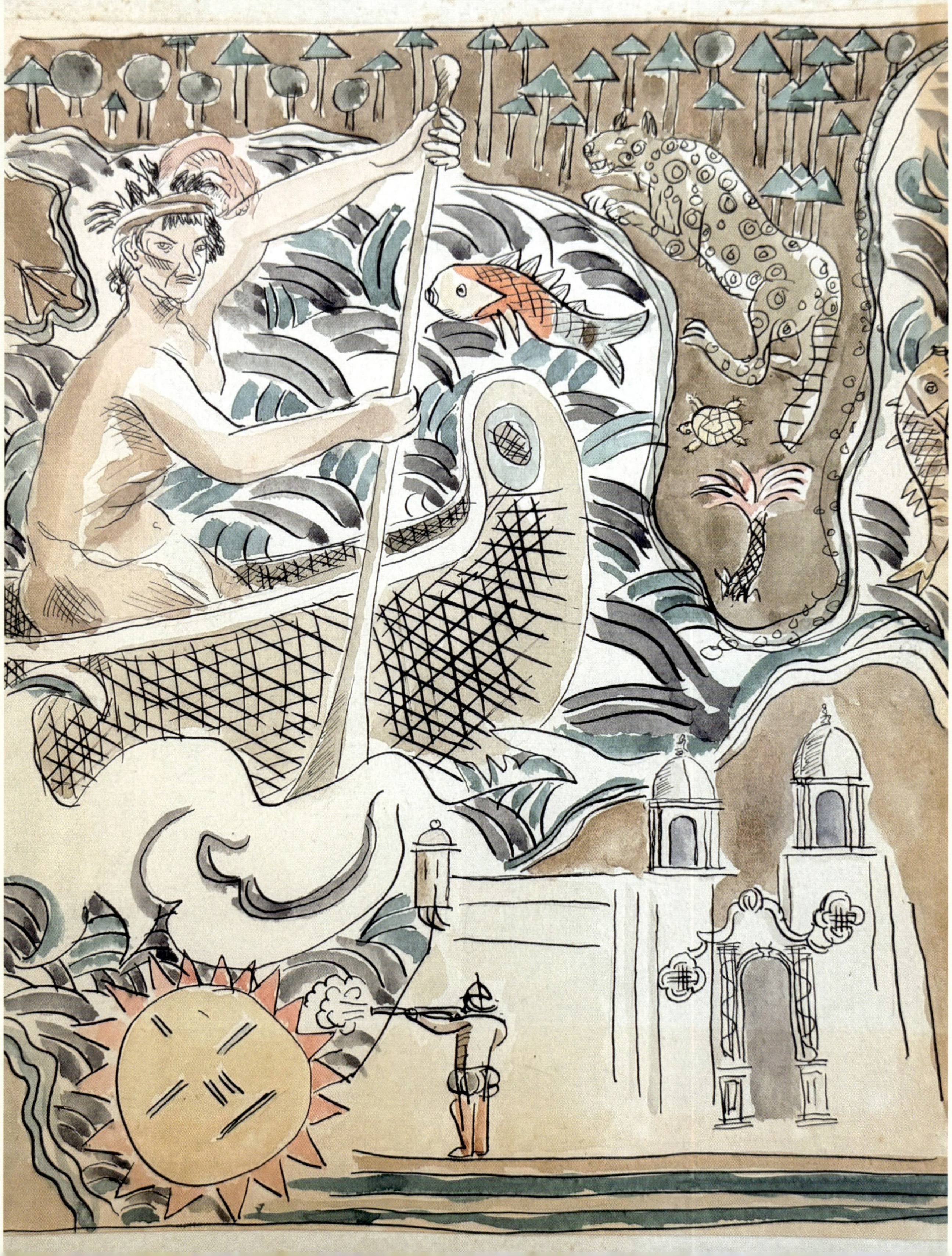

➢ During Haynes's years in New York, Art Deco and the influence of Mexican art, particularly that of muralist Diego Rivera, came to the forefront of the art scene. In one of his most visually stunning watercolors, Haynes reveals his interest in Art Deco in this portrayal of Florida. Outside the Castillo de San Marcos in St. Augustine, a Spanish soldier fires his weapon. An implacable, stylized sun sets in the west beneath a fast-approaching Seminole in his dugout. All around the peninsula the water churns, with fish leaping from the waves. The land is studded with stylized pines and palms. And that icon of the pre-Columbian South—a great spotted cat (perhaps an ocelot or jaguar)—slinks north up Florida's spine. Even a turtle makes an appearance, apparently headed west to the Gulf of Mexico.

Bartram visited St. Augustine numerous times, both with his father and later on his own, and was quite interested in the construction materials used in the Castillo.

> *The stone was cut out of quarries, on St. Anastatius [Anastasia] Island, opposite St. Augustine: it is of a pale redish brick colour, and a testacious composition, consisting of small fragments of sea-shells and fine sand. It is well adapted to the constructing of fortifications. It lies in horizontal masses in the quarry, and constitutes the foundation of that island. The castle at St. Augustine, and most of the buildings of the town, are of this stone. (80)*

He also described the importance of the symbolism of the wildcat to the Seminoles as well as the ancestors of the Southeastern tribes.

> *Tobacco and pipes are brought. The skin of a wild cat or young tyger stuffed with Tobacco is brought, and laid at the king's feet, with the great or royal pipe beautifully adorned; the skin is usually of the animals of the king's family or tribe, as the wild-cat, otter, bear, rattle-snake, &c. (453)*

Ocelots ranged as far east as western Louisiana during the 1800s. Based on fossils and preserved trackways, the extinct ancestors of today's jaguars were present as far east as Tennessee from the Early Pleistocene to the Early Holocene (1.8 million years ago to 10,000 years ago) overlapping in time with early human occupation of the Southeast. Examples of spotted cat imagery are found among cultural artifacts dating to the Middle Woodland to Mississippian periods (100 BCE to 1600 CE). Often these artifacts are found interred with the deceased.

For more information on spotted cat imagery, see W. Raymond Wood, "The Jaguar Gorget: The Missouri State Artifact," *Missouri Archaeological Society Quarterly* 17, no. 2 (April–June 2000): 8–11, https://anthromuseum.missouri.edu/e-exhibits/jaguar-gorget-missouri-state-artifact.

Bartram is seated next to his interpreter, taking in the festive activities in preparation for a ball-play contest the following day.

> *About the close of the evening I accompanied Mr. Galahan and other white traders to the rotunda, where was a grand festival, music and dancing. This assembly was held principally to rehearse the ball-play dance, this town being challenged to play against another the next day.*
>
> *The people being assembled and seated in order, and the musicians having taken their station, the ball opens, first with a long harangue or oration, spoken by an aged chief, in commendation of the manly exercise of the ball-play, recounting the many and brilliant victories which the town of Cowe had gained over the other towns in the nation, not forgetting or neglecting to recite his own exploits, together with those of other aged men now present, coadjutors in the performance of these athletic games in their youthful days.*
>
> *This oration was delivered with great spirit and eloquence, and was meant to influence the passions of the young men present, excite them to emulation and inspire them with ambition.*
>
> *This prologue being at an end, the musicians began, both vocal and instrumental, when presently a company of girls, hand in hand, dressed in clean white robes and ornamented with beads, bracelets and a profusion of gay [ribbons], entering the door, immediately began to sing their responses in a gentle, low and sweet voice, and formed themselves in a semicircular file or line, in two ranks, back to back, facing the spectators and musicians, moving slowly round and round; this continued about a quarter of an hour, when we were surprised by a sudden very loud and shrill whoop, uttered at once by a company of young fellows, who came in briskly after one another, with rackets or hurls in one hand. These champions likewise were well dressed, painted and ornamented with silver bracelets, gorgets and wampum, neatly ornamented with moccasins and high waving plumes in their diadems, who immediately formed themselves in a semicircular rank also, in front of the girls, when these changed their order, and formed a single rank parallel to the men, raising their voices in responses to the tunes of the young champions, the semicircles continually moving round. There was something singular and diverting in their step and motions, and I imagine not to be learned to exactness but with great attention and perseverance; the step, if it can be so termed, was performed after the following manner, i.e. first, the motion began at one end of the semicircle, gently rising up and down upon their toes and heels alternately, when the first was up on tip-toe, the next began to raise the heel, and by the time the first rested again on the heel, the second was on tip toe, thus from one end of the rank to the other, so that some were always up and some down, alternately and regularly, without the least baulk or confusion; and they at the same time, and in the same motion, moved on obliquely or sideways, so that the circle performed a double or complex motion in its progression, and at stated times exhibited a grand or universal movement, instantly and unexpectedly to the spectators, by each rank turning to right and left, taking each others places; the movements were managed with inconceivable alertness and address, and accompanied with an instantaneous and universal elevation of the voice and shrill short whoop.* (369–371)
>
> *These people like all other nations, are fond of music and dancing: their music is both vocal and instrumental; but of the latter they have scarcely any thing worth the name, the tambour, rattle-gourd, and a kind of flute, made of a joint of reed or the tibia of the deers leg: on this instrument they perform badly, and at best it is rather a hideous melancholy discord, than harmony; it is only young fellows who amuse themselves on this howling instrument, but the tambour and rattle, accompanied with their sweet low voices, produces a pathetic harmony, keeping exact time together, and the countenance of the musician, at proper times, seems to express the solemn elevated state of the mind; at that time there seems not only a harmony between*

him and his instrument, but instantly touches the feelings of the attentive audience, as the influence of an active and powerful spirit; there is then an united universal sensation of delight and peaceful union of souls throughout the assembly.

Their music, vocal and instrumental, united, keeps exact time with the performers or dancers.

They have an endless variety of steps, but the most common, and that which I term the most civil, and indeed the most admired and practiced amongst themselves, is a slow shuffling alternate step; both feet move forward one after the other, first the right foot foremost, and next the left, moving one after the other, in two opposite circles, i.e. first a circle of young men, and within a circle of young women moving together opposite ways, the men with the course of the sun, and the females contrary to it, the men strike their arm with the open hand, and the girls clap hands, and raise their shrill sweet voices, answering an elevated shout of the men at stated times of termination of the stanzas; and the girls perform an interlude or chorus separately.

They have songs to accompany their dances, of different classes, as martial, bacchanalian and amorous, which last I must confess, are extravagantly libidinous, and they have moral songs, which seem to be the most esteemed and practised, and answer the purpose of religious lectures. (504–506)

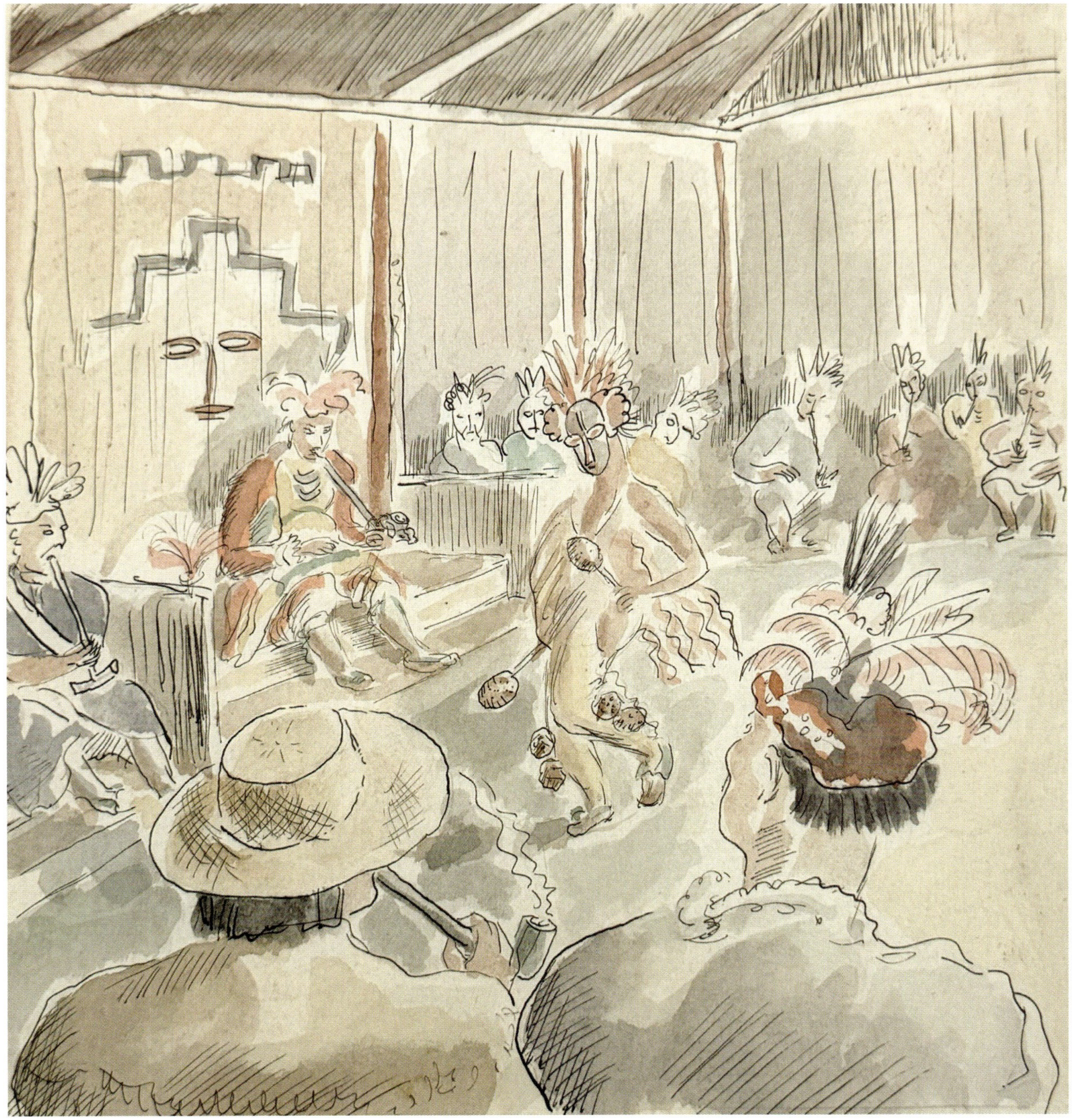

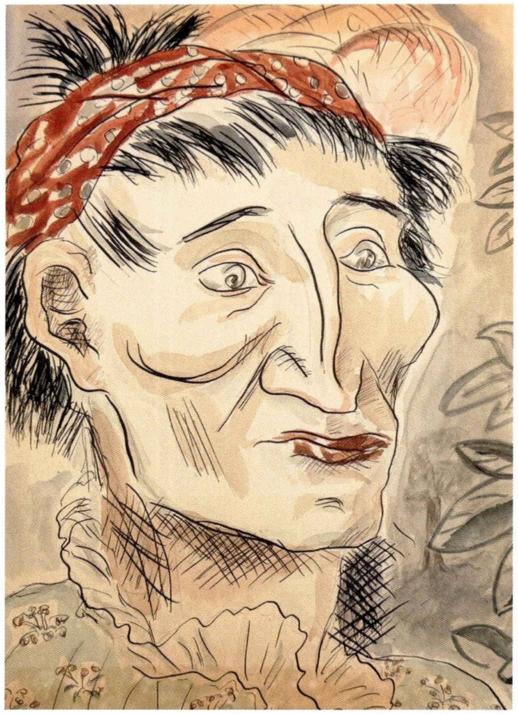

This is Haynes's full-face caricature of the interpreter seated next to Bartram in the rotunda. Note here that Haynes shows more detail in the man's dress, clearly incorporating the printed cloth, ruffled shirt, and Haynes's highly prized red feathers seen in other of his paintings (see, e.g., page 114). It may be based on his earlier portrait of Tachee (page 104), this time imagined as a much older, wizened man.

The Seminoles used narrow dugouts that easily slipped between the tall reeds in Florida's coastal swamps. They also conducted a thriving trade with the Spanish in Cuba. Using double-hulled canoes, they maneuvered coastwise south along the Florida peninsula and then erected a stepped mast to sail and paddle the ninety-mile crossing through the Florida Straits. They traded animal skins, bear oil, and honey in exchange for tobacco and liquor. For more details, see James W. Covington, "Trade Relations between Southwest Florida and Cuba, 1600–1840," *Florida Historical Quarterly* 38, no. 2 (1959): 114–128.

Haynes painted Seminoles paddling a very large "voyaging" canoe. Unfortunately, he pictured the canoes with a high curved bow and stern, a design like those used by the French voyageurs in North America, not those used by the Seminoles.

These Indians have large handsome canoes, which they form out of the trunks of Cypress trees (Cupressus disticha) some of them commodious enough to accom[m]odate twenty or thirty warriors. In these large canoes they descend the river on trading and hunting expeditions on the sea coast, neighbouring islands and keys, quite to the point of Florida, and sometimes cross the gulph, extending their navigations to the Bahama islands and even to Cuba: a crew of these adventurers had just arrived, having returned from Cuba just a few days before our arrival, with a cargo of spiritous liquors, Coffee, Sugar, and Tobacco. One of them politely presented me with a choice piece of Tobacco, which he told me he had received from the governor of Cuba.

They deal in the way of barter, carrying with them deer skins, furs, dry fish, bees-wax, honey, bear's oil and some other articles. They say the Spaniards receive them very friendly, and treat them with the best spiritous liquors. (227)

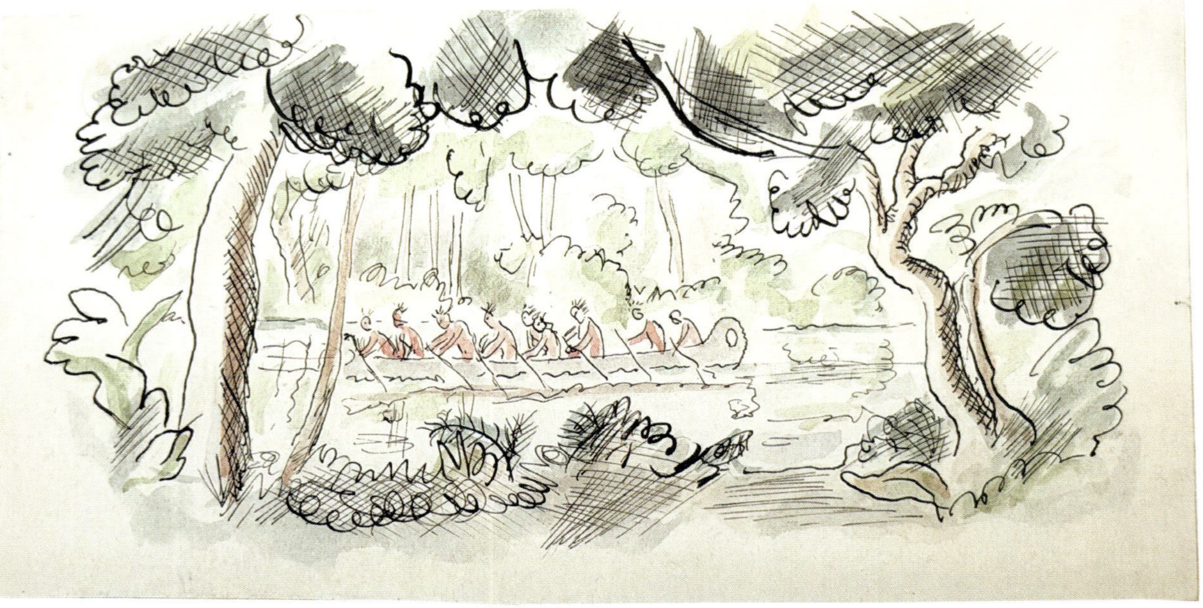

Haynes painted this serene scene near Whatoga, as Bartram is invited to enjoy Cherokee hospitality, resting beneath a pavilion with a beautiful view of the mountain landscape. Note the red bird again in flight.

During my continuance here, about half an hour, I experienced the most perfect and agreeable hospitality conferred on me by these happy people; I mean happy in their dispositions, in their apprehensions of rectitude with regard to our social or moral conduct: O divine simplicity and truth, friendship without fallacy or guile, hospitality disinterested, native, undefiled, unmodifyed by artificial refinements.

My venerable host gracefully and with an air of respect, led me into an airy, cool apartment, where being seated on cabins, his women brought in a refreshing repast, consisting of sodden venison, hot corn cakes, &c. with a pleasant cooling liquor made of hommony [sic] well boiled, mixed afterwards with milk; this is served up either before or after eating in a large bowl, with a very large spoon or ladle to sup it with.

After partaking of this simple but healthy and liberal collation and the dishes cleared off, Tobacco and pipes were brought, and the chief filling one of them, whose stem, about four feet long, was sheathed in a beautiful speckled snake skin, and adorned with feathers and strings of wampum, lights it and smoaks a few whiffs, puffing the smoak first towards the sun, then to the four cardinal points and lastly over my breast, hands it towards me, which I cheerfully received from him and smoaked, when we fell into conversation;

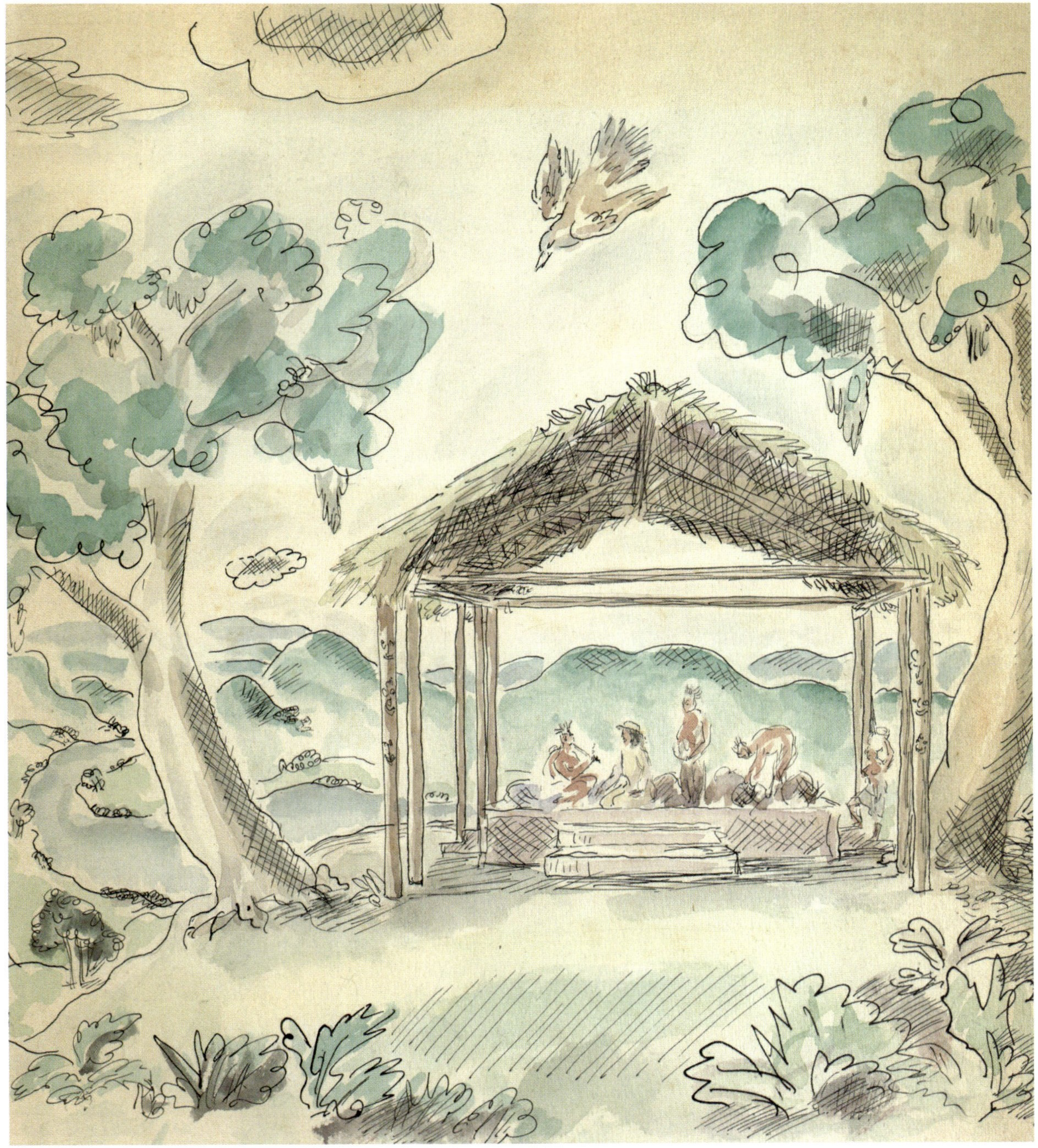

he first enquired if I came from Charleston? if I knew John Stewart, Esq,? how long since I left Charleston? &c. Having satisfied him in my answers in the best manner I could, he was greatly pleased, which I was convinced of by his attention to me, his cheerful manners and his ordering my horse a plentiful bait of corn, which last instance of respect is conferred on those only to whom they manifest the highest esteem, saying that corn was given by the Great Spirit only for food to man.

I acquainted this ancient prince and patriarch of the nature and design of my peregrinations, and that I was now for Cowe[e], but having lost my road in the town, requested that I might be informed. He cheerfully replied, that he was pleased I was come in their country, where I should meet with friendship and protection, and that he would himself lead me into the right path.

After ordering my horse to the door we went forth together, he on foot and I leading my horse by the bridle, thus walking together near two miles, we shook hands and parted, he returning home and I continuing my journey for Cowe[e]. (350–352)

➢ Bartram and a Seminole stand together in a deep forest, with the Carolina parakeet overhead. In his discussion of the bald cypress, Bartram indicated he was very familiar with the bird's food preferences. "Paroquets are commonly seen hovering and fluttering on their tops: they delight to shell these balls, its seed being their favourite food" (91–92).

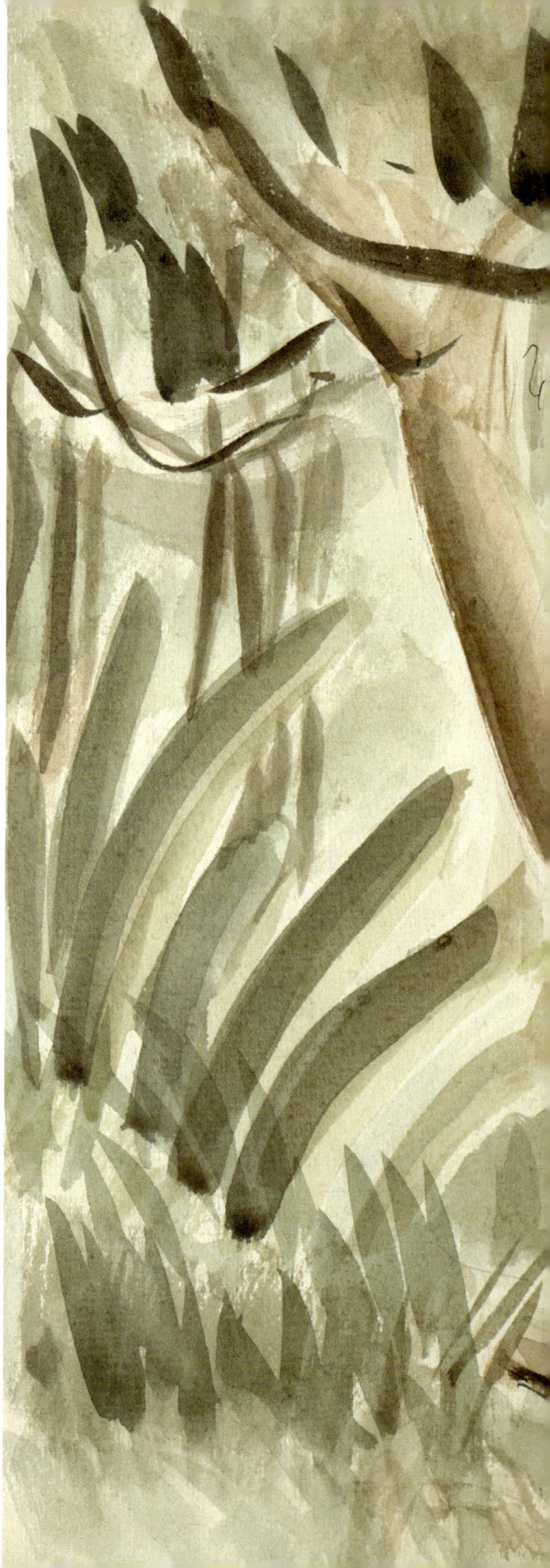

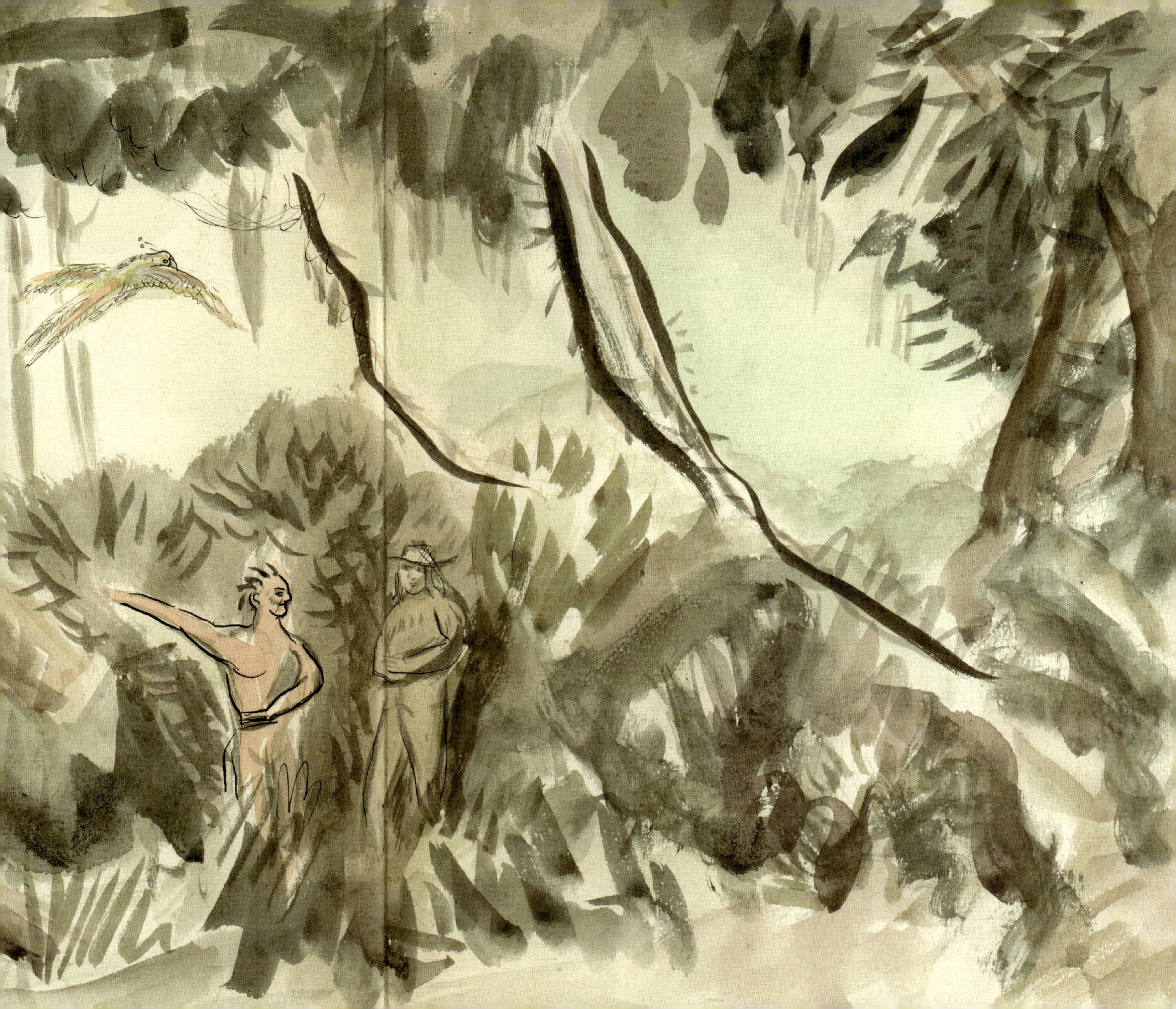

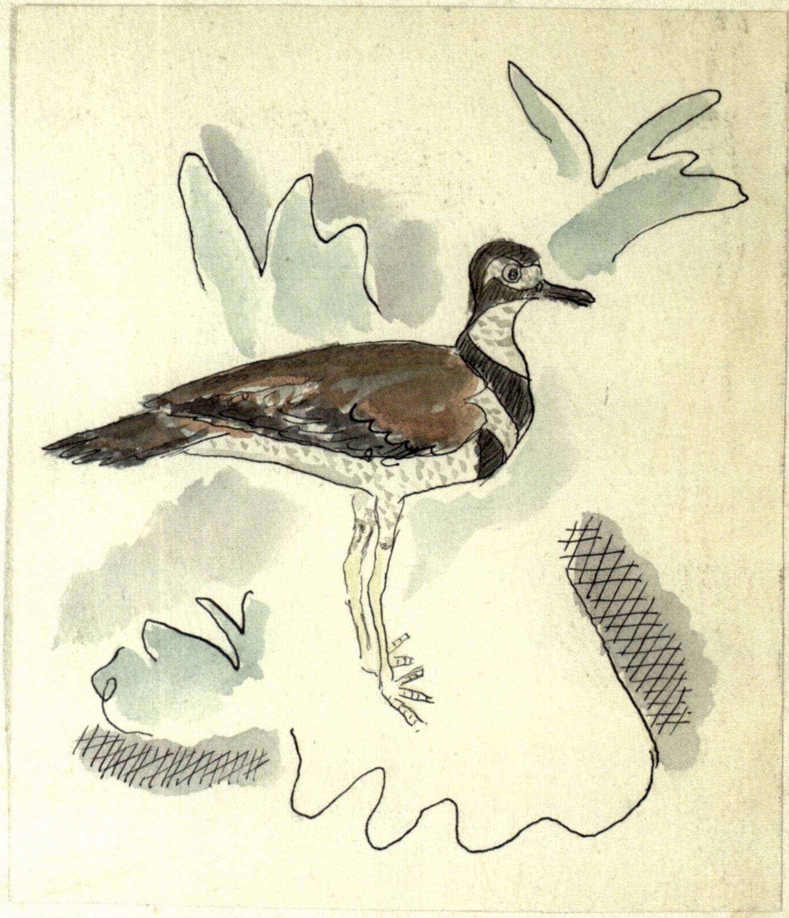

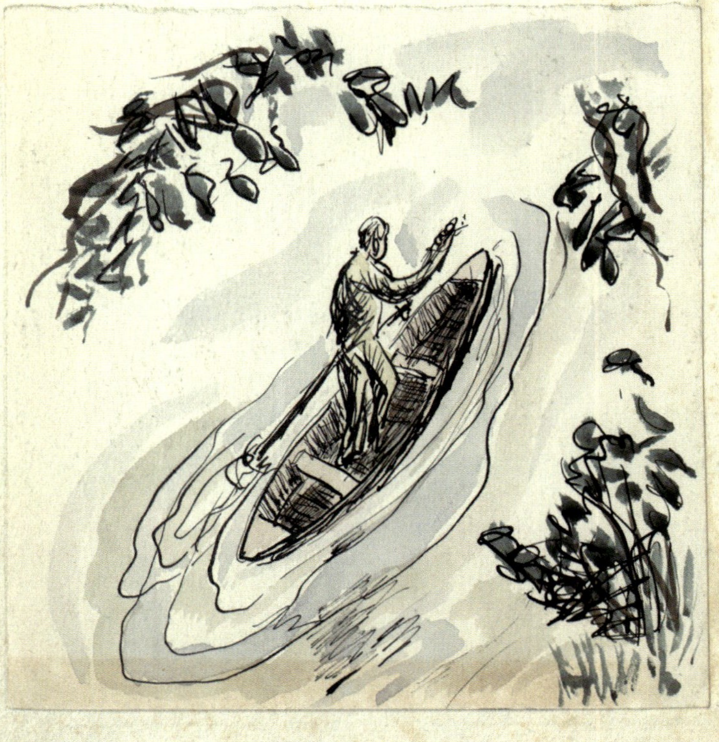

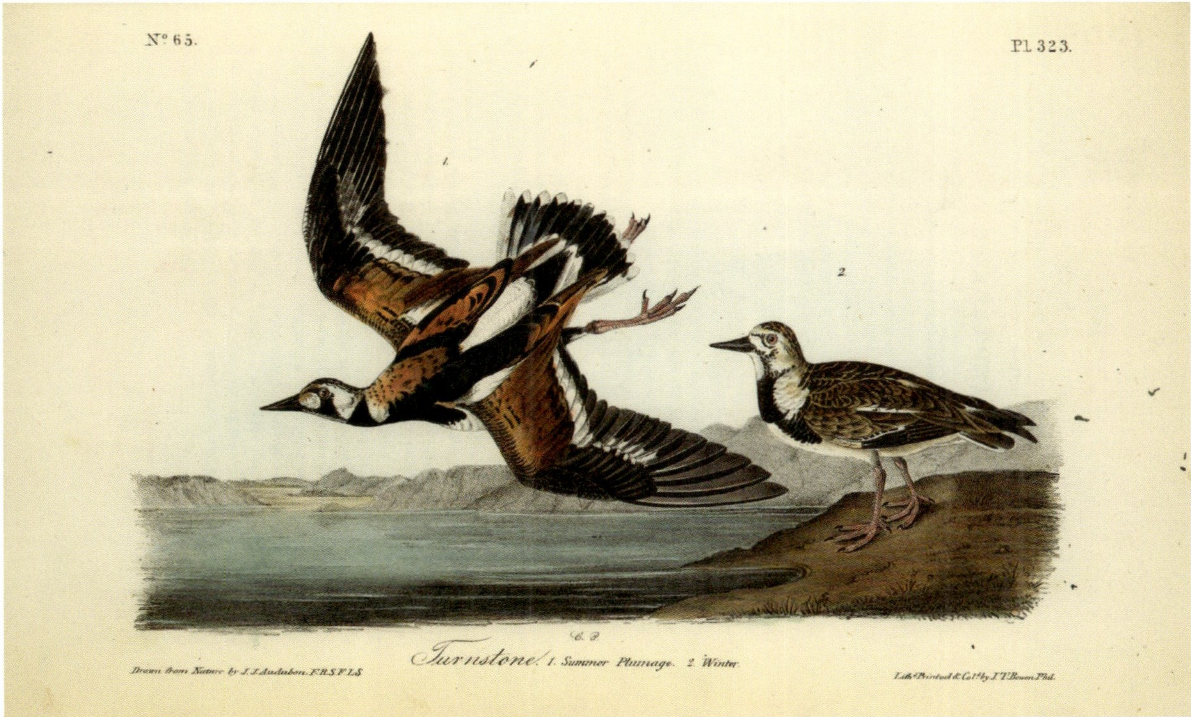

John James Audubon, *Ruddy Turnstone*, courtesy of New York Public Library.

The ruddy turnstone, a familiar shorebird of the Southeast coast, is listed only by Bartram at page 294, genus *Morinella*. At the bottom of the facing page, Bartram stands poling a bateau upstream. Again, Haynes's bird portrait is similar to that of Audubon.

➛ Beneath a magnolia tree, Bartram cuts a yucca flower stalk for his collection.

> *Just without the trees, betwixt them, the water and marshes, is a barricade of Palmetto royal (Yucca gloriosa) or Adam's needle, which grows so thick together, that a rat, or bird, can scarcely pass thro' them; and the stiff leaves of this Sword plant, standing nearly horizontally, are as impenetrable to man, or any other animal, as if they were a regiment of grenadiers with their bayonets pointed at you. The Palmetto royal is, however, a very singular and beautiful production. It may be termed a tree, from its durability and magnitude, as likewise from the ligneous quality of its stem, or trunk, when old; yet from its form and texture, I should be inclined to rank it amongst the herbaceous plants, for even the glorious Palm, although it rises to the altitude of a tree, and even transcends most of them, yet it bears the characters of the herbaceous ones: and this, like the Palm tree, rises with a strait, erect stem, about ten or twelve feet high, crowned with a beautiful chaplet of sword or dagger-like leaves, of a perfect green colour, each terminated with a stiff, sharp spur, and their edges finely crenated. This thorny crown is crested with a pyramid of silver white flowers, each resembling a tulip or lilly. These flowers are succeeded by a large fruit, nearly of the form and size of a slender cucumber, and when ripe, is of a deep purple colour, the skin smooth and shining, its pulp soft, very juicy, and of an agreeable aromatic flavour but rather bitter to the taste; it is, however, frequently eaten, but if eaten to excess, proves violently purgative. The seeds are numerous, flat and lunated.*
>
> *The plant, or tree, when grown old, sometimes divides into two or three stems, which seem of equal height and thickness, and indeed nearly of the same thickness with the main stem; but generally, when they arrive to this age and magnitude, their own weight brings them to the ground, where they soon decay, the heart or pith first, leaving a hollow fibrous reticulated trunk or sleeve, which likewise soon after decays, and in fine, all is again reduced to its original earth, and replaces the vegetative mould. But the deceased are soon replaced by others, as there are younger ones of all ages and stature, ready to succeed their predecessors, and flourish for a time, with the same regal pomp and splendor. These plants are so multitudinous, wherever they get a footing, that the earth is completely occupied with them, and scarcely any other vegetable is to be seen, where they are; yet they are sometimes scattered amongst other trees and vegetables. (71)*

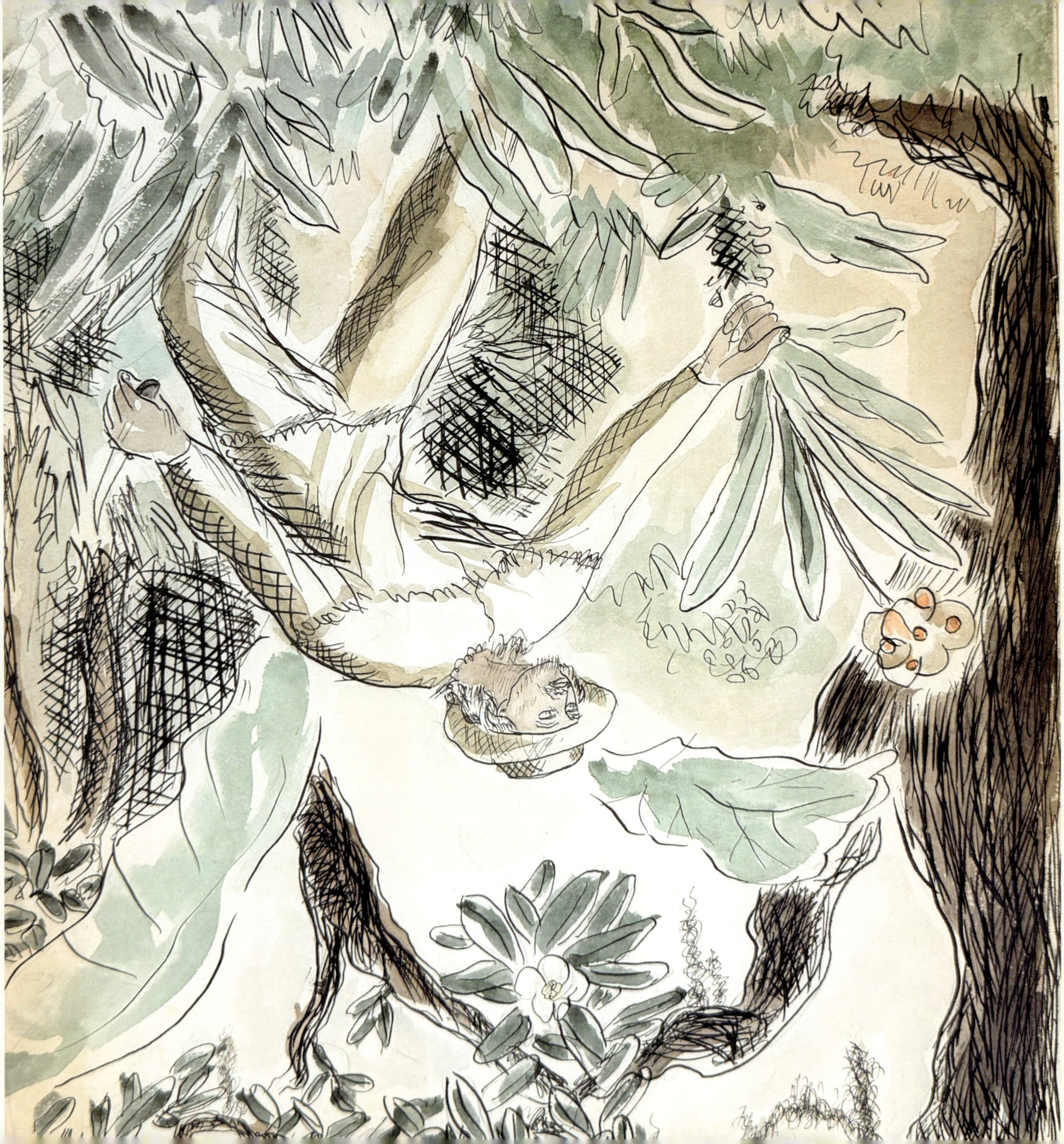

Perhaps Bartram's most famous find in Georgia is the shrub *Franklinia alatamaha*, named to honor both Benjamin Franklin and the Altamaha River ecosystem that supported the only known population ever found.

Fortunately, he sent seeds back to his family's botanical garden near Philadelphia where the Bartrams succeeded in cultivating *Franklinia* and sent specimens to plant collectors around the world. Despite diligent searches, botanists have not seen *Franklinia* in its wild Altamaha home since 1803. Every *Franklinia* we see today exists because of Bartram's small gesture of saving its seeds. Bartram described the showy, flowering shrub he saw in the summer of 1776, near Ft. Barrington in McIntosh County.

> *On first observing the fructification and habit of this tree, I was inclined to believe it a species of Gordonia, but afterwards, upon stricter examination, and comparing its flowers and fruit with those of the Gordonia lasianthus, I presently found striking characteristics abundantly sufficient to seperate it from that genus, and to establish it the head of a new tribe, which we have honoured with the name of the illustrious Dr. Benjamin Franklin, Franklinia Alatamaha.*
>
> *It is a flowering tree, of the first order for beauty and fragrance of blossoms: the tree grows fifteen or twenty feet high, branching alternately; the leaves are oblong, broadest towards their extremities, and terminate with an acute point, which is generally a little reflexed; they are lightly serrated, attenuate downwards and sessile, or have very short petioles; they are placed in alternate order, and towards the extremities of the twigs are crouded together, but stand more sparsedly below; the flowers are very large, expand themselves perfectly, are of a snow-white colour, and ornamented with a crown or tassel of gold coloured refulgent staminae in their centre; the inferior petal or segment of the corolla is hollow, formed like a cap or helmet, and entirely includes the other four, until the moment of expansion; its exterior surface is covered with a short silky hair; the borders of the petals are crisped or plicated: these large, white flowers stand single and sessile in the bosom of the leaves, which being near together towards the extremities of the twigs, and usually many expanded at the same time, make a gay appearance; the fruit is a large, round, dry, woody apple or pericarpe, opening at each end oppositely by five alternate fissures, containing ten cells, each replete with dry woody cuniform seed. This very curious tree was first taken notice of, about ten or twelve years ago, at this place, when I attended my father (John Bartram) on a botanical excursion; but, it being then late in the autumn, we could form no opinion to what class or tribe it belonged.*
>
> *We never saw it grow in any other place, nor have I ever since seen it growing wild, in all my travels, from Pennsylvania to Point Coupe, on the banks of the Mississip[p]i, which must be allowed a very singular and unaccountable circumstance; at this place there are two or three acres of ground where it grows plentifully. (467–468)*

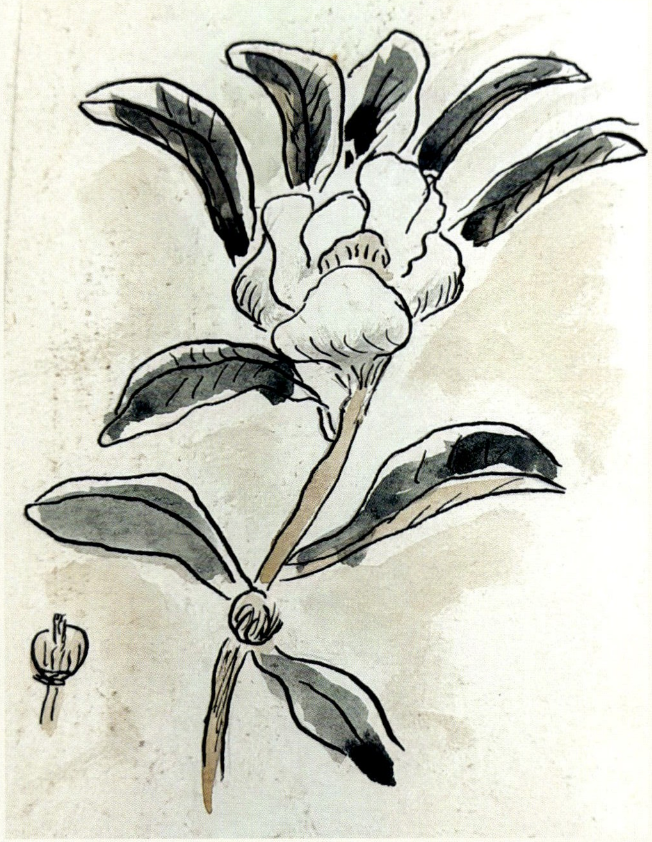

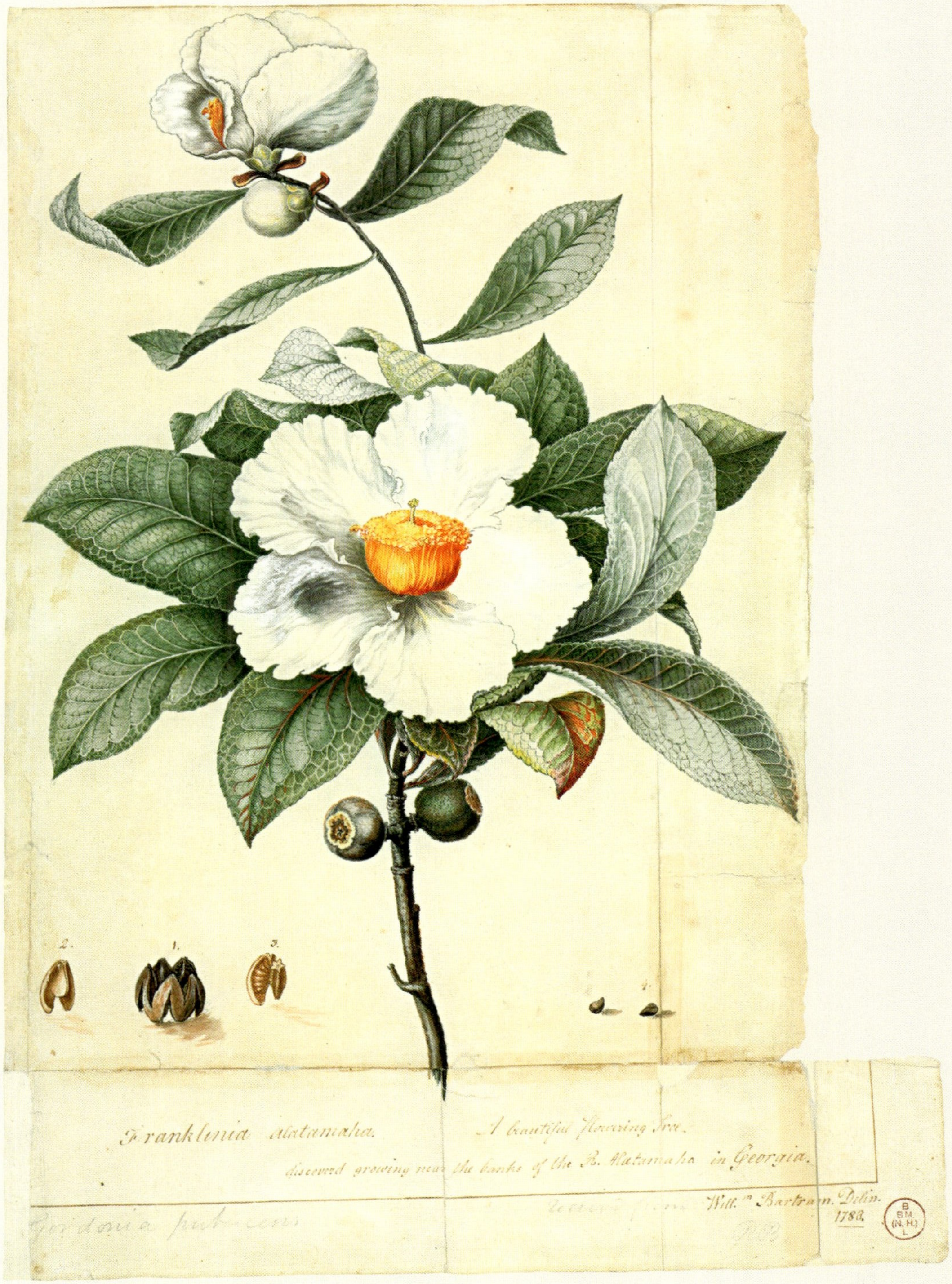

Trustees of the Natural History Museum, London.

Haynes includes a very abstract presentation of Indians beneath a palm tree, perhaps influenced by the modernist artists with whom he was acquainted in New York.

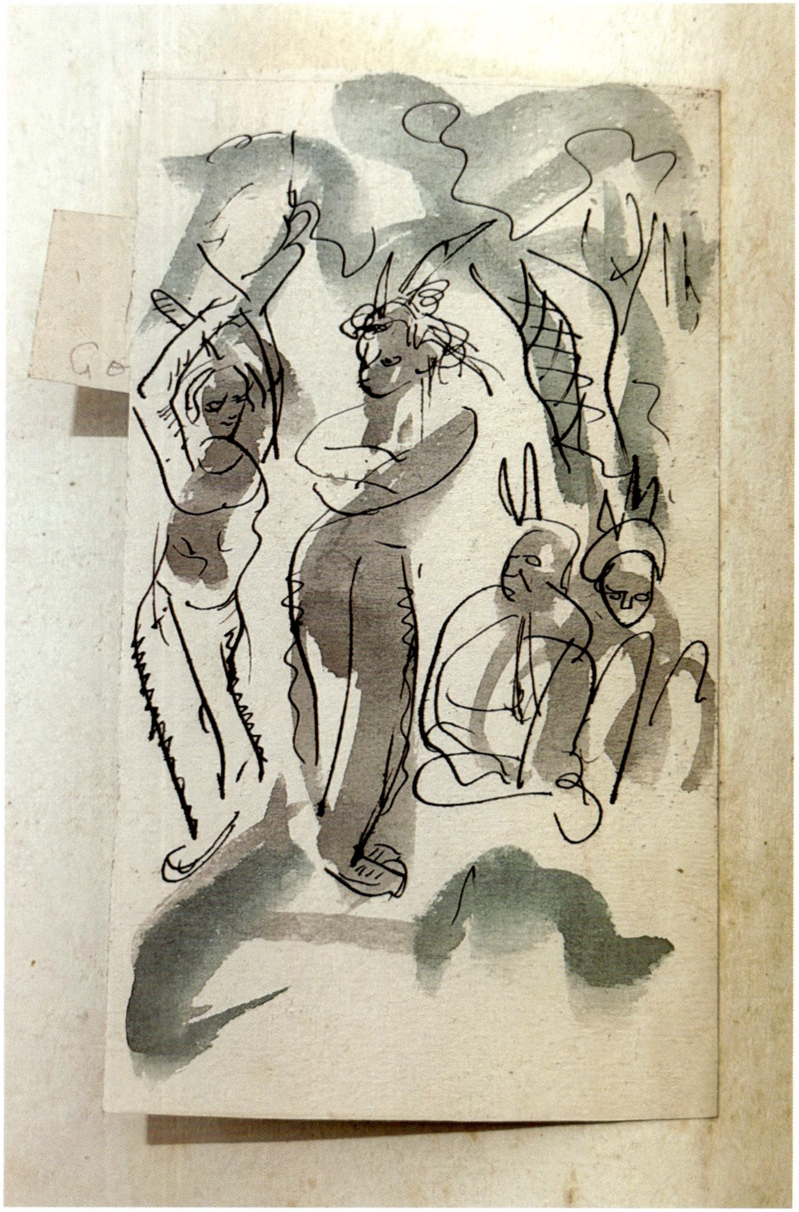

William Bartram greets a Seminole at the edge of the St. Johns River beneath a cypress.

On our return to camp in the evening, we were saluted by a party of young Indian warriors, who had pitched their camp on a green eminence near the lake, and at a small distance from our camp, under a little grove of Oaks and Palms. This company consisted of seven young Siminoles, under the conduct of a young prince or chief of Talahasochte, a town Southward in the isthmus, they were all dressed and painted with singular elegance, and richly ornamented with silver plates, chains, &c. after the Siminole mode, with waving plumes of feathers on their crests. On our coming up to them they arose and shook hands; we alighted and sat a while with them by their cheerful fire. (244)

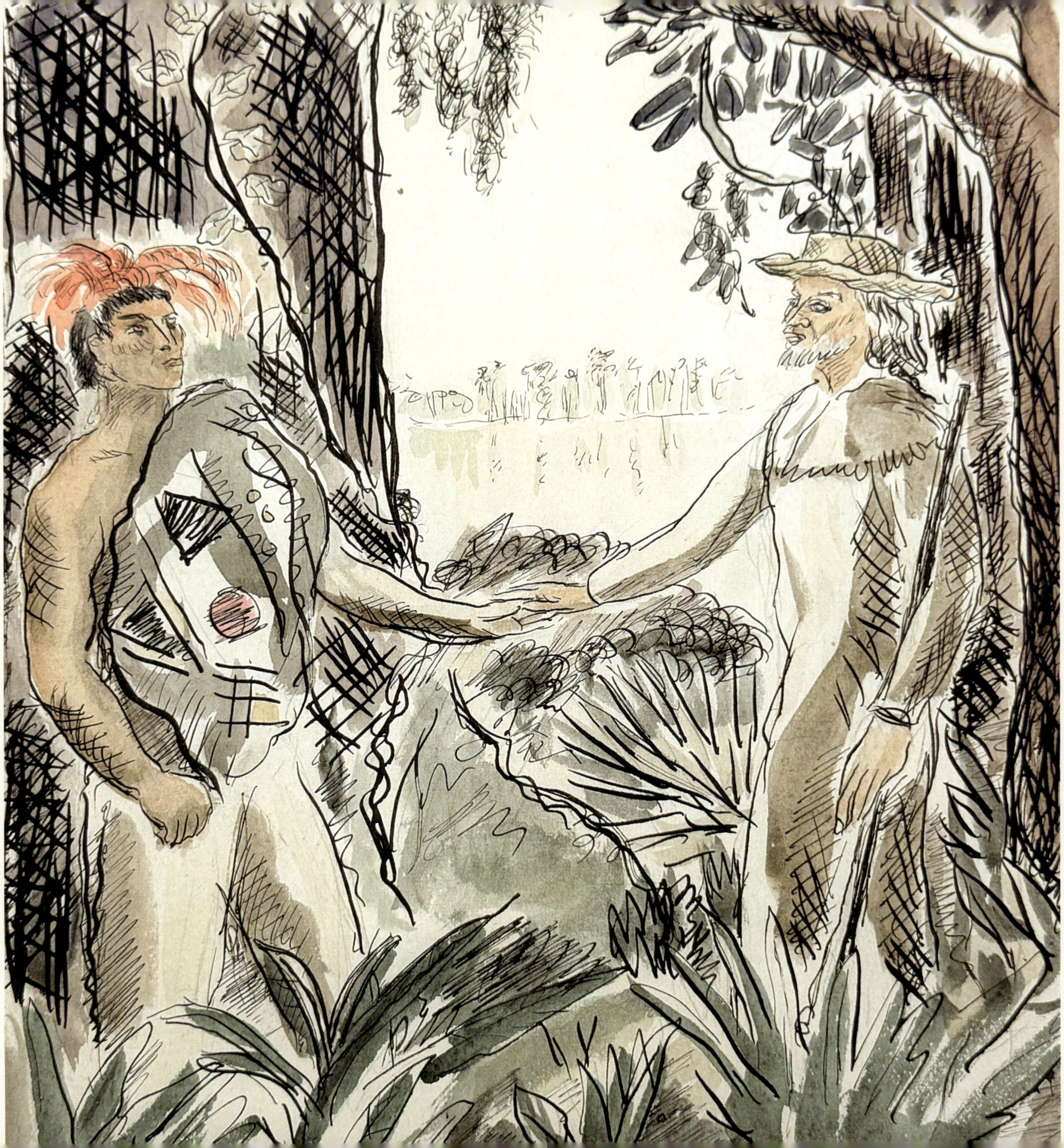

Haynes closes his collection of paintings in the same style as William Bartram: "Finis"—adding an oval enclosing a *Franklinia* blossom, dead duck (perhaps a blue-wing teal), "fusee" (or gun), Bartram's hat, and shoulder bag.

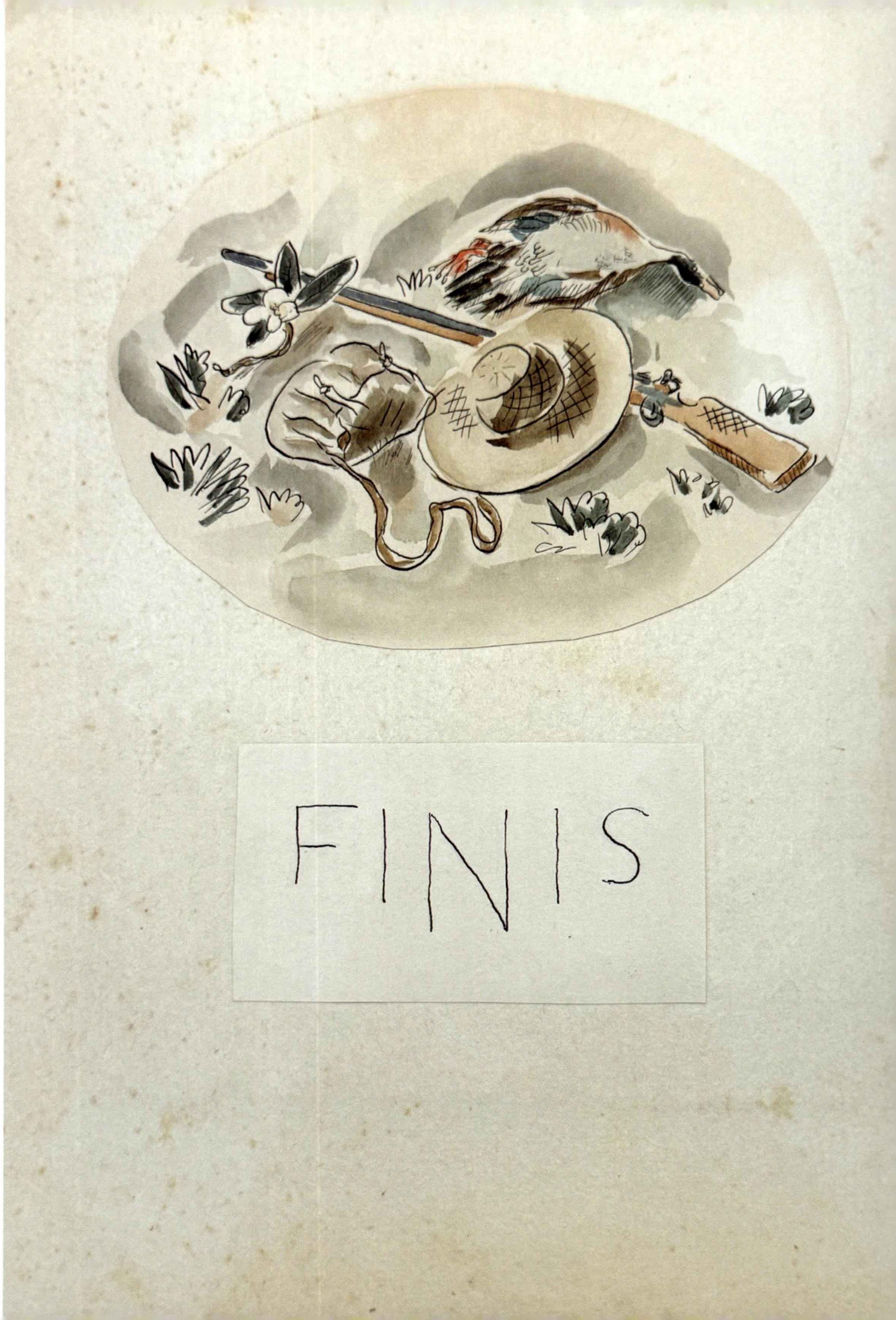

ACKNOWLEDGMENTS

The University of Georgia's Hargrett Rare Book and Manuscript Library is an Aladdin's cave of riches for scholars of all interests. Not just Bill Haynes's art but also a substantial archive of Haynes family material resides in safekeeping there. We would like to thank the library's director, Katherine Stein, exhibition coordinator Jan Hebbard, digital imaging coordinator Mary Palmer Linneman, and the tireless staff who helped make these materials available to us. Special thanks go to Julie Sowell, whose experience was invaluable in sorting the stacks of material left by the Haynes family and organizing the Hargrett Library's collection as well as ephemera that remain at the Ashantilly Center Archives. We also deeply appreciate Dr. P. Toby Graham, university librarian and associate provost, for his enthusiastic support for our project.

We also wish to acknowledge the following institutions for providing materials in their collections to tell this story of the two Williams: the Natural History Museum, London; the American Museum of Natural History, New York; the Trustees of the British Museum; the American Philosophical Society; the U.S. National Park Service; the National Library of Sweden; the Arader Galleries (Philadelphia and New York); the New York Public Library for their Audubon bird illustrations; and the Georgia Forestry Commission.

Additionally, we wish to thank members of the Bartram Trail Conference and the supporters of the Ashantilly Center for their enthusiasm for this project.

From Dorinda Dallmeyer

Many of the ideas in my chapters and captions in this book grew out of the opportunities I have had over the last twenty years to think and write about William Bartram. I would like to express my gratitude to the following friends and collaborators: Dr. Marc Jolley, director of the Mercer University Press, published my edited anthology *Bartram's Living Legacy: The* Travels *and the Nature of the South* (2010; 2nd ed., 2019). The book features the entire *Travels* manuscript along with essays contributed by seventeen Southern nature writers, attesting to Bartram's continuing influence on how we view these landscapes across the centuries.

Among those contributors is the artist Philip Juras, whose paintings graced his chapter in the Mercer book, "A Glimpse of the Southern Frontier." He returned the favor by asking me to compare his artistic vision with that of William Bartram for Philip's exhibition catalog *The Southern Frontier: Landscapes Inspired by Bartram's* Travels (2011). Exhibited at the Telfair Museum in Savannah and then at the Morris Museum of Art in Augusta in 2011, his paintings are cherished in American collections and abroad.

By September 2014, the Mercer anthology had made it into the hands of Eric Breitenbach, a filmmaker and professor at the Southeast Center for Photographic Studies at Daytona State College. Transplanted from New York, in the early 1990s he read *Travels* for the first time, which inspired him to envision a documentary combining Bartram's words with contemporary writers in much the same way as the Mercer anthology. Along with Eric's longtime collaborator and professional videographer Scott Auerbach, I knew that I was working with true professionals. We spent the next five years creating a film that told the Bartram story through six individuals whom we saw as "modern-day Bartrams." Among many tasks, it was my pleasure to write the film's narration for the inimitable Bailey White. In addition to Eric and Scott and the myriad of individuals involved in the production process, special thanks go to all the contributors who financed the film.

Finally, our collaboration with South Carolina Educational Television was indispensable in premiering the film in September 2020 on PBS stations nationwide. *Cultivating the Wild: William Bartram's Travels* continues to be available on the PBS website.

NOTES

CHAPTER 1. Why Bartram Matters

1. Both Philadelphia and Boston vied for the title "The Athens of America." For a comprehensive examination of the elements leading to Philadelphia's nickname, see Amy R. W. Meyers, ed., *Knowing Nature: Art and Science in Philadelphia, 1740–1840* (Yale University Press, 2011). Two chapters focus specifically on the Bartrams: Joel T. Fry, "America's Ancient Garden: The Bartram Botanic Garden, 1728–1850," 60–96; and Amy R. W. Meyers, "From Nature and Memory: William Bartram's Drawings of North American Flora and Fauna," 128–159.

2. The youthful drawing appears in a catalog prepared by Alison Petretti, Arader Galleries, New York and Philadelphia. The catalog is a goldmine of rare natural history illustrations collected by Peter Collinson. About this seaside image, Ms. Petretti provides the following details:

> WILLIAM BARTRAM
>
> Sanderling or curwillet with shell (*Calidris alba*) with *Hirundo rustica*, Barn Swallow, in the background {Sanderling drawn with winter plumage} Signed "William Bartram" center right
>
> Inscribed "the sanderling or Curwillet Se Willaghby/(is English) yet is America Pa-303/&Pensilvania/Not in Catesby" (by Peter Collinson and another hand). Pen and ink and watercolor on laid paper, 6½ × 8¼ inches [early 1750s].

According to Ms. Petretti:

> This early drawing stands out amongst Bartram's work for several scientific and artistic reasons. At first, a cursory analysis of this field sketch in watercolor and ink drawing would be sanderling on a shell-strewn beach. Upon further investigation, one sees several additional designs. In the bottom left-hand corner, there is a sketch of a military figure in a boat holding a telescope toward a bird rising from the water. A sailing ship graces the central horizon line. A barn swallow swoops downward with wings spread in the background. And scattered throughout the foreground are single and flocks of sanderling. Within the sanderling sketches, Bartram appears to be lightly sketching migratory bird flight patterns. This early observation, and quirky arrangement, is clearly influenced by Mark Catesby.

The "mature" seaside image appears in Joseph Ewan, ed., *William Bartram: Botanical and Zoological Drawings* (American Philosophical Society, 1968), plate 18, p. 57.

3. George Edwards, *Gleanings of Natural History*, vol. 6, chap. 67, plate 277, the spotted Tringa and the Pine-Creeper, Royal College of Physicians, London, England (1760). For a delightful discussion of Edwards's life and art, see A. Stuart Mason, *George Edwards: The Bedell and His Birds* (Royal College of Physicians of London, 1992).

4. John Bartram, "Diary of a Journey through the Carolinas, Georgia, and Florida from July 1, 1765, to April 10, 1766" (annotated by Francis Harper), *Transactions of the American Philosophical Society* 33, part 1, iv + 120, frontisp., 8 maps, 35 fig. (1942).

5. That a Quaker would even consider enslaving others seems incongruous. Later in his life, Bartram penned a strong statement denouncing slavery as it continued to be practiced in the new nation. Among his papers, on the back of a "Catalogue of American Trees, Shrubs and Herbacious Plants growing in John Bartram's Garden," are scribbled some notes for a speech or a petition. There is no record that the petition was ever shared with others.

> Ye Chiefs of this Nation whome the people have chosen and appointed as Watchmen . . . for their safety. . . . Recollect the fundamental principle, the first articles of the constitution of the United States, viz. We hold it as a sacred truth, that all men are born free, and have an equal unalienable right to Life, Liberty and property, etc. . . . Do we not continue in

a woefull predicament by suffering the Black People who are fellow citizens of our Nation to be held in perpetuall Bondage and slavery, being drag'd in chains from Africa their native Land many most of them for no crime whatever & none for any crime or harm that they have rendered us: incredible that an enlightened People as we would feign be should continue to afflict them. . . . Ye chiefs in the National Council, do you not confess while ye sit in the Assembly that those poor illtreated People are fellow citizens. Consider God is no respector of Persons & that the Black White Red & Yellow People are equally dear to him and under his protection and favour & that sooner or later ye must render full retribution. . . . Americans ye do not know your own interests by keeping these inocent people in bondage against their will.

The draft appeal ends with a prophecy of the day when these "afflicted" people will have full satisfaction for their oppressions. The full text of his statement appears in Kerry Waters, "All Equally Dear to God: William Bartram's Anti-Slavery Manuscript," in *William Bartram: The Search for Nature's Design: Selected Art, Letters and Unpublished Writings*, ed. Thomas Hallock and Nancy E. Hoffman, 372–380 (University of Georgia Press, 2010). Waters also provides a description of the evolution of abolitionism among American Quakers in the eighteenth century.

6. All page numbers cited herein come from the online site https://docsouth.unc.edu/nc/bartram/bartram.html. This online text is a transcription of the first edition of William Bartram's *Travels*, printed by James & Johnson, Philadelphia, 1791.

7. For the full list of plant and animal species first described, collected, or illustrated by William Bartram, see https://bartramtrailconference.wildapricot.org/Species-List.

8. See Haynes's watercolor of Bartram attempting to chase away an alligator, page 81.

9. *Travels*, 51–52.

The livid purple clouds thicken on the frowning brows of the morning; the tumultuous winds from the east now exert their power. O peaceful Alatamaha! gentle by nature! how thou art ruffled! thy wavy surface disfigures every object, presenting them obscurely to the sight, and they at length totally disappear, whilst the furious winds and sweeping rains bend the lofty groves, and prostrate the quaking grass, driving the affrighted creatures to their dens and caverns.

The tempest now relaxes, its impetus is spent, and a calm serenity gradually takes place; by noon they break away, the blue sky appears, the fulgid sun-beams spread abroad their animating light, and the steady western wind resumes his peaceful reign. The waters are purified, the waves subside, and the beautiful river regains its native calmness: so it is with the varied and mutable scenes of human events on the stream of life. The higher powers and affections of the soul are so blended and connected with the inferior passions, that the most painful feelings are excited in the mind when the latter are crossed: thus in the moral system, which we have planned for our conduct, as a ladder whereby to mount to the summit of terrestrial glory and happiness, and from whence we perhaps meditated our flight to heaven itself, at the very moment when we vainly imagine ourselves to have attained its point, some unforeseen accident intervenes, and surprises us; the chain is violently shaken, we quit our hold and fall: the well contrived system at once becomes a chaos; every idea of happiness recedes; the splendour of glory darkens, and at length totally disappears; every pleasing object is defaced, all is deranged, and the flattering scene passes quite away, a gloomy cloud pervades the understanding, and when we see our progress retarded, and our best intentions frustrated, we are apt to deviate from the admonitions and convictions of virtue, to shut our eyes upon our guide and protector, doubt of his power, and despair of his assistance. But let us wait and rely on our God, who in due time will shine forth in brightness, dissipate the envious cloud, and reveal to us how finite and circumscribed is human power, when assuming to itself independent wisdom.

10. The most extensive discussion of authors influenced by Bartram's *Travels* can be found in N. Bryllion Fagin, *William Bartram: Interpreter of the American Landscape* (Johns Hopkins Press, 1933), 128–198. Online at https://archive.org/details/cu31924103992644.

Over the course of seventy pages, Fagin details Bartram's influence on Samuel Taylor Coleridge and William Wordsworth as well as Dorothy Wordsworth, P. B. Shelley, Tennyson, Carlyle, and other British writers. The treatment of Bartram's influence on American writers is more abbreviated, with brief mentions of Emerson, Thoreau, Thomas Holly Chivers, and Lafcadio Hearn. As far as Continental writers go, Fagin focuses on Chateaubriand's *Le Voyage en Amérique* and *Les Natchez*, in which Chateaubriand passed off "most of the scenery and a good deal of the imagery as well as [Bartram's] Indian lore" (195) as his own observations, although Chateaubriand never visited the Southeast. In *Les Natchez* alone, Prof. Gilbert Chinard annotated fifty passages derived from Bartram's descriptions, ranging from the Cherokee maidens gathering strawberries to the battle of the crocodiles, as well as noting Bartram's stylistic influence on Chateaubriand's text. See Chateaubriand, *"Les Natchez," publiés avec une Introduction et des Notes par Gilbert Chinard*, 61 (Johns Hopkins Press, 1932) (cited in Fagin, 195–198).

11. Benjamin Smith Barton, *Elements of Botany* (1803). In the preface, Barton proclaims his esteem for Bartram:

> The greater number of the Plates, by which the work is illustrated, have been engraved from the original drawings of Mr. William Bartram of Kingsessing, in the vicinity of Philadelphia. While I thus publicly return my thanks to this ingenious naturalist, for his kind liberality in enriching my work, I sincerely rejoice to have the opportunity of declaring, how much of my happiness, in the study of natural history, has been owing to my acquaintance with him; how often I have availed myself of his knowledge in the investigation of the natural productions of our native country; how sincerely I have loved him for the happiest union of moral integrity, with original genius, and unaspiring science, for which he is eminently distinguished. "Sero in coelum redeat" (editor's note: translated from the Latin, "Let him return to heaven late").

See pages viii–ix, available online at https://babel.hathitrust.org/cgi/pt?id=hvd.hn4uf7&seq=9.

12. Ibid., viii. This image is from the first edition of *Elements of Botany* (1803), courtesy of the Hargrett Rare Book and Manuscript Library at the University of Georgia. For more details on the plant's continuing popularity in the present day, see https://medicinalgardens.web.unc.edu/yellow-root.

13. For more information on Titian Ramsey Peale II, one of Bartram's protégés, see pages 85–87.

CHAPTER 2. Bill Haynes

1. William Bartram, *Travels* (Philadelphia, 1791), 57, online at Documenting the American South, University of North Carolina, https://docsouth.unc.edu/nc/bartram/bartram.html.

2. Tabby is a building material deeply connected to the history of the Georgia coast. It is composed of equal parts of oyster shell, sand, water, lime derived from burning shells in ricks of wood, and the ash remaining from the shell-burning process. It can be poured into molds to make blocks and bricks. The Spanish introduced tabby construction methods during their colonization of the southeastern coast. It is an extremely durable building medium, especially when its outside surface is plastered to prevent weathering. For more information, see Susan Morris, "Tabby," *New Georgia Encyclopedia*, www.georgiaencyclopedia.org/articles/history-archaeology/tabby (last modified September 10, 2019).

3. Under a task labor system, an enslaved person was assigned a task, usually to complete the cultivation of a certain size parcel of land each day. Once the task was completed, that person could spend their time as they wished. Rice and sea-island cotton production, typical crops of coastal Georgia, operated on the task system. Tending these crops often required much more skill; also, the long experience that Africans had in rice cultivation meant that their owners learned from them how best to grow rice on this side of the Atlantic. In contrast, tobacco and sugar production were carried out by enslaved people who worked in gangs; they stopped only when the overseer announced that it was quitting time. For more details about task labor in the Low Country of South Carolina and Georgia, see "Slave Labor," at www.scencyclopedia.org/sce/entries/slave-labor.

4. Although enslaved, Bilali read and wrote Arabic fluently and also was quite adept at mathematics. In many cases, state laws prohibited the enslaved from learning to read and write in any language to avoid their "getting ideas." Bilali's skills were rare; even rarer was that he used them openly. Beyond keeping farm account books, Bilali wrote his own document regarding the proper observance of Islamic law. His bound text is now held by the Hargrett Rare Book and Manuscript Library. For a scholarly analysis of this remarkable document, see B. G. Martin, "Sapelo Island's Arabic Document: The 'Bilali Diary' in Context," *Georgia Historical Quarterly* 78, no. 3 (Fall 1994): 589–601.

5. This photograph and others of Ashantilly appear in the Historic American Buildings Survey, which may be viewed at the Library of Congress, www.loc.gov/pictures/search/?q=ashantilly%20plantation&co=hh&sg=true.

6. Susan Garrett Mason, "The Lord of Ashantilly," *Georgia Journal* 17 (May/June 1997): 20–21.

7. Jerry Merwin, *Coastyle*, Fall 1997, 16.

8. William G. Haynes and Clermont H. Lee, "William Bartram's Trails through Georgia," *Savannah*, August 1973, 12–15, at 13–14. It should be noted that, while Haynes undoubtedly had access to the 1928 Van Doren edition of Bartram's *Travels*, that book had none of Bartram's illustrations, unlike Van Doren's 1955 edition. Consequently, Haynes's illustrations were inspired by Bartram's words only.

9. Susan Garrett Mason, "The Lord of Ashantilly," 21, note 6.

10. Virginia Shields, "The Ashantilly Press," *Georgia Journal*, June/July 1982, 8.

11. The 1934 catalog advertising the Grand Central School of Art and its faculty can be found online: https://digital.wolfsonian.org/WOLF038341?search_api_fulltext=%22grand%20central%20school%20of%20art%22.

12. On the Zorachs, see the Zorach Collection, available at www.zorachart.com. For an insider's view on what it was like to study with Harvey Dunn, see Harvey Dunn, *An Evening in the Classroom: Notes Taken*

by Miss Taylor in One of the Classes of Painting (Dover, 2019).

13. See the wide range of Harvey Dunn's art at "Harvey Dunn Collection," *South Dakota Art Museum*, www.sdstate.edu/south-dakota-art-museum/harvey-dunn-collection.

14. "John Marin," *The Art Story*, www.theartstory.org/artist/marin-john. According to artist and researcher Jean Ershler Schatz: "[Marin] is to America what Paul Cézanne was to France—an innovator who helped to oppose the influence of the narrative painters, the illustrators who were more interested in subject than form, in surface than substance. Marin brought to his work a combination of values which, at the turn of the century, was unique in this country: an aliveness of touch, colors that have both sparkle and solidity, and forms that are vibrant with an energy characteristic of our age." For more of Haynes's New Guinea watercolors, see pages 20 and 54–55.

15. Ruth E. Fine, *John Marin* (Abbeville Press, 1990).

16. Quoted in Robert Torchia and Catherine Southwick, "Thomas Hart Benton," *National Gallery of Art*, August 17, 2018, https://grahamshay.com/artist/thomas-hart-benton.

17. Ninety years later, the full set of murals remains on display at Indiana University. See also Kathleen A. Foster, Nanette Esseck Brewer, and Margaret Contompasis, *Thomas Hart Benton and the Indiana Murals* (Indiana University Press, 2000) (Industrial Panel 3, "The Pioneers," 37).

18. It was reported that Benton had a particular affection for mules, once commenting, "You know, the mule is a damned dramatic animal" (https://thomashartbenton.org/ploughing-it-under/).

19. For a description of the amenities now available at the CCC park, see www.goldenisles.com/listing/blythe-island-regional-park/143.

20. See Shields, "The Ashantilly Press," 8, note 11.

21. Haynes seemed particularly delighted to illustrate the mischievous wildlife appearing in these Southern stories. In one undated charcoal sketch, Bruh Wasp has dropped by the sweet potato patch of his neighbor, Bruh Mosquito, who is hoeing in the field. After trading pleasantries, Bruh Wasp asks about the success of Bruh Mosquito's sweet potato crop. Bruh Mosquito says his potatoes are good but that Bruh Wasp should see the size of the potatoes at Bruh Mosquito's father's garden. Then Bruh Wasp asks how big they are, to which Bruh Mosquito responds, "They are bigger around than my leg," as he pulls up his pants leg for scale. Bruh Wasp takes one look at Bruh Mosquito's spindly leg and falls down laughing. He's laughing so hard, he has to squeeze in on his sides, and keeps laughing and squeezing, eventually reducing his midsection to a "wasp waist." That's why Bruh Wasp has such a terrible disposition to this day: because he's afraid that if he gets to laughing again, he will break himself in half. Fortunately, in 1949 Mr. Stoddard recorded a number of these folktales in dialect for the folklore collection of the Library of Congress. His recordings subsequently have been published, with the Gullah-Geechee version accompanied by standard English, and richly illustrated by other artists.

22. Approximately fifty of Haynes's index-card-sized, spiral-bound watercolor sketchbooks along with larger-format watercolor paintings from New Guinea are held in the Ashantilly Press Collection, Hargrett Rare Book and Manuscript Library.

23. Unfortunately, the print run was very limited. The three selected illustrations are the cover, one of the ornamental capitals showing native plants and birds Haynes encountered, and finally a decorative cartouche that features an attack by Japanese warplanes on a supply ship framed by wading birds, the face of a New Guinea man, and a boar around whose long tusks snakes are coiling, as well as a fish. Note in the illuminated "A" image Haynes's beautiful calligraphy. See more of his New Guinea paintings on pages 19–20 and 54–55.

24. Ashantilly Center Archives, online at https://newspaperarchive.com.

25. Ibid.

26. Ibid.

27. Ibid.

28. Ibid.

29. Ibid.

30. See Mason, "The Lord of Ashantilly," 20, note 6.

31. Ibid.

32. Merwin, *Coastyle*, 21, note 8.

33. Elfrida DeRenne Barrow and Laura Palmer Bell, *Anchored Yesterdays*, University of Georgia Press (first edition 1925, Ashantilly Press edition, reprinted 2001).

34. Merwin, *Coastyle*, 21, note 8.

35. Ibid.

36. Martha Jane Zachert, *Fine Printing in Georgia, 1950–1990: Six Prize-Winning Presses* (Press of the Nightowl, 1994), 15.

37. Ibid., 17 (quoting a 1997 letter to her from Charles F. Robertson).

38. Merwin, *Coastyle*, 22, note 8. Mrs. Barrow was a descendant of Noble Wimberly Jones whose home, Wormsloe, was on the Isle of Hope, south of Savannah. He hosted John and William Bartram in 1765. Jones was deeply involved in identifying crops that would grow well in Georgia. When the Bartrams departed, John Bartram noted that Jones sent them off with some "delitious [*sic*] pomegranates." John Bartram, "Diary of a Journey through the Carolinas, Georgia, and Florida from July 1, 1765, to April 10, 1766," ed. Francis Harper, *Transactions of the American Philosophical Society* 33, no. 1

(1942): 30. Another of Jones's Philadelphia connections was Benjamin Franklin, who sent seeds from Indochina to Jones for his agricultural experiments.

39. See Haynes's illustration of a storm-tossed boat at sea, page 58.

40. Note that Haynes followed Bartram's spelling "Alatamaha," the commonly used name in colonial Georgia. It has long been standardized as "Altamaha." See Bartram's description in *Travels*, https://docsouth.unc.edu/nc/bartram/bartram.html, 51–52.

41. William G. Haynes and Clermont Lee, *Savannah*, July 1973, 14.

42. Ibid. See also note 9.

43. The keynote speech by Joseph Ewan was a signal event. Ewan was an eminent botanist and historian of science who wrote extensively on the history of naturalists in America and their work during the seventeenth through nineteenth centuries. With more than four hundred publications, many consider Ewan's masterpiece to be *William Bartram: Botanical and Zoological Drawings, 1756–1788* (American Philosophical Society, 1968). Bartram took his journey on behalf of Dr. John Fothergill of London, supplying his patron with plant and seed samples as well as an album of detailed illustrations of American flora and fauna. Prior to the appearance of Ewan's book, most of Bartram's illustrations had never been made available to the public, and the so-called "Fothergill Album" eventually was archived at the British Museum. Nearly two hundred years later, the American Philosophical Society engaged Ewan to provide a historical introduction to Bartram's life and to the Fothergill Album itself. Particularly useful is that Ewan put his considerable skill and experience as a naturalist into identifying, introducing, and annotating each of Bartram's plates in chronological order. The detailed reproductions of Bartram's work occupy the bulk of this landmark volume.

44. William G. Haynes Jr., editor, "Conference: Man in the Landscape," a Bicentennial Project, sponsored by the Darien-McIntosh Bicentennial Committee, Darien, Georgia, November 13–14, 1976 (published 1977). Copy in Ashantilly Center Archives.

45. Ibid., title page.

46. Acceptance speech, Ashantilly Press papers, Hargrett Library, University of Georgia.

47. For more information, see the Ashantilly Center website, http://Ashantillycenter.org.

CHAPTER 3. Bartram's *Travels* Illustrated

1. Thomas P. Slaughter, *The Natures of John and William Bartram* (Alfred A. Knopf, 1996), 194.

2. David S. Shields, "Guinea Squash," *Carolina Gold Rice Foundation*, April 4, 2011, www.thecarolinagoldricefoundation.org/news/2016/6/4/guinea-squash.